T0344447

Integrating RegTech Solutions for Industry 4.0

Swati Gupta
Universal AI University, India

Smita Gupta
Galgotias University, India

Badri Narayanan Gopalakrishnan
University of Washington, USA

A volume in the Advances
in Finance, Accounting, and
Economics (AFAE) Book Series

Published in the United States of America by
    IGI Global
    Business Science Reference (an imprint of IGI Global)
    701 E. Chocolate Avenue
    Hershey PA, USA 17033
    Tel: 717-533-8845
    Fax: 717-533-8661
    E-mail: cust@igi-global.com
    Web site: http://www.igi-global.com

Library of Congress Cataloging-in-Publication Data

CIP DATA PROCESSING

2024 Business Science Reference
ISBN(hc) 9798369333228 | ISBN(sc) 9798369349830 | eISBN 9798369333235

British Cataloguing in Publication Data
A Cataloguing in Publication record for this book is available from the British Library.

All work contributed to this book is new, previously-unpublished material.
The views expressed in this book are those of the authors, but not necessarily of the publisher.

For electronic access to this publication, please contact: eresources@igi-global.com.

Advances in Finance, Accounting, and Economics (AFAE) Book Series

Ahmed Driouchi
Al Akhawayn University, Morocco

ISSN:2327-5677
EISSN:2327-5685

MISSION

In our changing economic and business environment, it is important to consider the financial changes occurring internationally as well as within individual organizations and business environments. Understanding these changes as well as the factors that influence them is crucial in preparing for our financial future and ensuring economic sustainability and growth.

The **Advances in Finance, Accounting, and Economics (AFAE)** book series aims to publish comprehensive and informative titles in all areas of economics and economic theory, finance, and accounting to assist in advancing the available knowledge and providing for further research development in these dynamic fields.

Coverage

- Managerial Accounting
- Behavioral Economics
- Economics of Migration and Spatial Mobility
- Fiscal Policy
- Economics of Risks, Uncertainty, Ambiguity, and Insurance
- Applied Accounting
- Labor Economics
- Economic Indices and Quantitative Economic Methods
- Entrepreneurship in Accounting and Finance
- Applied economics

IGI Global is currently accepting manuscripts for publication within this series. To submit a proposal for a volume in this series, please contact our Acquisition Editors at Acquisitions@igi-global.com or visit: http://www.igi-global.com/publish/.

Titles in this Series

For a list of additional titles in this series, please visit: www.igi-global.com/book-series

Decentralized Finance and Tokenization in FinTech
Luan Vardari (University "Ukshin Hoti" Prizren, Kosovo) and Isuf Qabrati (University "Ukshin Hoti" Prizren, Kosovo)
Business Science Reference • copyright 2024 • 392pp • H/C (ISBN: 9798369333464) • US $275.00 (our price)

Comparative Approach on Development and Socioeconomics of Africa
Baimba Yilla (Marymount University, USA)
Information Science Reference • copyright 2024 • 258pp • H/C (ISBN: 9798369324035) • US $255.00 (our price)

Impact of Renewable Energy on Corporate Finance and Economics
Ali Ahmadi (Higher Institute of Business Administration of Gafsa, Tunisia)
Business Science Reference • copyright 2024 • 288pp • H/C (ISBN: 9798369339329) • US $295.00 (our price)

Emerging Perspectives on Financial Well-Being
Dharmendra Singh (Modern College of Business and Science, Oman) Rohit Bansal (Rajiv Gandhi Institute of Petroleum Technology, India) Swati Gupta (K.R. Mangalam University, India) and Yasmeen Ansari (Saudi Electronic University, Saudi Arabia)
Business Science Reference • copyright 2024 • 339pp • H/C (ISBN: 9798369317501) • US $290.00 (our price)

Transforming the Financial Landscape With ICTs
Dharmendra Singh (Modern College of Business and Science, Oman) Garima Malik (Birla Institute of Technology Management, Greater Noida, India) and Shalini Aggarwal (Chandigarh University, India)
Business Science Reference • copyright 2024 • 345pp • H/C (ISBN: 9798369315033) • US $285.00 (our price)

701 East Chocolate Avenue, Hershey, PA 17033, USA
Tel: 717-533-8845 x100 • Fax: 717-533-8661
E-Mail: cust@igi-global.com • www.igi-global.com

Table of Contents

Detailed Table of Contents

Chapter 1

Anubha Anubha, Jaipuria Institute of Management, Ghaziabad, India

Based on the applications of various technologies like automation and artificial intelligence, RegTech enables institutions to comply with regulations and to improve client identification, fraud detection, rule adoption, and data collection. It assists them to be more efficient, accurate, and flexible in dealing with the ever-changing regulatory requirements. Accordingly, the chapter aims to explore the potential of RegTech in various sectors (for example, healthcare, insurance, banking). In other words, it intends to study the role of RegTech in simplifying the regulatory compliances. This study will bring significant insights to researchers and policymakers by exploring the potential benefits of RegTech in diverse sectors to have efficient compliance landscape including efficient risk management. The chapter will also explain the challenges of regulatory compliances and how such challenges can be combated by integrating technology and regulation, i.e., by adopting RegTech.

Chapter 2

Padma Iyenghar, Innotec GmbH, Germany

This chapter explores the economic implications of Regulatory Technology (RegTech) compliance in the context of Industry 4.0, Cyber-Physical Systems (CPS), cybersecurity, and functional safety. While RegTech offers significant economic benefits, concerns persist regarding implementation costs, regulatory uncertainties, and cybersecurity risks. This chapter conducts a comprehensive economic analysis of RegTech adoption, highlighting both positive and negative impacts on organizational performance. By examining the intersection of RegTech with Industry 4.0, CPS, and functional safety, this chapter provides actionable insights for navigating regulatory complexities. Future research avenues include exploring emerging technologies, regulatory sandbox frameworks, ethical and legal implications, and global regulatory convergence in RegTech. Overall, this chapter lays the groundwork for understanding the economic dynamics of RegTech adoption, empowering organizations to drive sustainable growth in a regulated business environment.

Chapter 3

Manali Agrawal, NSB Academy, India
Mohammad Irfan, NSB Academy, India
Anjali Goyal, Khalifa University, UAE

Fintech, which combines the words "financial" and "technology," refers to the integration of new technical developments with financial industry goods and services. The phrase refers to a quickly expanding sector that meets the needs of both companies and consumers in a variety of ways. Fintech offers a seemingly limitless range of uses, from cryptocurrencies and investment apps to mobile banking and insurance. Fintech is an essential component because of our increasing reliance on technology, large data sets, intricate networks of financial institutions, and affordable IT solutions like process automation software. The regulatory environment and industry have changed due to the growing use of FinTech solutions. Businesses that implement fintech are guaranteed to provide end customers with a secure environment in addition to good risk management. Digital payments, digital lending, InsurTech, and WealthTech are some of the major Fintech subsectors. In the upcoming years, each of these sectors is expected to have a significant uptrend.

Chapter 4

Mithilesh Kishor Gidage, Savitribai Phule Pune University, India
Shilpa Vasant Bhide, Savitribai Phule Pune University, India

This study examines the impact of fintech on India's financial landscape from 2021 to 2021. Using advanced regression techniques and accounting for various factors, the authors find a positive link between fintech and financial development, including improved access to loans and increased savings. They also highlight the potential of regtech in enhancing financial development. The findings stress the importance of balanced regulatory frameworks to foster fintech growth while managing risks. Additionally, they show how policy measures like interest rate liberalization can positively influence financial development. In conclusion, they propose a comprehensive policy framework to promote equitable fintech growth in developing nations.

Neha Khandelwal, Universal AI University, India
Abhishek Sahu, Universal AI University, India
Asha Bhatia, Universal AI University, India

The purpose of this study is to determine customers' attitudes toward financial technology in the banking sector based on challenges and impacts. Therefore, the study aims to develop hypotheses that relate to the challenges and impact of financial technology on customer attitudes. The survey instrument was sent to 200 customers in the banking sector. Overall, 182 valid responses were found suitable for the study with a 91.00% response rate. Statistical analyses were conducted to ensure the reliability and validity of the questionnaire. A structural equation modeling technique has been used to test the research hypothesis using AMOS 21 software. Consumer sentiments are positively affected by financial technology's global recognition, leading to an increased desire to use these innovative financial services. The findings of this study have practical implications for both the banking sector and the broader financial technology landscape, which may provide valuable insights for policymakers, practitioners, and researchers.

Priyanshu Sharma, Birla Institute of Technology Mesra, Jaipur, India
Jyoti Kumar Chandel, Birla Institute of Technology Mesra, Jaipur, India
Diksha Sinha, Birla Institute of Technology Mesra, Jaipur, India
Ramji Nagariya, Christ University, India
Abhineet Saxena, Amity University, India

This study aims to get an insight into the intellectual structure, current research themes, and future research directions on digital currency, cryptocurrency, and blockchain. Bibliometric analysis coupled with performance analysis and cluster analysis has been conducted on the digital currency articles, published between the years 2011 and 2023, filtered using PRISMA protocol, and extracted from the Web of Science and Scopus databases. Network analysis was carried out in the Biblioshiny package of R software and VOSviewer. The study highlights that the research of digital currency is classified into four broad categories: 'emerging technology', 'cryptocurrencies portfolios', 'cryptocurrencies as a medium of exchange and an asset class', and 'cryptocurrencies and financial risk'. The chapter presents an innovative model focusing on productive avenues for future research by synthesizing the latest research articles extracted from the databases, related to digital currency through bibliometric analysis.

Chapter 7

Mohammad Irfan, NSB Academy, India
Rui Dias, ISG, Business and Economics School, CIGEST, Portugal
Rosa Morgado Galvão, Instituto Politécnico de Setúbal, Portugal

This study tests whether the 2022 event has increased investor overreactions in the capital markets of eight Central and Eastern European countries (Romania, Bulgaria, Slovakia, Hungary, Croatia, Russia, the Czech Republic, and Slovenia). This chapter contributes to the existing literature on overreaction behavior in Central and Eastern European capital markets by introducing a new modeling technique that does not require specific threshold parameters. Instead, the analysis models the price overreaction as a price change based on 16-day lags. This approach differs from previous research that used statistical modeling of overreactions, selecting one or more arbitrary parameters. The research question is partially accepted since some studied regional markets show overreactions (4 out of 8 possible markets).

Chapter 8

S. Dhanabagiyam, NSB Academy, India
Boopathy Srihari, Christ University, Pune, India

In the contemporary business environment, marked by rapid changes, client acquisition stands out as a pivotal factor for companies aiming at sustained growth, particularly in sectors such as finance and real estate. The ability to attract and retain clients is not only a measure of a company's current success but also a fundamental driver for its future viability. This study focuses on Real Capital Ventures LLP, a company operating at the intersection of finance and real estate, aiming to unravel the intricacies of its client acquisition strategies. The overarching goal is to conduct an exhaustive examination of the current approaches employed by the firm and provide nuanced recommendations for refinement. By doing so, the study aspires to contribute to the enhancement of the effectiveness of Real Capital Ventures LLP's client acquisition, ensuring its continued success in a fiercely competitive market.

    P. C. Libeesh, CMR Institute of Technology, India
    Mohammad Irfan, NSB Academy, India
    Sylva Alif Rusmita, University of Airlangga, Indonesia
    Lissy George, Mount Tabor Training College, Pathanapuram, India

This research explores the dynamic interactions between artificial intelligence (AI) and start-ups, with a particular emphasis on sustainable aspects and a thorough investigation of their symbiotic relationship. In order to explore the various ways that AI technologies support the viability of start-ups in a variety of industries, the research uses a descriptive study approach. A detailed examination of the literature is incorporated into the investigation, which analyses accepted theories and models about sustainability, entrepreneurship, and artificial intelligence. The goal of the study is to provide a comprehensive understanding of how AI-driven innovations improve operational efficiency, encourage environmentally friendly practices, and support social inclusion within the entrepreneurial landscape by integrating existing evidence. This descriptive study offers insightful insights for academics and business practitioners alike, adding to the continuing conversation about the complex relationship between artificial intelligence (AI) and the sustainability of start-ups.

    Ruchika Rastogi, Pranveer Singh Institute of Technology, Kanpur, India
    Mohammad Ismail Iqbal, University of Technology and Applied
       Sciences, Oman

Regtech, or the use of technology in regulation, compliance, risk management, reporting, and monitoring, is driven by increasing regulatory requirements, rapid and continuous changes, and the digital dynamics of financial markets. The resulting multidimensional framework covers many dimensions. The first is regulation and technology, where technology (such as artificial intelligence, DLT, blockchain, smart contracts, apis) is used to meet one or more laws that do not require financial management. Regtech leverages technology for regulation, compliance, and risk management in finance, driven by regulatory demands and digital market dynamics. It utilizes AI, blockchain, and data automation for efficient data integration. Information sharing fosters an ecosystem benefiting stakeholders, offering increased efficiency, transparency, and reduced costs. Yet, risks like cyber threats and algorithmic bias persist.

In the digital age, the proliferation of technology has transformed the landscape of the music industry, enabling unprecedented access to music but also giving rise to rampant piracy. The chapter explores the intricate interplay between regulation and technology in combating digital music piracy. The analysis reveals that while regulatory interventions have played a crucial role in shaping the legal framework, technological advancements have simultaneously presented both opportunities and hurdles in the fight against piracy. Furthermore, the authors examine the strategic approaches adopted by industry players, policymakers, and technology innovators to mitigate piracy, including the development of DRM systems, subscription-based streaming services, and collaborative enforcement efforts.

This chapter examines various perspectives and challenges related to the integration of artificial intelligence (AI) in the transportation industry, particularly focusing on automated. The chapter also addresses the governance of AI, emphasizing the importance of responsible, ethical, and transparent control mechanisms. The chapter then explores AV 4.0, the latest guidance from the US Department of Transportation, which outlines efforts to support and advance autonomous vehicles while ensuring accountability. The legal status of automated vehicles is analysed under different regimes, including international conventions, national regulations, and state vehicle codes. The chapter recommends measures to increase legal certainty for automated vehicles, such as the development of common definitions and monitoring of relevant conventions.

Preface

In an era defined by relentless technological progress, the convergence of regulatory technology (regtech) with the transformative forces of Industry 4.0 represents a compelling narrative of adaptation and advancement. As editors of *Integrating RegTech Solutions for Industry 4.0,* we are honored to present a comprehensive exploration of this intersection, crafted by esteemed contributors from around the globe.

The landscape of financial compliance and regulation is undergoing a profound metamorphosis, propelled by the evolution of regtech solutions. At its essence, regtech leverages technology to streamline compliance and risk management processes within the financial sector. With the advent of Industry 4.0, characterized by automation, artificial intelligence, and machine learning, regtech is experiencing a paradigm shift, ushering in a new era of efficiency and effectiveness.

Through the pages of this edited volume, readers will embark on a journey through the intricate tapestry of regtech and Industry 4.0. From theoretical foundations to real-world applications, each chapter offers valuable insights gleaned from both scholarly research and practical experience. Our esteemed contributors have meticulously dissected the complexities of this dynamic landscape, shedding light on successes, challenges, and future prospects.

Part 1 of this book lays the groundwork, exploring the origins and evolution of regtech, the transformative effects of automation, the role of AI and machine learning in risk management, and the regulatory implications of emerging technologies such as blockchain and IoT.

Part 2 delves into real-world applications and case studies, offering a firsthand look at how leading financial institutions have integrated regtech solutions into their operations. From success stories to lessons learned, these chapters provide invaluable knowledge for practitioners and policymakers alike.

Part 3 confronts the regulatory implications and challenges inherent in the integration of regtech and Industry 4.0 technologies. Ethical considerations, data security, and the decentralized nature of blockchain are among the critical issues addressed in this section.

Finally, Part 4 peers into the future landscape of regtech, offering predictions, forecasts, and insights into emerging technologies that will shape the trajectory of regulatory compliance in the years to come.

As editors, our aim is to provide readers with a comprehensive resource that not only informs but also inspires further exploration and innovation. We extend our gratitude to all the contributors who have lent their expertise to this endeavor and hope that "RegTech Advancements in the Age of Industry 4.0" serves as a catalyst for meaningful dialogue and progress in this rapidly evolving field.

In this meticulously curated volume, *Integrating RegTech Solutions for Industry 4.0*, we embark on an illuminating journey through the evolving landscape of regulatory technology (regtech) within the context of Industry 4.0. Through the lens of esteemed scholars and practitioners, each chapter offers profound insights and actionable recommendations, shaping the discourse on the intersection of technology, regulation, and industry.

Chapter 1, "RegTech: An Effective Way To Regulatory Compliance," by Anubha Anubha, delves into the transformative potential of regtech across diverse sectors, elucidating its role in simplifying regulatory compliances. Drawing on applications of automation and artificial intelligence, this chapter offers valuable insights into enhancing risk management and regulatory adherence.

Chapter 2, "Economic Impact of RegTech Compliance," by Padma Iyenghar, provides a comprehensive economic analysis of RegTech adoption, shedding light on both its benefits and challenges within the context of Industry 4.0. By examining the intersection of RegTech with Industry 4.0, Cyber-Physical Systems (CPS), and functional safety, this chapter offers actionable insights for navigating regulatory complexities.

Chapter 3, "The Importance of Fintech in Promoting Regulatory Compliance in Major Fintech Subsectors," by Manali Agrawal, Mohammad Irfan, and Anjali Goyal, explores the symbiotic relationship between fintech and regulatory compliance, emphasizing its pivotal role across major subsectors. From digital payments to InsurTech, this chapter provides a holistic overview of fintech's transformative potential in ensuring regulatory adherence.

Chapter 4, "Fintech, RegTech, and Financial Development in India's Industry 4.0 Landscape," by Mithilesh Gidage and Shilpa Bhide, investigates the impact of fintech on India's financial landscape, highlighting the positive link between fintech adoption and financial development. By proposing a comprehensive policy framework, this chapter lays the groundwork for fostering equitable fintech growth in developing nations.

Chapter 5, "An Empirical Study on Continued Intention to Use Financial Technology in the Banking Sector," by Neha Khandelwal, Abhishek Sahu, and Asha Bhatia, offers valuable insights into customer attitudes toward financial technology in the banking sector. Through rigorous statistical analyses, this chapter underscores the positive impact of financial technology on consumer sentiments, paving the way for informed decision-making in the banking industry.

Chapter 6, "The Rise of Digital Currency: A Bibliometric Evaluation and Future Research Prospect," by Priyanshu Sharma, Jyoti Chandel, Diksha Sinha, Ramji Nagariya, and Abhineet Saxena, presents a comprehensive bibliometric analysis of digital currency research, outlining key themes and future research directions. By synthesizing the latest research articles, this chapter offers innovative avenues for advancing scholarly discourse on digital currency and blockchain technology.

Chapter 7, "Examining Investor Overreaction in Periods of Crisis: Evidence From Central and Eastern European Countries," Mohammad Irfan, Rui Dias, and Rosa Morgado Galvão, investigates investor overreactions in Central and Eastern European capital markets, offering insights into market dynamics during periods of crisis. By introducing a new modeling technique, this chapter enriches our understanding of investor behavior and market efficiency.

Chapter 8, "An Impact of AI and Client Acquisition Strategies in Real Capital Ventures," by S. Bagiyam and Boopathy Srihari, delves into the intricacies of client acquisition strategies in Real Capital Ventures LLP, offering nuanced recommendations for enhancing effectiveness in a competitive market landscape. Through a comprehensive examination of current approaches, this chapter provides actionable insights for sustainable growth.

Chapter 9, "The Application of AI in New Start-Ups: A Descriptive Inquiry That Emphasizes Sustainable Elements," by Libeesh P. C., Mohammad Irfan, Sylva Rusmita, and Lissy George, explores the symbiotic relationship between artificial intelligence (AI) and start-ups, with a focus on sustainability. By analyzing existing evidence, this descriptive study offers valuable insights for fostering environmentally friendly practices and social inclusion within the entrepreneurial landscape.

Chapter 10, "Data security and Privacy in RegTech," by Ruchika Rastogi and Mohammad Iqbal, delves into the multidimensional framework of regtech, highlighting the critical role of technology in regulation, compliance, and risk management. By addressing risks such as cyber threats and algorithmic bias, this chapter underscores the importance of information sharing and stakeholder collaboration in fostering a secure regulatory ecosystem.

Chapter 11, "The Nexus of Regulation and Technology: A Strategic Approach to Combating Digital Music Piracy," by Kiran Sharma, Shivangi Sharma, and Ansari Alam, explores the strategic approaches to combating digital music piracy, emphasizing the intricate interplay between regulation and technology. By examining DRM systems, subscription-based streaming services, and collaborative enforcement efforts, this chapter offers valuable insights for industry stakeholders and policymakers.

Chapter 12, "Automated Vehicles Landscape and India Through a Regulatory Lens," by Smita Gupta and Lavanya Bhagra, examines the integration of artificial intelligence (AI) in the transportation industry, with a focus on automated vehicles (AVs). By addressing governance, legal frameworks, and policy recommendations, this chapter provides a holistic perspective on the regulatory challenges and opportunities in the AV landscape.

As editors, we are privileged to present this diverse array of chapters, each contributing to a richer understanding of the complex dynamics between technology, regulation, and industry. We extend our sincere gratitude to all the contributors for their invaluable insights and scholarly contributions, shaping the discourse on regtech in the age of Industry 4.0.

In concluding this volume, *Integrating RegTech Solutions for Industry 4.0*, we reflect on the profound insights offered by our esteemed contributors and the significance of their collective work in shaping the future of regulatory technology (regtech).

Through the lens of each chapter, we have traversed the intricate landscape of regtech, exploring its transformative potential across diverse sectors and its symbiotic relationship with the forces of Industry 4.0. From the foundational principles of regulatory compliance to the empirical realities of real-world applications, each contribution has enriched our understanding of this dynamic intersection.

As editors, we are profoundly grateful to the scholars and practitioners whose expertise has illuminated these pages, offering valuable insights into the challenges, opportunities, and future prospects of regtech in the age of Industry 4.0. Their dedication to advancing knowledge and driving innovation serves as a beacon for progress in this rapidly evolving field.

As we bid farewell to this volume, we are filled with optimism for the future of regtech and its potential to revolutionize regulatory compliance in the digital era. We hope that *Integrating RegTech Solutions for Industry 4.0* serves as a catalyst for further dialogue, collaboration, and innovation, inspiring future generations to continue pushing the boundaries of technological advancement and regulatory excellence.

Swati Gupta
Universal AI University, India

Smita Gupta
Galgotias University, India

Badri Narayanan Gopalakrishnan
University of Washington, USA

Chapter 1
RegTech:
An Effective Way to Regulatory Compliance

Anubha Anubha
 http://orcid.org/0000-0002-2719-7697
Jaipuria Institute of Management, Ghaziabad, India

ABSTRACT

Based on the applications of various technologies like automation and artificial intelligence, RegTech enables institutions to comply with regulations and to improve client identification, fraud detection, rule adoption, and data collection. It assists them to be more efficient, accurate, and flexible in dealing with the ever-changing regulatory requirements. Accordingly, the chapter aims to explore the potential of RegTech in various sectors (for example, healthcare, insurance, banking). In other words, it intends to study the role of RegTech in simplifying the regulatory compliances. This study will bring significant insights to researchers and policymakers by exploring the potential benefits of RegTech in diverse sectors to have efficient compliance landscape including efficient risk management. The chapter will also explain the challenges of regulatory compliances and how such challenges can be combated by integrating technology and regulation, i.e., by adopting RegTech.

1. INTRODUCTION

"It's conceivable, not far in the future, that closed loop AI-driven financial eco-systems could emerge, where the extension of credit and other financial services, risk management and compliance through regtech, oversight through suptech, and

DOI: 10.4018/979-8-3693-3322-8.ch001

remedial actions, will all be made by AI applications communicating directly with each other."

Tobias Adrian (2021),
Financial Counsellor and Director,
Monetary and Capital Markets Department,
International Monetary Fund

For companies involved in the global market, rules and standards are essential to follow. They have to stick to strict regulations related to their industries. Failing which, they could lose customers, face fines, and get into legal trouble. Companies use a system called compliance management to comply with the rules and standards. However, because global regulations are always changing, it's tough for companies to stay updated. So, they are embracing automated monitoring and new technologies, which make up the world of RegTech(Chettri, 2022). Following rules is really important for all companies irrespective of their sizes. Regulations are getting more and more important worldwide. With technology advancing faster than ever, RegTech is predicted to be the protagonist of this decade by helping companies follow rules. By using automation to make things easier, work faster, and cost lesser, RegTech is likely to be a key player in the global economy (ibid.). As per the report of Bloomberg UK, by 2025, the global market for 'RegTech', will be worth $55 billion (Sian, 2023).

Regtech is the application of technology, especially information technology, to guarantee regulatory requirements are monitored and reported on in a way that is compliant (Bitterli, 2017). Regtech ensures that regulations are followed and streamlines regulatory procedures. This will be accomplished by implementing regulatory experts' control frameworks and standardizing processes across the entire company. Regtech is made up of two words, one, "technology" and another, "regulatory." This indicates that the regulatory compliance will be performed more accurately and efficiently with the help of technology. Regtech is thus, based on the use of technology to manage regulatory procedures in the financial sector. In another words, financial services firms can automate the process of managing compliance activities with Regtech.

The primary functions of Regtech include compliance, reporting, and regulatory monitoring. It is in fact a group of tech companies that use automation to address issues in a technologically driven economy. Regtech makes compliance rules clear and consistent. It sets standard procedures, clarifies unclear rules, and improves quality while cutting costs. It helps ensure regulations are followed. Regtech provides benefits to both financial institutions and regulators. It increases comfort levels and ensures that the supervision is automated. At the same time, it also ensured that the transparency is maintained in the application of regulations.

Real-time monitoring of activities is possible due to Regtech. This becomes more important for products that requires such kind of monitoring like self service desk. To automate the regulatory processes, RegTech uses various modern technologies like Big Data, Artificial Intelligence (AI) and Machine Learning. This leads to the efficient utilization of data. RegTech simplifies the work of reporting which in turn saves time and money. It provides the right information at the right place and hence reduces the manual work of a compliance team. Some of the major benefits of RegTech can be enumerated as follows:

- Monitoring internal controls and recognizing gaps
- Enhancing efficiency and commercial agility
- Recognizing and minimizing regulatory risks
- Mechanizing and restructuring the regulatory processes
- Minimizing costs of compliance management
- Confirming compliance in totality

RegTech is based on the applications of various of technology like automation and artificial intelligence which enables institutions to follow rules and regulations in an easier way. RegTech helps organizations to follow and comply with the rules and regulations. RegTech help businesses to comply with regulations. Businesses use new rules, understand what-if scenarios, and improve the regulatory framework to enable robust remedies. It improves client onboarding, fraud detection, rule adoption, data collecting, and analytics. It assists them be more efficient, accurate, and flexible in dealing with the ever-changing regulatory requirements. Regulation technology, or RegTech, uses smart technology like Machine Learning, Artificial Intelligence and Data Analytics to find possible problems and make compliance management easier. In India, banks, insurance companies, and investment firms are leading the way in using RegTech. These tools are designed to meet the rules set by regulators like the RBI, SEBI, and IRDAI effectively and efficiently. They help these companies manage things like knowing their customers, stopping money laundering, and making reporting simpler. Despite such a potential, the extant literature has not studied RegTech in comprehensive way which this chapter aims to do. Further, though a comprehensive and vast literature on RegTech exists (e.g., Sarabdeen, 2023; Yusoff et al., 2023; Zixuan, 2023; Kunhibava et al. 2023; Papantoniou, 2022; Muganyi et al., 2022; Ha, 2022; Utami & Septivani, 2022; Turki et al., 2020; Vivek et al., 2020; Buckley et al., 2020; Turki, et al., 2020). Most of the studies have been undertaken in the context of other countries. Only a few studies exist in Indian context (e.g., Narang, 2021). This indicates one more gap which the current study tries to fill.

Accordingly, the present chapter aims to explore the potential of RegTech in various sectors (for example, healthcare, insurance, banking). In other words, it intends to study the role of RegTech in simplifying the regulatory compliances. This study will bring significant insights to researchers and policymakers by exploring the potential benefits of RegTech in diverse sectors in order to have efficient compliance landscape including efficient risk management. The chapter will also explain the challenges of regulatory compliances and how such challenges can be combat by integrating technology and regulation, i.e., by adopting RegTech.

2. LITERATURE REVIEW

RegTech, an abbreviation for Regulatory Technology, is transforming how businesses in India navigate rules and regulations. By blending regulation and technology, it introduces innovative and effective methods for businesses to adhere to rules, handle risks, and maintain good governance. RegTech is gaining popularity in India because it leverages technology to simplify compliance procedures, automating tasks, enhancing accuracy, and facilitating easier rule adherence for businesses (Zixuan, 2023). RegTech is employed to automate daily tasks, enhance reporting accuracy, and manage risk in a better way across various sectors including not only finance but others too like real estate, healthcare and telecommunications to name few Kunhibava et al. 2023; Utami & Septivani, 2022). It is emerging as a significant innovation in India's business landscape which is going to be established as the most sought-after solution for regulatory compliances. The extent literature has tried to comprehended RegTech in several ways (Sarabdeen, 2023; Yusoff et al., 2023; Zixuan, 2023; Kunhibava et al. 2023; Papantoniou, 2022; Muganyi et al., 2022; Ha, 2022; Utami & Septivani, 2022; Turki et al., 2020; Vivek et al., 2020; Buckley et al., 2020; Turki, et al., 2020). However, most of the studies have been done in other countries, for example the study of Sarabdeen (2023) studies Regtech from the perspective of laws in Saudi Arabia. Yusoff et al. (2023) discusses the use of RegTech in money laundering preventation in Indonesia banking industry. Similarly, Utami & Septivani, 2022 verifies Regtech as a solution to prevent money laundering in Indonesia. In other studies, Muganyi et al. (2022) and Zixuan. (2023) have studied the development of RegTech in China. The study undertaken by Ha (2022) is focused on European countries. Buckley et al., (2020) has studied the adequacy of RegTech laws from the perspective of European Union. Few others have comprehended the role of RegTech in Islamic and conventional banking industry (Kunhibava et al. 2023; Turki, et al., 2020). The studies in the context of India are very limited (Narang, 2021). This indicates a gap which provides motivation to write this chapter.

3. RESEARCH METHODOLOGY

Data for this chapter has been collected from case studies, various newspapers, academic reports, government portals, government websites and consumers insights. An extensive literature review has also been done for the collection of appropriate data needed for realizing the objectives of this chapter. Therefore, the sources of data are secondary in nature. The analysis will focus on identifying key applications of RegTech in various sectors, best practices, benefits and advantages of RegTech. The data analysis will also identify the key challenges related to RegTech.

4. EVOLUTION OF REGTECH

The evolution of Regtech can be understood in the three phases. The first phase can be referred to as RegTech 1.0[1], a phase which started in 1967 and ended in 2008. This phase focused on analysing exchange-based activities. The scope of the activities in this phase was limited to the Basel II Quantitative risk management. The second phase is referred to as RegTech 2.0[2] (from 2008–Present) This phase consists of two stages, the first being facilitate compliance and the second one is to improve supervision and regulation. Both these stages require the use of technology. The primary emphasis of many RegTech applications has been enhancing consumer protection and addressing unethical practices, particularly through the improvement of 'know your customer' (KYC) procedures. The third stage can be referred to as Regtech 3.0. The financial sector is approaching RegTech 3.0[3], shifting its focus from 'know your customer' to 'know your data. For financial institutions, risk and regulatory compliances are the most important issues to be tackled. These institutions treat these issues as data which they feel that can be better managed with the help of technology. This chapter now discusses the various types of RegTech which are available and can be used for automated regulatory compliance.

4.1 Regulatory Intelligence-Oriented RegTech

Regulatory intelligence oriented RegTech helps businesses stay informed about new rules and updates. Some platforms that offer this kind of intelligence are Thomson Reuters, Clarivate's Cortellis Regulatory Intelligence™[4], and Freyr Solutions.

4.2 Transaction Monitoring and Reporting-Oriented RegTech

Anti-money laundering tools are examples of transaction monitoring and reporting oriented RegTech. These tools use artificial intelligence to find transactions that might be malign or against the rules (Papantoniou, 2022; Ha, 2022). They can detect such transactions anywhere in the world. Some companies in this area are Jumio, Accuity, Comply advantage, and Seon.

4.3 Risk-Oriented RegTech

RegTech that focuses on risks helps spot possible problems with rules and finds holes in how a company does things. A few companies that offer help in this area are Albany Group, 360factors, and Axiomsl.

4.4 KYC (Know Your Customer)-Oriented RegTech

KYC oriented RegTech improves efficiency by ensuring the observance of regulatory requirements and thus ensures that companies follow all regulatory compliances. This type of RegTech includes the verification of customers' ID. It helps businesses follow rules about stopping money laundering (AML) and knowing their customers (KYC). Companies that sell online products often use these tools to make it easier for sellers to start selling. Some of the companies that offer these tools are Agreement Express, and Accuity.

5. RATIONALE BEHIND THE ADOPTION OF REGTECH

The financial industry has seen new technologies cause big changes. But besides Blockchain and Fintech, many of these disruptive technologies didn't last long. It's normal to doubt new technologies, especially since a lot of such technologies fade away quickly. However, Regtech showed that it's sticking around. Thanks to advances in Artificial Intelligence and Distributed Ledger Technology, supported by cloud computing, the financial industry, now, has digital ways to follow rules and report things (Papantoniou, 2022). Regtech emerged in response to the problems of existing regulatory framework. First, companies use a system called compliance management to comply with the rules and standards. However, because global regulations always keep on changing, it is very difficult for companies to stay updated (Firmansyah & Arman, 2023). Second, if the compliance and reporting work is done manually, it requires substantial investment of time along with huge costs. Further, it is more prone to errors and mistakes. Also, when different parts of a company report separately, they might end up giving the same information twice, which makes it hard for both the company and the regulators to understand and comply with (Vivek et al., 2020). This made financial companies to search for an alternative way of compliance. Here is where RegTech came into picture.

As mentioned above, RegTech, is becoming more necessary because rules for businesses are getting more complicated. Doing compliance work manually may require more time and is prone to several mistakes, making it hard for companies to follow all the rules. RegTech helps with this by using technology, like automation and artificial intelligence, to make compliance processes smoother and automatic. This way, companies can easily keep up with the newest rules. The motivation behind using RegTech arises due to several challenges and complexities associated with regulatory compliance in various industries. The RegTech results in saving money and time for the businesses as with it the mundane tasks related to regulatory compliance that need to be performed on routine basis can be done easily and automatically with AI. AI helps in the automation of regulatory tasks which reduces the number of errors which could have been possible with manual doing. The adoption of RegTech offers tremendous benefits to the user businesses. Globalization has accelerated the need for RegTech. Businesses nowadays operate in several countries, each with different rules and regulations to be followed. RegTech offers compliance solutions which though are standardised, can be customised as per the requirements of varied locations in different countries.

6. APPLICATIONS OF REGTECH

The following section discusses the applications of Regtech in detail. While the Financial Conduct Authority (FCA) of UK sees RegTech as a part of fintech, it's actually a technology that helps businesses to handle their regulatory compliances in more efficient manner (Yusoff et al., 2023). RegTech has mostly been used in the financial sector. This could be due to the fact that non-compliance of statutory rules may lead to heavy losses and penalties. However, RegTech can work perfectly in any industry which require to follow regulatory compliances. This means not only financial industry but another industry like healthcare, insurance and banking, will also be equally benefitted from the adoption of RegTech.

RegTech is changing the game for businesses in India. It uses technology to help companies follow rules and manage risks better. By combining technology and regulations, RegTech is shaking things up in India, offering high-tech solutions to make regulatory compliance easier. It automates tasks, improves accuracy, and makes sure companies stick to the rules. RegTech simplifies complex rules in different industries and places worldwide, making it a big deal for businesses in India. Many industries, like healthcare, insurance and banking are using RegTech to automate tasks, make reports more accurate, and manage risks better.

6.1 Regtech and Healthcare

Automation offers the potential to improve the efficiency and accuracy of regulatory compliance in the healthcare industry. Regulatory compliance refers to the process of meeting the requirements set by regulatory agencies such as the Ministry of Health and Family Welfare (MoHFW), Central Council for Indian Medicine, Indian Nursing Council to name few. Following regulatory compliances set by such regulatory agencies is important to ensure patient safety and to deliver the quality healthcare services. Regtech can help healthcare sector in meeting the regulatory compliance in many ways. First, using technology, RegTech may help in the management of data which is very important in the healthcare sector. Automation can make it easier to comply the rules (McGraw & Mandl, 2021). Regtech can simplify the process of data collection and data reporting. For instance, there's a new rule that says on request, patient records must be shared electronically. Doing this manually can take a lot of time and may sometimes result in some errors. But technology can help by gathering and organizing data from electronic records faster and more accurately without leaving a scope for any error (Paul, et al., 2023).

Second, data privacy and security are also crucial in healthcare, especially with laws like HIPAA- (Health Insurance Portability and Accountability Act) (Kapasi, 2023). Technology can automatically check who's accessing sensitive information and raise alerts if something goes wrong. This is important because cyberattacks are a growing threat in healthcare. Third, RegTech can also help spot compliance issues early. For example, smart systems can analyse data and find patterns that might suggest a problem. This helps healthcare professionals fix issues before they become big problems. Apart from this, automated systems can quickly update rules based on new regulations. This in turn, reduces the need for staff training. Fourth, with RegTech, healthcare sector can reduce mistakes. RegTech ensures that everyone follows the rules in a consistent manner without violation (McGraw & Mandl, 2021). This becomes more important during pandemic times like the recent COVID-19 when health guidelines kept on changing frequently. Lastly, RegTech can provide valuable insights across different parts of a healthcare organization. By analysing data from different areas, like supply chains and patient experiences, automation can help organizations make better decisions (Mbonihankuye et al., 2019).

6.2 RegTech and Insurance

RegTech adoption can offer equal or even better benefits to the insurance sector which is witnessing tremendous changes due to new technologies and regulations by Insurance Regulatory and Development Authority (IRDA), the primary regulatory body for insurance sector. RegTech by using technology can facilitate insurance sector by offering low lost and easier insurance options to people with low incomes or who live far away from cities. This tech-driven change will enable insurance sector to save money, to work in a better way and to offer better services to their customers. The global Insurtech (insurance managed by technology) market which was worth $9.42 billion in 2022 is expected to grow to $159 billion by 2031, showing a great potential for Regtech adoption.

Regtech has great potential in the insurance sector. Know Your Customer" (KYC) work can be simplified by the adoption of RegTech. KYC is all about checking who the customer is and understanding what they need. It's also known as customer due diligence. KYC can be referred to as the process of verifying customer identity (Kulkarni, et al., 2021). RegTech can ensure the protection of customer in the insurance sector by ruling out the possibility of unfair pricing models which will help in the enhancement of explainability of pricing models. Data privacy is a big deal as more things are done online. The latest rule in India about protecting data, known as the India Digital Personal Data Protection Act (DPDP Act or DPDPA) came into effect in August 2023 (Sabharwal, 2023). DPDPA has made it tougher for insurance companies to follow all the rules they need to. At the same time, RegTech helps in keeping the data confidential, hence ensure data privacy. However, with the application of technology, RegTech can help companies follow data protection laws like DPDPA better. It can be used to keep track of information notices and collect data wisely i.e. collect only needed amount of data. It ensures that the insurance companies meet the data minimization principle. Technology can also track requests for data access, making it easier to follow the rules (Nicoletti & Nicoletti, 2021). With Regtech, insurance companies can use digital tools to perform the task of customer identification. RegTech can help lower risks by creating a secure record of all KYC steps, thus RegTech facilitates the assessment of customer risk more efficiently and accurately.

6.3 RegTech and Banking

The Reserve Bank of India (RBI) and other regulatory bodies keep introducing and updating regulations to make sure the Indian banking system stays strong and trustworthy. Accordingly, Indian banks have to follow a lot of rules about things like stopping money laundering, knowing who their customers are, keeping data private, and protecting against cyber-attacks. Following these rules is really important but also quite tough. Therefore, figuring out how to follow all these rules properly needs creative solutions. RegTech is one such solution. RegTech helps banks sign up new customers more easily by automating the process. This ensures that customer's verification is done properly. RegTech can help in the identification of any suspicious activities faster. Using automation saves time and money needed for these important checks. RegTech by using advanced data analytics helps banks to assess and manage risks more effectively. Predictive analysis can spot patterns and irregularities, helping them to avoid problems before they happen.

With the advent of technology, cyberattacks have become more common. In such a scenario, RegTech helps a lot by automating how banks keep their systems safe from cyber threats. This means constantly checking computer systems, making sure data is encrypted, and finding and fixing any vulnerability that could be exploited by hackers. Furthermore, financial transaction refers to a mutual agreement or communication between a purchaser and vendor, aiming to swap goods, services, or assets for payment (Chen, 2023). It results in an alteration of the financial status of two or more entities, whether they are businesses or individuals (Freij, 2020). The accuracy of all financial transactions can be easily verified with the adoption of RegTech, hence RegTech can be considered as an effective way of meeting regulatory compliance in banking sector too. Since long back, internal controls have long been the centre of auditors' risk assessments as they try to verify that the system is operating efficiently to reduce the possibility of fraud in any financial transactions. The industry has witnessed the evolution of new standards to identify frauds, Similarly, we have observed advanced technology that can easily identify frauds. Artificial intelligence (AI), blockchain, and robotic process automation (RPA) are such innovations that can help detect fraud. Hence, Regtech can help in fulfilling all the statutory compliance in banking sector in more accurate and more efficient way.

7. CHALLENGES FACED DURING THE ADOPTION OF REGTECH

Adoption of Regtech may pose several challenges which are of high concern. These challenges must be tackled efficiently in order to fully capitalize the potential of RegTech. This section deliberates these challenges in detail. It also discusses the ways to handle them. First, using RegTech to handle sensitive customer information makes people worry about keeping that data private and secure. Complying with data protection laws, like India's Digital Personal Data Protection Act (DPDPA) is really difficult while using RegTech (Haris & Dhobale, 2023). Second, lots of sectors like insurance, healthcare and banking use old computer systems that might not work well with new RegTech tools. Trying to put new technologies like RegTech, without causing problems for the old systems is really a big challenge. Third, the regulatory framework in India needs to advance so that the use of RegTech can be recognized formally. They need to standardize the use of RegTech, which otherwise may prove to be a challenge for regulatory compliance. Regulators in India might need to change the rules to officially approve and set standards for using RegTech. Having explicit standards and guidelines will help various sectors like insurance, healthcare and banking know how to use these new technologies efficiently and effectively. Lastly, the use of RegTech requires that employees should be trained enough to understand and use these new tools. The companies in different sectors need to follow effective change management strategies. As these strategies will help employees to accept the changes occurred due to automated compliance processes.

To overcome all the abovementioned challenges, first, it is important that both regulators and representatives of various sectors should work together to make sure that everyone understands how RegTech works. Having regular deliberations will help everyone to get on the same pace. It will help everyone to use these new technologies like RegTech in an easier way. Second, both regulators and representatives should allocate some budget on research and development which can help them to mitigate the challenges of adopting with new regulatory compliance. This includes supporting incubators, innovation hubs, and RegTech startups.

8. CONCLUSION

As India is becoming more digital, adopting RegTech well will be crucial for making sure that all the regulatory compliances are followed without any error. Regtech assists financial institutions to be more efficient, accurate, and flexible in dealing with the ever-changing regulatory requirements. By using RegTech, companies can reduce the amount of manual work, and improve how they check for risks. The future of RegTech for knowing your customer (KYC) and stopping money laundering (AML) looks bright because it offers innovative solutions for the finance industry. Adopting RegTech is indispensable for staying ahead in a swiftly altering regulatory landscape and and for keeping the financial system sound and robust.

REFERENCES

Bitterli, M. (2017). Is Regtech "The next big thing"? First part. Available at: https://blogs.deloitte.ch/banking/2017/11/is-regtech-the-next-big-thing-first-part.html

Chen, J. (2023). Transaction. Available at: https://www.investopedia.com/terms/t/transaction.asp

Chettri, Y. (2022). RegTech-A Beginner's Guide to Regulation Technology. Available at: https://signalx.ai/blog/a-beginners-guide-to-regtech/

Freij, Å. (2020). Using technology to support financial services regulatory compliance: Current applications and future prospects of regtech. *Journal of Investment Compliance*, 21(2/3), 181–190. 10.1108/JOIC-10-2020-0033

Ha, L. T. (2022). Effects of digitalization on financialization: Empirical evidence from European countries. *Technology in Society*, 68(C), 101851. 10.1016/j.techsoc.2021.101851

Hanley-Giersch, B. J. (2019). *RegTech and Financial Crime Prevention*. The RegTech Book. 10.1002/9781119362197.ch4

Haris, M., & Dhobale, S. (2023). Revolutionising Compliance: The Role Of RegTech In Reshaping India's Regulatory Landscape. Available at: https://www.news18.com/business/revolutionising-compliance-the-role-of-regtech-in-reshaping-indias-regulatory-landscape-8645348.html#:~:text=The%20Future%20of%20RegTech%20in%20India&text=In%20the%20coming%20years,%20we,stay%20ahead%20of%20the%20curve

Kapasi, S. (2023). The Effects of Data Privacy Bills on Healthcare: Safeguarding Patient Information. Available at:_https://health.economictimes.indiatimes.com/news/health-it/the-effects-of-data-privacy-bills-on-healthcare-safeguarding-patient-information-in-the-digital-age/100748897

Kulkarni, V., Sunkle, S., Kholkar, D., Roychoudhury, S., Kumar, R., & Raghunandan, M. (2021). Toward automated regulatory compliance. *CSI Transactions on ICT*, 9(2), 95–104. 10.1007/s40012-021-00329-4

Li, Z. (2023). Digitalization of RegTech - Critical Review in China. *Journal of Applied Economics and Policy Studies.*, 1(1), 57–65. 10.54254/2977-5701/1/2023006

Mbonihankuye, S., Nkunzimana, A., & Ndagijimana, A. (2019). Healthcare data security technology: HIPAA compliance. *Wireless Communications and Mobile Computing*, 2019, 1–7. 10.1155/2019/1927495

McGraw, D., & Mandl, K. D. (2021). Privacy protections to encourage use of health-relevant digital data in a learning health system. *NPJ Digital Medicine*, 4(1), 2. 10.1038/s41746-020-00362-833398052

Mengfei, L. I. U., Jie, F. E. N. G., & Xiaowei, L. U. O. (2022). RegTech: Theory and Practice in Technology Driven Financial Regulation. *Frontiers of Economics in China*, 17(1).

Muganyi, T., Yan, L., Yin, Y., Sun, H., Gong, X., & Taghizadeh-Hesary, F. (2022). Fintech, regtech, and financial development: Evidence from China. *Financial Innovation*, 8(1), 1–20. 10.1186/s40854-021-00313-6

Nicoletti, B., & Nicoletti, B. (2021). Future of Insurance 4.0 and Insurtech. *Insurance 4.0: Benefits and Challenges of Digital Transformation*, 389-431.

Papantoniou, A. A. (2022). Regtech: Steering the regulatory spaceship in the right direction? *Journal of Banking and Financial Technology*, 6(1), 1–16. 10.1007/s42786-022-00038-9

Paul, M., Maglaras, L., Ferrag, M. A., & AlMomani, I. (2023). *Digitization of healthcare sector: A study on privacy and security concerns*. ICT Express.

Ryan, P., Crane, M., & Brennan, R. (2021). GDPR compliance tools: best practice from RegTech. In *International Conference on Enterprise Information Systems* (pp. 905-929). Cham: Springer International Publishing. 10.1007/978-3-030-75418-1_41

Sabharwal, A. (2023). India's Digital Personal Data Protection Act (DPDPA) Demystified. Available at: https://www.forbes.com/sites/forbestechcouncil/2023/11/15/indias-digital-personal-data-protection-act-dpdpa-demystified/?sh=6651b27c5c1c

Sian, D. (2023). RegTech adoption is accelerating fast, but who's in the driving seat? Available at: https://iqeq.com/insights/regtech-adoption-accelerating-fast-whos-driving-seat/

Teichmann, F., Boticiu, S., & Sergi, B. S. (2023). RegTech–Potential benefits and challenges for businesses. *Technology in Society*, 72, 102150. 10.1016/j.techsoc.2022.102150

Vivek, D., Rakesh, S., Walimbe, R. S., & Mohanty, A. (2020). The Role of CLOUD in FinTech and RegTech. *Annals of the University Dunarea de Jos of Galati: Fascicle: I, Economics & Applied Informatics, 26*(3).

Von Solms, J. (2021). Integrating Regulatory Technology (RegTech) into the digital transformation of a bank Treasury. *Journal of Banking Regulation*, 22(2), 152–168. 10.1057/s41261-020-00134-0

ENDNOTES

[1]   https://www.cfainstitute.org/-/media/documents/article/rf-brief/rfbr-v3-n4-1
.ashx

[2]   https://assets.kpmg.com/content/dam/kpmg/uk/pdf/2018/09/regtech-revolution
-coming.pdf

[3]   https://www.cfainstitute.org/-/media/documents/article/rf-brief/rfbr-v3-n4-1
.ashx

[4]   https://clarivate.com/slp/cortellis-regulatory-intelligence-solutions/

Chapter 2
Economic Impact of RegTech Compliance

Padma Iyenghar
http://orcid.org/0000-0002-1765-3695
Innotec GmbH, Germany

ABSTRACT

This chapter explores the economic implications of Regulatory Technology (RegTech) compliance in the context of Industry 4.0, Cyber-Physical Systems (CPS), cybersecurity, and functional safety. While RegTech offers significant economic benefits, concerns persist regarding implementation costs, regulatory uncertainties, and cybersecurity risks. This chapter conducts a comprehensive economic analysis of RegTech adoption, highlighting both positive and negative impacts on organizational performance. By examining the intersection of RegTech with Industry 4.0, CPS, and functional safety, this chapter provides actionable insights for navigating regulatory complexities. Future research avenues include exploring emerging technologies, regulatory sandbox frameworks, ethical and legal implications, and global regulatory convergence in RegTech. Overall, this chapter lays the groundwork for understanding the economic dynamics of RegTech adoption, empowering organizations to drive sustainable growth in a regulated business environment.

1. INTRODUCTION

In today's rapidly evolving regulatory landscape, organizations across various industries face increasing challenges in meeting compliance requirements efficiently and effectively. The emergence of Regulatory Technology (RegTech) solutions offers a promising avenue for addressing these challenges by leveraging advanced technologies to streamline regulatory compliance processes (Teichmann et all 2023). This

DOI: 10.4018/979-8-3693-3322-8.ch002

article explores the economic impact of RegTech compliance amidst the backdrop of Industry 4.0, Cyber-Physical Systems (CPS), cybersecurity and functional safety.

RegTech refers to the use of technology-driven solutions to ensure adherence to relevant regulatory requirements and standards. By harnessing automation, Artificial Intelligence (AI), Machine Learning (ML), and data analytics, RegTech solutions empower organizations to navigate the complexities of regulatory compliance with greater agility and precision. From financial transactions to data protection and environmental regulations, RegTech solutions offer a diverse range of functionalities aimed at enhancing compliance effectiveness and efficiency.

The advent of Industry 4.0 (Yang & Gu 2021), characterized by the integration of digital technologies with manufacturing and industrial processes, has further underscored the importance of regulatory compliance in safeguarding the integrity and resilience of digital ecosystems. With the proliferation of IoT, AI, robotics, and cloud computing technologies, organizations must navigate a myriad of regulatory requirements related to data privacy, cybersecurity, intellectual property, and product safety. RegTech solutions play a pivotal role in enabling organizations to comply with industry-specific regulations and standards, thereby facilitating market expansion and fostering innovation.

Similarly, the evolution of Cyber-Physical Systems (CPS) has introduced new challenges and opportunities in ensuring the security and reliability of interconnected digital systems (Pivoto et al 2021). As CPS integrates physical components with digital technologies to monitor, control, and optimize physical processes, organizations must address cybersecurity risks associated with unauthorized access, data breaches, and system failures. RegTech solutions offer automated threat detection, incident response, and compliance monitoring capabilities to mitigate these risks and enhance the resilience of CPS environments.

Furthermore, functional safety remains paramount in industries where system failures could result in harm to individuals, damage to property, or adverse environmental impact (11)[1]. Standards such as ISO 26262 and IEC 61508 provide guidelines for ensuring the safety and reliability of safety-critical systems. RegTech solutions streamline compliance processes related to functional safety standards, reducing the time and resources required for safety analysis, documentation, and verification.

While RegTech compliance offers significant economic benefits, organizations must also consider potential implementation costs, regulatory uncertainty, and cybersecurity risks associated with RegTech adoption. This article provides a comprehensive analysis of the economic implications of RegTech compliance across various technological domains, highlighting both the positive and negative impacts on organizational performance and resilience.

By examining the intersection of RegTech compliance with Industry 4.0, CPS, and functional safety, this article aims to provide valuable insights into the economic dynamics shaping regulatory compliance in the digital age. Through a nuanced understanding of the opportunities and challenges inherent in RegTech adoption, organizations can navigate regulatory complexities more effectively and drive sustainable growth in an increasingly regulated business environment. Future research could explore emerging technologies, regulatory sandbox frameworks, ethical and legal implications, global regulatory convergence, and the long-term economic impact of RegTech to further enhance understanding in this field.

The remainder of this article is organized as follows. Following this introduction section, an introductory overview of key concepts essential to understanding the subsequent discussions on the economic impact of RegTech compliance amidst Industry 4.0, Cyber physical systems (CPS), and functional safety is provided in section 2. An economic analysis of RegTech adoption is provided in section 3. The economic implications of RegTec compliance across technological domains is provided in section 4. Potential for future research is discussed in section 5. A conclusion is provided in section 6.

2. BACKGROUND

In this section, we provide an introductory overview of key concepts essential to understanding the subsequent discussions on the economic impact of RegTech compliance amidst Industry 4.0, Cyber- physical systems (CPS), and functional safety. This comprehensive background sets the stage for a detailed analysis of the economic implications of RegTech compliance across various technological do- mains, providing valuable insights for organizations navigating regulatory complexities and harnessing the potential of advanced technologies in regulatory compliance.

2.1 RegTech and Related

2.1.1 What Is RegTech?

Regulatory Technology (RegTech) refers to the use of technology, particularly advanced software, and data analytics, to streamline regulatory compliance processes and help organizations meet their regulatory obligations more efficiently and effectively. *RegTech* solutions leverage automation, artificial intelligence, machine learning, and other technologies to address regulatory challenges across various industries, including finance, healthcare, manufacturing, and beyond.

RegTech solutions offer a range of functionalities, including regulatory reporting, compliance monitoring, risk assessment, identity verification, transaction monitoring, and audit trail management. By automating manual tasks, improving data accuracy, and providing real-time insights, RegTech enables organizations to reduce compliance costs, minimize regulatory risks, enhance operational efficiency, and maintain regulatory compliance in an increasingly complex and fast-paced regulatory environment (Teichmann et al 2023). Thus, RegTech plays a crucial role in helping organizations navigate regulatory complexities, adapt to regulatory changes, and stay competitive in today's highly regulated business landscape.

2.1.2 Regulatory Landscape

The regulatory landscape encompasses laws, regulations, and standards governing various industries and activities. Key aspects include:

- Laws and Regulations: Formal rules established by legislative bodies or regulatory agencies to ensure compliance and public safety.
- Regulatory Bodies: Government entities responsible for implementing and enforcing regulations within specific sectors.
- Compliance Frameworks: Guidelines and best practices for organizations to ensure adherence to regulatory requirements.
- Industry Standards: Established by associations and international bodies to promote consistency and quality within sectors.
- International Regulations: Cross-border regulations addressing global issues like trade, finance, and cybersecurity.
- Technological Advancements: Shaping regulations to address emerging risks and opportunities posed by new technologies.
- Regulatory Enforcement: Mechanisms such as inspections and penalties to ensure compliance and deter non-compliance.

2.1.3 Regulatory Compliance

RegTech compliance, short for Regulatory Technology compliance, refers to the use of technology- driven solutions to ensure that businesses adhere to relevant regulatory requirements and standards. These regulations can encompass a wide range of areas, including financial transactions, data protection, consumer rights, environmental regulations, and more. RegTech compliance solutions leverage advanced technologies such as artificial intelligence, machine learning, data analytics, and automation to streamline and enhance compliance processes (Teichmann et al 2023). RegTech compliance solutions offer several benefits, including:

- Automation: RegTech solutions automate various compliance processes, reducing manual effort and minimizing the risk of human error. This includes tasks such as data collection, monitoring, reporting, and audit preparation.
- Efficiency: By automating routine tasks and providing real-time insights into compliance status, RegTech solutions help organizations improve operational efficiency and resource allocation. This allows businesses to focus their efforts on value-added activities rather than spending time on administrative tasks.
- Accuracy: RegTech solutions enable more accurate and timely compliance reporting by ensuring data consistency, integrity, and completeness. This reduces the risk of compliance errors and discrepancies, helping organizations maintain regulatory compliance more effectively.
- Scalability: RegTech solutions are scalable, allowing organizations to adapt to changing regulatory requirements and business needs more easily. Whether an organization is a small startup or a large multinational corporation, RegTech solutions can be tailored to meet specific compliance needs and scale with the business.
- Risk Management: By providing real-time insights into compliance status and potential risks, RegTech solutions help organizations proactively identify and mitigate compliance risks. This allows businesses to avoid non-compliance penalties, reputational damage, and other negative consequences associated with regulatory violations.

Thus, RegTech compliance solutions play a crucial role in helping businesses navigate the complex regulatory landscape efficiently and effectively. By leveraging technology to automate and enhance compliance processes, organizations can reduce costs, improve efficiency, and mitigate compliance risks, ultimately driving business success and sustainability.

Figure 1. Pillars of Industry 4.0 (Pivoto et al., 2021) and an example of connected IoT devices[2]

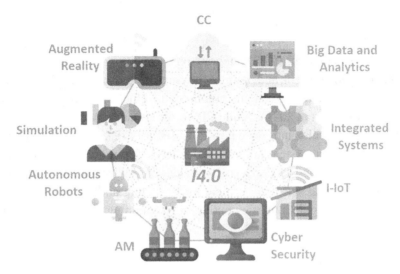

2.2 Technology

In this section, we delve into the technological landscape shaping modern industries and regulatory frameworks. The convergence of digital advancements with traditional industrial processes has ushered in a new era of Industry 4.0 (Pivoto et al 2021). This paradigm shift introduces cyber-physical systems (CPS) and underscores the importance of functional safety and cybersecurity in ensuring the integrity, security, and resilience of digital ecosystems (cf. Figure. 1). Several of the aspects are explained in brief below.

2.2.1 Industry 4.0

Industry 4.0 represents the fusion of digital technologies with manufacturing and industrial processes, revolutionizing how products are designed, produced, and delivered (Yang & Gu 2021). Innovations such as the Internet of Things (IoT), artificial intelligence (AI), robotics, data analytics, and cloud computing form the backbone of Industry 4.0, driving unprecedented efficiency, agility, and connectivity across supply chains and production networks (Pivoto et al 2021). However, this digital transformation also introduces new regulatory challenges related to data privacy, cybersecurity, intellectual property, product safety, and environmental sustainability[3]. Regulators must adapt existing regulations and develop new policies to address these challenges, ensuring responsible and ethical deployment of Industry 4.0 technologies.

2.2.2 Cyber Physical Systems (CPS)

Cyber-physical systems (CPS) integrate physical components with digital technologies to monitor, control, and optimize physical processes in real time. Examples include smart manufacturing systems, autonomous vehicles, smart grids, and healthcare devices (Pivoto et al 2021). While CPS offer immense potential for efficiency and innovation, they also introduce new cybersecurity risks, such as unauthorized access, data breaches, system failures, and safety-critical vulnerabilities. Regulators need to develop robust cybersecurity regulations and standards to protect CPS from cyber threats and safeguard critical infrastructure and services. Compliance with cybersecurity regulations is essential for maintaining trust and confidence in digital ecosystems.

2.2.3 Functional Safety

Functional safety is paramount in industries where system or component failures could result in harm to individuals, damage to property, or adverse environmental impact[4]. Standards such as ISO 26262 (automotive), IEC 61508 (industrial), and ISA/IEC 62443 (industrial control systems) provide guidelines for ensuring the safety and reliability of safety-critical systems (cf. Figure. 2). Regulators may require organizations to comply with these standards to mitigate risks associated with functional safety hazards. Compliance with functional safety standards is essential for obtaining regulatory approvals, certifications, and licenses to operate in safety-critical industries.

Figure 2. Overview of functional safety standards[5]

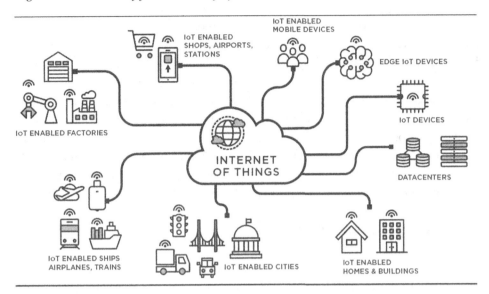

2.2.4 Cybersecurity

Cybersecurity challenges encompass the myriad threats and risks organizations face in safeguarding their digital assets, systems, and networks from malicious activities (Rohani et al 2023). These challenges evolve continuously as cyberattackers develop new tactics, techniques, and procedures (TTPs) to exploit vulnerabilities and breach defenses. Common cybersecurity challenges include phishing attacks, malware infections, ransomware, data breaches, insider threats, and denial-of-service (DoS) attacks. Organizations must adopt proactive cybersecurity measures to mitigate these risks effectively and comply with relevant regulations, such as the General Data Protection Regulation (GDPR), Health Insurance Portability and Accountability Act (HIPAA), Payment Card Industry Data Security Standard (PCI DSS), and the NIST Cybersecurity Framework.

Thus, Industry 4.0, CPS, functional safety, and cybersecurity are integral components of the regulatory landscape, influencing the development, implementation, and enforcement of regulations and standards across various emerging sectors. Regulators, policymakers, and industry stakeholders must collaborate to address the regulatory challenges and opportunities presented by these transformative technologies, ensuring that regulatory frameworks remain adaptive, responsive, and effective in promoting safety, security, and innovation in the digital age.

3. ECONOMIC ANALYSIS OF REGTECH ADOPTION

This section provides an analysis of the economic impacts associated with the adoption of RegTech solutions for regulatory compliance. It discusses both the positive and negative economic implications of implementing RegTech across various industries undergoing digital transformation. The section primarily focuses on the broader application of RegTech solutions, rather than limiting the discussion to specific technological domains. The section covers various aspects of RegTech compliance, including its potential to generate cost savings, mitigate risks, and facilitate market expansion. It also addresses the challenges and drawbacks associated with RegTech adoption, such as implementation costs, regulatory uncertainty, cybersecurity risks, integration challenges, regulatory overreach, and vendor dependence.

3.1 Positive Economic Impacts

- Cost savings: RegTech solutions can streamline compliance processes, reducing the time and resources required for manual tasks such as documentation, reporting, and audit preparation. Studies have shown that RegTech adoption can lead to cost savings of up to 50% in some cases[6].
- Risk mitigation: By automating compliance monitoring and risk assessment processes, RegTech solutions help organizations identify and address regulatory issues in a timely manner, reducing the likelihood of non-compliance fines, legal fees, and reputational damage. According to IBM, cost of a data breach report from 2023[7], the average cost of a data breach reached an all-time high in 2023 of $4.45 million globally, emphasizing the economic value of effective risk mitigation. Taking a long-term view, the average cost has increased 15.3% in 2023 in comparison with the cost of USD 3.86 million mentioned in the 2020 report.
- Market expansion: Compliance with regulations is often a prerequisite for entering new markets and securing contracts with customers. RegTech solutions that facilitate compliance with industry-specific regulations can enable organizations to expand their market reach and pursue business opportunities in sectors where safety and regulatory compliance are critical. While specific numerical data may vary, market expansion can lead to increased revenue and profitability for organizations.
- Efficiency gains: Various industry reports and case studies suggest that RegTech solutions can lead to significant efficiency gains by automating manual processes, reducing errors, and improving workflow management. For example, a study conducted by IBM (2023) found that RegTech adoption

can result in efficiency improvements of up to 50% in compliance-related tasks.

- Enhanced customer trust: Regulatory compliance and transparency are important factors in building customer trust and loyalty. RegTech solutions that help organizations demonstrate compliance with regulations can contribute to enhancing customer trust and reputation, ultimately leading to increased revenue and market share[8].

- Competitive advantage: Industry reports and surveys highlight the importance of regulatory compliance as a source of competitive advantage in today's business landscape. Organizations that invest in RegTech solutions to streamline compliance processes, reduce risks, and enhance operational efficiency are better positioned to outperform competitors and capture market opportunities (Teichmann et al 2023).

3.2 Negative Economic Impacts

- Implementation costs: While RegTech solutions can lead to cost savings in the long run, there may be initial implementation costs associated with software procurement, customization, integration, and training. According to an article in HBS[9], the initial investment required for RegTech implementation can range from tens of thousands to millions of dollars, depending on the size and complexity of the organization.

- Regulatory uncertainty: The regulatory landscape is constantly evolving, with new regulations, standards, and enforcement actions being introduced regularly. This uncertainty can create challenges for organizations seeking to implement RegTech solutions, as they may need to adapt to changes in regulatory requirements and compliance expectations. According to Thomson Reuters[10], regulatory change management costs financial institutions an average of $17.1 million per year.

- Cybersecurity risks: RegTech solutions often rely on digital technologies and data processing systems, making them vulnerable to cybersecurity threats such as data breaches, malware attacks, and insider threats. The economic impact of cybersecurity incidents can be significant, with studies estimating that the average cost of a data breach exceeds $3.8 million globally[11].

- Integration challenges: Further, industry surveys and case studies often highlight the complexity and costs associated with integrating RegTech solutions with existing IT systems and infrastructure. These challenges can result in delays, cost overruns, and disruptions to business operations, impacting financial performance and project outcomes.

- Regulatory overreach: Academic research and policy analysis on regulatory burden and compliance costs shed light on the potential negative economic impacts of excessive or poorly designed regulations. While the exact economic impact may vary by industry and jurisdiction, studies suggest that regulatory burdens can hinder innovation, entrepreneurship, and economic growth, imposing significant costs on businesses and consumers (IBM Report 2023).
- Vendor Dependence: Reports and articles on vendor risk management and outsourcing highlight the economic risks associated with heavy reliance on third-party RegTech vendors for compliance solutions. These risks, as mentioned in Global Cybersecurity Outlook 2024, include vendor lock-in, service disruptions, data breaches, and contractual disputes, which can lead to financial losses, reputational damage, and legal liabilities for organizations.

Thus, the economic implications of adopting RegTech solutions to address regulatory challenges and compliance requirements within industries undergoing digital transformation and embracing advanced technologies are discussed above.

4. ECONOMIC IMPLICATIONS OF REGTECH COMPLIANCE ACROSS TECHNOLOGICAL DOMAINS

This section provides an in-depth analysis of the economic implications associated with the adoption of RegTech solutions within the context of Industry 4.0, Cyber-Physical Systems (CPS), cybersecurity and Functional Safety compliance. The section examines both the positive and negative economic impacts of integrating RegTech solutions into compliance processes across these technological domains, highlighting both the opportunities and challenges associated with adopting RegTech solutions in these domains.

4.1 Positive Economic Impacts

- Cost Savings in functional safety compliance: RegTech solutions can streamline compliance processes related to functional safety standards such as ISO 26262 and IEC 61508, reducing the time and resources required for safety analysis, documentation, and verification.
- Efficiency gains in Industry 4.0 compliance: RegTech solutions enable organizations to comply with regulations specific to Industry 4.0 technologies, such as data privacy requirements under GDPR and cybersecurity standards like NIST Cybersecurity Framework, more efficiently through automation and real-time monitoring. Research by the European Union Agency

for Cybersecurity (ENISA) indicated that RegTech adoption in Industry 4.0 compliance processes could improve efficiency by up to 40% (Ewens et al 2024).

- Risk Mitigation in CPS security compliance: RegTech solutions help organizations address cybersecurity risks associated with CPS, such as unauthorized access, data breaches, and system failures, by providing automated threat detection, incident response, and compliance monitoring capabilities. According to a report by the World Economic Forum (WEF), effective RegTech adoption in CPS security compliance can reduce the likelihood of cybersecurity incidents by up to 50% (Yang & Gu 2021).
- Security awareness: Security awareness training empowers employees to identify and mitigate cybersecurity threats effectively, resulting in significant cost savings. Research indicates that organizations with comprehensive security awareness programs experience up to 50% fewer security incidents, translating into substantial financial benefits (Teichmann et al 2023). By reducing the frequency and severity of cyberattacks, businesses can save millions in remediation costs, regulatory fines, and reputational damage. Additionally, heightened security awareness fosters a culture of compliance and vigilance, enhancing operational efficiency and bolstering customer trust. These economic benefits underscore the critical role of security awareness in driving sustainable growth and competitive advantage in today's digital landscape.
- Cybersecurity governance: Effective cybersecurity governance frameworks play a crucial role in enhancing positive economic outcomes for organizations. By aligning cybersecurity objectives with broader business goals, these frameworks ensure that investments in cybersecurity contribute to overall organizational resilience and competitiveness. According to a study by the Ponemon Institute (2019), companies with strong cybersecurity governance experience lower average costs of cybercrime incidents by as much as 40% compared to those with weak governance structures. Furthermore, robust cybersecurity governance helps organizations maintain compliance with regulatory requirements, avoiding costly fines and penalties associated with non-compliance. For example, research by the International Data Corporation[12] (IDC) suggests that companies with comprehensive cybersecurity governance frameworks can reduce the risk of regulatory penalties by up to 50%, resulting in potential cost savings of millions of dollars annually.

4.2 Negative Economic Impacts

- Implementation Costs for Industry 4.0 Compliance: While RegTech solutions offer long-term cost savings, there may be initial implementation costs associated with software procurement, customization, integration, and training, particularly in the context of Industry 4.0 compliance. McKinsey estimates that the initial investment required for RegTech implementation in Industry 4.0 compliance can range from $100,000 to $10 million, depending on the size and complexity of the organization (as per GDPR).

- Regulatory uncertainty in functional safety compliance: The evolving regulatory landscape for functional safety standards may introduce uncertainty for organizations seeking to implement RegTech solutions, as they must adapt to changes in regulatory requirements and compliance expectations. A survey by Deloitte found that 70% of organizations cited regulatory change as a top challenge in compliance management (e.g. cybersecurity, functional safety), highlighting the impact of regulatory uncertainty on compliance costs and resource allocation.

- Cybersecurity risks in CPS compliance: RegTech solutions in CPS compliance may introduce new cybersecurity risks, such as reliance on third-party vendors for software and data storage, potential vulnerabilities in automated systems, and increased exposure to sophisticated cyberattacks. Reports from several independent institutes estimate that the average cost of a cyberattack on CPS systems is $6.39 million, emphasizing the economic impact of cybersecurity incidents on organizations adopting RegTech solutions in CPS compliance.

- Incident response: Effective incident response planning is crucial for mitigating the financial and reputational consequences of cybersecurity incidents. Inadequate incident response procedures can result in prolonged downtime, data breaches, and operational disruptions, leading to significant financial losses and reputational damage for organizations. According to a report by IBM, the average cost of a data breach reached $4.45 million globally in 2023, with costs increasing by 15.3% compared to the previous year. These costs include expenses related to incident investigation, remediation, regulatory fines, legal fees, and loss of customer trust. Furthermore, organizations that fail to respond effectively to cybersecurity incidents may face regulatory consequences, such as penalties for non-compliance with data protection regulations like GDPR. For example, the European General Data Protection Regulation (GDPR) allows regulators to impose fines of up to 4% of a company's annual global revenue or €20 million, whichever is higher, for serious violations. Thus, ineffective incident response procedures can have severe negative economic impacts, including financial losses, reputational damage, and regulatory consequences. Organizations must prioritize incident response planning and invest in robust response capabilities to minimize the adverse effects of cybersecurity incidents.

Overall, it is observed that RegTech compliance offers specific economic impacts in the context of Indus- try 4.0, functional safety, and cyber-physical systems, encompassing cost savings, efficiency gains, and risk mitigation. While RegTech solutions can streamline compliance processes, enhance operational efficiency, and mitigate regulatory and cybersecurity risks, organizations must also consider potential implementation costs, regulatory uncertainty, and cybersecurity risks associated with RegTech adoption in these domains.

This section has delved into various aspects of RegTech compliance, including cost savings, efficiency gains, risk mitigation, implementation costs, regulatory uncertainty, cybersecurity risks, and incident response. It elucidates how RegTech solutions can streamline compliance processes, improve operational efficiency, and mitigate regulatory and cybersecurity risks, thus fostering positive eco- nomic outcomes for organizations. Nevertheless, it also underscores the importance of acknowledging the potential challenges and drawbacks of implementing RegTech solutions, such as initial implementation costs, regulatory uncertainty, cybersecurity vulnerabilities, and the necessity of effective incident response planning.

5. POTENTIAL FOR FUTURE RESEARCH

As the landscape of regulatory compliance continues to evolve alongside advancements in technology, numerous opportunities for future research emerge. Exploring these avenues can provide valuable insights into the economic implications of RegTech compliance and drive innovation in regulatory frameworks. Below are several potential areas for future research:

5.1 Impact of Emerging Technologies

- Research could investigate the impact of blockchain technology on RegTech compliance, examining its potential to enhance data integrity, transparency, and regulatory reporting. For instance, a study by Deloitte found that blockchain-based RegTech solutions could reduce compliance costs by up to 50% (Corallo et al 2022).
- Similarly, exploring the implications of quantum computing on regulatory risk assessment and compliance monitoring could provide valuable insights.

A report by McKinsey estimates that quantum computing could enable organizations to analyse complex regulatory datasets up to 100 times faster.

- Additionally, research into the application of Augmented Reality (AR) (Chen et al 2019) in regulatory inspections and audits could offer innovative solutions for enhancing regulatory compliance processes. Studies done by Accenture[13] have shown that AR technology can improve task efficiency by up to 30% in industrial settings.

5.2 Regulatory Sandbox Frameworks

- A comparative analysis of regulatory sandbox frameworks across different jurisdictions could assess their effectiveness in promoting innovation and regulatory compliance. For example, a study by the World Bank identified key success factors for regulatory sandboxes, including stakeholder engagement, regulatory flexibility, and clear exit strategies (Pivoto et al 2021).
- Investigating the impact of regulatory sandboxes on RegTech startups and fintech ecosystems could provide insights into the scalability and sustainability of innovative solutions. Research by the Financial Conduct Authority (FCA) in the UK found that participating in a regulatory sandbox increased the likelihood of a fintech startup receiving funding by 25% (Shanaey et al 2020).

5.3 Ethical and Legal Implications

- Research could examine the ethical considerations of using AI and machine learning algorithms in RegTech compliance, addressing concerns related to algorithmic bias, fairness, and interpretability. For instance, a study by the AI Now Institute highlighted the need for transparency and accountability in AI systems used for regulatory decision-making[14].
- Legal analysis of data privacy regulations such as the General Data Protection Regulation (GDPR) and their implications for RegTech compliance could provide guidance for organizations. Research by the European Data Protection Supervisor (EDPS) offers insights into the intersection of data protection and emerging technologies.

5.4 Global Regulatory Convergence

- A longitudinal study tracking regulatory developments and convergence efforts in key sectors such as finance, healthcare, and manufacturing could assess progress towards global regulatory harmonization. Reports by organizations like the International Organization of Securities Com- missions (IOSCO) provide updates on regulatory convergence initiatives in the financial sector.

- Analysing the economic impact of regulatory divergence versus convergence on multinational corporations could quantify the costs and benefits of regulatory compliance across different jurisdictions. Research by the International Monetary Fund (IMF) highlights the challenges and opportunities of regulatory harmonization for global businesses (Rohani et al 2023).

5.5 Long-Term Economic Impact

- Longitudinal studies tracking the financial performance and regulatory compliance outcomes of organizations before and after implementing RegTech solutions could provide empirical evidence of long-term economic impact. For example, a study by PricewaterhouseCoopers (PwC) found that companies with advanced RegTech capabilities outperformed their peers by 20% in terms of revenue growth over a five-year period.

- Surveys and interviews with industry stakeholders could capture qualitative insights into the strategic benefits and challenges of RegTech adoption over time.

The examples illustrate the potential avenues for future research in understanding the economic implications of RegTech compliance and advancing regulatory innovation in an increasingly digitalized and interconnected world. Thus, future research in these areas would further advance our understanding of the economic implications of RegTech compliance and contribute to the development of innovative solutions for addressing regulatory challenges in an increasingly digitized and interconnected world.

6. CONCLUSION

In conclusion, this article provides a comprehensive analysis of the economic impact of RegTech compliance within the domains of Industry 4.0, CPS, and functional safety. It elucidates the significant opportunities offered by RegTech solutions in streamlining compliance processes, reducing costs, and enhancing efficiency, while also addressing the challenges such as implementation costs, regulatory uncertainty, cybersecurity vulnerabilities, and integration complexities. Moreover, future research avenues, including the exploration of emerging technologies, regulatory sandbox frameworks, ethical and legal implications, global regulatory convergence, and the long-term economic impact of RegTech, present promising areas for further investigation in the field.

REFERENCES

Accenture-Going beyond extended reality. (n.d.). https://www.accenture.com/de -de/about/ going-beyond-extended-reality

AI Now Institute. (n.d.). https://ainowinstitute.org/

Chen, Y., Wang, Q., Chen, H., Song, X., Tang, H., & Tian, M. (2019, June). An overview of augmented reality technology. *Journal of Physics: Conference Series*, 1237(2), 022082. 10.1088/1742-6596/1237/2/022082

Corallo, A., Lazoi, M., Lezzi, M., & Luperto, A. (2022). Cybersecurity awareness in the context of the Industrial Internet of Things: A systematic literature review. *Computers in Industry*, 137, 103614. 10.1016/j.compind.2022.103614

European Data Protection Supervisor. (n.d.). https://www.edps.europa.eu/_en

European Union Agency for Cybersecurity (ENISA). (n.d.). https://www.enisa.europa .eu/ publications/industry-4-0-cybersecurity-challenges-and-recommendations

Ewens, M., Xiao, K., & Xu, T. (2024). Regulatory costs of being public: Evidence from bunching estimation. *Journal of Financial Economics*, 153, 103775. 10.1016/j. jfineco.2023.103775

Functional safety standards-An overview. (n.d.). https://www.tuvsud.com/en-us/ services/ functional-safety/about

GDPR-fines and penalties. (n.d.). https://gdpr.eu/fines/

IBM. (n.d.). Cost of a Data Breach Report 2023. https://www.ibm.com/reports/ data-breach/

IDC spending guide forecasts. (n.d.). https://www.idc.com/getdoc.jsp?containerId =prUS50386323

IoT Security Best Practices. (n.d.). https://codalien.com/blog/ internet-of-things-io t-security-best-practices/

Key Data From Regulatory Sandboxes Across The Globe. (n.d.). https://www .worldbank.org/ en/topic/fintech/brief/key-data-from-regulatory-sandboxes-acros s-the-globe

Lim, M. K., Li, Y., Wang, C., & Tseng, M. L. (2021). A literature review of block-chain technology applications in supply chains: A comprehensive analysis of themes, methodologies and industries. *Computers & Industrial Engineering*, 154, 107133. 10.1016/j.cie.2021.107133

Pivoto, D. G., de Almeida, L. F., da Rosa Righi, R., Rodrigues, J. J., Lugli, A. B., & Alberti, A. M. (2021). Cyber-physical systems architectures for industrial internet of things applications in Industry 4.0: A literature review. *Journal of Manufacturing Systems*, 58, 176–192. 10.1016/j.jmsy.2020.11.017

Ponemon Institute. (2019). Global State of Cybersecurity in Small to Medium-sized Businesses Report. Author.

Quantum Computing for the Quantum Era. (n.d.). McKinsey & Company. https://www.mckinsey.com/featured-insights/the-rise-of-quantum-computing

RegTech. (n.d.). A New Way to Manage Risks. https://www.hbs.edu/faculty/Shared%20Documents/ conferences/2022-imo/Andrew%20Sutherland%20paper.pdf

RegTech Survey: PricewaterhouseCoopers. (n.d.). https://www.pwc.com/us/en/ industries/ financial-services/regulatory-services/regtech.html

Regulatory Divergence. (n.d.). Costs, Risks and Impacts. https://www. ifac.org/ knowledge-gateway/contributing-global-economy/publications/

Regulatory sandbox lessons learnt-report. (n.d.). https://www.fca.org.uk/publication/ research-and-data/regulatory-sandbox-lessons-learned-report.pdf

Rohan, R., Pal, D., Hautamäki, J., Funilkul, S., Chutimaskul, W., & Thapliyal, H. (2023). A systematic literature review of cybersecurity scales assessing information security awareness. *Heliyon*, 9(3), e14234. 10.1016/j.heliyon.2023.e1423436938452

Shanaev, S., Sharma, S., Ghimire, B., & Shuraeva, A. (2020). Taming the block-chain beast? Regulatory implications for the cryptocurrency Market. *Research in International Business and Finance*, 51, 101080. 10.1016/j.ribaf.2019.101080

Teichmann, F., Boticiu, S., & Sergi, B. S. (2023). RegTech–Potential benefits and challenges for businesses. *Technology in Society*, 72, 102150. 10.1016/j.tech-soc.2022.102150

The Role of RegTech in Organizations. (n.d.). https://www.doxee.com/blog/regtech/ the-role-of-regtech-in-organizations/

Thriving in a digital world. (n.d.). https://kpmg.com/xx/en/home/about/corporate -reporting/ thriving-in-a-digital-world.html

Tips for Selecting RegTec Solutions. (n.d.). https://infobelt.com/ tips-for-selecting-regulatory-technology-regtech-solutions/

WEF. (n.d.-a). Global cybersecurity outlook, 2024. https://www.weforum.org/ publications/ global-cybersecurity-outlook-2024/

WEF. (n.d.-b). Regulatory technology for the 21st century. https://www.weforum .org/publications/ regulatory-technology-for-the-21st-century/

Yang, F., & Gu, S. (2021). Industry 4.0, a revolution that requires technology and national strategies. *Complex & Intelligent Systems*, 7(3), 1311–1325. 10.1007/ s40747-020-00267-9

ENDNOTES

[1]   Functional safety standards-An overview. https://www.tuvsud.com/en-us/ services/functional-safety/about. Accessed: 9.02.2024.

[2]   IoT Security Best Practices. https://codalien.com/blog/internet-of-things-iot -security-best-practices/. Accessed: 9.02.2024.

[3]   IoT Security Best Practices. https://codalien.com/blog/internet-of-things-iot -security-best-practices/. Accessed: 9.02.2024.

[4]   Functional safety standards-An overview. https://www.tuvsud.com/en-us/ services/functional-safety/about. Accessed: 9.02.2024.

[5]   Functional safety standards-An overview. https://www.tuvsud.com/en-us/ services/functional-safety/about. Accessed: 9.02.2024.

[6]   The Role of RegTech in Organizations. https://www.doxee.com/blog/regtech/ the-role-of-regtech-in-organizations/. Accessed: 09.02.2024.

[7]   IBM: Cost of a Data Breach Report 2023. https://www.ibm.com/reports/data -breach/. Accessed: 09.02.2024.

[8]   Thriving in a digital world. https://kpmg.com/xx/en/home/about/corporate -reporting/thriving-in-a-digital-world.html. Accessed: 05.02.2024.

[9]   RegTech: A New Way to Manage Risks . https://www.hbs.edu/faculty/Shared %20Documents/conferences/2022-imo/Andrew%20Sutherland%20paper.pdf. Accessed: 09.02.2024.

[10]   Cost of Compliance 2021: Shaping the Future: Thompson Reuters report. https://legal.thomsonreuters.com/content/dam/ewp-m/documents/legal/en/ pdf/reports/shaping-the-future.pdf. Accessed: 9.02.2024

[11]   IDC spending guide forecasts. https://www.idc.com/getdoc.jsp?containerId= prUS50386323. Accessed: 9.02.2024.

[13]   Accenture-Going beyond extended reality. https://www.accenture.com/de-de/ about/going-beyond-extended-reality. Accessed: 9.02.2024.

[14]   AI Now Institute. https://ainowinstitute.org/. Accessed: 9.02.2024.

Chapter 3
The Importance of Fintech in Promoting Regulatory Compliance in Major Fintech Subsectors

Manali Agrawal
http://orcid.org/0009-0003-7283-3079
NSB Academy, India

Mohammad Irfan
http://orcid.org/0000-0002-4956-1170
NSB Academy, India

Anjali Goyal
Khalifa University, UAE

ABSTRACT

Fintech, which combines the words "financial" and "technology," refers to the integration of new technical developments with financial industry goods and services. The phrase refers to a quickly expanding sector that meets the needs of both companies and consumers in a variety of ways. Fintech offers a seemingly limitless range of uses, from cryptocurrencies and investment apps to mobile banking and insurance. Fintech is an essential component because of our increasing reliance on technology, large data sets, intricate networks of financial institutions, and affordable IT solutions like process automation software. The regulatory environment and industry have changed due to the growing use of FinTech solutions. Businesses that implement fintech are guaranteed to provide end customers with a secure environment in addition to good risk management. Digital payments, digital lending, InsurTech,

DOI: 10.4018/979-8-3693-3322-8.ch003

and WealthTech are some of the major Fintech subsectors. In the upcoming years, each of these sectors is expected to have a significant uptrend.

INTRODUCTION

The word "RegTech," which is a combination of "regulatory" and "technology," refers to the application of technology to regulatory compliance, reporting, and monitoring.4 Process automation makes it possible to identify risks more effectively and comply with regulations (Arner et al., 2018). It is possible to link the precipitous growth of India's fintech industry to the government's ambition for a cashless economy, which accelerated the use of digital payments—particularly during the demonetization period. have surely been the pioneers of the Indian Fintech field. The COVID-19 pandemic further increased the necessity for the digitalization of financial services and fueled the demand for fintech firms. The Indian Banks' Association and the Reserve Bank of India launched the National Payments Corporation of India (NPCI), which served as the foundation for many payment systems. Indian fintechs that specialize in payments have expanded significantly in recent years, attributed in a significant way to United Payment Interface (UPI).

India Stack, a single software platform designed to provide "presence-less," "paperless," and cashless service delivery to the nation's citizens, was reinforced by fintech. Financial services have become more accessible with the advent of digital payments and e-government services. Programs like the Pradhan Mantri Jan Dhan Yojana garnered a group of prospective clients who were on the hunt for easily available financial services. In conjunction with this, fintech has become an effective means of reaching rural and underprivileged people (Cycles & Text, n.d.).

Indian FinTech Startups Could Change the Financial Services Industry

FinTech firms have the potential to lower expenses while elevating the standard of financial services. Customers can profit from streamlined operating models since they are not encumbered by costly physical networks, IT systems, or legacy processes. The FinTech sector will create distinctive and pioneering risk assessment models. Financial services will become more widely available in India if big data, machine learning, and alternative data are used to evaluate credit and provide credit scores for clients with little credit history. The financial services industry will become more stable, safe, and diverse as a result of fintech. Compared to traditional banks, fintech companies are less homogeneous and provide excellent learning models for enhancing competencies and culture.

The majority of Indian banks and financial services providers have long-standing best practices in risk and internal controls, operational excellence, compliance culture, and employee engagement that fintech startups are able to snap up and implement (*Fintechs in India*, n.d.).

Key Enabling Technologies Used by FinTech

There are various technologies which can be used in order to enable FinTech. These technologies help by adding chatbots to virtual customer service to answer inquiries and provide suggestions. Utilizing AI algorithms to look for unusual activities and stop fraud. Natural language processing, or NLP, is being implemented to improve client engagement and allow human-like interactions with virtual assistants.

Figure 1. Key enabling technologies used by FinTechs

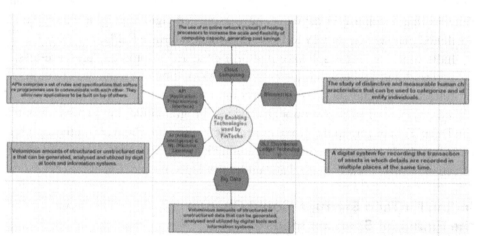

With the aid of automated and embedded security controls, cloud computing integration improves security. It's critical to keep in mind that retaining sensitive data entails risk, particularly in light of industry regulations. Blockchain has the enormous potential to completely destroy the existing banking system. Distributed ledger technology allows data to be stored, transferred, and synchronized in real time across several data repositories (DLT).

Categories of FinTechs

- **Digital payments:** Remittances and merchant payments are covered by electronic payment systems, which also include enterprise payments.
- **Digital lending:** Technology-enabled solutions to traditional credit scoring (for credit procedures) to offer loans to underprivileged retail customers and MSME*
- **InsurTech:** Solutions that reimagine insurance products to meet the specific needs of various consumer types and increase their distribution through the use of new technology.
- **WealthTech:** Technology-based solutions that make investing and managing personal money easier. These include robo-advisory solutions, which automate investment advice using artificial intelligence technologies.

Figure 2. Categories of FinTech

- **RegTech:** The application of new technology to more effectively and efficiently address regulatory and compliance needs. Organizations are being equipped with regulatory technology (RegTech) with a goal to ensure the longevity and efficiency of their regulatory compliance operations. An increasingly complicated regulatory environment, particularly for financial services firms, has fueled the growth of RegTech by necessitating the development of more effective compliance strategies. RegTech is likely to push standards, boost transparency between regulators and market players, and keep fabricating value for shareholders.

RegTech and FinTech are frequently misinterpreted and conflated. RegTech is the application of new technologies to address the increasingly complex data landscape needed to fulfill regulatory compliance concerns, whereas FinTech is the use of technologies and software to deliver financial services.

Application of RegTech

RegTech is applied in three major areas: Risk Management, Regulatory Compliance and Governance.

Figure 3. Application of RegTech

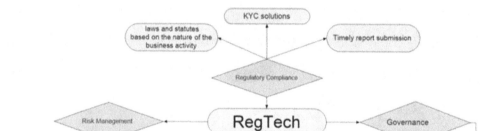

Regulatory Compliance

The fundamental problems that RegTech aims to solve are those related to regulatory compliance. To ensure compliance within the context of regulation, submitting reports, identity management.

Governance

To guarantee the operations of an ethical, transparent, and responsible manner, effective governance is necessary. It entails putting in place rules, guidelines, and other measures that create a framework for responsibility, risk management, and decision-making. Prospects for RegTech solutions aim to move away from traditional governance methods and toward helping senior management by enabling quicker, more collaborative, and well-informed decision-making.

Risk Management

- RegTech-based risk management strategies employ creative, data-driven solutions to reduce and manage risks.
- AI and ML technologies are used for projecting loan defaults, continuous consumer analysis and monitoring, and credit underwriting assessment.
- Market Risk Management Tools are used by regulatory organizations to detect, track, and quantify the risk of loss from changes in market pricing.
- Anti-money laundering risks are analyzed by making use of both structured and unstructured data. Screening, negative media searches, and network analytics, NLP, and ML algorithms are made use of to uncover suspicious transactions and linkages amongst organizations.
- RegTech products facilitate the provision of a centralized platform for the collection and management of ESG data, which facilitates the tracking of ESG parameters over time. They aim to offer a thorough understanding of ESG, which includes determining and evaluating the possible effects of ESG risks on the regulated company.
- Platforms evaluate the degree of risk based on pertinent data and enable comparison against preset thresholds, which helps with the quantification and monitoring of operational hazards.

LITERATURE REVIEW

India recorded the highest amount of real-time internet transactions worldwide in 2020, with over 25 billion. India has the fastest rate of expansion in FinTech markets with the in the world and has third largest FinTech ecosystem globally. In 2020, this industry in India was projected to be valued at a total of USD 50-60 billion. It is projected that the FinTech sector would be valued between $150 and 160 billion USD by 2025 (*Fintech opportunities*, n.d.).

It is obvious that innovation and the continued prosperity of the financial services sector, and particularly FinTech, depend on effective financial regulation. Additionally, there are unparalleled chances to reshape regulations and, in the process, launch new companies. Examples include encouraging a new generation of "RegTech" companies to provide the regulatory/compliance software and streamlining regulatory online reporting and analytics using "big data" (Arner et al., 2016).

FinTech is a subset of the financial industry that provides funding to businesses and private persons alike. This market can be further subdivided into FinTechs, whose services rely on the involvement of several contributors (the subsegment known as crowdfunding) and those that provide credit or factoring services outside of the crowd (the credit and factoring subsegment) (Dorfleitner et al., 2017).

Agile financial technology developers can support regulators in better enforcing prudential regulation and overseeing financial institutions, in addition to helping financial corporations comply with regulations (Anagnostopoulos, 2018).

Regulators need to make a concerted effort to keep their oversight capable of defending consumers and the economy from technological assaults. Cybersecurity and regtech are still at the forefront of the instruments used to keep the FinTech sector secure and profitable. Alongside FinTech products and services, cybersecurity and regtech must develop to maintain financial stability and consumer protection (Naviglia 2018).

A particular segment of the fintech industry known as "RegTech" is dedicated to developing technology that could make it easier and more efficient to fulfill regulatory obligations than what is now possible (Anagnostopoulos, 2018).

Fintech is an umbrella term for describing cutting-edge financial services enabled by technology and the business models that support them. Fintech, to put it simply, is the term for any innovation related to how organizations want to enhance the provision, utilization, and process of financial services (Mention, 2019).

Information technology (IT) known as "regtech" enables compliant business systems and data, helps control and manage financial and non-financial risks, and helps firms identify the impacts of regulatory provisions on business models, products and services, functional activities, policies, operational procedures, and controls. It also helps firms manage regulatory requirements and compliance imperatives. Finally, regtech performs regulatory compliance reporting (Butler & O'Brien, 2019).

The impact of cost and time on the effectiveness of money laundering prevention is strengthened by RegTech's ability to process massive amounts of data in real time, which lowers costs and increases accuracy in the screening of high volumes of transactions. Despite a moderately favorable association between the factors, the study shows that RegTech's computerized know your customer service has no discernible effect on preventing money laundering (Turki et.al., 2020).

Numerous financial organizations are having difficulty keeping up with the ever-changing regulatory landscape and the growing number of complex regulations. These regulations may contradict one another, be implemented locally, and be interpreted differently by different courts. Institutions that fail to control illicit and over-the-counter trading activities face severe penalties and multimillion dollar fines for noncompliance or failing to fulfill deadlines (Mohamed & Yildirim, 2021).

The final outcome of the financial development will improve with the emergence of finTech in the area of financial regulation (Muganyi et al., 2022).

Because of the higher risk and requirement for regulatory compliance, the development of RegTech was aided by the expansion of FinTech through recently founded FinTech businesses (Basdekis et al., 2022).

Fintech firms seek to deliver financial services that are more convenient, personalized, and focused on the needs of the customer than those provided by traditional suppliers. They do this by utilizing cutting-edge technology like blockchain, big data, artificial intelligence, and biometrics (Muganyi et al., 2022).

Regtech needed to adapt in opposition to Fintech in order to keep up with its rapid progress and development. It is also possible to argue that "the need for Regtech has been elicited by Fintech growth". Regtech ensures that financial service providers' business models are adequately solid by putting in place automated monitoring and regulatory compliance software. At the same time, Regtech enables regulators to effectively oversee and denounce any possible Fintech exploitation (Papantoniou, 2022).

Large software solutions or intricate cyber-physical solutions, or regtech, are made up of two different types of organizations: producers of goods and services and regulators/supervisors who keep an eye on the producers. In general, there are many producers with conflicting interests and few regulators who need to be objective toward all producers while also figuring out how to raise industry performance as a whole. Supervisors and producers have a one-to-many interaction in this fashion (Li et al., 2023).

A crucial component in the battle against these illegal operations has been regtech. RegTech solutions have helped handle the rising compliance burden as financial institutions have been under pressure to serve more customers and weather the epidemic. By using computers to monitor real-time data, RegTech solutions enable risk management activities to be automated. This allows for the detection of threats and hazards and the timely notification of individuals in charge of risk management. Additionally, machine learning is employed to forecast dangers like signs of money laundering (Teichmann et al., 2023).

DISCUSSION AND INTERPRETATION

FinTech, as an industry, is broadly defined as using technology to improve the efficiency of financial processes and financial service delivery. A new business model, application, procedure, or product that could have a significant impact on financial markets, institutions, and the provision of financial services is what is meant to be understood as "technologically enabled financial innovation" (FSB, 2019).

FinTechs are defined as "start-ups and other businesses that use technologies (Table 1) to carry out the core tasks performed by financial services, influencing the ways in which customers move, pay, save, borrow, invest, and safeguard their funds." Customers want a seamless experience and are less worried about getting all of their services from a single source in today's app-centric world. FinTechs are beginning to "unbundle" numerous services as they become aware of this new value expectation. FinTech companies are beginning to "unbundle" many of the conventional financial solutions as they become aware of this new value expectation (Basole and Patel, 2018). Simultaneously, FinTechs are offering a variety of non-financial services in addition to financial services, which makes it possible to deliver services through application software in an easy-to-use manner (Bank of Japan, 2018). To give an example, ride-sharing services are bundled by taxi aggregators with quick fare payment upon destination (*Reserve Bank of India - RBI Bulletin*, n.d.).

Table 1. Number of FinTechs founded in recent years

Years	Digital Payment	InsurTech	WealthTech	RegTech	Digital lending
2014	91	23	90	10	44
2015	165	36	163	10	131
2016	109	28	176	10	130
2017	75	28	81	8	67
2018	66	12	53	2	59
2019	26	2	16	1	26

Source:(Fintechs in India, Deloitte Report)

Figure 4. Number of FinTechs founded in recent years (Eviews data file)

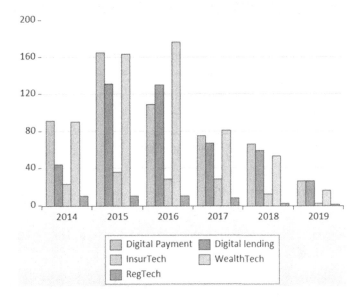

As per data in Table 1 Number of WealthTech companies are founded the maximum followed by Digital Payments and lending companies. As is evident from the figures given in Table 1 the number of RegTech companies is still increasing and slowly growing in numbers. For continuous three years the same numbers of companies were operating in the market and then in 2019 we can see 1 new company coming up. In the RegTech market today, there are businesses like ACTICO GmbH, Jumio Corporation, MetricStream, Inc., NICE Ltd., Thomson Reuters Corporation, Wolters Kluwer N.V., IBM Corporation, Deloitte Touche Tohmatsu Limited, Broadridge Financial Solutions Inc., and Trulioo, Inc. According to region, North America had the quickest rate of growth in the global regtech market in 2020 and is expected to maintain its dominating position through 2027.

Table 2. Global fintech investments

Year	Funding Amount Billion US ($)	Number of Equity Funding Rounds
2010	5	420
2011	4.39	661
2012	4.62	814
2013	12.4	1188
2014	16.8	1763

continued on following page

Table 2. Continued

Year	Funding Amount Billion US ($)	Number of Equity Funding Rounds
2015	42.4	2237
2016	37	2394
2017	39	2532
2018	73.3	2786
2019	78.3	2544
2020	22	1085

Source: RBI Bulletin-FinTech: The Force of Creative Disruption

Figure 5. Global fintech investments

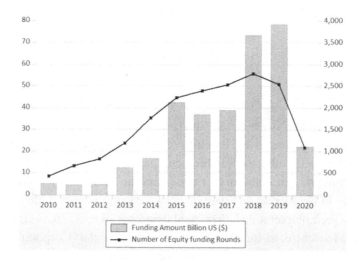

In light of the expanding acceptance during the previous ten years, numerous start-ups have developed a wide range of cutting-edge FinTech products. Investors have backed them passionately; from $5 billion in 2010 to $78 billion in 2019, investments in the sector have increased. During 2020 there is a sudden drastic fall in the Funding amounts because of reasons associated with Covid Pandemic.

Compliance is a collection of guidelines and practices that businesses must follow to abide by the laws and rules governing the FinTech sector. Consequently, FinTech companies: show their dedication to safe data storage and use, reassure industry bodies and end users that they will handle sensitive data responsibly, and protect themselves from hefty fines and audits.

CONCLUSION

It is anticipated that the fintech industry will continue to expand quickly driven by continued technical developments, shifting customer preferences, and governmental support. Notwithstanding the fact that customers are growing more and more enticed to the speed and convenience of mobile payment options, digital payments are probably going to stay a significant development. Investment in digital platforms are rising in popularity as more people look to handle their funds online. In addition, as these developments alter the financial landscape, the growth of digital assets and neo banking is probably going to continue. In general, it is anticipated that the fintech industry will continue to be inventive and dynamic, with new products and services appearing to satisfy changing customer demands. FinTech business models are scrutinized by RegTech for regulatory compliance and consumer protection. RegTech also offers consumer protection. RegTech is a product line that aims to alleviate legal compliance issues, particularly those brought on by the widespread use of FinTech. Networks and digital data facilitate better decision-making. FinTech and RegTech both employ the same technologies. RegTech business models are created using technologies like blockchain, cloud computing, machine learning, biometrics, big data analytics, data mining, robotics, artificial intelligence, automation, and application programming interfaces.

REFERENCES

Anagnostopoulos, I. (2018). Fintech and regtech: Impact on regulators and banks. *Journal of Economics and Business*, 100, 7–25. 10.1016/j.jeconbus.2018.07.003

Arner, D. W., Barberis, J., & Buckey, R. P. (2016). FinTech, RegTech, and the Reconceptualization of Financial Regulation. *Northwestern Journal of International Law & Business*, 37, 371.

Arner, D. W., Barberis, J., & Buckley, R. P. (2018). RegTech: Building a Better Financial System. In Lee Kuo Chuen, D., & Deng, R. (Eds.), *Handbook of Blockchain, Digital Finance, and Inclusion* (Vol. 1, pp. 359–373). Academic Press. 10.1016/B978-0-12-810441-5.00016-6

Basdekis, C., Christopoulos, A., Katsampoxakis, I., & Vlachou, A. (2022). FinTech's rapid growth and its effect on the banking sector. *Journal of Banking and Financial Technology*, 6(2), 159–176. 10.1007/s42786-022-00045-w

Butler, T., & O'Brien, L. (2019). Understanding RegTech for Digital Regulatory Compliance. In Lynn, T., Mooney, J. G., Rosati, P., & Cummins, M. (Eds.), *Disrupting Finance: FinTech and Strategy in the 21st Century* (pp. 85–102). Springer International Publishing. 10.1007/978-3-030-02330-0_6

Dorfleitner, G., Hornuf, L., Schmitt, M., & Weber, M. (2017). Definition of FinTech and Description of the FinTech Industry. In Dorfleitner, G., Hornuf, L., Schmitt, M., & Weber, M. (Eds.), *FinTech in Germany* (pp. 5–10). Springer International Publishing., 10.1007/978-3-319-54666-7_2

Fintech. (2018). Regtech and the importance of cybersecurity. *Issues in Information Systems*. Advance online publication. 10.48009/3_iis_2018_220-225

Fintechs in India. (n.d.). Deloitte India. Retrieved January 7, 2024, from https://www2.deloitte.com/in/en/pages/financial-services/articles/in-banking-fintechs-in-india-key-trends-noexp.html

Li, J., Maiti, A., & Fei, J. (2023). Features and Scope of Regulatory Technologies: Challenges and Opportunities with Industrial Internet of Things. *Future Internet*, 15(8), 8. Advance online publication. 10.3390/fi15080256

Mention, A.-L. (2019). The Future of Fintech. *Research Technology Management*, 62(4), 59–63. 10.1080/08956308.2019.1613123

Mohamed, H., & Yildirim, R. (2021). RegTech and Regulatory Change Management for Financial Institutions. In Hamdan, A., Hassanien, A. E., Razzaque, A., & Alareeni, B. (Eds.), *The Fourth Industrial Revolution: Implementation of Artificial Intelligence for Growing Business Success* (pp. 153–168). Springer International Publishing. 10.1007/978-3-030-62796-6_8

Muganyi, T., Yan, L., Yin, Y., Sun, H., Gong, X., & Taghizadeh-Hesary, F. (2022). Fintech, regtech, and financial development: Evidence from China. *Financial Innovation*, 8(1), 29. 10.1186/s40854-021-00313-6

Papantoniou, A. A. (2022). Regtech: Steering the regulatory spaceship in the right direction? *Journal of Banking and Financial Technology*, 6(1), 1–16. 10.1007/s42786-022-00038-9

Reserve Bank of India—RBI Bulletin. (n.d.). Retrieved January 24, 2024, from https://www.rbi.org.in/Scripts/BS_ViewBulletin.aspx?Id=19899

Teichmann, F., Boticiu, S., & Sergi, B. S. (2023). RegTech – Potential benefits and challenges for businesses. *Technology in Society*, 72, 102150. 10.1016/j.techsoc.2022.102150

The regulatory technology "RegTech" and money laundering prevention in Islamic and conventional banking industry—PMC. (n.d.). Retrieved January 8, 2024, from https://www.ncbi.nlm.nih.gov/pmc/articles/PMC7550909/

Turki, M., Hamdan, A., Cummings, R. T., Sarea, A., Karolak, M., & Anasweh, M. (2020, October 8). The regulatory technology "RegTech" and money laundering prevention in Islamic and conventional banking industry. *Heliyon*, 6(10), e04949. 10.1016/j.heliyon.2020.e0494933083582

Chapter 4
FinTech, RegTech, and Financial Development in India's Industry 4.0 Landscape

Mithilesh Kishor Gidage

http://orcid.org/0009-0003-7894-5143

Savitribai Phule Pune University, India

Shilpa Vasant Bhide

http://orcid.org/0000-0001-8928-6356

Savitribai Phule Pune University, India

ABSTRACT

This study examines the impact of fintech on India's financial landscape from 2021 to 2021. Using advanced regression techniques and accounting for various factors, the authors find a positive link between fintech and financial development, including improved access to loans and increased savings. They also highlight the potential of regtech in enhancing financial development. The findings stress the importance of balanced regulatory frameworks to foster fintech growth while managing risks. Additionally, they show how policy measures like interest rate liberalization can positively influence financial development. In conclusion, they propose a comprehensive policy framework to promote equitable fintech growth in developing nations.

DOI: 10.4018/979-8-3693-3322-8.ch004

INTRODUCTION

Fintech, a portmanteau of 'financial' and 'technology,' embodies the utilization of novel technologies and inventive business approaches to deliver financial services, as defined by Nicoletti (2017). India stands prominently within Asia as a burgeoning epicenter for fintech innovation, boasting a plethora of pioneering fintech enterprises. The intersection of fintech and financial development remains a burgeoning field of inquiry, hindered thus far by data constraints. Financial development encompasses a spectrum of dimensions, including accessibility, depth, efficiency in service provision, and stability, as delineated by Sahay et al. (2015), Sun and Muganyi (2019), and Sun et al. (2020a, b). This study addresses three dimensions of financial development through proxy variables. While the intuitive expectation is for fintech expansion to bolster financial development by enhancing inclusivity and accessibility, as noted by Leong et al. (2017), Jagtiani and Lemieux (2018), and Cole et al. (2019), it's imperative to acknowledge that fintech adoption introduces a new facet of risk into financial markets.

2021 saw India shine brightly on the global stage, showcasing its remarkable strides in the FinTech realm, aligning with the burgeoning momentum of this industry worldwide. India proudly holds its position as the third largest FinTech market globally, trailing only behind the US and the UK. The landscape is adorned with a constellation of FinTech unicorns, burgeoning startups, and a vibrant funding ecosystem, underscoring India's undeniable presence and influence in the global FinTech arena (EY, 2022).

The landscape of fintech is in a state of constant evolution, marked by the emergence of various trends such as digital payments, investments, capital raising, assets, and neobanking (Cole et al., 2019; Jagtiani & Lemieux, 2018; Leong et al., 2017; Sahay et al., 2015). Among these, digital payments have experienced a remarkable surge, driven by consumer reliance on mobile payment solutions. Simultaneously, digital investment platforms are gaining popularity for their accessibility and affordability (Cole et al., 2019). Moreover, digital capital raising has become an efficient avenue for startups and SMEs to secure funding (Jagtiani & Lemieux, 2018). The advent of digital assets, including cryptocurrencies and NFTs, has introduced novel opportunities for investors (Cole et al., 2019). Neobanks have disrupted traditional banking by offering innovative, customer-centric solutions tailored to modern consumers (Leong et al., 2017). This growth is propelled by several factors. Firstly, the widespread adoption of smartphones and the internet has made fintech solutions more accessible, spurring consumer demand (Cole et al., 2019). Secondly, the COVID-19 pandemic has accelerated the transition to digital payments and investments, prompting consumers to embrace remote and contactless transactions (Cole et al., 2019). Thirdly, regulatory changes have empowered fintech firms to compete with traditional financial institutions (Sahay et al., 2015). Lastly, technological advancements like AI and blockchain have catalyzed fintech innovation (Cole et al., 2019). The trajectory of the fintech market is expected to remain upward, fueled by ongoing technological progress, shifting consumer preferences, and regulatory encouragement. Digital payments are forecasted to maintain their dominance as consumers prioritize convenience and speed (Cole et al., 2019). Digital investment platforms will continue to attract users seeking online financial management solutions (Cole et al., 2019). Additionally, the ascent of digital assets and neobanking is anticipated to reshape the financial landscape (Leong et al., 2017). Overall, the fintech sector is poised to remain dynamic and inventive, continually introducing new services to meet evolving consumer demands.

Numerous inquiries into fintech have emphasized its potential to serve as a driving force for financial inclusion and access (Leong et al., 2017). However, empirical investigations regarding the causal relationship between fintech and metrics of financial development remain sparse. This study presents a distinctive contribution to this discourse in three significant ways. Firstly, we delve into the impact of fintech on various dimensions of financial development- specifically, access, depth, and stability- across 180 cities in India. Secondly, we illuminate the potential of regtech to enhance the effectiveness of financial regulation. Thirdly, we underscore the role of active policy initiatives such as interest rate liberalization in bolstering financial development outcomes.

LITERATURE REVIEW

India's FinTech Ecosystem

The Indian FinTech landscape has emerged as a formidable global player, solidifying its position as one of the largest markets worldwide. Notably, it boasts one of the most robust digital payments ecosystems in terms of both value and volume, alongside impressive growth in consumer and SME digital credit access, and a notable surge in retail investor participation in the stock market. These achievements serve as compelling evidence that Indian FinTech enterprises are charting a promising trajectory.

Recent findings from EY and Chiratae's study project a staggering 10X growth in the Indian FinTech market over the next decade, aiming to reach $1 trillion in assets under management and $200 billion in revenues. As of July 2022, the Tracxn database indicates a thriving FinTech startup scene in India, with over 7,300 ventures supported by a total funding volume of $30.2 billion, with 35% of these funds raised in the past sixteen months.

This remarkable growth is fueled by a myriad of supportive initiatives from the government and regulatory bodies, coupled with a buoyant funding environment and a strengthened venture capital ecosystem. Furthermore, India's massive demographic dividend, coupled with high FinTech adoption rates and abundant access to technology and talent, provides fertile ground for entrepreneurial endeavors catering to the evolving needs of the nation. The collaborative spirit within the FinTech ecosystem is evident as banks and insurers actively engage in partnerships with FinTech firms. This symbiotic relationship leverages the shared commitment to secure data sharing and monetization opportunities, fostering innovation and driving industry progress. However, amidst this growth, there are pertinent concerns to address. These include potential risks associated with data security and privacy in partnership scenarios, disparities in the adoption of digital financial services across demographic groups, insufficient financial literacy and awareness, as well as challenges such as IPO underperformance and cautiousness among institutional investors due to global geopolitical and macroeconomic uncertainties. Additionally, the dynamic regulatory landscape poses a continual challenge, necessitating agility and adaptability from FinTech companies to navigate changing regulations effectively (EY, 2022).

Looking ahead, the expansive scope of opportunities for FinTech far surpasses the challenges it faces. The government remains steadfast in its commitment to financial inclusion, particularly crucial given the underrepresentation of traditional financial services (FS) players in rural areas, among aging populations, and within the unorganized and gig economy segments. This presents a fertile ground for FinTech innovation to address gaps and cater to diverse customer needs, with a focus on delivering enhanced customer experiences and tailored products. Neo-banking emerges as a prime example, offering novel models that resonate with evolving consumer preferences. Despite promising growth in insurance and wealth sectors, significant untapped potential remains, indicating ample room for expansion. The supportive regulatory environment, coupled with a proactive stance from regulators, has been instrumental in propelling the FinTech industry forward at an impressive pace. Furthermore, FinTech companies have succeeded in attracting top talent from a wide array of industries, bolstering their capabilities and ensuring continued growth and innovation. As the industry evolves, these skilled professionals will play a pivotal role in driving further advancements and solidifying FinTech's position as a transformative force within the financial sector (EY, 2022).

Fintech and Financial Development Nexus

Assessing financial development presents a formidable challenge, as noted by Levine (2005). Much of the empirical research in this area relies heavily on approximating financial development through metrics such as the private credit-to-GDP ratio. However, this simplistic approach fails to capture the multidimensional essence of the concept, as highlighted by Svirydzenka (2016). While the World Bank employs various indexes to evaluate financial development on a national scale, researchers continue to grapple with defining its diverse dimensions and devising suitable measurement methods.

Nevertheless, there is a widespread acknowledgment that financial development is intricately intertwined with economic growth, facilitating capital accumulation and enhancing efficiency in resource allocation, as suggested by Dobson and Westland (2018). Furthermore, financial development plays a pivotal role in mitigating volatility in consumption, investment growth, and overall economic output, as underscored by Dabla-Norris and Srivisal (2013).

The rise of fintech ushers in a fresh array of prospects and obstacles for financial systems worldwide. Despite its growing prominence, fintech's exact role in shaping India's financial development remains ambiguous, prompting this study to delve into the intricate relationship between the two.

Drawing upon the theoretical framework outlined above, we propose the following hypotheses:

I.   Fintech exerts a favorable influence on financial development across dimensions such as access, depth, and stability.
II. The adoption of regulatory technology (regtech) contributes significantly to enhancing financial development outcomes.

These hypotheses serve as guiding principles for our exploration into the interplay between fintech, regulatory technology, and financial development within the Indian context.

RESEARCH METHODOLOGY

Sample and Econometric Modeling

For this study, panel data encompassing 180 Indian cities and 18 states spanning the timeframe from 2021 to 2023 serves as the foundation. Previous empirical research suggests that financial development indicators are most accurately forecasted utilizing lagged independent and control variables (Ryan et al., 2014; Li et al., 2016; Berger et al., 2017; Sheng, 2020). To explore the impact of fintech and regtech on financial development, we adopt the following foundational model.

$$FD_{i,t} = \alpha_0 + \alpha_1 Fintech_{i,t-1} + \alpha_2 Fintech_{i,t-1}$$
$$+\alpha_3 Fintech_{i,t-1} \times Finreg_{i,t-1} + \alpha_c Control_{i,t-1} + \eta_t + \lambda_t + \varepsilon_{i,t}$$

....

$$(1)$$

In this study, we establish a model where $\alpha_{i,s}$ represent the model parameters, with i and t denoting the city and year, respectively. The dependent variable, $FD_{i,t}$, signifies the financial development indicator for city i in year t. Given the complex nature of measuring financial development holistically (Akçay, 2019), we adopt a multidimensional approach to offer a comprehensive analysis of how predictor variables influence specific facets of financial development. We segment it into three dimensions: access, depth, and stability, each represented by distinct proxy variables- $FD_{(D)i,t}$, $FD_{(A)i,t}$, and $FD_{(S)i,t}$, respectively.

The depth dimension of financial development, $FD_{(D)i,t}$, is approximated by the level of deposits in financial institutions within each city. Similarly, $FD_{(A)i,t}$ serves as a proxy for the access dimension, utilizing the balances of loans from financial institutions. The stability dimension, denoted by $FD_{(S)i,t}$, is gauged through the levels of rural and urban savings.

The degree of fintech development in each city is denoted by Fintech, while Finreg represents expenditures on financial regulation. The interaction term $Fintech_{i,t-1} \times Finreg_{i,t-1}$ captures the convergence of fintech and financial regulation, representing regtech in our foundational model.

Control variables accounting for factors influencing financial development include the level of economic activity, industrialization, and financial openness in each city (Rajan and Zingales, 2003; Shahbaz et al., 2017). To account for economic activity and market size, GDP per capita, denoted as GDPpc, is employed. Financial openness (FOP) is defined as foreign investment, while industrialization (IND) is measured by the proportion of value-added secondary industries to GDP. The estimation equation is articulated as follows: ($FD_{(A)}$)

$$FD_{i,t} = \alpha_0 + \alpha_1 Fintech_{i,t-1} + \alpha_2 Fintech_{i,t-1} + \alpha_3 Fintech_{i,t-1}$$
$$\times Finreg_{i,t-1} + \alpha_4 GDPpc_{i,t-1} + \alpha_5 FOP_{i,t-1} + \alpha_6 IND_{i,t-1} + \eta_t + \lambda_t + \varepsilon_{i,t}$$

.... $$(2)$$

Data for Study

The Reserve Bank of India's Financial Inclusion Index (FI-Index) stands out as the prime gauge of fintech advancement in India, offering a holistic assessment encompassing a spectrum of dimensions. This comprehensive index, as outlined by the RBI (2021), provides insights into the breadth and depth of coverage, utilization levels, and penetration of fintech services. It meticulously tracks key indicators such as mobile payments, insurance accessibility, monetary fund management, investment avenues, credit availability, credit investigation efficiency, and the overall level of digitization within the financial ecosystem.

The FI-Index serves as our primary metric for assessing fintech development, given its unparalleled comprehensiveness in capturing the dynamic evolution of fintech in India throughout the analysis timeframe. This dataset stands out for its extensive coverage, offering detailed insights at the county, city, and provincial levels. In Table 1, we present an overview of the average characteristics and summary statistics derived from our dataset, shedding light on the key dimensions of fintech development under examination.

Table 1. Description of variables

Variable	Measurement	Source
Financial Depth ($FD_{(D)}$)	the ratio of liquid liabilities to GDP or the ratio of private credit to GDP (log)	CMIE Prowess and World Bank Open Data
Financial Access ($FD_{(A)}$)	Financial institutions loans (log)	CMIE Prowess and Reserve Bank of India
Financial Stability ($FD_{(s)}$)	Urban and rural residents' savings (log)	Reserve Bank of India
Fintech Index (Fintech)	The Reserve Bank of India's Financial Inclusion Index (FI-Index)	Reserve Bank of India
Financial Regulation (Finreg)	Fiscal expenditure on fnancial regulatory matters (log)	Reserve Bank of India
GDP per capita (GDPpc)	GDP per capita in Rs	World Bank Open Data
Financial Openness (FOP)	Actual foreign investment USD 10,000 (log)	World Bank Open Data
Industrialization (IND)	Secondary industry value added as a % of GDP (log)	Reserve Bank of India and World Bank Open Data
Mobile phone users (Mpu)	Number of mobile phone users (log)	Statista

Addressing Data Issues

Addressing cross-sectional dependency is crucial in econometric analysis of panel datasets, as failure to do so can result in misleading parameter estimates and erroneous inference (Sarafidis and Wansbeek, 2011). Among the various tests available for detecting cross-sectional dependency, the Breusch and Pagan (1980) LM statistic is widely recognized and frequently employed in economic literature.

Endogeneity poses a significant challenge in social science research, leading to spurious correlations and inaccurate estimations of causal relationships. Sources of endogeneity include omitted variable bias, simultaneity, model misspecification, and selection bias (Wooldridge, 2010; Zaefarian et al., 2017). To mitigate endogeneity issues in panel data analyses, instrumental variable (IV) approaches are commonly utilized.

Given the prevalent usage of consumer fintech platforms through mobile applications, we employ the number of mobile users as an instrumental variable for fintech to address its endogenous nature. Under this framework, we acknowledge the endogeneity of the fintech variable and specify it as follows:

$$Fintech_{i,t} = \pi_0 + \pi_1 Mpu_{i,t-1} + \pi_2 FI_{i,t-1} + \theta_{i,t}$$

$$\dotfill (3)$$

In this equation, $Mpu_{i,t}$ signifies the count of mobile phone users in a specific city, while $FI_{i,t-1}$ denotes the lagged value of the proxy variable indicating financial openness. This formulation acknowledges the influence of mobile phone usage on the fintech variable and incorporates the lagged value of financial openness to account for temporal effects.

DATA ANALYSIS, RESULTS, AND DISCUSSIONS

Results of Test for Cross-sectional Dependency

Addressing cross-sectional dependency is paramount in econometric analyses utilizing panel datasets, as overlooking this issue can lead to potentially misleading parameter estimates and erroneous conclusions (Sarafdis and Wansbeek, 2011). The Breusch and Pagan (1980) LM statistic stands as a widely employed tool in economic research for detecting cross-sectional dependency. Following a Hausman test and accounting for city and year fixed effects, we examine weak cross-sectional dependency across all three models using the Pesaran (2014) CD test, which is applicable when the number of entities (N) exceeds the time periods (T). The results, as detailed in Table 2, indicate significant cross-sectional dependence across all models, likely stemming from shifts in financial regulatory policies and other industry-related shocks during the study period.

Table 2. Results of test for weak cross-sectional dependence

Model 1 ($FD_{(D)}$)		Model 2 ($FD_{(A)}$)		Model 3 ($FD_{(s)}$)	
CD statistic	P value	CD statistic	P value	CD statistic	P value
189.239***	0.0000	217.290***	0.0000	382.390***	0.0000

Note: The null hypothesis (H0) assumes weak cross-sectional dependency. The CD statistic follows a normal distribution (CD ~ N(0, 1)). Significance at the 1% level is denoted by ***.Top of Form

To address cross-sectional dependence, we employ a fixed effects model with standard errors clustered at the city level. Acknowledging the potential endogeneity of Fintech$_{i,t}$ as specified in Eq. (3), we conduct an instrumental variable (IV) regression and perform post-estimation tests to assess endogeneity, under-identification, weak instruments, and over-identifying restrictions. These tests affirm the relevance, explanatory power, and validity of our chosen instruments. The estimation results for both the fixed effects and IV-two-stage least square (2SLS) approaches are presented in Table 3.

Table 3. Regression results

Variables	Model 1 Criterion ($FD_{(D)}$)		Model 2 Criterion ($FD_{(A)}$)		Model 3 Criterion ($FD_{(S)}$)	
	FE	IV-2SLS	FE	IV-2SLS	FE	IV-2SLS
Fintech$_{i,t-1}$	0.108***	0.381***	0.411***	0.912***	0.183***	0.588***
	(0.000)	(0.000)	(0.000)	(0.000)	(0.000)	(0.000)
Finreg$_{i,t-1}$	0.036	-0.288***	-0.006	-0.177***	0.082	- 0.122**
	(0.261)	(0.006)	(0.185)	(0.011)	(0.450)	(0.138)
Fintech$_{i,t-1}$ × Finreg$_{i,t-1}$	-0.014	0.182***	0.073	0.581***	0.0008	0.173**
	(0.681)	(0.004)	(0.048)	(0.099)	(0.100)	(0.481)
GDPpc$_{i,t-1}$	0.412***	0.184	0.382***	0.419***	0.175*	0.382***
	(0.000)	(0.000)	(0.000)	(0.000)	(0.000)	(0.000)
F OP$_{i,t-1}$	-0.026***	-0.027***	-0.028	-0.004	-0.28***	-0.078***
	(0.015)	(0.000)	(0.167)	(0.218)	(0.002)	(0.000)
NDi,t-1	-0.328***	-0.218***	-9.188***	-0.381.23	-2.481***	-0.218
	(0.000)	(0.000)	(0.046)	(0.382)	(0.000)	(0.000)

continued on following page

Table 3. Continued

Variables	Model 1 Criterion $(FD_{(D)})$		Model 2 Criterion $(FD_{(A)})$		Model 3 Criterion $(FD_{(S)})$	
	FE	IV-2SLS	FE	IV-2SLS	FE	IV-2SLS
City FE						
Year FE						
No. of Obs.	390	288	390	288	390	288
F-Stat	1183.09***	1859.03***	529.02*	631.89**	1842.03***	1329.49
R-Squared	0.781	0.824	0.889	0.691	0.781	0.910

Note: For clarity, p-values are provided in parentheses. Standard errors are clustered at the city level. R-squared values are reported as "R-squared (within)" for fixed effects (FE) models and are centered for instrumental variable two-stage least squares (IV-2SLS) models. Significance levels are denoted by ***, **, and *, indicating significance at the 1%, 5%, and 10% levels, respectively.

Results of Post-Estimation

The outcomes of post-estimation tests validate the reliability of the instruments employed in this study, as elaborated in the subsequent sections. These tests affirm that the instrumental variable (IV) regression estimation yields the most appropriate results for our model.

Endogeneity Test

Examining endogeneity, the null hypothesis is decisively rejected at the 1% significance level across all three models. This rejection implies that the Fintech$_{i,t}$ variable is indeed endogenous and cannot be regarded as exogenous. Detailed results of the endogeneity test are presented in Table 4.

Table 4. Results of endogeneity test

Model 1 $(FD_{(D)})$		Model 2 $(FD_{(A)})$		Model 3 $(FD_{(s)})$	
Chi-sq (1)	P value	Chi-sq (1)	P value	Chi-sq (1)	P value
14.298***	0.0007	18.293***	0.0006	8.039**	0.0418

Note: The null hypothesis (H0) posits that specified endogenous regressors can be treated as exogenous. Significance at the 1% level is denoted by ***.

Assessment of Underidentification

We perform a rigorous examination to determine if the equation is underidentified, employing tests for both underidentification and weak identification. The null hypothesis suggesting underidentification is robustly refuted at the 1% significance level, as evidenced across all three models. Detailed findings are elaborated in Table 5.

Table 5. Weak identification test: Anderson canon. Corr. LM statistic

LM statistic	P value	Outcome
173.294***	0.00000	Reject H_0

Note: The null hypothesis (H0) suggests that the model is underidentified. Significance at the 1% level is denoted by ***.

Evaluation of Weak Instruments

Our analysis of weak identification reveals that our chosen instruments exhibit strong explanatory power for the endogenous regressor. The Cragg–Donald Wald F statistic significantly exceeds the critical values from the Stock–Yogo weak identification test, validating the appropriateness of our instrument selection. These findings, presented in Table 6, hold true for all three models.

Table 6. Results of weak instrument test

Cragg-Donald Wald F statistic	89.021
Stock-Yogo weak ID test critical values	
10% Maximal IV size	23.109
15% Maximal IV size	18.23
20% Maximal IV size	11.201
25% Maximal IV size	8.39

Note: The null hypothesis (H0) indicates weak instruments. The outcome rejects H0.

Validation of Instruments

To ascertain the validity of our instruments, we conduct the Sargan–Hansen test of overidentifying restrictions under the null hypothesis that our instruments are indeed valid. This hypothesis suggests that the instruments are uncorrelated with the residuals and can be safely omitted from the model. The results, detailed in Table 7, consistently fail to reject the null hypothesis at the 5% significance level across all three models.

Table 7. Result of Sargan-Hansen TEST

Model 1 ($FD_{(D)}$)			Model 2 ($FD_{(A)}$)			Model 3 ($FD_{(s)}$)	
Sargan statistic	P value		Sargan statistic	P value		Sargan statistic	P value
0.71	0.2481		0.0099	0.5729		4.218	0.0547

Note: The null hypothesis (H0) proposes that instruments are valid. The outcome fails to reject H0 at the 1% and 5% significance levels, respectively.

Analysis of Fintech Impact on Financial Development

The estimation findings reveal a significant positive influence of fintech across all dimensions of financial development. Notably, fintech exhibits the most pronounced effect on financial access, reflected by a coefficient of 0.912. This implies that a 10% increase in fintech development corresponds to a notable 9.12% enhancement in financial access, as measured by loan balances at financial institutions. This underscores the pivotal role of India's rapidly expanding fintech sector in driving both financial inclusion and access.

Furthermore, coefficients for financial depth and stability stand at 0.381 and 0.588, respectively, all statistically significant at the 1% level. These results indicate that the advent of fintech has facilitated Indian financial institutions in attracting increased deposits and savings from consumers across both rural and urban areas. Such outcomes can be attributed to synergies forged between traditional banks and fintech service providers. Additionally, the substantial investments made by traditional financial service providers in their digital transformations and fintech subsidiaries likely contribute to these observed trends.

Impact of Regtech on Financial Development

The analysis of the regtech variable, reflecting fintech's integration into financial regulation, demonstrates a significantly positive influence on all three dimensions of financial development under scrutiny. Notably, regtech exhibits its most substantial impact on financial access, boasting a coefficient of 0.581, statistically significant at the 1% level. Furthermore, coefficients for financial depth (0.182) and stability (0.173) are statistically significant at the 1% and 5% levels, respectively.

These findings underscore the dual role of fintech in financial markets, where it not only introduces new dimensions of risk but also offers avenues to mitigate such risks, as exemplified by regtech's emergence. Specifically, regtech plays a crucial role in addressing risks associated with areas like subprime lending. Leveraging advancements in artificial intelligence (machine learning) algorithms, regtech enables regulators to access more comprehensive data on financial markets. This, in turn, facilitates better insights from vast datasets, aiding policymakers in making more targeted and effective decisions.

India's progressive strides in the application of regtech surpass those of many other nations, owing to factors such as less stringent privacy laws and advancements in big data analytics, cloud computing, and artificial intelligence. Such advancements position India as a frontrunner in harnessing the potential of regtech to bolster financial regulation and foster a more resilient financial ecosystem.

Impact of Financial Openness and Industry 4.0

Noteworthy findings emerge regarding the influence of control variables representing financial openness and the degree of industrialization on the dimensions of financial development. These variables exhibit significant positive coefficients, particularly in relation to the depth and stability dimensions of financial development.

Financial openness, characterized by greater access to international financial markets and foreign investment, plays a pivotal role in enhancing the depth and stability of financial systems. Increased financial openness fosters competition, encourages capital inflows, and facilitates access to diverse financial products and services, thereby deepening financial markets and enhancing their stability. Similarly, the level of industrialization, indicative of a nation's economic diversification and technological advancement, positively impacts financial development. A more industrialized economy tends to offer greater employment opportunities, higher income levels, and increased demand for financial services. This, in turn, stimulates the growth of financial markets, promoting both their depth and stability. In summary, the significant positive coefficients observed for financial openness and industrialization underscore their crucial roles in fostering the depth and stability of financial systems, thereby contributing to overall financial development and economic growth.

CONCLUSION

India's fintech industry has experienced remarkable growth during the period examined in this study, with analysts projecting continued positive momentum and increased maturity and consolidation in the sector (Ernst and Young, 2019). Regulators have been diligently seeking the optimal balance between fostering fintech growth and effectively managing the associated risks. This study contributes to these efforts by providing valuable insights into the intricate relationship between fintech and various dimensions of financial development.

The question of whether fintech acts as a complement to or a substitute for financial development warrants further rigorous analytical examination. Nonetheless, the findings of this study indicate a positive causal relationship between fintech and diverse aspects of financial development. This finding holds significant implications, particularly for emerging markets, in shaping a robust fintech policy framework.

By gaining a deeper understanding of the interplay between fintech and financial development, regulators can craft more effective policies to foster fintech growth while safeguarding financial system stability. Furthermore, assessing the implications of new and emerging technologies will be critical in ensuring the resilience and adaptability of financial systems to evolving market dynamics and technological advancements.

A comprehensive understanding of the intricate relationship between fintech and financial development empowers regulators to craft more effective policies that foster fintech growth while ensuring the stability of financial systems. Moreover, diligent assessment of the implications of new and emerging technologies, including artificial intelligence, big data analytics, cloud computing, machine learning, blockchain, 5G, the Internet of Things, biometrics, and others, enables regulators to adapt to the rapid pace of fintech evolution.

Regtech emerges as a crucial tool in maintaining financial stability and mitigating risks associated with digital financial services, offering financial institutions and fintech companies the means to navigate regulatory challenges effectively. While the empirical findings of this study may not fully substantiate the following recommendations, the outlined regulatory strategies for fintech in India and other emerging markets hold significant importance:

1. Accelerate the development and implementation of regulatory frameworks tailored to the fintech industry.
2. Foster international collaboration with global regulators in the fintech domain to enhance regulatory harmonization.
3. Embrace regtech solutions and leverage emerging technologies to effectively regulate the digital financial service industry.
4. Support traditional banks in their digital transformation journey to remain competitive in the evolving fintech landscape.
5. Encourage collaboration between traditional financial institutions and fintech entities, particularly in financial intelligence, to mitigate risks and promote sustainable growth.
6. Invest in artificial intelligence and big data analytics to bolster financial system stability.

7. Strengthen fintech services catering to underserved market segments and promote collaboration with incumbent banks.
8. Address deficiencies in the financial service industry that contribute to the emergence of shadow banking practices.
9. Foster fundamental research in emerging technologies to drive fintech sector growth and develop a talent strategy based on sustainable and ethical practices.
10. Establish research institutions dedicated to fintech development and foster global cooperation to advance quality research initiatives.

In conclusion, embracing these recommendations and adopting a forward-thinking approach to fintech regulation will be instrumental in promoting a resilient and inclusive financial ecosystem conducive to sustainable growth and innovation.

Our findings contribute significantly to the existing literature on the role of fintech in advancing financial access and inclusion, offering pertinent policy implications. Firstly, regulators are encouraged to formulate and implement a comprehensive policy framework that fosters balanced growth within the fintech sector. Secondly, policymakers should strategize on the optimal utilization of regtech to effectively mitigate risks associated with fintech activities. Thirdly, our study underscores the importance of active policy initiatives aimed at financial liberalization in achieving financial development.

LIMITATIONS AND FURTHER RESEARCH DIRECTIONS

Despite the valuable insights gleaned from our study, several limitations warrant acknowledgment. The scarcity of available data posed constraints on the scope of our econometric analysis, thereby influencing the depth of our findings. However, our study serves as a significant contribution to the literature, particularly for policymakers in emerging markets grappling with the rapid ascent of fintech.

Moving forward, there is a compelling need for further empirical research to comprehensively understand the multifaceted impact of fintech on various dimensions of financial development. While theoretical frameworks highlighting the role of fintech in promoting financial inclusivity exist, empirical investigations remain relatively nascent. Our study stands as one of the few empirical analyses shedding light on the positive contributions of fintech to financial development.

Future research endeavors should prioritize mapping the inherent risks posed by fintech to incumbent financial systems, providing critical insights to inform more robust regulatory strategies. As fintech continues to disrupt the global financial landscape, researchers should extend their focus beyond inclusion to explore its broader implications. Investigating how fintech can facilitate sustainable financial development and stability in developing countries represents a crucial avenue for future inquiry.

By addressing these limitations and embarking on further research endeavors, we can deepen our understanding of fintech's role in shaping the future of financial systems and pave the way for more effective regulatory approaches that foster sustainable and inclusive financial development.

REFERENCES

Accenture. (2018). Mind the gap: the challenges to fintech adaptation. In *FinTech Innovation Lab*. Accenture.

Akçay, S. (2019). Remittances and financial development in Bangladesh: Substitutes or complements? *Applied Economics Letters*, 27(16), 1206–1214.

Anagnostopoulos, I. (2018). Fintech and regtech: Impact on regulators and banks. *Journal of Economics and Business*, 100, 7–25. 10.1016/j.jeconbus.2018.07.003

Ansari, S., & Krop, P. (2012). Incumbent performance in the face of a radical innovation: towards a framework for incumbent challenger dynamics. SSRN *Electronic Journal, 41*, 1357–1374. 10.2139/ssrn.2034266

Berger, A. N., Bouwman, C. H. S., & Kim, D. (2017). Small bank comparative advantages in alleviating financial constraints and providing liquidity insurance over time. *Review of Financial Studies*, 30(9), 3416–3454. 10.1093/rfs/hhx038

Breusch, T., & Pagan, A. (1980). The Lagrange multiplier test and its application to model specification in econometrics. *The Review of Economic Studies*, 47(1), 239–253. 10.2307/2297111

Chiratae. (2024). *FinTech Report 2024*. Retrieved from https://www.chiratae.com/fintech-report-2024/

Christensen, C. M. (2016). *The innovator's dilemma: When new technologies cause great firms to fail*. Harvard Business Review Press.

Cole, R. A., Cumming, D. J., & Taylor, J. R. (2019). Does FinTech compete with or complement bank finance? *SSRN*. 10.2139/ssrn.3302975

Cole, R. A., Gao, L., & Strobel, J. (2019). Fintech credit markets around the world: Size, drivers and policy issues. *Journal of Financial Stability*, 42, 100–113.

Dabla-Norris, E., & Srivisal, N. (2013). *Revisiting the link between finance and macroeconomic volatility*. IMF Working Paper, 13/29.

Diemers, D., Lamaa, A., Salamat, J., & Stefens, T. (2015). *Developing a FinTech ecosystem in the GCC*. Strategy.

Ding, D., Chong, G., & Chuen, L. K. D., & Cheng, T. L. (2018). From Ant Financial to Alibaba's rural Taobao strategy—how Fintech is transforming social inclusion. In D. Lee & R. H. Deng (Eds.), *Handbook of blockchain, digital finance, and inclusion* (Vol. 1, pp. 19–35). Academic Press.

Dobson, W., & Westland, T. (2018). Financial liberalisation and trade: An examination of moving up value chains in the Asia-Pacific region. In Armstrong, S., & Westland, T. (Eds.), *Asian economic integration in an era of global uncertainty*. ANU Press. 10.22459/AEIEGU.01.2018.05

Drasch, B. J., Schweizer, A., & Urbach, N. (2018). Integrating the 'Troublemakers': A taxonomy for cooperation between banks and fintechs. *Journal of Economics and Business*, 100, 26–42. 10.1016/j.jeconbus.2018.04.002

Drummer, D., Jerenz, A., Siebelt, P., & Thaten, M. (2016). *Fintech—challenges and opportunities. How digitization is transforming the financial sector*. McKinsey & Company.

Ernst & Young. (2019). *EY 2019 global fintech adoption index*. Author.

EY. (2022). *$1 Tn India FinTech Opportunity: Chiratae Ventures-EY FinTech Report*. Retrieved from https://assets.ey.com/content/dam/ey-sites/ey-com/en_in/topics/financial-services/2022/ey-one-trillion-dollars-india-fintech-opportunity-chiratae-ventures-ey-fintech-report_v1.pdf

Gabor, D., & Brooks, S. (2016). The digital revolution in financial inclusion: International development in the fintech era. *New Political Economy*, 22(4), 423–436. 10.1080/13563467.2017.1259298

Goode, A. (2018). Biometrics for banking: Best practices and barriers to adoption. *Biometric Technology Today*, 2018(10), 5–7. 10.1016/S0969-4765(18)30156-5

Gopalan, S., & Sasidharan, S. (2020). Financial liberalization and access to credit in emerging and developing economies: A firm-level empirical investigation. *Journal of Economics and Business*, 107, 105861. 10.1016/j.jeconbus.2019.105861

Haddad, C., & Hornuf, L. (2018). The emergence of the global fintech market: Economic and technological determinants. *Small Business Economics*, 53(1), 81–105. 10.1007/s11187-018-9991-x

Huang, Y., & Ji, Y. (2017). How will financial liberalization change the Chinese economy? Lessons from middle-income countries. *Journal of Asian Economics*, 50, 27–45. 10.1016/j.asieco.2017.04.001

Insights, C. (2019). *Global Fintech Report Q2 2019*. CB Insights.

Jagtiani, J., & Lemieux, C. (2018). Do fintech lenders penetrate areas that are underserved by traditional banks? *Journal of Economics and Business*, 100, 43–54. 10.1016/j.jeconbus.2018.03.001

Jagtiani, J., & Lemieux, C. (2018). *Fintech Lending: Financial Inclusion, Risk Pricing, and Alternative Information*. Federal Reserve Bank of Philadelphia Working Paper, (18-20).

Lee, C.-C., Lin, C.-W., & Zeng, J.-H. (2016). Financial liberalization, insurance market, and the likelihood of financial crises. *Journal of International Money and Finance*, 62, 25–51. 10.1016/j.jimonfin.2015.12.002

Lee, I., & Shin, Y. J. (2018). Fintech: Ecosystem, business models, investment decisions, and challenges. *Business Horizons*, 61(1), 35–46. 10.1016/j.bushor.2017.09.003

Leong, C. W., Tan, G. W., Chong, S. C., Ooi, K. B., & Lin, B. (2017). Predicting the determinants of users' intention for using mobile-based financial services: A structural equation modeling (SEM) approach. *International Journal of Information Management*, 37(3), 252–261.

Levine, R. (2005). Finance and growth: Theory and evidence. In Aghion, P., & Durlauf, S. (Eds.), *Handbook of Economic Growth* (pp. 865–934). Elsevier.

Li, G. Z., Xiong, D. H., & Liu, L. (2016). How does SMBs' development affect SMEs' financing? *Journal of Financial Research*, 12, 78–94.

Li, H., Tao, Q., Xiao, H., & Li, G. (2019). Money market funds, bank loans and interest rate liberalization: Evidence from an emerging market. *Finance Research Letters*, 30, 426–435. 10.1016/j.frl.2019.04.020

Mahoney, J. (2019). *The rise of Chinese fintech: Lessons for the United States*. Colombia Business School.

Makina, D. (Ed.). (2019). *Extending financial inclusion in Africa*. Academic Press.

Meijering, E. (2002). A chronology of interpolation: From ancient astronomy to modern signal and image processing. *Proceedings of the IEEE*, 90(3), 319–342. 10.1109/5.993400

Nicoletti, B. (2017). Financial services and fintech. In B. Nicoletti, W. Nicoletti, & Weis (Eds.), *The Future of FinTech* (pp. 3–29). Springer. 10.1007/978-3-319-51415-4_2

Pesaran, M., & Yamagata, T. (2008). Testing slope homogeneity in large panels. *Journal of Econometrics*, 142(1), 50–93. 10.1016/j.jeconom.2007.05.010

Pesaran, M. H. (2004). *General diagnostic tests for cross section dependence in panels*. Cambridge Working Papers in Economics. University of Cambridge, Faculty of Economics.

Pesaran, M. H. (2014). Testing weak cross-sectional dependence in large panels. *Econometric Reviews*, 34(6-10), 1089–1117. 10.1080/07474938.2014.956623

Rajan, R. G., & Zingales, L. (2003). The great reversals: The politics of financial development in the twentieth century. *Journal of Financial Economics*, 69(1), 5–50. 10.1016/S0304-405X(03)00125-9

Ryan, R. M., O'Toole, C. M., & McCann, F. (2014). Does bank market power affect SME financing constraints? *Journal of Banking & Finance*, 49, 495–505. 10.1016/j.jbankfin.2013.12.024

Sahay, M. R., Cihak, M. M., N'Diaye, M. P., Barajas, M. A., Kyobe, M. A., Mitra, M. S., Mooi, M. N., & Yousef, M. R. (2015). *Rethinking financial deepening: Stability and growth in emerging markets*. IMF Working Paper, SDN.

Sahay, R., Čihák, M., N'Diaye, P., Barajas, A., Bi, R., Ayala, D., & Yousefi, S. R. (2015). *Rethinking financial deepening: Stability and growth in emerging markets*. International Monetary Fund.

Salampasis, D., & Mention, A.-L. (2018). FinTech: Harnessing innovation for financial inclusion. In Chuen, D. L., & Deng, R. H. (Eds.), *Handbook of Blockchain, Digital Finance, and Inclusion* (Vol. 2, pp. 451–461). Academic Press. 10.1016/B978-0-12-812282-2.00018-8

Sarafidis, V., & Wansbeek, T. (2011). Cross-sectional dependence in panel data analysis. *Econometric Reviews*, 31(5), 483–531. 10.1080/07474938.2011.611458

Shahbaz, M., Bhattacharya, M., & Mahalik, M. K. (2017). Financial development, industrialization, the role of institutions and government: A comparative analysis between India and China. *Applied Economics*, 50(17), 1952–1977. 10.1080/00036846.2017.1383595

Sheng, T. (2020). The effect of fintech on banks' credit provision to SMEs: Evidence from China. *Finance Research Letters*, 39, 101558. 10.1016/j.frl.2020.101558

Sun, H., Edziah, B. K., Kporsu, A. K., Sarkodie, S. A., & Taghizadeh-Hesary, F. (2021). Energy efficiency: The role of technological innovation and knowledge spillover. *Technological Forecasting and Social Change*, 167, 120659. 10.1016/j.techfore.2021.120659

Sun, H., Kporsu, A. K., Taghizadeh-Hesary, F., & Edziah, B. K. (2020). Estimating environmental efficiency and convergence: 1980 to 2016. *Energy*, 208, 118224. 10.1016/j.energy.2020.118224

Sun, Y., Chen, L., Sun, H., & Taghizadeh-Hesary, F. (2020). Low-carbon financial risk factor correlation in the belt and road PPP project. *Finance Research Letters*, 35, 101491. 10.1016/j.frl.2020.101491

Svirydzenka, K. (2016). *Introducing a new broad-based index of financial development*. IMF Working Paper.

Tianhong. (2019). http://www.thfund.com.cn/en/about.html

Wooldridge, J. M. (2010). *Econometric Analysis of Cross Section and Panel Data*. The MIT Press.

World Bank. (2018). *Global Financial Inclusion (Global Findex) Database*. https://www.worldbank.org/en/publication/gfdr/data/global-financial-development-database

Zaefarian, G., Kadile, V., Henneberg, S. C., & Leischnig, A. (2017). Endogeneity bias in marketing research: Problem, causes and remedies. *Industrial Marketing Management*, 65, 39–46. 10.1016/j.indmarman.2017.05.006

ADDITIONAL READING

Basdekis, C., Christopoulos, A., Katsampoxakis, I., & Vlachou, A. (2022). FinTech's rapid growth and its effect on the banking sector. *J Bank Financ Technol*, 6(2), 159–176. 10.1007/s42786-022-00045-w

Chishti, S., & Barberis, J. (2016). *The FinTech Book: The Financial Technology Handbook for Investors, Entrepreneurs and Visionaries*. Wiley. 10.1002/9781119218906

Drescher, D. (2017). *Blockchain Basics: A Non-Technical Introduction in 25 Steps*. APress.

Sironi, P. (2016). *Fintech Innovation: From Robo-Advisors to Goal-Based Investing and Gamification*. Wiley. 10.1002/9781119227205

Skinner, C. (2014). *Digital Bank: Strategies to Launch or Become a Digital Bank*. MC.

William, J. (2016). *Fintech: The Beginner's Guide to Financial Technology*. Createspace Independent Pub.

KEY TERMS AND DEFINITIONS

Financial Access: Financial access, also known as financial inclusion, refers to the ability of individuals and businesses to access and use financial services effectively. It encompasses access to banking services, savings accounts, credit, insurance, payment systems, and other financial products and services. Improving financial access is essential for promoting economic participation, reducing poverty, and fostering inclusive growth.

Financial Depth: Financial depth refers to the level of financial intermediation and the size of financial markets relative to the overall economy. It measures the breadth and depth of financial services available, including banking services, capital markets, insurance, and other financial instruments. Greater financial depth indicates a more developed financial system capable of mobilizing savings, allocating capital efficiently, and facilitating economic growth.

Financial Development: Financial development refers to the process of improving the efficiency, depth, accessibility, and stability of financial systems within an economy. It encompasses the development of financial institutions, markets, infrastructure, regulations, and services to support economic growth, investment, savings, and risk management.

Financial Openness: Financial openness refers to the degree of integration and liberalization of a country's financial system with the global economy. It encompasses policies and measures that facilitate cross-border capital flows, foreign investment, trade in financial services, and participation in international financial markets. Greater financial openness can promote economic growth, efficiency, and risk-sharing but may also increase vulnerability to external shocks and contagion.

Financial Stability: Financial stability refers to the condition in which the financial system functions smoothly and can absorb shocks without disruption to its core functions. It encompasses the resilience of financial institutions, markets, and infrastructures to withstand external stresses, such as economic downturns, market volatility, credit crises, and systemic risks. Maintaining financial stability is a key objective of financial regulation and supervision.

FinTech (Financial Technology): FinTech refers to the innovative use of technology to deliver financial services and products. It encompasses a wide range of applications, including digital banking, mobile payments, peer-to-peer lending, robo-advisors, blockchain, and cryptocurrencies. FinTech aims to enhance efficiency, accessibility, and affordability in financial services, often disrupting traditional banking and finance sectors.

Industry 4.0: Industry 4.0, also known as the Fourth Industrial Revolution, refers to the integration of digital technologies into industrial processes to create "smart factories" and interconnected systems. It encompasses the use of advanced technologies such as the Internet of Things (IoT), artificial intelligence (AI), robotics, big data analytics, and cloud computing to optimize manufacturing and production processes, improve efficiency, and enable new business models.

NeoBanks: Neobanks, also known as digital banks or challenger banks, are financial institutions that operate exclusively online or through mobile applications, without traditional physical branches. They leverage digital technologies and innovative business models to offer a range of banking services, such as savings accounts, payments, loans, and financial management tools, often targeting tech-savvy and digitally native consumers. Neobanks typically provide streamlined, user-friendly experiences and may specialize in niche markets or innovative products.

RegTech (Regulatory Technology): RegTech refers to the use of technology to facilitate regulatory compliance, monitoring, and reporting for financial institutions. It encompasses solutions such as automated compliance checks, regulatory reporting tools, risk management systems, and anti-money laundering (AML) software. RegTech helps financial institutions navigate complex regulatory requirements efficiently, reducing compliance costs and risks associated with non-compliance.

Chapter 5
An Empirical Study on Continued Intention to Use Financial Technology in the Banking Sector

Neha Khandelwal
Universal AI University, India

Abhishek Sahu
https://orcid.org/0000-0001-6481-6728
Universal AI University, India

Asha Bhatia
https://orcid.org/0000-0003-3665-6864
Universal AI University, India

ABSTRACT

The purpose of this study is to determine customers' attitudes toward financial technology in the banking sector based on challenges and impacts. Therefore, the study aims to develop hypotheses that relate to the challenges and impact of financial technology on customer attitudes. The survey instrument was sent to 200 customers in the banking sector. Overall, 182 valid responses were found suitable for the study with a 91.00% response rate. Statistical analyses were conducted to ensure the reliability and validity of the questionnaire. A structural equation modeling technique has been used to test the research hypothesis using AMOS 21 software. Consumer sentiments are positively affected by financial technology's global recognition, leading to an increased desire to use these innovative financial services. The findings of this study have practical implications for both the banking sector and

DOI: 10.4018/979-8-3693-3322-8.ch005

the broader financial technology landscape, which may provide valuable insights for policymakers, practitioners, and researchers.

1. INTRODUCTION

Over the last decade, the FinTech has had a significant impact on the global financial services industry. According to the report given by Ministry of Finance, India is amongst the fastest growing FinTech market in the world. The market size of the Indian FinTech industry is projected to reach 150 Billion $ by 2025, up from 50 Billion $ in 2021. Government has taken numerous steps to increase investment in the Fintech industry. The objective of the FinTech industry is to increase financial inclusion in India by assisting beneficiaries in opening new bank accounts for direct benefits transmission and access to a variety of financial services applications. This has enabled Fintech entrepreneurs to develop technology products for India's vast consumer market. With a Fintech adoption rate of 87% compared to the global average of 64%, India has become one of the world's largest digital markets. India's Fintech Sector has enormous potential, supported by an enabling policy and digital infrastructure (Sakhare et al., 2023). Despite this growth, a relatively small proportion of market customers still use FinTech services. The majority of service providers have yet to demonstrate profitability. According to EY's, the payments landscape in India is expected to reach $ 100 Tn in transaction volume and $ 50 Bn in terms of revenue by 2030.

This study examines how consumers view the use of FinTech services in order to comprehend how consumers perceive technology use and the factors that contribute to it. To keep current customers happy and draw in new ones, it is important to look at numerous factors that affect how FinTech services are adopted. To create successful plans, promote a wider adoption of FinTech services, and enhance financial services, politicians, experts, and business owners must be aware of these forces. However, reliable study findings that pinpoint the variables affecting the actual acceptance and utilisation of FinTech services are lacking. With an emphasis on consumer behaviour and their aspirations to use FinTech, some researches have attempted to investigate the barriers to embracing and utilising FinTech (Leong et al., 2017; Cheng et al., 2006; Tan and Leby, 2016). Any technology must be embraced by potential users and used to its full potential before it can be successful and widely adopted (Rogers, 1983). Due to their importance in prior studies on technology adoption, gender and age are also included as control factors (Boonsiritomachai and Pitchayadejanant, 2019).

According to Park (2009), FinTech technological developments that give clients access to a range of financial products and services. The main objective of these services is to make traditional financial services more effective, timely, and useful (Hu et al., 2019). Due to its ongoing development, FinTech is playing a significant part in the profound and broad transformation that the global financial industry is currently through. The banking and finance industry has undergone a FinTech transformation, which presents a challenge to established financial institutions (McWaters et al., 2015). Customers have been lured away from traditional payment methods by the superior and more effective customer experience it provides. A wide range of services are currently offered by FinTech companies, including insurance, crowdfunding, bill payment, portfolio management, and payment banking. These businesses have fundamentally altered the way financial services are provided, making them quicker, more accessible, and more sophisticated technologically. Further, E-banking and the digitization of conventional financial services only represent a small percentage of the influence of FinTech services. Instead, the industry's primary focus is on creating and implementing cutting-edge solutions that satisfy consumers' financial needs and demands. This technical development in the banking sector in India is aligned with the goal of the Indian government to promote financial inclusion.

Therefore, the purpose of the study is to identify the potential factors for the successful adoption of FinTech and to enhance performance of the banking sector. The novelty of this study is the implementation of the analysis of moment structure structural equation modeling (AMOS-SEM) approach for evaluating critical factors affecting FinTech adoption in the Indian banking sector. The present study identifies the critical factors and items that facilitate the adoption of FinTech and develops a hypothesis to evaluate its relationships with the adoption phenomenon. Prior to or initially, the identified factors are validated by a group of FinTech field experts to determine their real-time applicability and relevance. Using SEM methodology, the validity of the causal relationship is determined by examining the goodness-of-fit statistics. Kaiser-Meyer-Olkin, Bartlett's Test of Sphericity is used in conjunction with the supported relationships of the SEM to predict FinTech adoption intentions. Empirical research analysing the customer attitude towards FinTech in the banking sector would be extremely valuable. Therefore, the proposed study may attempt to achieve the aforementioned research objectives.

- To develop a conceptual framework and research model of FinTech implementation in the banking sector.
- To analysis of FinTech-induced challenges and their impact on customer attitudes in the banking sector

The remainder part of article is organized as follows. Section 2 describes the existing literature review on financial technology in the banking sector, and impact on FinTech on customer attitude. Hypotheses development is explained in Section 3. Research methodology utilized for the proposed study including data collection and data analysis are described in Section 4. Results are analyzed and discussed in Section 5. Section 6 discusses conclusion, research implications and future research directions for the study.

2. LITERATURE REVIEW

Existing research reveals a variety of perspectives regarding the impact of investing in financial technology on the profitability of a banking sector. According to Bhutto et al. (2023), the FinTech develops the relationship among human resource expertise, service innovation, and business expansion. The study, which involved 55 US institutions, found that adoption of FinTech is fuelled by strong human resource competences, which promote service innovation and commercial expansion. Riaz et al. (2023) concluded that how banking sector customers use FinTech services, emphasising the role of social connections. According to the findings, social network word-of-mouth and trust in services are what propel FinTech adoption. Customers who are informed are more inclined to adopt FinTech, especially if they receive favourable recommendations from friends and family. Building trust and utilising social networks should be a top priority for service providers in underdeveloped areas to encourage the adoption of FinTech. Further, Al-Khawaja et al. (2023) examined that People used financial technologies to transact during the COVID-19 pandemic. This study looks at how it has affected Jordan's banking industry. Results of a consumer survey of 2450 people indicate a good relationship between pandemic perception and FinTech, influencing factors like usability and privacy. The study highlights how electronic banking helps people visit fewer branches less frequently and recommends coordinating technological advancement with client satisfaction.

However, Aggarwal et al. (2023) did a study adoption of FinTech by India's GenY demographic is examined in this study. It adds new elements, such as information quality and desire to pay, to the planned behaviour hypothesis. Smart PLS 4 software was used to analyse data from 349 students, proving the theory's viability and emphasising the significance of information quality in the adoption of FinTech. The study deepens our understanding of planned behaviour and how it affects Gen Y's use of FinTech in India, providing information that can be used to create more user-friendly financial goods and services. Alkhawaldeh et al. (2023) looked at how Jordanian customers' financial performance and satisfaction are affected by FinTech adoption. The adoption of FinTech has a favourable impact on financial performance, with customer happiness serving as a mediator, according to an analysis of data from 500 SMEs using PLS-SEM. Customers who are satisfied often experience higher financial results. In the context of Jordan and other nations undergoing significant FinTech growth, the research emphasises the significance of comprehending consumer satisfaction and FinTech adoption. Zhang et al. (2023) investigated the variables affecting Pakistani banks' adoption of FinTech services. It examines data from 297 banking users using the Technology Acceptance Model. The findings indicate that perceived data security, usefulness, ease of use, and customer trust all have a positive impact on consumers' intentions to use FinTech. The study highlights the value of data protection and open communication for boosting acceptance of FinTech, which is advantageous to both regulators and FinTech developers. Jugurnath et al. (2023) examined the role of FinTech in banking is expanding. This Mauritius study looks at the elements that affect consumer acceptance of FinTech and finds that while perceived risk does not affect attitudes, subjective norms, utility, usability, and trust do. The TAM framework can be used to personalise FinTech services with the help of this understanding. Roh et al. (2023) concluded that FinTech robo-advisors help with distant financial services, but trust and security issues still exist. We examine user adoption by fusing UTAUT and TRA. Positive attitudes are influenced by antecedents such as performance, effort, and social influence. Use of robo-advisors is influenced by TRA factors, including security, privacy, and trust. These impacts are confirmed in testing with 638 Chinese users, which clarifies adoption and trust dynamics. Rangaswamy et al. (2023) analysed of changes in Singaporean consumer behaviour is prompted by the digital boom, particularly in the banking industry. The study examines elements including perceived danger, value, and emotions in digital consumer behaviour using critical realism and descriptive research. Positive effects are observed; however they are unrelated to consumer behaviour. The emphasis of recommendations is on protecting customers from online risks. Ediagbonya and Tioluwani (2023) investigated that the how financial inclusion is aided by FinTech in emerging nations like Nigeria. It evaluates the roles of the government, institutions, and FinTech using sociological and doctrinal approaches. Despite digital initiatives, inclusion is hampered by issues including infrastructure and illiteracy. Ganguly and Arcot (2023) looked at the current state, businesses, investments, and growth of FinTech in India. It examines technological adoption theories, focusing in particular on India's FinTech industry, identifying knowledge gaps and offering suggestions for further research.

The impact of FinTech on consumer sentiments has also been discussed by a number of authors. In their study on customer impressions of FinTech, Smith and Johnson (2022) discovered that ease of use and privacy and security concerns are both important factors in determining how customers feel. Another study by Lee et al. (2021) examined how FinTech affects customer satisfaction and found that convenience, lower costs, and the conformity of FinTech services with social trends all have a favourable impact on consumers' perceptions. In conclusion, client views in the banking industry are significantly impacted by the difficulties and effects of FinTech. To successfully navigate the FinTech landscape and satisfy customer expectations and preferences, financial institutions must have a thorough understanding of these variables. The current status of FinTech in banking sector are reviewed and presented in Table 1.

Table 1. Summarized literature review of FinTech in banking sector

Authors	Contributions	Models, Frameworks, Architecture	Application
Bhutto et al. (2023)	Human resource practises aimed at enhancing employee competencies	Structural Equation Modeling	Banking sector
Bian et al. (2023)	This study investigate the impact of InsurTech on the Chinese insurance industry.	Instrumental variables	Insurance sector
Mirza et al. (2023)	The role of FinTech in promoting green finance, and profitability.	Regression model	Banking sector
Renduchintala et al. (2022)	Application of bockchain technology in banking sector	SLR	FinTech sector
Wen et al. (2023)	This study investigates the extraordinary risk spill overs between traditional financial and FinTech institutions in the United States using complex network analysis techniques,	GARCH-Copula-CoVaR approach	Insurance and FinTech sector
Tut et al. (2023)	The study measures the effect COVID-19 on financial and consumers adoption using FinTech payments banks.	Normalized Herfindahl–Hirschman Index	Electronic payment systems
Junarsin et al. (2023)	The study seeks to investigate the effects of the expansion of FinTech lending on bank risk-taking.	GMM regression	Banking sector

2.1 Current Challenges of Fintech on Customer Attitude

The financial industry has unquestionably been transformed by FinTech, which provides technological breakthroughs that enable consumers to access a range of financial goods and services. However, there have been challenges with this transition. The annoyance that customers feel when attempting to complete activities electronically is one important obstacle. This is particularly valid for those who might lack technological sophistication or have only limited access to online resources. Additionally, in some areas, internet restrictions can make it difficult for FinTech services to be adopted smoothly, thereby reducing their potential reach and accessibility.

The lack of expertise and understanding among some customer segments is another problem. Navigating FinTech platforms and services might be frightening for older people or people who are unfamiliar with technology, which discourages people from embracing new technologies. FinTech may also result in decreased personal efficiency for some clients who prefer more individualised contacts in traditional financial settings, despite the fact that it increases work efficiency through automation and digital processes. This trend towards digitalization might not suit everyone's tastes, which might make some people hesitant to completely embrace FinTech solutions.

Additionally, clients may develop unfavourable attitudes as a result of worries about the excessive fees associated with various FinTech services. Users may be wary or hesitant about fully utilising these services because they are concerned about hidden fees or unforeseen charges. FinTech organisations must concentrate on enhancing user experience, streamlining interfaces, offering user-friendly education and support, and assuring transparent pricing models in order to overcome these difficulties. By removing these obstacles, FinTech can continue to shape a positive client mentality and advance the financial sector's growth.

2.2 Impact of Fintech on Customer Attitude

FinTech's influence on consumer attitudes has taken many different forms. On the one hand, some users of FinTech services raise worries about the elevated risk of fraud and con games brought on by these services, as the digital nature of transactions might leave personal data open to unauthorised access. These worries can be reduced and client trust can be increased by addressing security measures and offering comprehensive data protection.

On the plus side, FinTech has helped to lessen work backlogs by providing streamlined and effective processes that improve customer experiences. Many users of FinTech appreciate the comfort and simplicity it gives to financial transactions and find it to be simple to use. However, some buyers continue to worry about wasting money when making purchases online. Some users can be reluctant to fully embrace FinTech services due to the perception of the risk of going over budget or running into hidden costs. These issues can be addressed by ensuring transparent pricing structures and explicit explanation of transaction fees.

The impact of FinTech on customer attitude varies, with advantages in efficiency and convenience alongside challenges related to security, transaction costs, and overspending apprehensions. FinTech companies must continue to prioritize security, transparency, and user-friendly interfaces to foster positive customer attitudes and encourage broader adoption of their services.

2.3 Variables Extracted

After conducting an extensive review of the existing literature, specific variables have been recognized that warrant further investigation. Table 2 presents the various constructs and variables considered in this study. It is found from the literature review and expert's opinion customer attitude, challenges of FinTech, and impact of FinTech are the major constructs.

Table 2. Summary of construct with measurement items

Constructs	Variables	References
Customer Attitude	BA11- Lack of IT infrastructure BA9- I find FinTech banking services beneficial. BA12- Information will not be kept private. BA10- I believe FinTech services have a long-lasting nature. BA7- FinTech service is in line with ongoing trend in the society. BA8- FinTech provides greater convenience and reduce cost. BA6- I am learning better use of FinTech services from other's experiences	Laksamana et al. (2023); Vijai et al. (2023); Chouhan et al. (2023)
Challenges of FinTech	BA15- Frustration in getting work done electronically. BA16- Internet barriers BA14- Lack of skill and knowledge BA17- Increased work efficiency but reduced personal efficiency. BA13- I feel charges are high	Gopal et al. (2023); Verma et al. (2023); Kim (2023); Junarsin et al. (2023)
Impact of FinTech	BA3- FinTech increases the risk of fraud and scam. BA4- It has reduced back-log of work. BA2- I find it easy to use. BA1- I am scared of excessive expenditure during online transaction. BA5- Concerned about paying transaction charges	Renduchintala et al. (2022); Asif et al. (2023); Ergashev (2023); Soon (2023);

2.4 Research Gaps

Certainly, there exists a notable research gap when it comes to thoroughly understanding the challenges that arise from utilizing FinTech and the subsequent impact it has on users within the banking sector. While certain studies acknowledge the presence of challenges and advantages associated with FinTech adoption, a more comprehensive exploration is needed to delve into the specific obstacles that users encounter when engaging with FinTech tools and services in the banking context. This gap is significant as it hampers a complete grasp of the user experience, thereby impeding the development of effective strategies to address challenges and enhance the overall adoption of FinTech solutions.

Moreover, existing research often focuses on high-level outcomes such as convenience and accessibility in relation to the impact of FinTech on users. However, a research gap remains in examining the broader and more intricate effects of FinTech on users' financial behaviors, decision-making processes, and overall financial well-being. Bridging this gap is crucial to gain a more holistic perspective on how FinTech shapes user interactions and financial outcomes. This, in turn, enables a more informed approach to designing and implementing FinTech solutions that are attuned to users' needs and preferences, while simultaneously maximizing positive impact and minimizing potential risks.

3. ESTABLISHMENT OF HYPOTHESES

The subsequent hypothesis is formulated to determine whether the challenges and impact of FinTech have a notable influence on consumer attitudes;

H_{01}: There is not significant role of challenges of FinTech in determining customer attitude.

H_{A1}: There is a significant role of challenges of FinTech in determining customer attitude.

H_{02}: There is not significant impact of FinTech on customer attitude.

H_{A2}: There is a significant impact of FinTech on customer attitude.

4. RESEARCH METHODOLOGY AND DESIGN OF THE STUDY

This section demonstrates the interrelationships between the variables using a structural equation model (SEM). SEM integrates both regression analysis and factor analysis, making it possible to fully understand the correlations. To choose the right factors and variables for the structural model, confirmatory factor analysis (CFA), a preliminary step in structural equation modelling, is utilised. After that, the regression weights between the independent variables—the difficulties and effects of FinTech—and the dependent variable—customer attitude—are determined using multiple regression analysis. Please see the site below for the AMOS SEM results.

The SEM technique is a robust statistical method for analysing complex relationships between observed and latent variables. It is utilised extensively in numerous disciplines, including psychology, sociology, economics, and other social sciences, as well as marketing, education, and epidemiology. It incorporates elements of factor analysis and multiple regression at its foundation to investigate the causal relationships between latent constructs and their observed indicators. The primary objective of SEM is to test and refine theoretical models by assessing how well the hypothesised relationships match the observed data. Further, it can be viewed as an extension of linear regression, with an emphasis on estimating the relationships between variables while incorporating measurement error and latent variables (Agrawal and Singh, 2019).

Figure 1. Model of hypothesized relationship

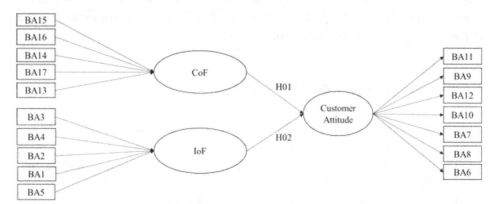

In this study, a descriptive study design was used to thoroughly understand customers' desires to adopt FinTech goods and services in the banking industry. A systematic questionnaire was used to collect primary data. Respondents were asked to score their beliefs on a five-point Likert scale, with 1 denoting strongly disagree and 5 denoting strongly agree. The survey, which primarily targeted the study's individual bank customers, had 182 participants. The sampling method in this experiment was random sampling.

4.1 Data Collection Procedure

Customers with high school, undergraduate, graduate, postgraduate, and doctoral degrees make up the study's intended demographic. The questionnaire was distributed to participants electronically using the Google Docs online format. Numerous emails with links to the survey's questions and invitations to take part were sent to the participants. Due to certain missing or incomplete answers on some of the 200 sent questionnaires, only 182 were useful for analysis.

4.2 Data Analysis

Using AMOS 21 software, confirmatory factor analysis (CFA) was identified as the best method for measuring and evaluating the FinTech-related components. Six fundamental metrics were used to evaluate the model's overall goodness of fit: "Chi-Square/Degree of Freedom ratio, Normed Fit Index (NFI), Non-Normed Fit Index (NNFI), Comparative Fit Index (CFI), Root Mean Square Error of Approximation (RMSEA), and Standardised Root Mean Square Residual (SRMSR)" (Hair et al., 2010; Kline, 2010).

Additionally, the study employed SEM for statistical analysis of the collected data. The objective was to examine the interactions among the three subscales: students' customer attitude items (n=7), challenges of FinTech items (n=5), and impact on FinTech items (n=5). The results of SEM provided a path analysis of the hypothesized model, exploring the relationships between challenges, impact of FinTech, and customer attitudes.

5. RESULTS AND DISCUSSION

The study included 182 participants, 92 of whom (50.5%) were men and 90 (49.5%) were women. The respondents' age distribution was as follows: 30 of the participants were under the age of 18, 48 were between the ages of 18 and 24, 52 were between the ages of 25 and 30, 29 were between the ages of 31 and 40, and 23 were beyond 40. 16 participants were in high school, 46 were undergraduates, 45 were graduates, 45 were postgraduates, 15 were pursuing doctorates, and 15 were categorised as "others" in terms of their educational background. 126 respondents said they were married, 40 said they were single, 8 said they were widowed, and 8 said they had divorced. The participants represented a variety of professions, with 8 respondents representing students, 38 representing employees of the private sector, 8 representing employees of the government, 45 representing employees of businesses, 16 representing employees of the self-employed, and 67 representing respondents who fell into the "other" category.

5.1 Evaluation of Model Fit

In order to conduct a factor analysis, it is necessary for the variables to exhibit correlations. Since every pair of variables has a correlation, the correlation matrix includes diagonal elements. This sample size makes it possible to run a factor analysis on it. Depending on whether factor analysis can be performed on the data, it ranges from 0.5 to 1 is shown in Table 3. Factors cannot be applied to the data if this statistic is less than 0.5. The factor analysis is adequate for the data, according to a KMO statistic of 0.905. This statistic is used to determine factor analysis models as well as Bartlett's test outcomes. The Bartlett's test for the population's correlation matrix yields an identity matrix. Based on the KMO and Bartlett tests, factor analysis seems reasonable. Table 4 displays the initial and extracted communalities for each variable. All variables are given a default value of one at the beginning, which is displayed in the table's initial communality column. Yet, an estimate of the variance for each variable is provided by the recovered communalities. A variable may need to be removed from the analysis if it does not fit the factor solution well.

Table 3. KMO and Bartlett's test

KMO and Bartlett's Test		
Kaiser-Meyer-Olkin Measure of Sampling Adequacy.		**0.905**
Bartlett's Test of Sphericity	Approx. Chi-Square	3052.020
	df	136
	Sig.	0.000

Table 4. Communalities values

Communalities		
	Initial	**Extraction**
BA1	1.000	0.772
BA2	1.000	0.795
BA3	1.000	0.883
BA4	1.000	0.868
BA5	1.000	0.716
BA6	1.000	0.951
BA7	1.000	0.676
BA8	1.000	0.707
BA9	1.000	0.889
BA10	1.000	0.786
BA11	1.000	0.834
BA12	1.000	0.800
BA13	1.000	0.824
BA14	1.000	0.885
BA15	1.000	0.871

continued on following page

Table 4. Continued

Communalities		
	Initial	**Extraction**
BA16	1.000	0.904
BA17	1.000	0.790

Extraction Method: Principal Component Analysis

Three components were found using principal component analysis. The first component of the starting variables, which may be integrated linearly, explains the most variance overall. The analysis demonstrated that these three components collectively explained 78.694 percent of the overall variation as shown in Table 5. In the case of factor analysis, the plot retains the number of components indicated. When examining the components with steep slopes, it was determined that three components should be retained for factor extraction.

By choosing the smallest number of components required, a factor analysis seeks to pinpoint the factors that contribute the most to the variability in the data. There are several ways to choose how many components to keep when completing a factor analysis. The eigenvalue technique was used in this work to extract the factors. This method takes into account variables with eigenvalues greater than one. Three components were added to the model because their eigenvalues were greater than one. The factor structure of the model was then optimised using varimax orthogonal rotation.

Factor rotation establishes a relationship between variables and factors. Factor loadings represent the association between elements and variables within a factor. In the provided table, factor loadings highlight items that exhibit a strong correlation with a particular factor. These items contribute to the characterization of the factors. Consequently, the following variables were derived: F1 = Customer Attitude, F2 = Challenges of FinTech, F3 = Impact of FinTech.

Table 5. Total variance explained

Component	Initial Eigenvalues			Extraction Sums of Squared Loadings			Rotation Sums of Squared Loadings		
	Total	% of Variance	Cumulative %	Total	% of Variance	Cumulative %	Total	% of Variance	Cumulative %
1	8.219	48.348	48.348	8.219	48.348	48.348	5.122	30.127	30.127
2	3.391	19.947	68.295	3.391	19.947	68.295	4.211	24.770	54.897
3	1.768	10.400	78.694	1.768	10.400	78.694	4.046	23.798	78.694
4	0.573	3.370	82.064						
5	0.501	2.947	85.011						
6	0.421	2.475	87.486						

continued on following page

Table 5. Continued

Component	Initial Eigenvalues			Extraction Sums of Squared Loadings			Rotation Sums of Squared Loadings		
	Total	% of Variance	Cumulative %	Total	% of Variance	Cumulative %	Total	% of Variance	Cumulative %
7	0.367	2.161	89.646						
8	0.321	1.890	91.536						
9	0.259	1.525	93.062						
10	0.225	1.321	94.383						
11	0.200	1.175	95.558						
12	0.177	1.039	96.597						
13	0.161	0.946	97.543						
14	0.139	0.815	98.358						
15	0.108	0.633	98.991						
16	0.091	0.535	99.526						
17	0.081	0.474	100.000						

Extraction Method: Principal Component Analysis

The graphic in Figure 2 shows how many components are optimized to extract for factor analysis. Three elements should be incorporated, according to the analysis of the slope's steepness. The number of elements that should be preserved for the analysis is indicated by the slope's levelling-off point.

Figure 2. Screen plot graph

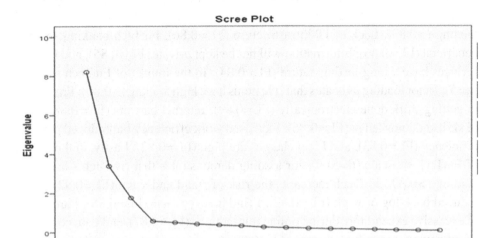

5.2 Validity and Reliability

The study evaluated a number of the measurement features and the reliability of the used items (instrument). The researchers calculated the loading factor (LF) of each item and tested its convergent validity. They also assessed each construct's internal consistency, validity, reliability, and multicollinearity potential.

Composite reliability (CR) was used to calculate the internal consistency of the constructs, and average variance extracted (AVE) was used to calculate the validity of the constructs. Cronbach's alpha was calculated in order to assess the constructions' consistency. Due to the fact that all of these parameters fell within the acceptable range, the results showed strong internal reliability, validity, and consistency.

In particular, the "Cronbach's alpha values varied from 0.86 to 0.90, and the composite reliability values ranged from 0.90 to 0.93, supporting good internal reliability. The constructs' validity was supported by the AVE values, which varied from 0.83 to 0.86". Additionally, the estimated construct loadings were in the range of 0.672 to 0.924, strengthening the study's convergent validity even more. The study met the requirements for convergent validity, and it was determined that the items' measurement characteristics and validity were reliable and consistent within the allowed range.

Table 6 presents the classification of the three subscales of FinTech based on factor loading (FL) into two groups: high loading and medium loading. In the customer attitude subscale (n=7), factor loading reveals that four items have high loading (>0.80): Lack of IT infrastructure (FL=0.86), FinTech banking services beneficial (FL=0.86), Information will not be kept private (FL=0.85), and FinTech services have a long-lasting nature (FL=0.84). In the impact of FinTech subscale (n=5), factor loading indicates that five items have high loading (>0.80): Frustration in getting work done electronically (FL=0.89), Internet barriers (FL=0.88), Lack of skill and knowledge (FL=0.86), Increased work efficiency but reduced personal efficiency (FL=0.83), and I feel charges are high (FL=0.82). Lastly, in the impact of FinTech subscale (n=5), factor loading demonstrates that five items have high loading (>0.80): FinTech increases the risk of fraud and scam (FL=0.92), It has reduced back-log of work (FL=0.92), I find it easy to use (FL=0.88), I am scared of excessive expenditure during online transactions (FL=0.87), and I am concerned about paying transaction charges (FL=0.82).

Table 6. Result of confirmatory factor analysis

Construct	Code and Item	Alpha	Standardized Factor Loading	AVE	CR
Customer Attitude (n=7)	BA11- Lack of IT infrastructure BA9- I find FinTech banking services beneficial BA12- Information will not be kept private BA10- I believe FinTech services have a long lasting nature BA7- FinTech service is in line with ongoing trend in the society BA8- FinTech provides greater convenience and reduce cost BA6- I am learning better use of FinTech services from other's experiences	0.90	0.869 0.867 0.851 0.848 0.771 0.739 0.672	0.84	0.92
Challenges of FinTech (n=5)	BA15- Frustration in getting work done electronically BA16- Internet barriers BA14- Lack of skill and knowledge BA17- Increased work efficiency but reduced personal efficiency BA13- I feel charges are high	0.89	0.890 0.886 0.861 0.832 0.821	0.86	0.90
Impact of FinTech (n=5)	BA3- FinTech increases the risk of fraud and scam BA4- It has reduced back-log of work BA2- I find it easy to use BA1- I am scared of excessive expenditure during online transaction BA5- Concerned about paying transaction charges	0.86	0.924 0.901 0.884 0.871 0.828	0.83	0.93

Table 7 presents the findings of discriminant validity between various constructs. Elements in the matrix diagonal that were greater than off-diagonal components in the corresponding row and column served as placeholders for the square roots of the AVEs. Each construct in this analysis therefore validated the discriminant validity of the data.

Table 7. Discriminant validity test (Fornell and Larcker criteria)

Construct	CA	COF	IOF
CA	0.815		
COF	0.555	0.791	
IOF	0.230	0345	0.715

Figure 3 demonstrates a weakly positive correlation (R=0.41) between challenges and the impact of FinTech on consumer views. This implies a direct relationship between the three subscales and that customer perceptions of the challenges and effects of FinTech are related.

This model has 115 degrees of freedom (DF), a Chi-Square value of 217.303, and a p-value of less than 0.000. It should be mentioned that chi-square is sensitive to sample size (Kline, 2010). The Goodness of Fit Index (GFI), which is high and measures 0.980, indicates high levels of "satisfactory fit". GFI values near 1 indicate an excellent match. The Comparative Fit Index (CFI) score of 0.966 indicates a very good fit. According to statistically significant fit tests, the hypothesised model fits the data well, as evidenced by the Root Mean Square Error of Approximation (RMSEA), which is 0.050 with a 95% confidence interval. These figures provide confirmation that the model is accurate and that no further improvements are feasible.

Figure 3. CFA measurement model of challenges and impact of FinTech on customer attitude

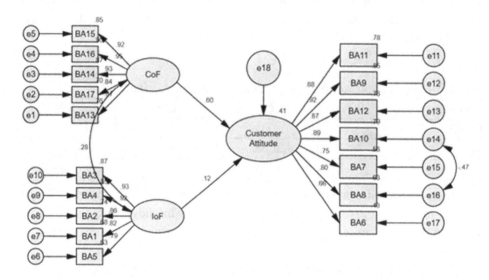

Table 8 presents the study examines the relationship between independent and dependent variables, a connection highlighted through regression analysis. The dependent variable in this context is customer attitude, while the independent variable encompasses challenges and the influence of FinTech. To validate the hypothesis, a structure equation modeling was employed. In this test, a p-value exceeding 0.05 indicates rejection of the alternative hypothesis, whereas a p-value below 0.05 leads to the rejection of the null hypothesis. In this instance, due to the significance values of all factors falling below 0.05, the null hypothesis can be rejected. Hence, the test results highlight the noteworthy influence that both the challenges faced in adopting FinTech and the broader impact of FinTech itself exert on shaping customer attitudes. This suggests that the interplay between these factors significantly contributes to the way customers perceive and respond to financial technology innovations.

Table 8. Regression weight (default model)

			Estimate	S.E.	C.R.	P
Customer Attitude	<---	CoF	.588	.071	8.335	***
Customer Attitude	<---	IoF	.127	.068	1.866	***

FinTech, as a transformative force in the financial landscape, exerts a significant influence on how consumers perceive and approach various financial aspects. This impact extends beyond mere convenience, extending its reach to shape the overall attitude that consumers hold towards financial technology. This can manifest in the way consumers view digital banking, online payment methods, and other techno- logical innovations within the financial sector.

Moreover, the influence of FinTech on consumer attitude is intricately intertwined with the specific concerns and apprehensions that individuals associate with these technological advancements. These FinTech-related concerns, which encompass issues such as data security, privacy, and the potential disruptions brought about by technological changes, serve as pivotal determinants in molding customer attitudes. Consumers' perceptions of risk, trustworthiness, and the perceived benefits of Fin- Tech play a crucial role in forming their overall attitude towards these innovations.

In essence, the profound influence of FinTech on consumer attitude underscores the multifaceted nature of this relationship. It is not solely about the convenience or efficiency that FinTech offers, but also about addressing and mitigating the legit- imate concerns and uncertainties that consumers may harbour. By understanding and addressing these concerns, financial institutions and technology providers can effectively shape a positive consumer attitude towards FinTech, fostering a more re- ceptive environment for its adoption and integration into everyday financial activities.

6. CONCLUSION

Several macroeconomic factors, including India's booming economic growth with rising disposable income, a large unbanked and under-banked population, government and regulatory initiatives, a growing young adult population, improving internet access and smartphone penetration, and a rapidly expanding e-commerce market, all contribute to the growth of the Indian FinTech market. FinTech, an emerging sector in the financial industry, leverages technology and innovation to offer financial services through digital platforms, encompassing various applications, workflows, products, and business models conducted entirely over the internet. Numerous studies have shown that customer perceptions are greatly impacted by the use of FinTech in the banking industry. Moreover, customers' attitudes are also shaped by the challenges and difficulties associated with FinTech. In conclusion, this study reveals that the challenges and impact of FinTech have a substantial effect on customers' attitudes. Some of the challenges identified include frustration with electronic processes, barriers to internet access, lack of skills and knowledge, per- ceived high charges, increased risks of fraud and scams, reduced personal efficiency despite improved work efficiency, concerns regarding excessive expenditures during online transactions, lack of adequate IT infrastructure, worries about the privacy of personal information, belief in the long-term viability of FinTech services, alignment with societal trends, greater convenience, cost reduction, and learning from others' experiences in utilizing FinTech services.

The impact of FinTech on consumer sentiments has also been discussed by a number of authors. In their study on customer impressions of FinTech, Smith and Johnson (2022) discovered that ease of use and privacy and security concerns are both important factors in determining how customers feel. Another study by Lee et al. (2021) examined how FinTech affects customer satisfaction and found that convenience, lower costs, and the conformity of FinTech services with social trends all have a favourable impact on consumers' perceptions. In conclusion, client views in the banking industry are significantly impacted by the difficulties and effects of FinTech. To successfully navigate the FinTech landscape and satisfy customer expectations and preferences, financial institutions must have a thorough understanding of these variables.

6.1 Research Implications

The findings of this study have practical implications for both the banking sector and the broader financial technology landscape. By understanding the factors influencing customers' intention to continue using financial technology, banks can design targeted strategies to enhance user engagement and retention. Moreover, these insights can guide the development of user-centric FinTech solutions that address the identified determinants, ultimately fostering a more seamless and satisfactory customer experience. Additionally, the study contributes to the existing body of knowledge by shedding light on the dynamic nature of customer intentions in the rapidly evolving realm of financial technology, providing valuable insights for policymakers, practitioners, and researchers alike.

6.2 Limitations and Further Research Direction

However, it's important to acknowledge certain limitations inherent to this study. Firstly, the research focuses solely on the banking sector, potentially limiting the generalizability of the findings to other industries within the FinTech domain. Secondly, the study's reliance on empirical data might not capture the entirety of complex behavioural and psychological factors that influence users' intention to continue using FinTech. Lastly, the study's cross-sectional design may not fully capture the dynamics of changing user intentions over time. These limitations emphasize the need for further research to explore a broader spectrum of contexts, factors, and variables that may impact users' continued intention to use financial technology.

Future research should focus on how trust and security concerns affect customers' intentions to adopt FinTech. A deeper comprehension of how privacy, data security, and customer trust in FinTech platforms affect customers' continued usage is required, even though few research have touched on these topics. Further investigation is required on how user experience and interface design affect the desire to utilise FinTech in the banking industry. Optimising FinTech services may require a thorough understanding of how user-friendliness and ease of use impact client happiness and willingness to utilise these technologies repeatedly.

REFERENCES

Aggarwal, M., Nayak, K. M., & Bhatt, V. (2023). Examining the factors influencing fintech adoption behaviour of gen Y in India. *Cogent Economics & Finance*, 11(1), 2197699. 10.1080/23322039.2023.2197699

Agrawal, S., & Singh, R. K. (2019). Analyzing disposition decisions for sustainable reverse logistics: Triple Bottom Line approach. *Resources, Conservation and Recycling*, 150, 104448. 10.1016/j.resconrec.2019.104448

Al-Khawaja, H. A., Yamin, I., & Alshehadeh, A. (2023). The COVID-19 Pandemic's Effects on Fintech in Banking Sector. *Revue d'Economie Financiere*, 21, 1.

Alkhawaldeh, B., Alhawamdeh, H., Al-Afeef, M., Al-Smadi, A., Almarshad, M., Fraihat, B., & Alaa, A. (2023). The effect of financial technology on financial performance in Jordanian SMEs: The role of financial satisfaction. *Uncertain Supply Chain Management*, 11(3), 1019–1030. 10.5267/j.uscm.2023.4.020

Asif, M., Khan, M. N., Tiwari, S., Wani, S. K., & Alam, F. (2023). The impact of fintech and digital financial services on financial inclusion in India. *Journal of Risk and Financial Management*, 16(2), 122. 10.3390/jrfm16020122

Bhutto, S. A., Jamal, Y., & Ullah, S. (2023). FinTech adoption, HR competency potential, service innovation and firm growth in banking sector. *Heliyon*, 9(3), e13967. 10.1016/j.heliyon.2023.e1396736915496

Boonsiritomachai, W., & Pitchayadejanant, K. (2019). Determinants affecting mobile banking adoption by generation Y based on the Unified Theory of Acceptance and Use of Technology Model modified by the Technology Acceptance Model concept. *Kasetsart Journal of Social Sciences*, 40(2), 349–358.

Cheng, T. E., Lam, D. Y., & Yeung, A. C. (2006). Adoption of internet banking: An empirical study in Hong Kong. *Decision Support Systems*, 42(3), 1558–1572. 10.1016/j.dss.2006.01.002

Chouhan, V., Ali, S., Sharma, R. B., & Sharma, A. (2023). The effect of financial technology (Fin-tech) on the conventional banking industry in India. *International Journal of Innovative Research and Scientific Studies*, 6(3), 538–544. 10.53894/ijirss.v6i3.1578

Ediagbonya, V., & Tioluwani, C. (2023). The role of fintech in driving financial inclusion in developing and emerging markets: Issues, challenges and prospects. *Technological Sustainability*, 2(1), 100–119. 10.1108/TECHS-10-2021-0017

Ergashev, A. (2023). Financial technologies in the remote banking system. *Science and Innovation,2*(A6), 197-201.

Ganguly, A. K., & Arcot, P. P. (2023). Models of technology adoption and growth of fintech in India: A review. *European Chemical Bulletin*, 12, 2153–2168.

Gopal, S., Gupta, P., & Minocha, A. (2023). Advancements in Fin-Tech and Security Challenges of Banking Industry. *4th International Conference on Intelligent Engineering and Management (ICIEM)*, 1-6 10.1109/ICIEM59379.2023.10165876

Hair, J. F., Jr., & Black, W. C. (2010). *Multivariate data analysis* (7th ed.). Pearson Prentice Hall.

Hu, Z., Ding, S., Li, S., Chen, L., & Yang, S. (2019). Adoption intention of fintech services for bank users: An empirical examination with an extended technology acceptance model. *Symmetry*, 11(3), 340. 10.3390/sym11030340

Jugurnath, B., Hemshika, P., & Štraupaitė, S. (2023). Fintech challenges and opportunities in banking. *Management/Vadyba,39*(1), 16487974.

Kim, S. J. (2023). An Overview of Fintech, Pandemic and the Financial System: Challenges and Opportunities. *Fintech, Pandemic, and the Financial System. Challenges and Opportunities*, 22, 3–9.

Kline, R. (2010). *Principles and practice of structural equation modelling*. The Guilford Press.

Laksamana, P., Suharyanto, S., & Cahaya, Y. F. (2023). Determining factors of continuance intention in mobile payment: Fintech industry perspective. *Asia Pacific Journal of Marketing and Logistics*, 35(7), 1699–1718. 10.1108/APJML-11-2021-0851

Lee, C., Kim, S., & Park, J. (2021). The Impact of Fintech on Customer Satisfaction in the Banking Sector. *Journal of Financial Services*, 25(3), 129–147.

Leong, C., Tan, B., Xiao, X., Tan, F. T. C., & Sun, Y. (2017). Nurturing a FinTech ecosystem: The case of a youth microloan startup in China. *International Journal of Information Management*, 37(2), 92–97. 10.1016/j.ijinfomgt.2016.11.006

McWaters, R. J., Bruno, G., Lee, A., & Blake, M. (2015). The future of financial services: How disruptive innovations are reshaping the way financial services are structured, provisioned and consumed. *World Economic Forum,125*, 1-178.

Park, S. Y. (2009). An analysis of the technology acceptance model in understanding university students' behavioral intention to use e-learning. *Journal of Educational Technology & Society*, 12(3), 150–162.

Rangaswamy, E., Yong, W. S., & Joy, G. V. (2023). The evaluation of challenges and impact of digitalisation on consumers in Singapore. *International Journal of System Assurance Engineering and Management*, 1-13.

Riaz, M., Mehmood, A., Shabbir, U., & Kazmi, S. M. A. (2023). Social Interactions Leading Role in Adopting the Fintech: A Case of Banking Sector. *Pakistan Journal of Humanities and Social Sciences*, 11(2), 1467–1476. 10.52131/pjhss.2023.1102.0449

Rogers, E. M. (1983). *Diffusion of Innovation* (3rd ed.). Academic Press.

Roh, T., Park, B. I., & Xiao, S. S. (2023). Adoption of AI-enabled Robo-advisors in Fintech: Simultaneous Employment of UTAUT and the Theory of Reasoned Action. *Journal of Electronic Commerce Research*, 24(1), 29–47.

Sakhare, C. A., Somani, N. N., Patel, B. L., Khorgade, S. N., & Parchake, S. (2023). What drives FinTech Adoption? A study on Perception, Adoption, and Constraints of FinTech Services. *European Economic Letters*, 13(3), 1216–1230.

Smith, A., & Johnson, B. (2022). Customer Perceptions of Fintech Services. *Journal of Financial Innovation*, 10(2), 75–92.

Soon, L. K. (2023). A review of literature on the impact of fintech firms on the banking industry. *Informative Journal of Management Sciences,2*(2).

Tan, E., & Leby Lau, J. (2016). Behavioural intention to adopt mobile banking among the millennial generation. *Young Consumers*, 17(1), 18–31. 10.1108/YC-07-2015-00537

Verma, A., Tiwari, D., Lohchab, P., Khan, M., & Pandey, A. (2023). *Fintech and digital finance: opportunities and challenges in Indian banking sector*. Academic Press.

Vijai, C., Bhuvaneswari, L., Sathyakala, S., Dhinakaran, D. P., Arun, R., & Lakshmi, M. R. (2023). The Effect of Fintech on Customer Satisfaction Level. *Journal of Survey in Fisheries Sciences*, 10(3S), 6628–6634.

Zhang, W., Siyal, S., Riaz, S., Ahmad, R., Hilmi, M. F., & Li, Z. (2023). Data security, customer trust and intention for adoption of fintech services: An empirical analysis from commercial bank users in Pakistan. *SAGE Open*, 13(3). 10.1177/21582440231181388

Chapter 6
The Rise of Digital Currency:
A Bibliometric Evaluation and Future Research Prospect

Priyanshu Sharma
Birla Institute of Technology Mesra, Jaipur, India

Jyoti Kumar Chandel
https://orcid.org/0000-0003-2051-9654
Birla Institute of Technology Mesra, Jaipur, India

Diksha Sinha
https://orcid.org/0000-0002-5058-8012
Birla Institute of Technology Mesra, Jaipur, India

Ramji Nagariya
https://orcid.org/0000-0002-2739-9838
Christ University, India

Abhineet Saxena
Amity University, India

ABSTRACT

This study aims to get an insight into the intellectual structure, current research themes, and future research directions on digital currency, cryptocurrency, and blockchain. Bibliometric analysis coupled with performance analysis and cluster analysis has been conducted on the digital currency articles, published between the years 2011 and 2023, filtered using PRISMA protocol, and extracted from the Web of Science and Scopus databases. Network analysis was carried out in the Biblioshiny

DOI: 10.4018/979-8-3693-3322-8.ch006

package of R software and VOSviewer. The study highlights that the research of digital currency is classified into four broad categories: 'emerging technology', 'cryptocurrencies portfolios', 'cryptocurrencies as a medium of exchange and an asset class', and 'cryptocurrencies and financial risk'. The chapter presents an innovative model focusing on productive avenues for future research by synthesizing the latest research articles extracted from the databases, related to digital currency through bibliometric analysis.

1. INTRODUCTION

The performance of modern organizations is largely influenced by the effective utilization of information and communication technology (ICT) in the contemporary competitive world (Müller and Antoni, 2020). Applications of ICT and Blockchain Technologies have enhanced financial performance, innovation, supply chain, value creation, competitiveness, decision-making, strategy formulation, strategy implementation, sustainability, and overall management of the organizations (Eze *et al.*, 2019; Inegbedion, 2021). Cryptocurrency is a decentralized digital currency that utilizes blockchain technology. It exists as virtual currency without any physical form, ensuring secure and invisible transactions. Examples of cryptocurrencies include Bitcoin, Ethereum, Litecoin, and Monero. Satoshi Nakamoto introduced blockchain through Bitcoin. Blockchain is a digital data storage system that uses cryptography to create a linear chain of records. Cryptocurrencies are protected by cryptography and enable decentralized digital ledgers. Bitcoin and Ether, used in the Ethereum blockchain, are currently the most widely adopted cryptocurrencies (Khan and Hakami, 2022).

Digital Currency, Crypto Currency, and Blockchain are significantly evolving research domains in the contemporary techno-economic sphere and have started disrupting traditional financial systems. Digital Currency is an electronic form of currency. These currencies are considered assets that are influenced by various supply and demand factors. To record the transactions of encrypted digital currencies, blockchain technology is being broadly utilized (Ahluwalia *et al.*, 2020). Blockchain technology has potential applications far beyond cryptocurrencies which are witnessed in many sectors primarily at the nascent stage. The core focus of the first-generation blockchain technology has been on the applications in cryptocurrencies (Tönnissen *et al.*, 2020). Blockchain is an underlying technology on which most cryptocurrencies rely. It provides a secure mechanism for fast, economical, and reliable financial transactions (Duan and Guo, 2021). Blockchain technology is prominently used to develop digital currencies and cryptocurrencies in money transfer (Ali *et al.*, 2020) are traded in various crypto exchanges and electronic markets (Alt, 2020). Blockchain-based applications are significantly increasing in the evolving fintech segment (Chang *et al.*, 2020). The crypto marketplaces have a relationship with blockchain technology and shape the functioning of electronic trading (Alt and Wende, 2020).

A large number of research papers have been published in the areas of digital currencies, cryptocurrencies, and blockchain in recent years. The focus of researchers has shifted from Bitcoin to the broader cryptocurrency market (Jalal *et al.*, 2021). Research gaps in the domain of blockchain and cryptocurrency have been highlighted in many research studies. The dearth of research in cryptocurrency adoption with weak research methods in Bitcoin and cryptocurrency (Al-Amri *et al.*, 2019; Sharma *et al.*, 2019)along with the Lack of focused applied research in blockchain, insufficient systematic research in blockchain sustainability, with the scarcity of bibliometric reports on blockchain applications(Drljevic *et al.*, 2020; Esmaeilian, B., Sarkis, J., Lewis, K. and Behdad, 2020; Firdaus *et al.*, 2019) are prominent knowledge gaps recommended as future research directions. Following the future research direction suggested by Firdaus *et al.*, (2019) and Dashkevich *et al.*, (2020) apply the bibliometric analysis to get a better insight into the evolving structure of knowledge and potential research directions linked with blockchain, cryptocurrency, and digital currency.

The following research question is aimed to be investigated through this study focusing on the digital currency research papers published between 2010 and 2022:

● RQ. What are the intellectual structure, current themes, and future research directions in digital currency?

To address this research question and cater to the main objective of providing a holistic view of the development of literature and suggesting further research directions in digital currency, descriptive analysis is deployed to get the quantitative data of the selected articles(Shtovba *et al.*, 2020), citation analysis is done to reveal the most influential studies in the field, Keyword occurrence analysis and co-authorship analysis are done to present the current theme and intellectual structure of research, and lastly, content analysis is completed to know the current theme and suggest future research direction(Leonidou and Leonidou, 2011).

Through a bibliometric analysis, this study has identified key research themes (concentrated across four clusters) and the most influential authors, journals, and publications in the field of digital currency. Additionally, we provide a roadmap for future research by identifying gaps and areas requiring further investigation. Overall, this study provides valuable insights into the trends, patterns, and future research prospects on digital currency(Van Veldhoven and Vanthienen, 2023).

Different stakeholders keep constantly watching for insights into the evolving technological trends to facilitate proactive steps for gaining competitive advantages. This study contributed by offering deep insights into the domains of digital currency, cryptocurrency, and blockchain technology for practical applications(Abdullah *et al.*, 2022). The practical implications of this study are to offer deep insight into emerging trends in financial blockchain applications, to explore and identify opportunities in the domain of blockchain and digital currency, to develop cost-effective user-friendly financial blockchain applications, to assist investors through informed decision-making in portfolio investments and to gauge the possibility of using cryptocurrency as a medium of exchange.

Theoretically, the study contributes towards revealing the contemporary state of knowledge surrounding digital currency through four acknowledged clusters and paving the way for the further scope of research by addressing the gaps identified. Additionally, the academicians and researchers may benefit through further collaborations after learning about the prominent authors, institutions, journals, and citation and co-citation networks prevailing in the current state of literature on digital currency through bibliometric and network analysis. Major social implications are the evolution of an alternate financial system, higher speed of transactions, lower transaction costs, enhanced access to the financial system, ease of remittances, ease of participation in the financial system, and better social inclusion.

The remainder of the paper is structured as follows: Section 2 encapsulates the review of literature and theoretical background, Section 3 enumerates the search criteria and methodology, Section 4 provides the analyses and results, Section 5 portrays the discussion and implications of the study, Section 6concludes the study with limitations and future research directions.

2. THEORETICAL BACKGROUND

Blockchain, Cryptocurrencies, Digital Currencies, and Bitcoin have evolved as new domains of interdisciplinary research during the last two decades. Table 1 summarizes relevant studies related to digital currency, with cryptocurrency, bitcoin, or blockchain as their keywords and bibliometric analysis as their methodology. The disruptive nature of Blockchain technology has applications in all subjects and has also paved the way for the development of many cryptocurrencies (García-Corral *et al.*, 2022). Few bibliometric studies have been conducted to understand knowledge structure and future research directions.(Jalal *et al.*, 2021) have identified the determinants of cryptocurrency returns, the efficiency of cryptocurrencies, portfolio diversification, and regulatory aspects of cryptocurrencies as main streams of existing cryptocurrency literature. Tandon *et al.*, (2021) have identified inefficiencies of Bitcoin, multi-domain deployment, enablement and implication, strategy, and regulation as major research themes. Bitcoin-related research in various knowledge streams has grown significantly (Merediz-Solá and Bariviera, 2019). Implementing blockchain in Human Resource Management has offered Employee-Systems Interaction and Blockchain Framework for HR as major themes (Mohammad Saif and Islam, 2022). Blockchain applications in the Accounting domain have highlighted the need for new accounting and control processes (Lardo *et al.*, 2022). Blockchain has been identified to create a clear impact on auditing and accounting but its linkage with the area of accountability is unclear and needs further research (Secinaro *et al.*, 2021). (Lombardi *et al.*, 2022) have identified blockchain as a tool for auditors to save time; prevent fraud, enabling smart contracts and initial coin offerings. blockchain to notarize non-financial documents can benefit organizations and stakeholders by mitigating asymmetric information (Pizzi *et al.*, 2022). Information efficiency, price discovery, and price clustering under the domain of financial economics have evolved as main research themes (Bariviera and Merediz-Solà, 2021).

The contribution of blockchain technology toward sustainable development goals has been investigated and future research focus areas have been put forward (Parmentola *et al.*, 2022). Research on the sustainability of supply chain management in food, infrastructure, manufacturing, and healthcare through the adoption of blockchain technology has revealed many interesting future research areas (Sahoo *et al.*, 2022). The role of blockchain technology in the logistical and digital supply chains is worth exploring (Musigmann *et al.*, 2020). Framework for integrating blockchain technology with cloud computing and the Internet of Things has been investigated and new pathways for research have been recommended (Gorkhali *et al.*, 2020). (Nobanee and Ellili, 2023) studied Non-Fungible Tokens (NFTs) in the context of blockchain, cryptocurrency, and digital art. (Bajwa *et al.*, 2022) have identified crowd funding, mobile payments, Bitcoin, and digital currency streams as main themes in the Fin-Tech literature. The macroeconomic impact of cryptocurrency and legal digital currencies are likely to be future research hotspots (Yue *et al.*, 2021). All the previous studies have concentrated their keywords on bitcoin, cryptocurrency, or blockchain. In contrast, our study has combined all the combined keywords and presented the results more comprehensively. Both WOS and Scopus database has been used for searching the keywords in the title and abstract for the past decade 2011-2022, which has not been taken before. Previous studies have limited their focus to the application of blockchain in a particular domain like management and human resources (Mohammad Saif and Islam, 2022; Tandon *et al.*, 2021), whereas our study has taken a vast perspective on the application and development of digital currency in all the fields of social sciences.

Table 1. Overview of previous bibliometric studies related to digital currency

S.No	Previous Studies	Time period	Keywords	Focus of the study	Database
1.	(García-Corral *et al.*, 2022)	2010-early 2019	"Cryptocurrency," "Bitcoin," or "Ethereum"	Specifies the development and lines of related research	WOS and Scopus
2.	(Jalal *et al.*, 2021)		"Bitcoin"	Explore cryptocurrency literature in the areas of business and management	WOS
3.	(Merediz-Solá and Bariviera, 2019)		"Bitcoin"	study the scientific production only around bitcoin, excluding other blockchain application	WOS
4.	(Tandon *et al.*, 2021)		"blockchain or ethereum" OR "blockchain or distributed ledger technology" OR "blockchain or smart contracts"	Application of blockchain technology in Management domain	Scopus
5.	(Mohammad Saif and Islam, 2022)		Not specified	developing theoretical themes, useful for HR personnel	Scopus and WOS
6.	(Lardo *et al.*, 2022)		"Blockchain" OR "Cryptocurrency" OR "Smart Contract" OR "Initial Coin Offering" OR "Bitcoin") AND ("Account*")	Identify main research venues in managerial and accounting issues related to blockchain technology (BT)	Scopus database
7.	(Parmentola *et al.*, 2022)		(green) OR ("circular economy") OR (carbon) OR (sustainab*) OR (climate) OR (co2) OR ("ecol*") OR (emission*) OR ("natural environment*") OR (footprint) AND (cryptocurrency) OR (blockchain) OR (bitcoin)	attempts to identify how blockchain technology is considered able to affect environmental sustainability	Scopus database

3. METHODOLOGY

To address the objective of the study bibliometric analysis is conducted based on Preferred Reporting Items for Systematic Reviews and Meta-Analyses (PRISMA) model (Kim and So, 2022; Pahlevan-Sharif *et al.*, 2019; Pahlevan Sharif *et al.*, 2019). The PRISMA checklist is used for the review as depicted in Figure 1.

3.1. Data Extraction Process

The search criteria for the data retrieval process are based on the previous studies by (García-Corral *et al.*, 2022), (Sharma *et al.*, 2019), and (Ali *et al.*, 2020).After reviewing the previous studies and using the features of R software, the most relevant and frequently occurring keywords were selected for the study. All possible search strings of the term "Block Chain", "Digital Currency," and "Cryptocurrency" was chosen to analyze the Web of Science and Scopus database in December 2022. Multiple bibliographical databases are consulted for bibliometric analysis (Rodríguez-López *et al.*, 2020). After searching for the terms in the title, abstract, and keywords 13,329 records from the Web of Science and 42614 records from the

Scopus database were obtained initially. Then limiting the records to the English language and selecting 12 years of papers from 2011-2022 the documents were reduced to 13078 in Web of Science and 41033 in Scopus. Research publications before 2011 were minimalistic and not significantly related to the domain of management; hence these are not included in the study. Based on the subject category from Economics, Econometrics and Finance, Business Management and Accounting, Social Science, and Multidisciplinary total of 1817 documents were filtered from Web of Science and 9934 documents from Scopus. After merging the records from both the databases and removing duplicates a total of 10,751 records were identified. After the document identification process, a two- step screening process is used as per PRISMA checklist to include the most pertinent and relatable studies.

3.1.1 Initial Screening

After removing duplicate records, each study was screened for its applicability based on the relevance and contribution of the study, highlighting the development of digital currency in the modern context in the title and content of the abstract. A total of 5,019 records were filtered to be in included in the full-text review (Figure 1). For a study to be included in the full-text review, explicitly have an explicit focus on the management and financial aspect of digital currency. Several studies were excluded that do not focus on the efficacy and applicability of digital currency in the long run.

3.1.2 Secondary Screening

In-depth screening of full-text articles resulted in the inclusion of 1303 documents and subsequently, 85 non-related documents were excluded. The study whose outcomes did not match the context of our review and the models developed do not lie within the periphery of our study were excluded. In the final analysis; 1218 documents were included which comprised 1171 research articles and 47 review papers. Figure 1 shows the data retrieval process with the selection of articles as per PRISMA protocol to be included in the review from the databases.

3.2 Method

Bibliometrics introduced by Pritchard (Broadus, 1987; Pritchard, 1969) is a statistical analysis of the bibliographic data to extract the intellectual structure of any discipline (Broadus, 1987; Hota *et al.*, 2020; Kent Baker *et al.*, 2020) which reveals the structure of a research domain, highlights central themes, reveals correlations, and expresses scientific communication in quantities (Biancone *et al.*, 2020; Bollani and Chmet, 2020). This in-depth analysis incorporates the careful examination of the different dimensions of the scientific landscape and offers insight into research growth. The multi-dimensional construct of Bibliometric understanding analyses the authors, the author's keywords, the thematic category distribution, the publication models, the most frequently cited articles, and the country of publication (Bollani and Chmet, 2020). However, the bibliometric interpretation takes place in an institutional context. The bibliometric analysis conducts a comprehensive examination of the published literature in a specific research field by visualizing the literature structure over some time and the knowledge development that took place (Linnenluecke *et al.*, 2020). The bibliometric analysis delivers an objective measure of the scientific literature assessment and is helpful in literature reviews (Kim and So, 2022). Bibliometric analysis has evolved to handle big scientific data and produce high-impact research (Donthu *et al.*, 2021).

This study is based on bibliometrics because of its wide recognition, ability to process a large volume of scientific data, quantitative nature of this method, and high research impact (Donthu *et al.*, 2021; Ellegaard and Wallin, 2015; Kent Baker *et al.*, 2020). It extracts highly locally cited, globally cited, and prominent research papers in any research domain (Nagariya *et al.*, 2021).

Figure 1. Data retrieval process through PRISMA flow diagram

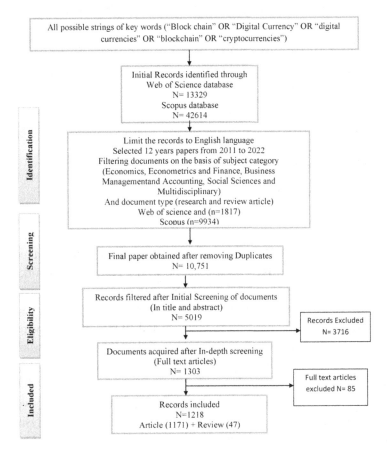

Figure 2. Analytical structure of bibliometric analysis

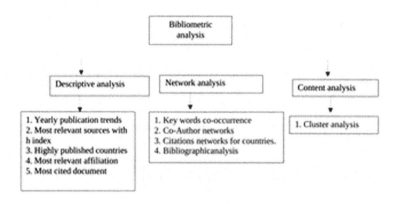

Bibliometric analysis of the literature on digital currency was conducted using several tools such as keywords co-occurrence networks, co-author networks, citations networks, and countries networks. For bibliometric analysis, data from the Web of Science database was extracted in Bibtex file format. The Biblioshiny package of R Software was deployed for descriptive analysis and VOSviewer software was used for network analysis because of its flexibility in visualizing the network which is easily adjustable to input data files (Nandan and Soni, 2023).

Figure 2demonstrates the analytical structure of the bibliometric analysis. The focus of bibliometric analysis is divided into three parts: (1) Descriptive Analysis (2) Network Analysis and (3) Content Analysis. The descriptive analysis accounts for the contribution of research yearly publication trends, relevant sources, highly published countries, relevant authors, relevant affiliations, and cited documents. The next section of the networking analysis highlights all the networks and bibliographic coupling. The last section is Content Analysis and it includes the Cluster Analysis.

4. ANALYSES AND RESULTS

Descriptive information about the data is presented in Table 2whichcontains the main information in five parts and includes results from the years 2011 to 2022. Part (a) exhibits the main information about data with 1218 documents and 45791 total numbers of references. Part (b) lists document types with 1012 articles and 41 reviews in the Web of Science dataset. Part (c) shows document contents with 1526 Keywords plus (ID) and 3254 Author's Keywords (DE). Part (d) highlights data about the authors. There are 2617 authors, 3455 author appearances, 177 authors of single-authored documents, and 2440 Authors of multi-authored documents in this bibliometric study on digital currency. Part (e) includes the results of the authors' collaboration. There are 204 single-authored documents, 0.465 Documents per Author, 2.15 Authors per Document, 2.84 Co-Authors per Document, and 2.41 Collaboration Index.

Table 2. Main information about data

	Description	Results
(a)	*Main information about data*	
	Timespan	2011-2022
	Sources (Journals, books, etc)	249
	Documents	1218
	References	45791
(b)	*Document types*	
	Article	1012
	Article; book chapter	2
	Article; early access	150
	Article; proceedings paper	7
	Review	41
	Review; early access	6
(c)	*Document contents*	
	Keywords plus (ID)	1526
	Author's keywords (DE)	3254
(d)	*Authors*	
	Authors	2617
	Author appearances	3455
	Authors of single-authored documents	177
	Authors of multi-authored documents	2440
(e)	*Authors collaboration*	
	Single-authored documents	204
	Co-Authors per documents	2.84
	Collaboration index	2.41

Source: Results extracted from VOSviewer

4.1 Annual Publication Trend

To understand the annual publication and citation pattern of digital currency articles, we analyzed the annual production and citations per year. Table 3 highlights the total number of citations as 1062 from the year 2011 to 2022. Figure-3 exhibits that during the early six years, only 12 citations happened in the next six years, the number of citations jumped to 1050 which shows significant growth. The average growth rate of the citations per year has been 56.71% indicating a significant growth of research interest and the filling of knowledge gaps faster.

Table 3. Annual publication and citation per year

Year	N	Mean TC per Art	Mean TC per Year	Citable Years
2011	1	2	0.18	11
2012	0	0	0	0
2013	0	0	0	0
2014	1	37	4.62	8
2015	3	142.67	20.38	7
2016	7	134.14	22.35	6
2017	26	97.03	19.40	5
2018	58	63.75	15.93	4
2019	182	37.07	12.35	3
2020	305	15.82	7.91	2
2021	422	4.85	4.85	1
2022	57	0.91	NA	0

Where, TC = Total Citation

Figure 3. Distribution of the number of citations (2021-2022)

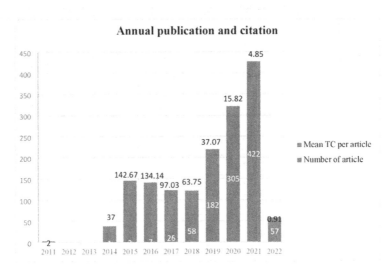

4.2 Relevant Authors' Impact Analysis

The most prolific published authors in the digital currency domain are listed in Table 4 with their affiliations. Table 4 lists the top 20 most published authors in the domain of digital currency. It sorts the authors based on the number of papers and respective h-index. Author Corbet has the highest 25 articles with an h-index of 12 followed by Bourie with 18 articles and 13 h-index, Choi with 14 articles and 9 as h- index. Results for other authors with a lesser number of papers can be referred to from the table by the readers.

Table 4. Most relevant authors with h-index

Authors	Articles	Articles Fractionalized	h Index	g Index	m Index	TC	PY Start
Corbet S	25	6.95	12	22	3.75	589	2019
Bouri E	18	5.17	13	17	NA	1261	NA
Choi TM	14	6.67	9	12	2.25	710	2019
Lucey B	11	2.93	9	10	2.25	410	2019
Roubaud D	11	3.17	11	11	1.833	806	2017
Sensoy A	11	3.02	7	9	1.75	142	2019
Katsiampa P	10	5.58	8	9	1.3333	741	2017

continued on following page

Table 4. Continued

Authors	Articles	Articles Fractionalized	h Index	g Index	m Index	TC	PY Start
Li Y	10	3.17	5	9	NA	81	NA
Urquhart A	10	4.75	7	10	1	869	2016
Li X	9	3.25	6	7	0.667	159	2014
Wang S	8	2.33	3	5	1	34	2020
Yarovaya L	8	2.10	5	7	1.667	118	2020
Zhang W	8	2.45	5	8	NA	111	NA
Grobys K	7	3.67	3	6	0.75	66	2019
Tiwari AK	7	2.08	5	6	1.25	115	2019
Treiblmaier H	7	4.53	4	6	NA	213	NA
Vidal-Tomas D	7	4.67	5	5	1	170	2018
XuanVinh Vo XVV	7	1.82	3	6	NA	60	NA
Zhang S	7	2.33	3	5	0.75	25	2019
Akyildirim E	6	1.43	4	5	1.333	58	2020

TC = Total Citation, PY Start- Starting of Publishing Year

4.3 Most Relevant Sources

Table 5 lists the top 20 influential and most productive journals linked with digital Currency which have been taken out of 249 journals. The progress and impact of reputable journals' research are also reflected in Table 5. Finance Research Letters is the top journal with 27 as h-index, 47 as g-index, 4.5 as m-index, and 2458 total citations. It is followed by *Technological Forecasting and Social Change* journal with 1860 total citations and 17 h-index.

Table 5. Most relevant sources

Sources	Articles	h_index	g_index	m_index	TC
Finance Research Letters	100	27	47	4.5	2458
Technological Forecasting And Social Change	58	17	34	3.5	1860
IEEE Transactions On Engineering Management	54	17	31	2.83	1156
Research In International Business And Finance	40	16	28	2.67	1085
Economics Letters	38	14	25	2.43	1026
International Review Of Financial Analysis	33	14	25	2	815
Financial Innovation	30	12	19	2	800
Transportation Research Part E-Logistics And Transportation Review	28	9	16	2	769
Applied Economics	23	9	15	1.8	584

continued on following page

Table 5. Continued

Sources	Articles	h_index	g_index	m_index	TC
Applied Economics Letters	23	8	13	1.67	549
Journal Of Enterprise Information Management	21	8	13	1.67	538
North American Journal Of Economics And Finance	18	8	12	1.6	512
Electronic Markets	17	8	12	1.6	489
Journal Of International Financial Markets Institutions \& Money	17	8	11	1.5	394
European Journal Of Finance	16	8	11	1.5	308
Electronic Commerce Research And Applications	15	8	10	1.33	305
Technology In Society	15	7	10	1.33	252
International Journal Of Finance \& Economics	14	7	10	1.25	237
Technology Analysis \& Strategic Management	14	6	10	1.25	220
Information Systems And E-Business Management	12	6	9	1.25	188

TC- Total Citation

4.4 Highly Contributing Countries With Citations

Publications from 20 countries contributed to the digital currency articles. The aggregate number of publications is 3523. Table 6 highlights the top publication and citation countries. The USA, United Kingdom, and China are the top three ranked countries with the highest number of citations 4415, 3571, and 2811 respectively, and have contributed 55.51% of citations. The aggregate number of citations in the domain of digital currency has come to 19451. Dwyer, (2015) has emphasized using peer-to-peer networks and open-source software to save and close transactions in digital currencies. Wang *et al.*, (2019) have offered valuable insight into the disruptive potential of blockchain technology in the area of the supply chain. Warner and Wäger(2019)have revealed the ongoing process of digital transformation through digital technologies to deliver agility for the strategic renewal of organizations.

Table 6. Most publication countries with citations

Country	Frequency	%	Country	Total Citations	Average Article Citations
China	717	58.87	USA	4415	23.12
USA	648	53.20	United Kingdom	3571	31.32
UK	407	33.42	China	2811	13.92
Germany	240	19.70	Australia	1611	29.83
Italy	172	14.12	Germany	1158	17.03
Australia	171	14.04	Lebanon	921	61.40

continued on following page

Table 6. Continued

Country	Frequency	%	Country	Total Citations	Average Article Citations
France	141	11.58	Ireland	748	27.70
India	121	9.93	Spain	517	15.67
Spain	109	8.95	France	495	16.50
Ireland	94	7.72	Canada	464	18.56
Canada	90	7.39	Italy	448	8.78
South Korea	89	7.31	Brazil	397	22.06
Turkey	86	7.06	Austria	326	25.08
Vietnam	85	6.98	India	274	8.56
Switzerland	70	5.75	Sweden	243	24.30
New Zealand	68	5.58	Switzerland	228	12.67
Netherlands	66	5.42	Netherlands	216	12.71
Greece	51	4.19	Denmark	207	15.92
Brazil	50	4.11	New Zealand	206	12.88
Denmark	48	3.94	Poland	195	24.38

Figure 4. Distribution of publications and country of origin

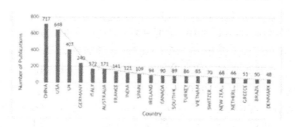

Figure 4 exhibits the distribution of publications regarding the country of origin. China (717), the USA (648), and the UK (407) have contributed to more than 50.29% of the publications in the domain of digital currency.

4.5 Most Relevant Affiliations

Table 7 lists the authors' affiliations and the University of Economics Ho Chi Minh City is the highest-yielding university with 48 papers, trailed by Dublin City University with 42 papers, Hong Kong Polytechnic University with 32, the University of Sydney with 28, and Montpellier Business School with 27 articles.

Table 7. Most relevant affiliations

S.No	Affiliations	Articles
1	University of Economics Ho Chi Minh City	48
2	Dublin City University	42
3	The Hong Kong Polytechnic University	32
4	The University of Sydney	28
5	Montpellier Business School	27
6	University of Vaasa	26
7	Tianjin University	25
8	Copenhagen Business School	24
9	University of Zurich	24
10	Southwestern University of Finance and Economics	22
11	University College Dublin	22
12	University of Waikato	22
13	University of Southampton	21
14	Holy Spirit University of Kaslik	20
15	Trinity College	20
16	University of Arkansas at Little Rock	18
17	Chinese Academy of Sciences	16
18	University of Reading	16
19	Bilkent University	15
20	Hunan University	15

4.6 Citation Network Analysis

Citation Network Analysis has contributed to knowing the most frequently cited articles of digital currency in other journals. In the citation network, there are two types of citations: global citation and local citation. Table-8 depicts the top 20 frequently cited articles on global and local platforms between 2011 and 2022. Citation of (Iansiti and Lakhani, 2017) topped the list with 521 citations, followed by (Urquhart, 2016) with 471 citations and (Bouri, Molnár, *et al.*, 2017) with 392 citations in the global citations category. (Iansiti and Lakhani, 2017) have concluded that blockchain will likely reduce transaction costs, remove intermediaries and transform economies. (Urquhart, 2016) has emphasized the inefficiency of the Bitcoin market. Similarly in local citations, (Urquhart, 2016) ranked first with 176 citations. (Katsiampa, 2017) ranked second with 118 citations, and (Bouri, Jalkh, *et al.*, 2017) with 117 citations ranked third. (Katsiampa, 2017) investigated the price volatility of Bitcoin through various GARCH models and recommended tools for portfolio and risk management. The visible data gap between global and local documents' citations signifies that the digital currency domain has received interest from both segments.

Table 8. Top 20 most cited global and local cited documents (citation network analysis)

Global Cited Document	Total Citations	Local Cited Document	Local Citation
(Iansiti&Lakhani,2017}	531	(Urquhart, 2016)	176
(Ur (Urquhart, 2016)	471	(Katsiampa, 2017)	118
(Bouri, Molnár, *et al.*, 2017)	392	(Bouri *et al.*, 2019)	117
(Katsiampa, 2017)	360	(Gandal *et al.*, 2018)	69
(Baur *et al.*, 2018)	330	(Klein *et al.*, 2018)	69
(Dwyer, 2015)	264	(Urquhart, 2017)	63
(Hawlitschek *et al.*, 2018)	222	(Fry & Cheah, 2016)	60
(Klein *et al.*, 2018)	213	(Ji *et al.*, 2019)	59
(Wang *et al.*, 2019)	211	(Wei, 2018)	58
(Gandal *et al.*, 2018)	199	(Phillip *et al.*, 2018)	55
(Warner & Wäger, 2019)	187	(Treiblmaier, 2018)	51
(Treiblmaier, 2018)	185	(Urquhart & Zhang, 2019)	50
(Gomber *et al.*, 2018)	180	(Bouri *et al.*, 2019)	49
(Fry & Cheah, 2016)	176	(Cong & He, 2019a)	47
(Min, 2019)	167	(Foley *et al.*, 2019)	46
(Urquhart, 2017)	164	(Treiblmaier, 2018)	39
(Cong & He, 2019b)	146	(Blau, 2017)	38
(Ji *et al.*, 2019)	146	(Caporale *et al.*, 2018)	38
(Treiblmaier, 2018)	146	(Cole *et al.*, 2019)	38
(Foley *et al.*, 2019)	140	(Bouri *et al.*, 2019)	37

To know the intellectual structure of the research in digital currency, we have analyzed the citation networks of 1218 articles. The citation network of countries reveals the intellectual structure of the research. The digital currency has attracted considerable attention from researchers in various countries. Figure-5 exhibits the top publishing countries on Digital currency as per the total citation, with the top five being England (4744), USA (5708), People's Republic of China (3266), France (2293), Germany (1962), and India (499) based on citation numbers.

Figure 5. Citation network on digital currency

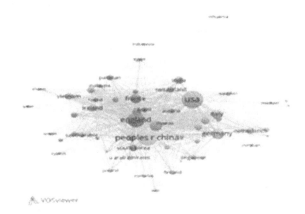

Figure 5 exhibits the citation network of Digital Currency using VOSviewer based on the number of citations with a threshold of at least 5 documents.

4.7 Keywords Co-Occurrence Networks

Figure-6 exhibits the keyword co-occurrence network and highlights authors' keywords and their frequencies. The minimum number of occurrences of keywords is five out of the 3436 keywords and 167 meet the threshold number of keywords to be selected and we get a total of 10 clusters. Keyword analysis of "Block Chain"," "Digital Currency"," "Blockchain" and "Cryptocurrencies" reveals high production of publications.

Figure 6. Keywords co-occurrence networks

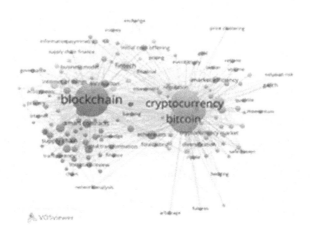

4.8 Frequently Occurring Keywords

Keyword analysis was conducted with the VOSviewer software to explore the most prevalent themes in Digital Currency. Table 9 shows the frequency of occurrences of various keywords. All the researchers have used multiple keywords related to digital currency. PageRank is calculated using the Louvain clustering algorithm. We have selected ten keywords. In this study, we have used three main keywords: Blockchain, Digital Currency, and Cryptocurrency. In Table 9, the two most similar keywords in the digital currency articles are cryptocurrency and cryptocurrencies. Out of 3436 keywords, 167 are selected following the threshold of having a minimum of 5 occurrences. As shown in the table, 'blockchain' 'cryptocurrency' and 'bitcoin' are the most frequently occurring keywords.

Table 9. Frequently occurring keywords

S.no	Words	Occurrences	PageRank
1	Blockchain	440	0.174
2	Cryptocurrency	300	0.110
3	Bitcoin	290	0.128
4	Cryptocurrencies	141	0.042
5	blockchain technology	62	0.014
6	Volatility	44	0.021

continued on following page

Table 9. Continued

S.no	Words	Occurrences	PageRank
7	Fintech	40	0.023
8	Technology	37	0.011
9	covid-19	35	0.013
10	Ethereum	33	0.023

4.9 Co-Author Network Analysis

To reveal the co-authorship collaboration of digital currency articles, the Co-Authors network exhibits the existing state of collaborations and identifies the most prolific authors on digital currency research collaborations. Research collaboration is a well-established way of intellectual associations among scholars. We have analyzed here the scale of collaboration among scholars and identified the most prolific authors within collaborative research. Figure-7 highlights the dominating authors in terms of collaboration as Urquhart –England (635), Katsiampap –Sheffield (463), Hawlitscheky- Berlin (233), Blanbm – USA (153), Choi Tm – Chinese (230). The co-authorship network is exhibiting the collection of a few fairly closed networks that reveal few interactions among themselves.

Figure 7. Co-authors network

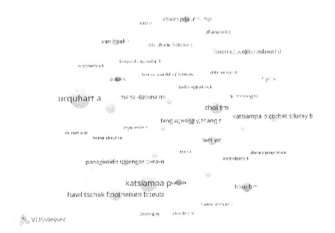

4.10 Content Analysis

Content analysis determines the presence of certain themes and concepts within the data, which is replicable and rigorous. To get insight into the current theme of research, VOSviewer software has been used for data analysis and four clusters have evolved. The minimum number of 30 citations of a document is considered to meet the threshold of Co-citations. Overall 192 items have been found in the four clusters. In the first cluster ninety-four items, the second cluster has sixty-five items, the third cluster has twenty-five items, and the fourth cluster has eight items.

Cluster 1: Emerging Technology

Blockchain is an emerging technology and has started receiving considerable attention but its applications are still evolving and being developed (Angelis and Ribeiro da Silva, 2019). Companies feel compelled to adopt innovative approaches to deal with the challenges of evolving digital technologies (Abdullah *et al.*, 2022). The adaption of technological innovations brings digital transformations in organizations and enhances organizational performance(Moraes *et al.*, 2022). Management of many organizations is curiously looking to accept blockchain technology for enhanced value creation. Distributed digital ledger is the concept around which blockchain technology has been developed and cryptocurrency is its first major application (Babich and Hilary, 2020; Belotti *et al.*, 2019). It is seen as a game-changer technology that will likely make life safe and simple by eliminating the scope of information loss, data theft, hacking, and fraud (Attaran and Gunasekaran, 2019). Cost efficiency and distributed ledger features of blockchain with high trust and security can decrease transaction costs significantly and benefit stakeholders in entrepreneurial ecosystems (Ahluwalia *et al.*, 2020). The role of middlemen may not exist with blockchain technology (Andreassen *et al.*, 2018). Applications of Blockchain 3.0 are being studied in identity management, healthcare records management, decentralized notary, electronic voting, supply chain management, and intellectual property protection for in-depth analysis, requirements, adoption, and proposed solutions to the problems (Di Francesco Maesa and Mori, 2020). An integrated framework of disruptive technologies with elements of AI, IoT, industry 4.0, IoMT, VR, big data, autonomous robots, 5G, drone technology, and blockchain has been proposed to enhance governance in a complex and challenging environment (Abdel-Basset *et al.*, 2021).

Cluster 2: Cryptocurrencies Portfolios

Cryptocurrencies have evolved as an option from the point of view of portfolio management in recent years. Asset correlation is one indicator used to develop efficient portfolios by considering the positive correlation among Cryptocurrencies, the stable correlation across time with Monero, and the negligible correlation between traditional financial assets and cryptocurrencies (Aslanidis, N., Bariviera, A. F., & Martínez-Ibañez, 2019). The risk of Cryptocurrency portfolios can be reduced and better risk-adjusted returns could be generated (Borri, 2019). Combining the advanced Black-Litterman model with variance-based constraints (VBCs) is likely to yield superior risk-adjusted returns at lower risks (Platanakis and Urquhart, 2019). Portfolios could be optimized by maximizing the Sharpe ratio and forming a global minimum variance-based portfolio (Schellinger, 2020).Using data from the trades on crypto exchanges is advised to examine crypto market efficiency, hedging, portfolio optimization, and trading applications instead of coin ranking sites' data (Alexander and Dakos, 2020). Cryptocurrencies appear to be decoupled from traditional financial assets and are used by investors for portfolio diversification as a new investment class (Gil-Alana *et al.*, 2020). Bitcoin and Ethereum dominate the cryptocurrency market and services for potential hedging opportunities through dynamic hedge ratios and portfolio weights (Antonakakis *et al.*, 2019). However, smaller cryptocurrencies tend to deliver higher returns (Shen *et al.*, 2020).Cryptocurrencies have the potential to form an optimal portfolio as a single investment (Inci and Lagasse, 2019).

Cluster 3: Cryptocurrencies as a Medium of Exchange and an Asset Class

Cryptocurrencies demonstrate unique features of a separate asset class by exhibiting strong internal correlation and no correlation with any traditional asset class (Krueckeberg and Scholz, 2019). The liquidity of Bitcoin is decoupled with other asset classes and seen as a speculative asset (Klose, 2022). Cryptocurrencies are evolving as a mode of exchange but Bitcoin has only been demonstrated as a value storage instrument due to its low supply resulting from distributed protocol and large processing power as compared with other Cryptocurrencies having lax requirements (Ammous, 2018). (Shibano and Mogi, 2022)have proposed conditions that are required for cryptocurrencies to attain monetary function. Bitcoin is a speculative investment, a mode of exchange but not an alternative currency while it is also uncorrelated with bonds, commodities, and stocks (Baur *et al.*, 2018). Returns from Bitcoin are related to other assets, particularly commodities, and spillovers are exhibited with high reception of volatility than transmission (Bouri, Jawad, *et al.*,

2018). Bitcoin has shown dissimilar dynamic correlations between extreme upward and downward movements (Bouri, Jalkh, *et al.*, 2017). Cryptocurrencies have also posed many ethical challenges to their use in money laundering, the dark net, and shadow banking (Dierksmeier and Seele, 2018).

Cluster 4: Cryptocurrencies and Financial Risks

The value of blockchain networks is related to the number of active users (Alabi, 2017). Bitcoin has been considered a viable currency despite the contribution of speculation to create asset bubbles and price destabilization of Bitcoin (Blau, 2017). Cryptocurrency markets are inherently risky and risk management remains unclear as of now (Fry, 2018). Cryptocurrencies inherit market risk, cyber risk, operational risk, liquidity risk, and general perceived risk (Angerer *et al.*, 2020). A few cryptocurrencies (DOGE, USDT, VTC, XEM, XLM, XRP) are suitable for portfolio diversification and hedging (Huynh *et al.*, 2022). Users also anticipate risks of fraud and cyber-attack (Rejeb *et al.*, 2021). Money laundering is an apprehension by law enforcement agencies (Shahbazi and Byun, 2022). Therefore, market participants need to exercise caution in cryptocurrency markets (Corbet *et al.*, 2019).Herding behavior visible in the cryptocurrency markets helps to identify Bitcoin contagion to other Cryptocurrencies (P.V.J. da Gama Silva, M.C. Klotzle, 2019). Herding behavior has been detected in cryptocurrency markets through the multi-fractal de-trended fluctuation approach (Mnif *et al.*, 2020)and during low volatility period in Decentralized Finance (DeFi) assets (Yousaf and Yarovaya, 2022). Bubble behavior(Haykir and Yagli, 2022)and risk spillovers(Cui and Maghyereh, 2022) have been commonly witnessed in the cryptocurrency market. The hierarchical Risk Parity method has delivered better results in cryptocurrency risk management (Shahbazi and Byun, 2022).

5. DISCUSSION AND IMPLICATIONS

5.1 Contribution to the Economy and Society

The social implications of the blockchain and digital currencies are manifold. These are likely to facilitate the growth of alternate financial systems propelled with higher speeds of domestic and international transactions at reduced costs. Better access to the financial system, ease of remittances, involvement of many segments of the population in the financial system and social inclusion are likely positive implications. However, apprehensions of money laundering and digital crimes call for stringent regulations and guidelines for cryptocurrency participants, while blockchain technology's disruptive and innovative natures are calling for an open-minded workable regulatory framework (Yin *et al.*, 2019). Scrutiny of societal security, labor practices, equality, and health in the social domain linked with cryptocurrencies needs to be considered for decision-making (de Vries *et al.*, 2021). Cryptocurrencies are likely to disrupt traditional monetary systems and social structures as well (Caliskan, 2020).

5.2 Contributions and Implications to Theory and Knowledge

This study offers five major theoretical implications to advance knowledge in digital currency through our findings. First, the results of this study reveal the current knowledge boundaries and possibilities of future research in the area of digital currency by knowing issues with different levels of potentiality. Second, researchers will learn about the eminent researchers and institutions in this field that may benefit from research collaborations. Third, it will help academicians and researchers understand the present status and structure of digital currency research through four identified clusters viz. cryptocurrencies as a medium of exchange and an asset class, cryptocurrencies and financial risks, blockchain as an emerging technology, and cryptocurrencies' portfolios. Clusters based on the content analysis highlight the significant information about the influential research papers which future researchers may view as a broad classification and foundation of research areas. Identified thematic clusters also suggest prominent research areas which future researchers may undertake through informed decisions. Fourth, it will help to facilitate a more refined research conceptualization focused on the peculiar issues delivered by citation, co-citation, and network analysis. Fifth, this study has addressed the gaps of inadequate systematic literature reviews in blockchain applications and the scarcity of bibliometric reports on blockchain in the context of digital currency reported by (Dashkevich *et al.*, 2020) and (Firdaus *et al.*, 2019) respectively.

5.3 Contributions and Implications to Practice and Management

This study's results benefit the applied researchers and practitioners from the industry. Applications of digital currency are likely to benefit the industry in data management, human resource management, financial management, risk management, and portfolio management. Blockchain technology is anticipated to impact transparency, digital identity, supply chain, personal data protection, compliance, legitimacy, and trust. We propose four practical implications for practitioners and policymakers regarding digital currency.

First, applications of blockchain, cryptocurrencies, and digital currencies have exponentially increased over the last few years. These applications are potentially disruptive and have started influencing the technological, social, economic, legal, and political environment. Hence, different stakeholders need to examine changes and prepare to adjust effectively to a new environment. This paper offers a comprehensive insight into this field to all stakeholders. This paper may also give insight to technology entrepreneurs about the current status and emerging trends to develop cost-effective user-friendly applications by integrating blockchain technology. Organizations may utilize our research findings in understanding and find suitable opportunities with the use of blockchain technology and digital currency.

Second, this paper's results may help investors analyze cryptocurrencies as an asset class and decide on effective portfolio investments. Insight into the relationships between traditional financial assets and cryptocurrencies is more likely to help in refined decision-making in portfolio management.

Third, this research work may help to gauge the possibility of using cryptocurrency as a medium of exchange and act as a game changer in transactions of various assets. Cryptocurrencies' characteristics of peer-to-peer transactions, independence of banking systems, low transaction costs, and high anonymity facilitate their adoption and growth (Parino *et al.*, 2018).

Fourth, the market participants may benefit from understanding financial risks, challenges, opportunities, and potential future trends associated with cryptocurrencies for informed decision-making.

6. CONCLUSION, LIMITATIONS, AND FUTURE RESEARCH DIRECTIONS

This research paper is a bibliometric study and VoSviewer software has been used. VoSviewer has generated descriptive, network, and content analyses for the research articles published between 2011 and 2022. The annual scientific production growth rate in digital currency is 56.71% a healthy growth rate for a promising research domain. The USA, the United Kingdom, and China have the top-ranking citations accounting for 55.51% of citations. Finance Research Letters holds the position of the top-ranked journal with an h-index of 27 and 2458 total citations. The field of digital currency has significant scope soon including cryptocurrencies and blockchain technology as found out by the VOSviewer using visualization diagrams of keywords. From descriptive analysis, the year publication trend per year has come to 56.71% and in the year 2021, the highest number of 422 research papers has been published till March 2022. (Iansiti and Lakhani, 2017) holds the record with the most relevant papers with an h-index of 12 with 25 research articles. England has 635 highest number of authors and the highest number of 48 papers affiliated with the University of Economics Ho Chi Minh City. Citation network analysis resulted in 176 local citations and 521 global citations. VOSviewer produces four clusters through bibliometric analysis. Each cluster has different research sub-themes. Cluster 1 is about Blockchain as an Emerging Technology. Cluster 2 is about Cryptocurrencies' Portfolios. Cluster 3 is about Cryptocurrencies as a mode of exchange and an asset class. Cluster 4 is about Cryptocurrencies and Financial Risks.

6.1 Limitations of the Study

This study has a few limitations. Firstly, only research and review articles are selected from the database for inclusion in the analysis. Other document types like books, proceedings, and conference papers could be taken for further research that could bring more comprehensive insight into the study. The medium of our selected publications has been English only. However, future research studies may also consider including papers published in other languages. Lastly, a different algorithm may be used for creating different clusters. New dimensions of challenges and issues need to be well-researched in the future.

6.2 Future Research Directions

Future aspects of research in the domain of digital currency have emerged in different directions. Figure 8 summarizes the theoretical model for future research directions paving the stream of further applications of blockchain technology, risk management in cryptocurrency, scrutinizing the relationship between cryptocurrency and other assets, and miscellaneous areas exploring ethical clarification and interdisciplinary domains. The following are broad areas of future research directions:

Figure 8. Theoretical model developed for future research directions

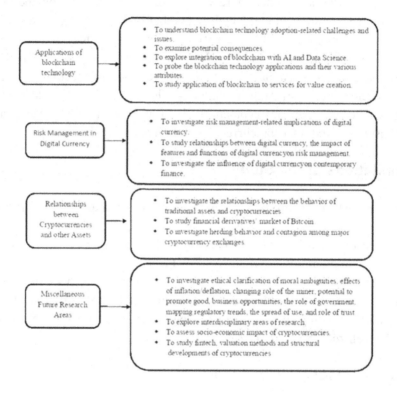

A model is developed to showcase future research directions (Ferenhof *et al.*, 2015; Jordão and Novas, 2017). Expansion of the number of cryptocurrencies and datasets, issues of asymmetrical information, theory development, alternate benefits and usage of cryptocurrencies, environmental challenges of cryptocurrencies, examination of various cryptocurrencies separately, the study of legal aspects, the study of regulatory and economic aspects have been suggested as future areas of research (Corbet *et al.*, 2019). The most promising area of research is also the trials of central bank-backed digital currencies (Hairudin *et al.*, 2020).

6.3 Applications of Blockchain Technology

Blockchain technology is emerging and seen as potentially disruptive (Babich and Hilary, 2020). However, potential consequences have to be examined and further research is required in this direction. Performance expectancy, facilitating condition, and effort expectancy factors are seen as significant predictors of adopting cryptocurrencies for transactions (TerJi-Xi, J., Salamzadeh, Y. and Teoh, 2021) blockchain technology adoption-related challenges and issues need to be thoroughly researched (Angelis and Ribeiro da Silva, 2019). Integrating blockchain with AI and Data Science requires exploration (Abdel-Basset *et al.*, 2021). Probing the blockchain technology applications and their various attributes to various areas of the business ecosystem is an area of future research (Ahluwalia *et al.*, 2020). The application of blockchain to services for value creation (Andreassen *et al.*, 2018) and capability development are opportunities to expand the knowledge horizon in services management (Noor, 2022).

6.4 Risk Management in Cryptocurrencies

Cryptocurrency research is nascent and should be rigorously researched with econometric techniques to establish facts (Gil-Alana *et al.*, 2020). Risk management-related implications require further investigation (Fry, 2018). Bivariate relationships between cryptocurrencies, the impact of features and functions of cryptocurrency on risk management, and their influence on contemporary finance need further research (Antonakakis *et al.*, 2019). Data calibration on any volatility model should be done from crypto exchange data for risk management (Alexander and Dakos, 2020).

6.5 Relationships Between Cryptocurrencies and Other Assets

Relationships between the behavior of traditional assets and cryptocurrencies require in-depth investigation (Aslanidis, N., Bariviera, A. F., & Martínez-Ibañez, 2019). After the decision of the United States Commodity Futures Trading Commission (CFTC) to acknowledge Bitcoin as a 'commodity'; financial derivatives of Bitcoin are likely to draw attention as a new domain of research (Bouri, Jalkh, *et al.*, 2017). The recent crumbling of the FTX crypto exchange has drawn attention to the role of CFTC in this episode and triggered a debate about future regulatory roles which needs rigorous future research. According to (Bouri, Gupta, *et al.*, 2018), "Future research should consider the determinants of significant return and volatility spillovers between Bitcoin and these other assets." Investigating herding behavior and contagion among major cryptocurrency exchanges is required (P.V.J. da Gama Silva, M.C. Klotzle, 2019).

6.6 Miscellaneous Future Research Areas

Future research in cryptocurrencies is also suggested in ethical clarification of moral ambiguities, research on effects of inflation/deflation, changing role of the miner, the potential to promote goods, business opportunities, the role of government, mapping regulatory trends, the spread of use, and role of trust (Dierksmeier and Seele, 2018). Interdisciplinary research areas are evolving as revisions and rectifications are taking place to handle problems in cryptocurrencies (García-Corral *et al.*, 2022). The socioeconomic impact of cryptocurrencies needs to be assessed (Jalal *et al.*, 2021). Fintech, valuation methods, and structural developments of cryptocurrencies are also new directions for research (Nasir *et al.*,2021). Management, energy, machine learning, and smart homes are some aspects of blockchain technology that need further investigation (Guo *et al.*, 2021). The recent collapse of the FTX crypto exchange has exposed the structural weaknesses of these exchanges and future research is required to find effective ways to strengthen these. Central Bank Digital Currency (CBDC) has been launched in 11 countries, and 15 countries are in the stage of pilot testing, 26 countries are in the development stage, 46 countries are in the research stage, ten countries are inactive and 2 countries have canceled it. CBDC being at an initial stage, many new dimensions have to be explored and considered for research.

REFERENCES

Abdel-Basset, M., Chang, V., & Nabeeh, N. A. (2021). An intelligent framework using disruptive technologies for COVID-19 analysis. *Technological Forecasting and Social Change*, 163, 120431. 10.1016/j.techfore.2020.120431

Abdullah, Z., Anumudu, C. E., & Raza, S. H. (2022). Examining the digital organizational identity through content analysis of missions and vision statements of Malaysian and Singaporean SME company websites. *The Bottom Line (New York, N.Y.)*, 35(2–3), 137–158. 10.1108/BL-12-2021-0108

Ahluwalia, S., Mahto, R. V. & Guerrero, M. (2020). Blockchain technology and startup financing: A transaction cost economics perspective. *Technological Forecasting and Social Change*. .10.1016/j.techfore.2019.119854

Al-Amri, R., Zakaria, N. H., Habbal, A., & Hassan, S. (2019). Cryptocurrency adoption: Current stage, opportunities, and open challenges. *International Journal of Advanced Computer Research*, 9(44), 293–307. 10.19101/IJACR.PID43

Alabi, K. (2017). Digital blockchain networks appear to be following Metcalfe's Law. *Electronic Commerce Research and Applications*, 24(June), 23–29. 10.1016/j. elerap.2017.06.003

Alexander, C., & Dakos, M. (2020). A critical investigation of cryptocurrency data and analysis. *Quantitative Finance*, 20(2), 173–188. 10.1080/14697688.2019.1641347

Ali, O., Ally, M., Clutterbuck, , & Dwivedi, Y. (2019). Clutterbuck and Dwivedi, Y. (2020), "The state of play of blockchain technology in the financial services sector: A systematic literature review. *International Journal of Information Management*, 54(August), 102199. 10.1016/j.ijinfomgt.2020.102199

Alt, R. (2020). Electronic Markets on sustainability. *Electronic Markets*, 30(4), 667–674. 10.1007/s12525-020-00451-2

Alt, R., & Wende, E. (2020). Blockchain technology in energy markets – An interview with the European Energy Exchange. *Electronic Markets*, 30(2), 325–330. 10.1007/s12525-020-00423-6

Ammous, S. (2018). Can cryptocurrencies fulfil the functions of money? *The Quarterly Review of Economics and Finance*, 70, 38–51. 10.1016/j.qref.2018.05.010

Andreassen, T. W., Lervik-Olsen, L., Snyder, H., Van Riel, A. C. R., Sweeney, J. C., & Van Vaerenbergh, Y. (2018). Business model innovation and value-creation: The triadic way. *Journal of Service Management*, 29(5), 883–906. 10.1108/JOSM-05-2018-0125

Angelis, J., & Ribeiro da Silva, E. (2019). Blockchain adoption: A value driver perspective. *Business Horizons*, 62(3), 307–314. 10.1016/j.bushor.2018.12.001

Angerer, M., Hoffmann, C. H., Neitzert, F., & Kraus, S. (2020). Objective and subjective risks of investing into cryptocurrencies. *Finance Research Letters*, 40, 101737. 10.1016/j.frl.2020.101737

Antonakakis, N., Chatziantoniou, I., & Gabauer, D. (2019). Cryptocurrency market contagion: Market uncertainty, market complexity, and dynamic portfolios. *Journal of International Financial Markets, Institutions and Money*, 61, 37–51. 10.1016/j.intfin.2019.02.003

Aslanidis, N., Bariviera, A. F., & Martínez-Ibañez, O. (2019). An analysis of cryptocurrencies conditional cross correlations. *Finance Research Letters*, 31, 130–137. 10.1016/j.frl.2019.04.019

Attaran, M., & Gunasekaran, A. (2019). Blockchain-enabled technology: The emerging technology set to reshape and decentralise many industries. *International Journal of Applied Decision Sciences*, 12(4), 424–444. 10.1504/IJADS.2019.102642

Babich, V., & Hilary, G. (2020). Distributed ledgers and operations: What operations management researchers should know about blockchain technology. *Manufacturing & Service Operations Management*, 22(2), 223–240. 10.1287/msom.2018.0752

Bajwa, I. A., Ur Rehman, S., Iqbal, A., Anwar, Z., Ashiq, M., & Khan, M. A. (2022). Past, Present and Future of FinTech Research: A Bibliometric Analysis. *SAGE Open*, 12(4), 1–22. 10.1177/21582440221131242

Bariviera, A. F., & Merediz-Solà, I. (2021). Where Do We Stand in Cryptocurrencies Economic Research? a Survey Based on Hybrid Analysis. *Journal of Economic Surveys*, 35(2), 377–407. 10.1111/joes.12412

Baur, D. G., Hong, K., & Lee, A. D. (2018). Bitcoin : Medium of Exchange or Speculative Assets? *Journal of International Financial Markets, Institutions and Money*, 54, 177–189. 10.1016/j.intfin.2017.12.004

Belotti, M., Božić, N., Pujolle, G., & Secci, S. (2019). A Vademecum on Blockchain Technologies: When, Which, and How. *IEEE Communications Surveys and Tutorials*, 21(4), 3796–3838. 10.1109/COMST.2019.2928178

Biancone, P., Saiti, B., Petricean, D., & Chmet, F. (2020). The bibliometric analysis of Islamic banking and finance. *Journal of Islamic Accounting and Business Research*, 11(9), 2069–2086. 10.1108/JIABR-08-2020-0235

Blau, B. M. (2017). Research in International Business and Finance Price dynamics and speculative trading in bitcoin. *Research in International Business and Finance*, 41(May), 493–499. 10.1016/j.ribaf.2017.05.010

Bollani, L., & Chmet, F. (2020). Bibliometric Analysis of Islamic Finance. *European Journal of Islamic Finance*, 19(1), 1–11.

Borri, N. (2019). Conditional Tail-Risk in Cryptocurrency Markets. *Journal of Empirical Finance*, 50, 1–19. 10.1016/j.jempfin.2018.11.002

Bouri, E., Gupta, R., & Roubaud, D. (2018). Spillovers between Bitcoin and other assets during bear and bull markets. *Applied Economics*, 50(55), 5935–5949. 10.1080/00036846.2018.1488075

Bouri, E., Jalkh, N., Molnár, P., & Roubaud, D. (2017). Bitcoin for energy commodities before and after the December 2013 crash : Diversifier, hedge or safe haven? *Applied Economics*, 49(50), 5063–5073. 10.1080/00036846.2017.1299102

Bouri, E., Jawad, S., Shahzad, H., & Roubaud, D. (2018). *"Co-explosivity in the cryptocurrency market", Finance Research Letters*. Elsevier Inc., 10.1016/j.frl.2018.07.005

Bouri, E., Molnár, P., Azzi, G., Roubaud, D., & Hagfors, L. I. (2017). On the hedge and safe haven properties of Bitcoin: Is it really more than a diversifier? Forthcoming in Finance Research Letters On the hedge and safe haven properties of Bitcoin: Is it really more than a diversifier? *Finance Research Letters*, 20, 1–12. 10.1016/j.frl.2016.09.025

Broadus, R. N. (1987). Toward a definition of 'bibliometrics'. *Scientometrics*, 12(5–6), 373–379. 10.1007/BF02016680

Caliskan, K. (2020). Data money: The socio-technical infrastructure of cryptocurrency blockchains. *Economy and Society*, 49(4), 540–561. 10.1080/03085147.2020.1774258

Chang, V., Baudier, P., Zhang, H., Xu, Q., Zhang, J., & Arami, M. (2020). How Blockchain can impact financial services – The overview, challenges and recommendations from expert interviewees. *Technological Forecasting and Social Change*, 158(June), 120166. 10.1016/j.techfore.2020.120166

Corbet, S., Lucey, B., Urquhart, A., & Yarovaya, L. (2019). Cryptocurrencies as a financial asset: A systematic analysis. *International Review of Financial Analysis*, 62, 182–199. 10.1016/j.irfa.2018.09.003

Cui, J., & Maghyereh, A. (2022). Time–frequency co-movement and risk connectedness among cryptocurrencies: New evidence from the higher-order moments before and during the COVID-19 pandemic. *Financial Innovation*, 8(1), 90. Advance online publication. 10.1186/s40854-022-00395-w

da Gama, P. V. J., Silva, M. C., & Klotzle, A. C. F. P. (2019). Herding Behavior and Contagion in the Cryptocurrency Market Pontifical Catholic University of Rio de Janeiro. *Journal of Behavioral and Experimental Finance*, 22, 41–50. 10.1016/j.jbef.2019.01.006

Dashkevich, N., Counsell, S., & Destefanis, G. (2020). Blockchain Application for Central Banks: A Systematic Mapping Study. *IEEE Access : Practical Innovations, Open Solutions*, 8, 139918–139952. 10.1109/ACCESS.2020.3012295

de Moraes, G. H. S. M., Pelegrini, G. C., de Marchi, L. P., Pinheiro, G. T., & Cappellozza, A. (2022). Antecedents of big data analytics adoption: An analysis with future managers in a developing country. *The Bottom Line (New York, N.Y.)*, 35(2/3), 73–89. 10.1108/BL-06-2021-0068

De Vries, A., Gallersdörfer, U., Klaaßen, L., & Stoll, C. (2021). The true costs of digital currencies: Exploring impact beyond energy use. *One Earth*, 4(6), 786–789. 10.1016/j.oneear.2021.05.009

Di Francesco Maesa, D., & Mori, P. (2020). Blockchain 3.0 applications survey. *Journal of Parallel and Distributed Computing*, 138, 99–114. 10.1016/j.jpdc.2019.12.019

Dierksmeier, C., & Seele, P. (2018). Cryptocurrencies and Business Ethics. *Journal of Business Ethics*, 152(1), 1–14. 10.1007/s10551-016-3298-0

Donthu, N., Kumar, S., Mukherjee, D., Pandey, N., & Lim, W. M. (2021). How to conduct a bibliometric analysis: An overview and guidelines. *Journal of Business Research*, 133(May), 285–296. 10.1016/j.jbusres.2021.04.070

Drljevic, N., Aranda, D. A., & Stantchev, V. (2020). Perspectives on risks and standards that affect the requirements engineering of blockchain technology. *Computer Standards & Interfaces*, 69, 103409. 10.1016/j.csi.2019.103409

Duan, R., & Guo, L. (2021). Application of Blockchain for Internet of Things: A Bibliometric Analysis. *Mathematical Problems in Engineering*, 2021, 1–16. 10.1155/2021/5547530

Dwyer, G. P. (2015). The economics of Bitcoin and similar private digital currencies. *Journal of Financial Stability*, 17, 81–91. 10.1016/j.jfs.2014.11.006

Ellegaard, O., & Wallin, J. A. (2015). *The bibliometric analysis of scholarly production: How great is the impact?Scientometrics*, *105*(3), 1809–1831. 10.1007/s11192-015-1645-z

Esmaeilian, B., Sarkis, J., Lewis, K., & Behdad, S. (2020). Blockchain for the future of sustainable supply chain management in Industry 4.0. *Resources, Conservation and Recycling*, 163, 105064. 10.1016/j.resconrec.2020.105064

Eze, S. C., Olatunji, S., Chinedu-Eze, V. C., Bello, A. O., Ayeni, A., & Peter, F. (2019). Determinants of perceived information need for emerging ICT adoption: A study of UK small service businesses. *The Bottom Line (New York, N.Y.)*, 32(2), 158–183. 10.1108/BL-01-2019-0059

Ferenhof, H. A., Durst, S., Zaniboni Bialecki, M., & Selig, P. M. (2015). Intellectual capital dimensions: State of the art in 2014. *Journal of Intellectual Capital*, 16(1), 58–100. 10.1108/JIC-02-2014-0021

Firdaus, A., Razak, M. F. A., Feizollah, A., Hashem, I. A. T., Hazim, M., & Anuar, N. B. (2019). *The Rise of "Blockchain": Bibliometric Analysis of Blockchain Study, Scientometrics* (Vol. 120). Springer International Publishing. 10.1007/s11192-019-03170-4

Fry, J. (2018). Booms, busts and heavy-tails: The story of Bitcoin and cryptocurrency markets? *Economics Letters*, 171, 225–229. 10.1016/j.econlet.2018.08.008

García-Corral, F. J., Cordero-García, J. A., de Pablo-Valenciano, J., & Uribe-Toril, J. (2022). A bibliometric review of cryptocurrencies: How have they grown? *Financial Innovation*, 8(1), 2. Advance online publication. 10.1186/s40854-021-00306-5

Gil-Alana, L. A., Abakah, E. J. A., & Rojo, M. F. R. (2020). Cryptocurrencies and stock market indices. Are they related? *Research in International Business and Finance*, 51, 101063. Advance online publication. 10.1016/j.ribaf.2019.101063

Gorkhali, A., Li, L., & Shrestha, A. (2020). Blockchain: A literature review. *Journal of Management Analytics, Taylor & Francis*, 7(3), 321–343. 10.1080/23270012.2020.1801529

Guo, Y. M., Huang, Z. L., Guo, J., Guo, X. R., Li, H., Liu, M. Y., Ezzeddine, S., & Nkeli, M. J. (2021). "A bibliometric analysis and visualization of blockchain", *Future Generation Computer Systems. Future Generation Computer Systems*, 116, 316–332. 10.1016/j.future.2020.10.023

Hairudin, A., Sifat, I. M., Mohamad, A., & Yusof, Y. (2020). Cryptocurrencies: A survey on acceptance, governance and market dynamics. *International Journal of Finance & Economics*, (December). Advance online publication. 10.1002/ijfe.2392

Haykir, O., & Yagli, I. (2022). Speculative bubbles and herding in cryptocurrencies. *Financial Innovation*, 8(1), 78. 10.1186/s40854-022-00383-0

Hota, P. K., Subramanian, B., & Narayanamurthy, G. (2020). Mapping the intellectual structure of social entrepreneurship research. *Journal of Business Ethics*, 166(1), 89–114. 10.1007/s10551-019-04129-4

Huynh, T. L. D., Shahbaz, M., Nasir, M. A., & Ullah, S. (2022). Financial modelling, risk management of energy instruments and the role of cryptocurrencies. *Annals of Operations Research*, 313(1), 47–75. 10.1007/s10479-020-03680-y

Iansiti, M., & Lakhani, K. R. (2017). The truth about blockchain. *Harvard Business Review*.

Inci, A. C., & Lagasse, R. (2019). Cryptocurrencies: Applications and investment opportunities. *Journal of Capital Markets Studies*, 3(2), 98–112. 10.1108/JCMS-05-2019-0032

Inegbedion, H. E. (2021). Digital divide in the major regions of the world and the possibility of convergence. *The Bottom Line (New York, N.Y.)*, 34(1), 68–85. 10.1108/BL-09-2020-0064

Jalal, R. N. U. D., Alon, I., & Paltrinieri, A. (2021). A bibliometric review of cryptocurrencies as a financial asset. *Technology Analysis and Strategic Management*, 0(0), 1–16. 10.1080/09537325.2021.1939001

Jordão, R. V. D., & Novas, J. C. (2017). Knowledge management and intellectual capital in networks of small- and medium-sized enterprises. *Journal of Intellectual Capital*, 18(3), 667–692. 10.1108/JIC-11-2016-0120

Katsiampa, P. (2017). Volatility estimation for Bitcoin : A comparison of GARCH models. *Economics Letters*, 158, 3–6. 10.1016/j.econlet.2017.06.023

Kent Baker, H., Pandey, N., Kumar, S., & Haldar, A. (2020). A bibliometric analysis of board diversity: Current status, development, and future research directions. *Journal of Business Research*, 108, 232–246. 10.1016/j.jbusres.2019.11.025

Khan, R., & Hakami, T. A. (2022). Cryptocurrency: Usability perspective versus volatility threat. *Journal of Money and Business*, 2(1), 16–28. 10.1108/JMB-11-2021-0051

Kim, H. & So, K.K.F. (2022). Two decades of customer experience research in hospitality and tourism: A bibliometric analysis and thematic content analysis. *International Journal of Hospitality Management*, 100. .10.1016/j.ijhm.2021.103082

Klose, J. (2022). Comparing cryptocurrencies and gold - a system-GARCH-approach. *Springer International Publishing*, 12(4), 653–679. 10.1007/s40822-022-00218-4

Krueckeberg, S., & Scholz, P. (2019). *Cryptocurrencies as an Asset Class?* Springer International Publishing., 10.2139/ssrn.3162800

Lardo, A., Corsi, K., Varma, A., & Mancini, D. (2022). Exploring blockchain in the accounting domain: A bibliometric analysis. *Accounting, Auditing & Accountability Journal*, 35(9), 204–233. 10.1108/AAAJ-10-2020-4995

Leonidou, C. N., & Leonidou, L. C. (2011). Research into environmental marketing/management: A bibliographic analysis. *European Journal of Marketing*, 45(1), 68–103. 10.1108/03090561111095603

Linnenluecke, M. K., Marrone, M., & Singh, A. K. (2020). Conducting systematic literature reviews and bibliometric analyses. *Australian Journal of Management*, 45(2), 175–194. 10.1177/0312896219877678

Lombardi, R., de Villiers, C., Moscariello, N., & Pizzo, M. (2022). The disruption of blockchain in auditing – a systematic literature review and an agenda for future research. *Accounting, Auditing & Accountability Journal*, 35(7), 1534–1565. 10.1108/AAAJ-10-2020-4992

Merediz-Solá, I., & Bariviera, A. F. (2019). A bibliometric analysis of bitcoin scientific production. *Research in International Business and Finance*, 50, 294–305. 10.1016/j.ribaf.2019.06.008

Mnif, E., Jarboui, A., & Mouakhar, K. (2020). How the cryptocurrency market has performed during COVID 19? A multifractal analysis. *Finance Research Letters*, 36, 101647. 10.1016/j.frl.2020.101647

Mohammad Saif, A. N., & Islam, M. A. (2022). Blockchain in human resource management: A systematic review and bibliometric analysis. *Technology Analysis and Strategic Management*, 2021(March), 1–16. 10.1080/09537325.2022.2049226

Müller, R., & Antoni, C. H. (2020). Individual Perceptions of Shared Mental Models of Information and Communication Technology (ICT) and Virtual Team Coordination and Performance — The Moderating Role of Flexibility in ICT Use. *Group Dynamica:Theory, Research, and Practices*, 24(3), 186–200. 10.1037/gdn0000130

Musigmann, B., Von Der Gracht, H., & Hartmann, E. (2020). Blockchain Technology in Logistics and Supply Chain Management - A Bibliometric Literature Review from 2016 to January 2020. *IEEE Transactions on Engineering Management*, 67(4), 988–1007. 10.1109/TEM.2020.2980733

Nagariya, R., Kumar, D., & Kumar, I. (2021). Service supply chain: From bibliometric analysis to content analysis, current research trends and future research directions. *Benchmarking*, 28(1), 333–369. 10.1108/BIJ-04-2020-0137

Nasir, A., Shaukat, K., Khan, K. I., Hameed, I. A., Alam, T. M., & Luo, S. (2021). What is Core and What Future Holds for Blockchain Technologies and Crypto-currencies: A Bibliometric Analysis. *IEEE Access : Practical Innovations, Open Solutions*, 9, 989–1004. 10.1109/ACCESS.2020.3046931

Nobanee, H., & Ellili, N. O. D. (2023). Non-fungible tokens (NFTs): A bibliometric and systematic review, current streams, developments, and directions for future research. *International Review of Economics & Finance*, 84(January), 460–473. 10.1016/j.iref.2022.11.014

Noor, A. (2022). Adoption of Blockchain Technology Facilitates a Competitive Edge for Logistic Service Providers. *Sustainability (Basel)*, 14(23), 15543. Advance online publication. 10.3390/su142315543

Pahlevan-Sharif, S., Mura, P., & Wijesinghe, S. N. R. (2019). A systematic review of systematic reviews in tourism. *Journal of Hospitality and Tourism Management*, 39(March), 158–165. 10.1016/j.jhtm.2019.04.001

Pahlevan Sharif, S., Mura, P. & Wijesinghe, S.N.R. (2019). *Systematic Reviews in Asia: Introducing the 'PRISMA' Protocol to Tourism and Hospitality Scholars*. .10.1007/978-981-13-2463-5_2

Parino, F., Beiró, M. G., & Gauvin, L. (2018). Analysis of the Bitcoin blockchain: Socio-economic factors behind the adoption. *EPJ Data Science*, 7(1), 38. Advance online publication. 10.1140/epjds/s13688-018-0170-8

Parmentola, A., Petrillo, A., Tutore, I., & De Felice, F. (2022). Is blockchain able to enhance environmental sustainability? A systematic review and research agenda from the perspective of Sustainable Development Goals (SDGs). *Business Strategy and the Environment*, 31(1), 194–217. 10.1002/bse.2882

Pizzi, S., Caputo, A., Venturelli, A., & Caputo, F. (2022). Embedding and managing blockchain in sustainability reporting: A practical framework. *Sustainability Accounting, Management and Policy Journal*, 13(3), 545–567. 10.1108/SAMPJ-07-2021-0288

Platanakis, E., & Urquhart, A. (2019). Portfolio management with cryptocurren-cies: The role of estimation risk. *Economics Letters*, 177, 76–80. 10.1016/j.econ-let.2019.01.019

Pritchard, A. (1969). Statistical bibliography or bibliometrics. *The Journal of Doc-umentation*, 25, 348.

Rejeb, A., Rejeb, K., & Keogh, , J. (2021). Cryptocurrencies in Modern Finance: A Literature Review. *Etikonomi*, 20(1), 93–118. 10.15408/etk.v20i1.16911

Rodríguez-López, M. E., Alcántara-Pilar, J. M., Del Barrio-García, S., & Muñoz-Leiva, F. (2020). A review of restaurant research in the last two decades: A bibliometric analysis. *International Journal of Hospitality Management*, 87(April), 102387. 10.1016/j.ijhm.2019.102387

Sahoo, S., Kumar, S., Sivarajah, U., Lim, W.M., Westland, J.C. & Kumar, A. (2022), *Blockchain for Sustainable Supply Chain Management: Trends and Ways Forward, Electronic Commerce Research*. Springer US. .10.1007/s10660-022-09569-1

Schellinger, B. (2020). Optimization of special cryptocurrency portfolios. *The Journal of Risk Finance*, 21(2), 127–157. 10.1108/JRF-11-2019-0221

Secinaro, S., Dal Mas, F., Brescia, V., & Calandra, D. (2021). Blockchain in the accounting, auditing and accountability fields: A bibliometric and coding analysis. *Accounting, Auditing & Accountability Journal*, 35(9), 168–203. 10.1108/AAAJ-10-2020-4987

Shahbazi, Z., & Byun, Y. C. (2022). Machine Learning-Based Analysis of Cryptocurrency Market Financial Risk Management. *IEEE Access : Practical Innovations, Open Solutions*, 10, 37848–37856. 10.1109/ACCESS.2022.3162858

Sharma, G. D., Jain, M., Mahendru, M., Bansal, S., & Kumar, G. (2019). Emergence of Bitcoin as an Investment Alternative: A Systematic Review and Research Agenda. *International Journal of Business and Information*, 14(1), 47–84. 10.6702/ijbi.201903

Shen, D., Urquhart, A. & Wang, P. (2020). A three-factor pricing model for cryptocurrencies. *Finance Research Letters*, *34*. .10.1016/j.frl.2019.07.021

Shibano, K., & Mogi, G. (2022). An analysis of the acquisition of a monetary function by cryptocurrency using a multi-agent simulation model. *Financial Innovation*, 8(1), 87. Advance online publication. 10.1186/s40854-022-00389-8

Shtovba, S., Shtovba, O., & Filatova, L. (2020). The current state of brand management research: An overview of leaders and trends in branding research over the past 20 years. *The Bottom Line (New York, N.Y.)*, 33(1), 1–11. 10.1108/BL-08-2019-0106

Tandon, A., Kaur, P., Mäntymäki, M., & Dhir, A. (2021). Blockchain applications in management: A bibliometric analysis and literature review. *Technological Forecasting and Social Change*, 166(January), 120649. Advance online publication. 10.1016/j.techfore.2021.120649

TerJi-Xi, J., Salamzadeh, Y., & Teoh, A. P. (2021). Behavioral intention to use cryptocurrency in Malaysia: An empirical study. *The Bottom Line (New York, N.Y.)*, 34(2), 170–197. 10.1108/BL-08-2020-0053

Tönnissen, S., Beinke, J. H., & Teuteberg, F. (2020). Understanding token-based ecosystems – a taxonomy of blockchain-based business models of start-ups. *Electronic Markets*, 30(2), 307–323. 10.1007/s12525-020-00396-6

Urquhart, A. (2016). The inefficiency of Bitcoin. *Economics Letters*, 148, 80–82. 10.1016/j.econlet.2016.09.019

Van Veldhoven, Z., & Vanthienen, J. (2023). Best practices for digital transformation based on a systematic literature review. *Digital Transformation and Society*, 2(2), 104–128. 10.1108/DTS-11-2022-0057

Wang, Y., Han, J. H., Beynon-davies, P., Wang, Y., Han, J. H., & Beynon-davies, P. (2019). Understanding blockchain technology for future supply chains : A systematic literature review and research agenda. *Supply Chain Management*, 24(1), 62–84. 10.1108/SCM-03-2018-0148

Warner, K. S. R., & Wäger, M. (2019). Building dynamic capabilities for digital transformation: An ongoing process of strategic renewal. *Long Range Planning*, 52(3), 326–349. 10.1016/j.lrp.2018.12.001

Yin, H. H. S., Langenheldt, K., Harlev, M., Mukkamala, R. R., & Vatrapu, R. (2019). Regulating Cryptocurrencies: A Supervised Machine Learning Approach to De-Anonymizing the Bitcoin Blockchain. *Journal of Management Information Systems*, 36(1), 37–73. 10.1080/07421222.2018.1550550

Yousaf, I., & Yarovaya, L. (2022). Herding behavior in conventional cryptocurrency market, non-fungible tokens, and DeFi assets. *Finance Research Letters*, 50, 103299. 10.1016/j.frl.2022.103299

Yue, Y., Li, X., Zhang, D., & Wang, S. (2021). How cryptocurrency affects economy? A network analysis using bibliometric methods. *International Review of Financial Analysis*, 77(71988101), 101869. 10.1016/j.irfa.2021.101869

Chapter 7
Examining Investor Overreaction in Periods of Crisis:
Evidence From Central and Eastern European Countries

Mohammad Irfan
http://orcid.org/0000-0002-4956-1170
NSB Academy, India

Rui Dias
http://orcid.org/0000-0002-6138-3098
ISG, Business and Economics School, CIGEST, Portugal

Rosa Morgado Galvão
http://orcid.org/0000-0001-8282-6604
Instituto Politécnico de Setúbal, Portugal

ABSTRACT

This study tests whether the 2022 event has increased investor overreactions in the capital markets of eight Central and Eastern European countries (Romania, Bulgaria, Slovakia, Hungary, Croatia, Russia, the Czech Republic, and Slovenia). This chapter contributes to the existing literature on overreaction behavior in Central and Eastern European capital markets by introducing a new modeling technique that does not require specific threshold parameters. Instead, the analysis models the price overreaction as a price change based on 16-day lags. This approach differs from previous research that used statistical modeling of overreactions, selecting one or more arbitrary parameters. The research question is partially accepted since

DOI: 10.4018/979-8-3693-3322-8.ch007

some studied regional markets show overreactions (4 out of 8 possible markets).

1. INTRODUCTION

On February 21, 2022, Vladimir Putin recognized the independence of the Donetsk People's Republic and the Lugansk People's Republic, both controlled by pro-Russia separatists in the Donbas. The following day, the Russian Federation Council approved using military force, resulting in Russian troops entering these regions. On February 24, Putin announced a "special military operation" to "demilitarize" and "denazify" Ukraine, followed by missile attacks throughout Ukrainian territory, including Kiev. There were also reports of attacks on border crossings. Russian ground forces entered Ukraine, prompting President Zelensky to declare martial law and call for general mobilization (Johannesson and Clowes, 2022; Appiah-Otoo, 2023; Khalfaoui et al., 2023).

According to the efficient market hypothesis, stock prices result from rationally assessing all available information. This means that it is difficult for investors to obtain abnormal returns, i.e., returns higher than expected, based on public information. However, several academic studies conducted since the 1980s suggest that the efficient market hypothesis is incorrect. One of those studies, by Bondt and Thaler (1985), found that it is possible to obtain abnormal long-term returns by investing in stocks that have performed poorly in the past (extreme early losers) and short-selling those that have performed very well (extreme early winners). Bondt and Thaler (1985) argue that this "opposite" approach to investment generates returns, as investors tend to overreact to information, leading to excessive optimism and pessimism in the market.

According to the authors De Bondt and Thaler (2012), it is conventional wisdom on Wall Street that academic research supports irrational exuberance. For example, Shiller's survey data on the 1987 stock market crash reveals that investors were reacting to each other's behavior rather than to hard economic news (Shiller, 2003). The authors Bondt & Thaler (1985) argued that average reversion in stock prices is evidence of overreaction, showing that stocks that were extreme losers during an initial 3 to 5 years period made excessive returns in subsequent years. In the 1987 paper, Bondt and Thaler (1987) showed that excess returns could not be easily attributed to changes in risk, tax effects or the small business anomaly. Instead, they argue that biased expectations of future returns could explain excess returns for losers. They show that the returns of losing companies fell sharply while their share prices lagged behind market performance but recovered strongly over the following years.

Given these events, this study aims to examine the overreactions in the capital markets of Romania (BET), Bulgaria (SOFIX), Slovakia (SAX 16), Hungary (BUX), Croatia (CROBEX), Russia (MOEX), the Czech Republic (PRAGUE SE PX) and Slovenia (SBI TOP), in the period from January 1, 2021, to November 23, 2023, i.e., in the period before and during the Russian invasion of Ukraine in 2022.

This study makes an important contribution to the existing literature on overreaction behavior in Central and Eastern European capital markets by introducing a new modeling technique that does not require specific threshold parameters. Instead, our analysis models the price overreaction as a price change based on 16-day lags. This approach contrasts with previous research that relies on statistical modeling of overreactions, which involves the selection of one or more arbitrary parameters.

This chapter is organized into five sections. Section 2 provides a literature review of studies on the overreaction hypothesis in international financial markets. Section 3 describes the methodology and data. Section 4 contains the results, and section 5 is the conclusion.

2. LITERATURE REVIEW

The swiftness with which new information is integrated into security prices is a fundamental characteristic of an efficient market. In such a market, prices quickly and exhaustively reflect new information, and there is no chance of gaining an advantage by using already public information. As a result, the market constantly adapts to new information, and the security prices change accordingly. In addition to assuming that the information available on the market is free, HME also assumes that market participants are rational and act in their best interests. This means they will make decisions based on all available information and that emotions or other irrational factors will not influence them. However, this assumption has been challenged by recent studies, which have shown that emotions and other psychological factors can play a significant role in financial decision-making (Fama, 1965, 1970; Fama and French, 1993).

Despite these challenges, the efficient market hypothesis remains a widely accepted theory in finance, and many investors use it as the basis for their investment strategies. However, it is important to remember that no theory is perfect and that financial markets can be influenced by a wide range of factors, including political events, economic conditions, and social trends. As such, it is crucial to approach investing with a level of caution and consider all available information before making any investment decisions (Dias et al., 2020; Dias, Horta, et al., 2022; Dias, Pereira, et al., 2022; Guedes et al., 2022; Santana et al., 2023; Dias et al., 2023).

Related Studies

In recent decades, a significant prevalence of overreaction has been witnessed in the financial markets, as evidenced by academic research and observations on Wall Street. Several scholars have analyzed investor behavior in various financial markets, identifying a propensity to overreact. Bondt and Thaler (1985) argue that the average reversal in stock prices manifests itself through exaggerated responses. On the other hand, Chen and Zhu (2005), examining the Chinese stock market, propose that investors tend to react disproportionately, possibly interpreting good news negatively and exaggerating bad news. The study by Antweiler and Frank (2011) supports the market efficiency hypothesis; however, it reveals evidence of reversals or overreactions in abnormal returns, both before and after significant corporate events. Subsequently, De Bondt and Thaler (2012) showed that the exceptional returns for companies that initially showed losses cannot be explained by risk, tax effects, or anomalies in small companies but rather by distorted expectations regarding future returns.

Caporale and Plastun (2019) explored the frequency of price overreactions in the US stock market, focusing on the Dow Jones Industrial Index from 1990 to 2017. The tested hypotheses are: whether or not the frequency of overreactions varies over time (H1), is informative about crises (H2) and/or price movements (H3), and exhibits seasonality (H4). The authors provide evidence to support market inefficiency since price predictability can allow investors to devise profitable trading strategies, and the fact that the frequency of overreactions varies over time is consistent with the Adaptive Expectations Hypothesis (AHE). In a complementary way, Huo and Qiu (2020) studied how China's stock market reacted to the outbreak of COVID-19 in 2020. The authors generally observed reversals at the industry and company level due to investors' overreactions to the pandemic lockdown. Thus, the reversal effects are mainly driven by industries and shares that overreact more positively to COVID-19 than others. Further investigation shows that overreactions are stronger for shares with lower institutional ownership, meaning that retail investors react more strongly to COVID-19.

Later, the authors Piñeiro-Chousa et al. (2022) examined the impact of Twitter sentiment on the returns of the S&P 500 stock indices, the VIX, and the MSCI World index, analyzing whether investors overreact to news that reaches the market. The authors show that Twitter users respond with different intensities in the case of rising or falling markets, but they cannot find evidence that the S&P 500 index and the VIX are relevant in supporting switching behavior. However, the MSCI World Index, to a certain extent, causes this relationship to diverge, i.e., investor overreactions influence prices. More recently, the author Saji (2023) tested the hypothesis of overreaction, i., whether the previous period's losers outnumber the previous period's winners in the stock markets. In this sense, the author tested this price reversal behavior in the Indian stock market. Consistent with previous evidence on market overreactions, the author concludes that losers outperform previous winners over a portfolio formation period of one to two years. The study observes the persistence of investor overreactions to price trends in both upward and downward price movements in the Indian stock market during the aftermath of the 2008 financial crisis.

In summary, this paper aims to provide information to investors and regulators in Central and Eastern European stock markets where individual and institutional investors seek diversification benefits, as well as to help promote the implementation of policies that contribute to the efficiency of these regional stock markets. Therefore, the context of this paper is to examine the market efficiency, in its weak form, and the predictability of these capital markets in this period of uncertainty in the global economy arising from the 2022 event.

3. MATERIALS AND METHODS

3.1 Data

The sample comprises the capital market indices of eight Central and Eastern European countries, namely the stock indices of Romania (BET), Bulgaria (SOFIX), Slovakia (SAX 16), Hungary (BUX), Croatia (CROBEX), Russia (MOEX), the Czech Republic (PRAGUE SE PX) and Slovenia (SBI TOP), from January 1, 2021 to November 23, 2023., The sample was divided into two sub-periods to ensure the reliability of the results:

- Pre-conflict period: from January 1, 2021 to February 23, 2022.
- Conflict period: from February 24, 2022 to November 23, 2023.

The daily prices were obtained from the Thomson Reuters Eikon platform and are denominated in the local currency of each country to avoid distortions caused by exchange rates.

3.2 Methodology

This research will be developed in several steps. In the first stage, descriptive statistical measures and the Jarque and Bera (1980) adherence test will be used to verify that the data follows a normal distribution. In the second step, graphs of the returns will be made to measure the evolution of the capital markets analyzed. To estimate stationarity, the Breitung (2000), Levin et al. (2002), and Im, Pesaran, and

Shin (2003) tests will be used, which postulate that the null hypothesis has unit roots. The Dickey and Fuller (1981) and Phillips & Perron (1988) - Fisher Chi-square and Choi Z-stat will be used for results validation. Fisher's chi-square version, also known as the Pesaran and Pesaran test, assesses the cross-sectional independence of panel data based on Fisher's chi-square statistic. The Choi Z-stat test, developed by Choi (2001), tests for the presence of cross-sectional dependence in panel data and is based on the Z statistic and helps determine whether there is a correlation or interdependence between the observations of the individuals in the panel.

In order to answer the research questions, the variance ratio methodology proposed by Lo and Mackinlay (1988) will be used to assess the autocorrelation between the yield series. This methodology can be classified as a parametric test. The weak form of the efficient market hypothesis states that predicting future prices based on historical prices is impossible. The author Rosenthal (1983) advocates that if a market is efficient in its weak form, then there should be no linear dependence between lagged returns in both the statistical sense (absence of autocorrelation) and the economic sense (absence of positive returns after taking transaction costs into account). The Lo and Mackinlay (1988) model defines P_t as the price of an asset in t and X_t as the natural logarithm of P_t, the random walk hypothesis is given by:

$$X_t = \mu + X_{t-1} + \epsilon_t$$

[1]

Where μ is an arbitrary movement parameter and ϵ_t is the random error term. The authors point out that an important characteristic of the random walk process is that the variance of the increments grows linearly according to the observation interval. In other words, the variance of $X_t - X_{t-2}$ is twice the variance of $X_t - X_{t-1}$. Thus, the validity of a random walk model can be tested by comparing variance estimators for returns at different frequencies. For example, the variance of the weekly returns series should be five times greater than the variance of the daily returns. The model tests whether the variance ratio for different intervals weighted by their duration is equal to one.

The variance of a q-differenced series $(X_t - X_{t-q})$ will be q times the variance of the series from the first differentiation $(X_t - X_{t-1})$. The variance ratio test is performed according to the heteroscedasticity-consistent estimator defined by Lo and Mackinlay (1988). In a sample with $nq + 1$ observations, where q is an integer greater than 1, the following estimators are defined:

$$\hat{\mu} \equiv \frac{1}{nq} \sum_{k=1}^{nq} (X_k - X_{k-1}) = \frac{1}{nq}(X_{nq} - X_0)$$

[2]

$$\bar{\sigma}_a^2 \equiv \frac{1}{nq} \sum_{k=1}^{nq} \left(X_k - X_{k-1} - \hat{\mu} \right)^2$$

[3]

$$\bar{\sigma}_c^2(q) \equiv \frac{1}{m} \sum_{k=1}^{n} \left(X_{qk} - X_{qk-q} - q\hat{\mu} \right)^2$$

[4]

Where:

$$m = q(nq - q + 1)\left(1 - \frac{q}{nq}\right)$$

[5]

The variance ratio is given by:

$$\widehat{VR}(q) = \frac{\bar{\sigma}_c^2(q)}{\bar{\sigma}_a^2}$$

[6]

The test statistic robust to heteroscedasticity is defined by:

$$z^*(q) = \frac{\sqrt{nq}\left(\widehat{VR}(q) - 1\right)}{\sqrt{\hat{\phi}(q)}}$$

[7]

Where:

$$\widehat{\phi}(q) = \sum_{j=1}^{q-1} \left[\frac{2(q-j)}{q} \right]^2 \widehat{\delta}(j)$$

[8]

$$\widehat{\delta}(j) = \frac{\sum_{t=j+1}^{nq} (X_k - X_{k-1} - \widehat{\mu})^2 (X_{k-j} - X_{k-j-1} - \widehat{\mu})^2}{\sum_{t=j+1}^{nq} (X_k - X_{k-1} - \widehat{\mu})^2}$$

[9]

4. RESULTS

Figure 1 shows the evolution, in returns, of the stock indices of Romania (BET), Bulgaria (SOFIX), Slovakia (SAX 16), Hungary (BUX), Croatia (CROBEX), Russia (MOEX), the Czech Republic (PRAGUE SE PX) and Slovenia (SBI TOP), from January 1, 2021, to November 23, 2023. Graphically, it can be seen that the stock indices show significant variations, highlighting the volatility to which these markets have been subject, especially in the first few months of 2022, a period coinciding with the Russian invasion of Ukraine.

Figure 1. Evolution, in returns, of the capital markets of eight Central and Eastern European countries from January 1, 2021, to November 23, 2023 (Own elaboration)

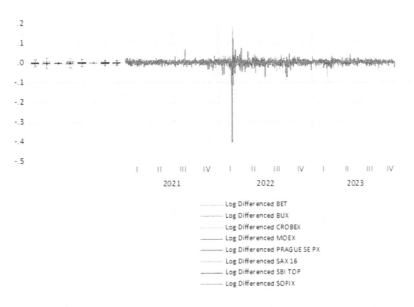

Tables 1 and 2 summarize the main measures of descriptive statistics, in daily returns, of the time series, referring to the stock indices of Romania (BET), Bulgaria (SOFIX), Slovakia (SAX 16), Hungary (BUX), Croatia (CROBEX), Russia (MOEX), the Czech Republic (PRAGUE SE PX) and Slovenia (SBI TOP), for the period from January 1, 2021, to November 23, 2023. When observing the statistical summary table, the mean returns are positive, except for the stock indices MOEX (-2.37e-05) and SAX 16 (-0.0001). Regarding risk, the stock index with the greatest difference from the mean is the MOEX index (0.02185), while the CROBEX capital market (0.00617) has the lowest standard deviation. To validate whether the time series have Gaussian distributions, the skewness, and kurtosis were estimated, and it was found that the values are different from the reference values (skewness zero and kurtosis 3). The capital markets analyzed have negative asymmetries, with the highest being the MOEX stock index (-8.0546), while the lowest value is in the BET market (-0.3831). Concerning the kurtosis statistical measure, the most significant value is found in the Russian market (165.0802) and the lowest in the PRAGUE stock index (8.4122), i.e., these are non-Gaussian distributions. For validation, the Jarque and Bera (1980) test was estimated, leading to the rejection of H_0 with a significance level of 1%. These results were expected due to the presence of fat tails, i.e. extreme values, resulting from the 2022 event. Those results are also validated by the authors Dias, Horta, et al. (2023), Dias et al. (2023), Dias et al. (2023), Dias et al. (2023), which show the presence of non-Gaussian distributions in the time series of international financial markets.

Table 1. Summary table of the main statistics on the capital markets of eight Central and Eastern European countries from January 1, 2021, to November 23, 2023

	BET	**BUX**	**CROBEX**	**MOEX**
Mean	0.00053	0.00039	0.00043	-2.37e-05
Std. Dev.	0.00898	0.01356	0.00617	0.02185
Skewness	-0.3831	-1.4082	-1.9227	-8.0546
Kurtosis	10.4484	15.4618	23.8899	165.0802
Jarque-Bera	1763.75	5135.00	14193.29	834572.43
Probability	0.0000	0.0000	0.0000	0.0000
Observations	755	755	755	755

Source: Own elaboration.

Table 2. Summary table of the main statistics on the capital markets of eight Central and Eastern European countries from January 1, 2021, to November 23, 2023

	PRAGUE	**SAX 16**	**SBI TOP**	**SOFIX**
Mean	0.0004	-0.0001	0.00039	0.00066
Std. Dev.	0.0093	0.0077	0.0084	0.0076
Skewness	-0.6651	-0.9825	-1.3381	-0.5612
Kurtosis	8.4122	28.2516	14.0953	12.8368
Jarque-Bera	977.18	20180.77	4098.03	3083.66
Probability	0.0000	0.0000	0.0000	0.0000
Observations	755	755	755	755

Source: Own elaboration.

In order to validate the stationarity assumption of the time series referring to the Central and Eastern European capital markets, namely the stock indices of Romania (BET), Bulgaria (SOFIX), Slovakia (SAX 16), Hungary (BUX), Croatia (CROBEX), Russia (MOEX), the Czech Republic (PRAGUE SE PX) and Slovenia (SBI TOP), for the period from January 1, 2021, to November 23, 2023, the summary table of the panel unit root tests will be used, namely the tests of Levin, Lin, and Chu (2002), Breitung (2000) and Im et al. (2003). The Dickey and Fuller (1981) and Phillips and Perron (1988) with Fisher Chi-square transformation were used for validation. In order to obtain stationarity, the logarithmic transformation in the first differences was used to smooth the time series so that the characteristics of white noise could be achieved (mean 0; constant variance), thus validating the assumption of stationarity by rejecting H_0 at a significance level of 1% (see table 3).

Table 3. Summary table of the unit root tests for the capital markets of eight Central and Eastern European countries from January 1, 2021, to November 23, 2023

Group unit root test: Summary				
			Cross-	
Method	Statistic	Prob.**	sections	Obs
Null: Unit root (assumes common unit root process)				
Levin, Lin & Chu t*	-135.1326	0.0000	8	6021
(Breitung, 2000) t-stat	-59.8085	0.0000	8	6013
Null: Unit root (assumes individual unit root process)				
Im, Pesaran and Shin W-stat	-83.9923	0.0000	8	6021
ADF - Fisher Chi-square	1924.7137	0.0000	8	6021
PP - Fisher Chi-square	2107.1263	0.0000	8	6024

*Note:*** Probabilities for Fisher tests are computed using an asymptotic Chi square distribution. All other tests assume asymptotic normality.

Source: Own elaboration.

In this study, the research question was answered using the variance ratio test proposed by Lo and Mackinlay (1988) to assess the autocorrelation between the yield series. This methodology can be classified as a parametric test.

In the pre-conflict period, the stock indices of Romania (BET), Bulgaria (SOFIX), Slovakia (SAX 16), Hungary (BUX), Croatia (CROBEX), Russia (MOEX), the Czech Republic (PRAGUE SE PX), and Slovenia (SBI TOP) can be observed in the period from January 1, 2021 to February 23, 2022. Based on the results, the capital markets of Russia (MOEX) and Slovakia (SAX 16) show negative serial autocorrelation, which means that price movements are not entirely random and are influenced by past price movements. This evidence could indicate exaggerated reactions on the part of investors to the information that reaches the market. In such a scenario, any positive/negative news or information about a particular asset traded on these markets can lead to an increase/decrease in its price as investors become more optimistic/pessimistic about its future prospects. In addition, it was also found that the capital markets of Romania (BET), Bulgaria (SOFIX), Hungary (BUX), Croatia (CROBEX), the Czech Republic (PRAGUE SE PX), and Slovenia (SBI TOP) are in equilibrium, showing that there is no autocorrelation in price formation and that investors will have difficulty achieving returns above market average without incurring additional risk. These findings are relevant for players operating in these regional markets.

Table 4. Summary table of the Lo and Mackinlay (1988) tests on the capital markets of eight Central and Eastern European countries from January 1, 2021, to February 23, 2022

Null Hypothesis: BET is a random walk			
Joint Tests	**Value**	**df**	**Probability**
Max |z| (at period 16)	1.2279	298	0.4466
Wald (Chi-Square)	8.8352	4	0.0592
Individual Tests			
Period	**Var. Ratio**	**Std. Error**	**z-Statistic**	**Probability**
2	1.0320	0.0579	0.5531	0.5773
4	1.1127	0.1083	1.0401	0.2943
8	0.9581	0.1713	-0.2440	0.7923
16	0.6869	0.2549	-1.2275	0.2184
Null Hypothesis: BUX is a random walk				
Joint Tests	**Value**	**df**	**Probability**	
Max |z| (at period 16)	0.8564	298	0.7064	
Wald (Chi-Square)	2.3512	4	0.6772	
Individual Tests				
Period	**Var. Ratio**	**Std. Error**	**z-Statistic**	**Probability**
2	1.0220	0.05792	-0.3800	0.7030
4	0.9397	0.1083	-0.555	0.5692
8	0.8584	0.1713	-0.8258	0.4143
16	0.7816	0.2549	-0.8564	0.4247
Null Hypothesis: CROBEX is a random walk				
Joint Tests	**Value**	**df**	**Probability**	
Max |z| (at period 2)	0.7218	298	0.8082	
Wald (Chi-Square)	1.6031	4	0.8165	
Individual Tests				
Period	**Var. Ratio**	**Std. Error**	**z-Statistic**	**Probability**
2	1.0418	0.0579	0.7218	0.4770
4	1.0231	0.1083	0.2131	0.8260
8	1.0705	0.1713	0.4115	0.6752
16	1.0765	0.2549	0.3001	0.7833
Null Hypothesis: MOEX is a random walk				
Joint Tests	**Value**	**df**	**Probability**	
Max |z| (at period 4)	2.0419	298	0.0886	

continued on following page

Table 4. Continued

Wald (Chi-Square)		12.1036	4	0.0245
Individual Tests				
Period	**Var. Ratio**	**Std. Error**	**z-Statistic**	**Probability**
2	0.9896	0.0579	-0.1789	0.8320
4	0.7785	0.1083	-2.0419	0.0296
8	0.6794	0.1713	-1.8708	0.0556
16	0.4971	0.2549	-1.9719	0.0374
Null Hypothesis: PRAGUE is a random walk				
Joint Tests		**Value**	**df**	**Probability**
Max |z| (at period 16)		1.1344	298	0.5235
Wald (Chi-Square)		5.4261	4	0.2614
Individual Tests				
Period	**Var. Ratio**	**Std. Error**	**z-Statistic**	**Probability**
2	1.0322	0.0579	0.5562	0.5780
4	1.0382	0.1083	0.3529	0.7110
8	0.9955	0.1713	-0.0260	0.9862
16	0.7107	0.2549	-1.1344	0.3036
Null Hypothesis: SAX 16 is a random walk				
Joint Tests		**Value**	**df**	**Probability**
Max |z| (at period 2)		3.9181	298	0.0014
Wald (Chi-Square)		17.7701	4	0.0030
Individual Tests				
Period	**Var. Ratio**	**Std. Error**	**z-Statistic**	**Probability**
2	0.7730	0.0579	-3.9181	0.0000
4	0.5901	0.1083	-3.7816	0.0010
8	0.4684	0.1713	-3.1023	0.0030
16	0.2760	0.2549	-2.8399	0.0010
Null Hypothesis: SBI TOP is a random walk				
Joint Tests		**Value**	**df**	**Probability**
Max |z| (at period 4)		0.7432	298	0.8057
Wald (Chi-Square)		0.6963	4	0.9662
Individual Tests				
Period	**Var. Ratio**	**Std. Error**	**z-Statistic**	**Probability**
2	1.0404	0.0579	0.6976	0.4982
4	1.0805	0.1083	0.7432	0.4756

continued on following page

Table 4. Continued

8	1.0796	0.1713	0.4649	0.6486
16	1.0534	0.2549	0.2096	0.8353

Null Hypothesis: SOFIX is a random walk				
Joint Tests		**Value**	**df**	**Probability**
Max |z| (at period 2)		1.1182	298	0.5353
Wald (Chi-Square)		7.8753	4	0.1127

Individual Tests				
Period	**Var. Ratio**	**Std. Error**	**z-Statistic**	**Probability**
2	0.9352	0.0579	-1.1182	0.2910
4	1.0208	0.1083	0.1920	0.8554
8	1.0145	0.1713	0.0846	0.9341
16	0.8074	0.2549	-0.7550	0.4889

Note: Standard error estimates assume no heteroscedasticity. User-specified lags: 2 4 8 16. Test probabilities computed using permutation bootstrap: reps = 1000.

Source: Own elaboration.

In the Conflict period, the stock indices of Romania (BET), Bulgaria (SOFIX), Slovakia (SAX 16), Hungary (BUX), Croatia (CROBEX), Russia (MOEX), the Czech Republic (PRAGUE SE PX), and Slovenia (SBI TOP) can be observed over the period from February 24, 2022 to November 23, 2023. Based on the results, it can be seen that Romania's capital market (BET) shows positive serial autocorrelation on days 2 and 4, but when looking at lags 8 and 16, the market is in equilibrium. The Russian market shows positive serial autocorrelation only for the 2-day lag; for the other lags, the market shows efficiency in its weak form. The Slovak stock index (SAX 16) shows negative serial autocorrelation for the lags from 2 to 16 days, showing that investors reacted negatively to the information that flowed into the market. In addition, it also found that the Slovenian capital market (SBI TOP) showed positive serial autocorrelation, which demonstrates the presence of exaggerated reactions on the part of investors to the new information that was flowing into this market. The markets of Bulgaria (SOFIX), Hungary (BUX), Croatia (CROBEX), and the Czech Republic (PRAGUE SE PX) did not reject the random walk hypothesis. In other words, these markets show that they are in equilibrium and that the existence of overreactions on the part of investors is not significant. The answer to the research question was partially accepted, i.e., the Russian invasion of Ukraine in 2022 led to the presence of overreactions in these regional markets (4 out of 8 possible markets).

Table 5. Summary table of the Lo and Mackinlay (1988) tests on the capital markets of eight Central and Eastern European countries from February 24, 2022, to November 23, 2023

Null Hypothesis: BET is a random walk			
Joint Tests	**Value**	**df**	**Probability**
Max |z| (at period 2)	3.6112	455	0.0030
Wald (Chi-Square)	15.6202	4	0.0050
Individual Tests			
Period	**Var. Ratio**	**Std. Error**	**z-Statistic**	**Probability**
2	1.1692	0.0468	3.6112	0.0020
4	1.2476	0.0877	2.8237	0.0040
8	1.1939	0.1386	1.3985	0.1736
16	1.2177	0.2063	1.0554	0.3157
Null Hypothesis: BUX is a random walk				
Joint Tests	**Value**	**df**	**Probability**	
Max |z| (at period 8)	1.0277	455	0.5510	
Wald (Chi-Square)	5.3968	4	0.2447	
Individual Tests				
Period	**Var. Ratio**	**Std. Error**	**z-Statistic**	**Probability**
2	1.0324	0.0468	0.6929	0.4734
4	0.9335	0.0877	-0.7578	0.4387
8	0.8574	0.1386	-1.0277	0.2919
16	0.84509	0.2063	-0.7508	0.4462
Null Hypothesis: CROBEX is a random walk				
Joint Tests	**Value**	**df**	**Probability**	
Max |z| (at period 16)	1.5495	455	0.2655	
Wald (Chi-Square)	2.6781	4	0.6473	
Individual Tests				
Period	**Var. Ratio**	**Std. Error**	**z-Statistic**	**Probability**
2	1.0349	0.0468	0.7463	0.4529
4	1.0761	0.0877	0.8667	0.3812
8	1.1608	0.1386	1.1599	0.2626
16	1.3197	0.2063	1.5495	0.1279
Null Hypothesis: MOEX is a random walk				
Joint Tests	**Value**	**df**	**Probability**	
Max |z| (at period 2)	2.4325	455	0.0393	

continued on following page

Table 5. Continued

	Wald (Chi-Square)		6.6885	4	0.1689
Individual Tests					

Period	Var. Ratio	Std. Error	z-Statistic	Probability
2	1.1149	0.0468	2.4325	0.0146
4	1.1269	0.0877	1.4469	0.1528
8	1.1168	0.1386	0.8428	0.4062
16	1.0891	0.2063	0.4319	0.6974

Null Hypothesis: PRAGUE is a random walk

Joint Tests	Value	df	Probability
Max |z| (at period 4)	1.6013	455	0.2397
Wald (Chi-Square)	5.7763	4	0.2159

Individual Tests

Period	Var. Ratio	Std. Error	z-Statistic	Probability
2	1.0115	0.0468	0.2471	0.8188
4	1.1404	0.0877	1.6013	0.1145
8	1.1998	0.1386	1.4408	0.1655
16	1.2292	0.2063	1.1107	0.2982

Null Hypothesis: SAX 16 is a random walk

Joint Tests	Value	df	Probability
Max |z| (at period 2)	3.6927	455	0.0012
Wald (Chi-Square)	15.6488	4	0.0044

Individual Tests

Period	Var. Ratio	Std. Error	z-Statistic	Probability
2	0.8268	0.0468	-3.6927	0.0000
4	0.6878	0.0877	-3.5589	0.0000
8	0.6230	0.1386	-2.7184	0.0030
16	0.5047	0.2063	-2.3999	0.0070

Null Hypothesis: SBI TOP is a random walk

Joint Tests	Value	df	Probability
Max |z| (at period 4)	3.9877	455	0.0000
Wald (Chi-Square)	16.8352	4	0.0040

Individual Tests

Period	Var. Ratio	Std. Error	z-Statistic	Probability
2	1.1762	0.0468	3.7592	0.0000
4	1.3497	0.0877	3.9877	0.0000

continued on following page

Table 5. Continued

8	1.4653	0.1386	3.3559	0.0010
16	1.5392	0.2063	2.6139	0.0050

Null Hypothesis: SOFIX is a random walk				
Joint Tests		**Value**	**df**	**Probability**
Max |z| (at period 16)		0.8045	455	0.7770
Wald (Chi-Square)		2.0293	4	0.7600
Individual Tests				
Period	**Var. Ratio**	**Std. Error**	**z-Statistic**	**Probability**
2	0.9843	0.0468	-0.3347	0.7370
4	0.9711	0.0877	-0.3285	0.7520
8	1.0245	0.1386	0.1770	0.8700
16	1.1660	0.2063	0.8045	0.4600

Note: Standard error estimates assume no heteroscedasticity. User-specified lags: 2 4 8 16. Test probabilities computed using permutation bootstrap: reps = 1000.

Source: Own elaboration.

5. CONCLUSION

The study aimed to assess whether the 2022 event triggered overreactions by investors in the capital markets of eight Central and Eastern European countries. The results revealed interesting patterns, especially during the period leading up to and following the Russian invasion of Ukraine. During the pre-conflict period, negative serial autocorrelation was found in the Russian and Slovak capital markets, indicating that price movements were not entirely random and were influenced by past movements. This suggests possible overreactions by investors to market information. During the Russian invasion of Ukraine in 2022, positive serial autocorrelations were observed on some specific days in the capital markets of Romania, Russia, Slovakia, and Slovenia, suggesting investor overreactions at those times. However, other markets, such as Bulgaria, Hungary, Croatia, and the Czech Republic, showed no significant evidence of overreactions. These results indicate that the answer to the research question is partial: the Russian invasion of Ukraine in 2022 provoked overreactions in some regional markets, but not uniformly. In practical terms, the study's conclusion suggests that investors operating in these regional markets should exercise caution and consider their risk tolerance before investing. Analyzing market trends and adapting investment strategies as necessary are recommended. In a context of geopolitical uncertainty, continuous attention to ongoing developments and prudence in decision-making are crucial for investors wishing to trade successfully in these markets.

REFERENCES

Antweiler, W., & Frank, M. Z. (2011). Do US Stock Markets Typically Overreact to Corporate News Stories? SSRN *Electronic Journal*. 10.2139/ssrn.878091

Appiah-Otoo, I. (2023). The Impact of the Russia-Ukraine War on the Cryptocurrency Market. *Asian Economics Letters*, 4(1). Advance online publication. 10.46557/001c.53110

Breitung, J. (2000). The local power of some unit root tests for panel data. *Advances in Econometrics*, 15, 161–177. Advance online publication. 10.1016/S0731-9053(00)15006-6

Caporale, G. M., & Plastun, A. (2019). On stock price overreactions: Frequency, seasonality and information content. *Journal of Applied Econometrics*, 22(1), 602–621. Advance online publication. 10.1080/15140326.2019.1692509

Chen, M. W., & Zhu, J. (2005). Do Investors in Chinese Stock Market Overreact? *Journal of Accounting and Finance Research*, 13(3).

Choi, I. (2001). Unit root tests for panel data. *Journal of International Money and Finance*, 20(2), 249–272. 10.1016/S0261-5606(00)00048-6

De Bondt, W. F. M., & Thaler, R. (1985). Does the Stock Market Overreact? *The Journal of Finance*, 40(3), 793–805. Advance online publication. 10.1111/j.1540-6261.1985.tb05004.x

De Bondt, W. F. M., & Thaler, R. H. (1987). Further Evidence on Investor Overreaction and Stock Market Seasonality. *The Journal of Finance*, 42(3), 557–581. Advance online publication. 10.1111/j.1540-6261.1987.tb04569.x

De Bondt, W. F. M., & Thaler, R. H. (2012). Do Analysts Overreact? *Heuristics and Biases*. 10.1017/CBO9780511808098.040

Dias, R., Chambino, M., & Rebolo Horta, N. (2023). Long-Term Dependencies in Central European Stock Markets: A Crisp-Set Analysis. *Economic Analysis Letters*, 2(February), 10–17. 10.58567/eal02010002

Dias, R., Horta, N., & Chambino, M. (2023). Clean Energy Action Index Efficiency: An Analysis in Global Uncertainty Contexts. *Energies*, 16(9), 3937. Advance online publication. 10.3390/en16093937

Dias, R., Horta, N., Chambino, M., Alexandre, P., & Heliodoro, P. (2022). A Multiple Fluctuations and Detrending Analysis of Financial Market Efficiency: Comparison of Central and Eastern European Stock Indexes. *International Scientific-Business Conference – LIMEN 2022:* Vol 8.*Conference Proceedings*, 11–21. 10.31410/LIMEN.2022.11

Dias, R., Horta, N. R., & Chambino, M. (2023). Portfolio rebalancing in times of stress: Capital markets vs. Commodities. *Journal of Economic Analysis*, 9(1), 129–151. 10.58567/jea02010005

Dias, R., Pereira, J. M., & Carvalho, L. C. (2022). Are African Stock Markets Efficient? A Comparative Analysis Between Six African Markets, the UK, Japan and the USA in the Period of the Pandemic. *Naše Gospodarstvo/Our Economy, 68*(1), 35–51. 10.2478/ngoe-2022-0004

Dias, R., Teixeira, N., Machova, V., Pardal, P., Horak, J., & Vochozka, M. (2020). Random walks and market efficiency tests: Evidence on US, Chinese and European capital markets within the context of the global Covid-19 pandemic. *Oeconomia Copernicana*, 11(4), 585–608. Advance online publication. 10.24136/oc.2020.024

Dias, R. M. T. S., Chambino, M., Alexandre, P., Morais da Palma, C., & Almeida, L. (2023). Unveiling Bitcoin's Safe Haven and Hedging Properties Beyond Diversification. *Advances in Web Technologies and Engineering*, (November), 380–410. Advance online publication. 10.4018/978-1-6684-9039-6.ch018

Dias, R. T., Chambino, M., Palma, C., Almeida, L., & Alexandre, P. (2023). Overreaction, Underreaction, and Short-Term Efficient Reaction Evidence for Cryptocurrencies. *Advances in Web Technologies and Engineering*, (November), 288–312. 10.4018/978-1-6684-9039-6.ch014

Dickey, D., & Fuller, W. (1981). Likelihood ratio statistics for autoregressive time series with a unit root. *Econometrica*, 49(4), 1057–1072. 10.2307/1912517

Fama, E. F. (1965). Random Walks in Stock Market Prices. *Financial Analysts Journal*, 21(5), 55–59. Advance online publication. 10.2469/faj.v21.n5.55

Fama, E. F. (1970). Efficient Capital Markets: A Review of Theory and Empirical Work. *The Journal of Finance*, 25(2), 383. Advance online publication. 10.2307/2325486

Fama, E. F., & French, K. R. (1993). Common risk factors in the returns on stocks and bonds. *Journal of Financial Economics*, 33(1), 3–56. 10.1016/0304-405X(93)90023-5

Guedes, E. F., Santos, R. P. C., Figueredo, L. H. R., Da Silva, P. A., Dias, R. M. T. S., & Zebende, G. F. (2022). Efficiency and Long-Range Correlation in G-20 Stock Indexes: A Sliding Windows Approach. *Fluctuation and Noise Letters*, 21(4), 2250033. Advance online publication. 10.1142/S021947752250033X

Huo, X., & Qiu, Z. (2020). How does China's stock market react to the announcement of the COVID-19 pandemic lockdown? *Economic and Political Studies*, 8(4), 436–461. Advance online publication. 10.1080/20954816.2020.1780695

Im, K. S., Pesaran, M. H., & Shin, Y. (2003). Testing for unit roots in heterogeneous panels. *Journal of Econometrics*, 115(1), 53–74. Advance online publication. 10.1016/S0304-4076(03)00092-7

Jarque, C. M., & Bera, A. K. (1980). Efficient tests for normality, homoscedasticity and serial independence of regression residuals. *Economics Letters*, 6(3), 255–259. 10.1016/0165-1765(80)90024-5

Johannesson, J., & Clowes, D. (2022). Energy Resources and Markets - Perspectives on the Russia-Ukraine War. *European Review (Chichester, England)*, 30(1), 4–23. 10.1017/S1062798720001040

Khalfaoui, R., Gozgor, G., & Goodell, J. W. (2023). Impact of Russia-Ukraine war attention on cryptocurrency: Evidence from quantile dependence analysis. *Finance Research Letters*, 52, 103365. Advance online publication. 10.1016/j.frl.2022.103365

Levin, A., Lin, C. F., & Chu, C. S. J. (2002). Unit root tests in panel data: Asymptotic and finite-sample properties. *Journal of Econometrics*, 108(1), 1–24. Advance online publication. 10.1016/S0304-4076(01)00098-7

Lo, A. W., & MacKinlay, A. C. (1988). Stock Market Prices Do Not Follow Random Walks: Evidence from a Simple Specification Test. *Review of Financial Studies*, 1(1), 41–66. Advance online publication. 10.1093/rfs/1.1.41

Phillips, P. C. B., & Perron, P. (1988). Testing for a unit root in time series regression. *Biometrika*, 75(2), 335–346. 10.1093/biomet/75.2.335

Piñeiro-Chousa, J., López-Cabarcos, M. Á., & Šević, A. (2022). Green bond market and Sentiment: Is there a switching Behaviour? *Journal of Business Research*, 141, 520–527. Advance online publication. 10.1016/j.jbusres.2021.11.048

Rosenthal, L. (1983). An empirical test of the efficiency of the ADR market. *Journal of Banking & Finance*, 7(1), 17–29. 10.1016/0378-4266(83)90053-5

Saji, T. G. (2023). Mean reversals and stock market overreactions: Further evidence from India. *Afro-Asian Journal of Finance and Accounting*, 13(4), 467–477. Advance online publication. 10.1504/AAJFA.2023.132959

Santana, T. P., Horta, N., Revez, C., Dias, R. M. T. S., & Zebende, G. F. (2023). Effects of Interdependence and Contagion on Crude Oil and Precious Metals According to ρDCCA: A COVID-19 Case Study. *Sustainability (Basel)*, 15(5), 3945. Advance online publication. 10.3390/su15053945

Shiller, R. J. (2003). From Efficient Markets Theory to Behavioral Finance The 1980s and Excess Volatility. *Journal of Economic Perspectives, 17*(1).

Chapter 8
An Impact of AI and Client Acquisition Strategies in Real Capital Ventures

S. Dhanabagiyam
http://orcid.org/0000-0002-5268-178X
NSB Academy, India

Boopathy Srihari
Christ University, Pune, India

ABSTRACT

In the contemporary business environment, marked by rapid changes, client acquisition stands out as a pivotal factor for companies aiming at sustained growth, particularly in sectors such as finance and real estate. The ability to attract and retain clients is not only a measure of a company's current success but also a fundamental driver for its future viability. This study focuses on Real Capital Ventures LLP, a company operating at the intersection of finance and real estate, aiming to unravel the intricacies of its client acquisition strategies. The overarching goal is to conduct an exhaustive examination of the current approaches employed by the firm and provide nuanced recommendations for refinement. By doing so, the study aspires to contribute to the enhancement of the effectiveness of Real Capital Ventures LLP's client acquisition, ensuring its continued success in a fiercely competitive market.

DOI: 10.4018/979-8-3693-3322-8.ch008

1. INTRODUCTION

In most countries, housing is the most widely held kind of wealth from a social perspective. Because of this and the way rental markets function, housing plays a significant role in determining the distribution of welfare as well as its average level (Ullah & Sepasgozar, 2020). It is also not surprising that all governments intervene in the housing market in some way through a variety of taxes, subsidies, regulations, and occasionally direct public provision because housing is a good that is characterized by significant external costs and benefits, i.e. costs and benefits that are not paid directly/received by individual market participants. However, the effectiveness of these therapies varies greatly (Manconi et al., 2012). National perspectives on sectoral growth in the real estate industry may range greatly depending on a multitude of factors, including current economic conditions, governmental laws, demographic trends, emerging technology, and more (Rahmawati et al., 2021). Keep the following things in mind to understand sectoral growth in the real estate sector from a national perspective: Numerous elements, such as technical improvements, market dynamics, and shifting, consumer tastes, have an impact on the worldwide perspectives on sectoral expansion of client acquisition techniques in the real estate business. The following are some significant developments and viewpoints about customer acquisition tactics in the real estate industry. The real estate sector has recently undergone a digital shift. The use of digital marketing techniques by real estate firms to attract customers is on the rise. These techniques include social media advertising, email marketing, and search engine optimization (SEO) (Rosenthal & Brito, 2017). Digital technologies for online transactions and virtual property tours have become more popular as a result of the COVID-19 epidemic. Strategies for acquiring new clients that are data-driven are becoming increasingly common. To better identify their target customers, hone their marketing messages, and improve their sales funnels, real estate businesses are using data analytics. They can more easily identify potential customers as a result (Dash & Chakraborty, 2021).

Technology and Urbanization as Key Drivers of Retail Business

Digital inclusion is the key issue due to the limited access of the rural communities (Ko et al., 2019) examined the application effects of information and communications technology (ICT) on rural community development with various sustainable developmental goals (SDGs, 2015) with various goals like literacy rate of technology (Goal-5), developing industry-infrastructure facilities (Goal-9).

Challenges been also identified to increase the skillset on usage of software and hardware. Reduced professional income.

The more intention and focus are required on the importance of rural population hence, Fennell et al. (2018) also examined the linkages between smart villages and smart cities in the Indian context. There is now a great deal of focus on creating smart cities. Using the new waves of ICTs, cities are being transformed. Both the soft and hard technologies are being looked into for providing the public services and managing the demand for those services. Often those endeavours remain concentrated within the urban areas.

The Emergence of Online Platforms and Switch to Online Retail

Technology can offer several advantages to address the challenges of urbanization and spatial inequalities (Steel et al., 2013). However, technology can also create further divides if the access is constrained. As discussed above, providing goods and services through digital technology driven channels is the key focus. The traditional marketplace is fast transforming into digital mega-market, reaching millions at a time and aiming to provide economic goods and services in a frictionless manner (Fornari et al., 2016). Retail business has been Real estate transactions might be streamlined and made safer and more transparent with the use of block chain technology. By easing the friction involved in real estate transactions, this technology can help speed up customer acquisition. Client interest in ecologically and socially responsible real estate investments is rising. Businesses that prioritize sustainability and environmental, social, and governance (ESG) principles in their initiatives may have a competitive edge in attracting new customers (Fennel et al., 2018). Many of the studies been highlighted about the physical stores and online stores and synergy effect on online shopping and instore shopping (Bosman et al., 2013). Examining linkages between smart villages and smart cities: Learning from rural youth accessing the internet in India. Because the real estate sector is so regionally focused, businesses are adjusting their client acquisition plans to fit certain areas. Success requires an understanding of the distinctive traits and requirements of local markets. Building strategic alliances with other companies, such mortgage brokers, home inspectors, and regional community groups, may be a successful customer acquisition approach. In the real estate industry, networking and recommendations are crucial.

Online real estate markets and platforms have grown in popularity, enabling customers to search homes and communicate directly with brokers or sellers (Baen, 2000). To properly compete on these platforms, real estate agents must have a strong online presence. Maintaining and gaining new clients depend on delivering excellent customer experiences. In order to handle customer contacts more efficiently and provide individualized services, real estate businesses are investing in CRM (Customer Relationship Management) systems.

Portfolio selection of customers been selected and widely used ever since. Nearly two types of decision making are required when it comes to stock selection like invest and divest. Spinning of non-core asset been used in Real Estate Investment Trusts (REITs) as well as property funds (Parker, 2016). Jones and Livingstone (2015) always examine the decrease of demand for many of the retail space near the future based on their empirical findings, the tiny retailers in their presence look into the valid empirical findings, due to the small space in the retail of the strategy. Real estate sector been highly significant in announcing the retail park sector. Which is evidenced by the retail property sector in 2020, the retail property investors adjust their portfolio against the tenants will be in onside of investing the investor. Hammerson (2020) has planned to optimize the London office reimagine retail which includes hotels, leisure and retail parks in October 2020 (Landsec, 2020).

2. BACKGROUND OF THE RESEARCH

There has been a significant trend in recent years toward online marketing and digital presence. To contact potential clients, real estate brokers and businesses are increasingly turning to websites, social media platforms, and online advertising. In order to effectively target particular demographics and geographic areas for national growth in this industry, digital marketing methods must be optimized.

The application of data analytics and artificial intelligence (AI) in the acquisition of real estate clients is growing (Marler & Boudreau, 2017). Data-driven insights are used to discover new customers, forecast industry trends, and customize marketing campaigns as part of the sector in national expansion. Lead generating services and platforms are frequently used by real estate professionals to find clients. These websites link buyers and sellers by collecting real estate listings. Developing more advanced lead generating technologies and methods is a must for national progress.

In 2023, Indian real estate developers working in the nation's largest cities are expected to complete over 558,000 residences, which will be a remarkable accomplishment (Chalutz Ben-Gal, 2019). In the first nine months of FY22, approximately 1,700 acres of land were transacted in India's top eight cities. From 2017 to 2021, there were 10.3 billion dollars in foreign investments in the commercial real estate market. Developers anticipate that with the replacement of the old SEZs legislation, demand for office spaces in SEZs would soar as of February 2022.

Using infrastructure and real estate investment trusts, Indian businesses are predicted to raise more than Rs.3.5 trillion (US$ 48 billion) in 2022, up from the US$ 29 billion raised so far.

The top six cities experienced 8.3 million square feet of net office absorption in the first quarter of 2023 (January to March).

In the first quarter of 2023 (January to March), new real estate debuts in India's top seven cities took home a 41% share, up from 26% during the same time period in 2014. Over 41% of the 1.14 lakh units sold in the top seven cities during the first quarter of 2023 were newly released products.

Between July and September 2021, the third quarter of 2021, there were 65,211 new housing units, an increase of 228% year over year among the top eight cities. The commercial sector is anticipated to see rising investments in 2021–2022. For instance,the Chintels Group announced in October 2021 that it would invest Rs.400 crores (US$ 53.47 million) in the development of a new commercial Complex.

In contrast to the required building pace of five houses per 1,000 people, according to the Economic Times Housing Finance Summit, only approximately three houses are created per 1,000 people annually. An estimated 10 million housing units are currently needed in urban areas. By 2030, the country would need an additional 25 million affordable dwelling units to accommodate the increase in the urban population.

Figure 1. Market of real estate in India (US$ billion)

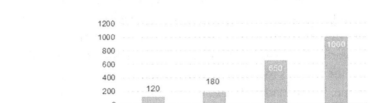

In 2023, Indian real estate developers working in the nation's largest cities are expected to complete over 558,000 residences, which will be a remarkable accomplishment. In the first nine months of FY22, approximately 1,700 acres of land were transacted in India's top eight cities. From 2017 to 2021, there were 10.3 billion dollars in foreign investments in the commercial real estate market. Developers anticipate that with the replacement of the old SEZs legislation, demand for office spaces in SEZs would soar as of February 2022.

Using infrastructure and real estate investment trusts, Indian businesses are predicted to raise more than Rs.3.5 trillion (US$ 48 billion) in 2022, up from the US$ 29 billion raised so far. The top six cities experienced 8.3 million square feet of net office absorption in the first quarter of 2023 (January to March).

In the first quarter of 2023 (January to March), new real estate debuts in India's top seven cities took home a 41% share, up from 26% during the same time period in 2014. Over 41% of the 1.14 lakh units sold in the top seven cities during the first quarter of 2023 were newly released products.

Between July and September 2021, the third quarter of 2021, there were 65,211 new housing units, an increase of 228% year over year among the top eight cities. The commercial sector is anticipated to see rising investments in 2021–2022. For instance, the Chintels Group announced in October 2021 that it would invest Rs.400 crores (US$ 53.47 million) in the development of a new commercial complex in Gurugram that would be 9.28 lakh square feet in size. In Q1 2023, commercial real estate transactions quadrupled to 1.5 million square feet.

In contrast to the required building pace of five houses per 1,000 people, according to the Economic Times Housing Finance Summit, only approximately three houses are created per 1,000 people annually. An estimated 10 million housing units are currently needed in urban areas. By 2030, the country would need an additional 25 million affordable dwelling units to accommodate the increase in the urban population. Castro (2023, "The residential real estate sector lags behind in terms of technical advancement."). Brokers must adjust to surroundings that are dynamic and reliant on technology. The best opportunity for businesses to survive is through innovation and retraining. This thesis discusses the appeal of the European market and examines the key technological advances in the sector. Additionally, the function of intermediaries is covered and connected to contemporary digital platforms. An insight on the broker's role is provided by evaluating the platform model environment in Europe. While marketplaces and multiple listing services may help brokers (Sihotang & Hudrasyah, 2023). Evaluation of customer journeys is required to show the points of contact that customers may have with businesses. Given the growing complexity of providing the services that customers need, it is crucial to comprehend the customer journey. The whole of a customer's digital engagements with a company is referred to as the "digital customer journey," which also includes information about transactions, browsing history across all platforms, and interactions with online customer support. Brands may create a communication strategy that converses with consumers by using digital customer journey mapping. The brand can observe existing and planned client journeys as well as crucial touch points across multiple marketing channels by monitoring its digital consumer journeys. Autio et al. (2023) was to pinpoint the strategic pillars upon which real estate investors build their plans. The present study presented the ideas for these strategic themes in the form of an IREM framework, which was based on prior research from CREM and real estate investment research, along with the ideas themselves. The purpose of the interviews was to see whether there may be support for both the IREM framework as a whole and for each individual proposition independently (Athira Azmil et al., 2021). Additionally, the Covid-19 pandemic's arrival has significantly shifted marketing strategies toward digital ones. Despite the enthusiasm for include VR in real estate marketing strategies, little is known about how this technology would affect prospective homebuyers' emotions and purchase intentions in comparison to traditional marketing methods employing physically constructed environments. The ambiance at physical stores or service providers may have a significant impact in evoking emotions that influence customers' favorable purchase behavior,

A study comparing the evaluations of participants on the atmosphere, enjoyment, and arousal feelings, as well as the purchase intention between a real environment and a virtual environment, was done with 60 actual prospective homebuyers. To test the proposed associations, partial least squares structural equation modeling (PLS-SEM) was used. The findings show that there is a considerable difference between the real and virtual environments in how prospective homebuyers assess the ambiance and buying intention. The PLS-SEM results showed that the environment considerably influences pleasure and arousal emotions, and that pleasure emotion greatly influences the intention to buy a house. The research's conclusions provide a significant contribution to improving the use of virtual reality in residential real estate marketing methods (Dash et al., 2021). An improvement to the old marketing model called marketing tries to take into account the effect of brand engagement in the digital era. This study analyzes 508 potential real estate first-time purchasers using structural equation modeling to determine the influence of marketing elements in increasing customer satisfaction and affecting purchase intentions. According to research, brand identity and brand image are crucial determinants of customer happiness and purchase intent. brand contact or integrity has no discernible impact on customers' pleasure or propensity to buy. This study offers significant insights into developing worldwide companies and their key future target market, taking into account the study's participants (Gen-Z/Millennial first-time homebuyers) and the foreign environment of the study (the northern Indian real estate market). Additionally, this study shows that a marketing strategy that emphasizes brand identification and brand image. As a result of the assessment of literature, identification of gaps in various sectors and as the world has recently been expanded to include socio-economic and financial kinds of entrepreneurial action (Dhanabagiyam et al., 2024).

3. RESEARCH QUESTIONS AND METHODOLOGY OF THE STUDY

How can real estate agents use digital marketing to attract new clients?

What are the essential phases and recommended methods for creating an effective customer acquisition strategy in the real estate sector

4. FINDINGS, SUGGESTION, AND CONCLUSION

How can real estate agents use digital marketing to attract new clients?

Figure 2. Use of customer relationship management (CRM) software of respondents to manage client acquisition

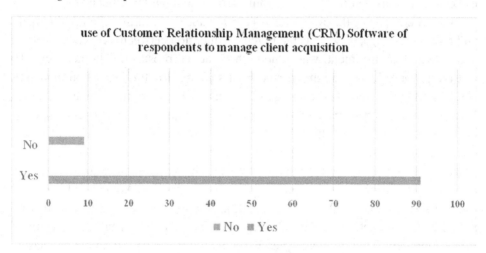

From the above (Figure 2) use of Customer Relationship Management (CRM) Software of respondents to manage client acquisition, out of a total of 100 respondents, the majority 91% of respondents are using Customer Relationship Management (CRM) software and the rest of the 9% respondents are using others sources for their client acquisition.

What are the essential phases and recommended methods for creating an effective customer acquisition strategy in the real estate sector.

Figure 3. Respondents of satisfied employees with their current client acquisition strategies

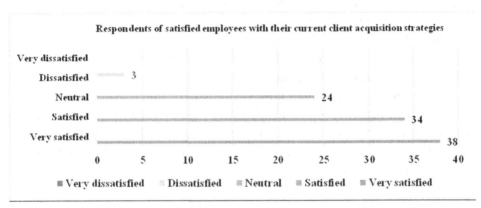

From the above (Figure 3), employees satisfied with their current client acquisition strategies, out of a total of 100 respondents, 38.4% employees are very satisfied with their current client acquisition strategies, 34.3% employees are satisfied with their current client acquisition strategies, 24.2% employees are neutral with their current client acquisition strategies, 3% employees are dissatisfied with their current client acquisition strategies and none of the employees is very dissatisfied with their current client acquisition strategies.

Determine Important Client Segments

To find possible client categories, examine the venture capital and real estate markets. Create thorough customer personas in order to comprehend the characteristics, inclinations, and problems of the intended audience.

Assess Present Approaches: To determine the advantages, disadvantages, opportunities, and threats associated with Real Capital Ventures LLP's current client acquisition strategy, do a SWOT analysis. Examine the company's online marketing initiatives, social media profiles, and website to see how well they draw in customers.

Competition Analysis: To find best practices for the industry, examine rivals' client acquisition methods in the real estate. Determine the unique selling proposition (USP) of Real Capital Ventures LLP and the ways in which their acquisition efforts emphasize these elements.

Digital Advertising Techniques: Investigate the efficacy of content marketing and search engine optimization (SEO) in drawing in online customers. Examine how social media advertising, particularly targeted marketing, affects the ability to contact prospective customers.

Client relationship management: CRM Systems, assess how well client interactions are managed and acquisition rates are increased by using CRM systems. Investigate the ways in which acquisition methods are improved by incorporating feedback from current clients.

Ethical Aspects: Moral Customer Acquisition Talk about the moral issues surrounding customer acquisition, making sure that the strategies used are just, open, and compliant with accepted practices in the field.

Suggestions and Upcoming Plans: On the basis of your research's conclusions, provide specific suggestions for enhancing Real Capital Ventures LLP's client acquisition tactics. upcoming trends Examine new developments in customer acquisition, such as Chabot's, AI-powered marketing, and customization, and suggest ways to incorporate them into the business's plans.

CONCLUSION

In summary, the research on client acquisition strategies, with special reference to Real Capital Ventures LLP, clarifies the important elements of gaining clients in the cutthroat business environment. The study examined the several approaches and strategies utilized by Real Capital Ventures LLP to successfully draw in and hold onto customers. Upon conducting an extensive examination of the organization's tactics, several significant conclusions have surfaced.

- It is clear that acquiring clients requires a multifaceted strategy. It's possible that using just one strategy won't produce the best outcomes. Real Capital Ventures LLP expanded its clientele through utilizing digital marketing, networking, and relationship development in an efficient manner that blended offline and online tactics.

- It is essential to comprehend the target audience. In order to determine the requirements, preferences, and pain points of its potential clientele, Real Capital Ventures LLP dedicated time and resources to market research. This comprehension made it easier to create customized plans that connected with the customers and built a solid rapport.

- It is impossible to exaggerate the importance of developing credibility and trust. Customers prefer to express themselves with an organization they are comfortable in. In order to build long-lasting relationships with its clients, Real Capital Ventures LLP placed a high value on openness, professionalism, and keeping their word.

- It is important to adjust to evolving trends and shifting market conditions. By using new technology and modifying their methods in response to market needs, Real Capital Ventures LLP showed flexibility. Their capacity to adapt allowed them to keep one step ahead of their competitors and satisfy their clients' changing requirements.

- The study highlights the importance of effective communication is. Real Capital Ventures LLP listened intently to their clients' opinions and concerns, keeping lines of communication open. In addition to quickly resolving problems, this two-way communication increased consumer loyalty and satisfaction.

- A comprehensive strategy that incorporates market knowledge, trust-building, flexibility, and first-rate communication is responsible for Real Capital Ventures LLP's success in client acquisition. Businesses looking to improve their customer acquisition tactics may learn a lot from Real Capital Ventures LLP's methods, which will help them maintain steady growth and a devoted clientele in the fast-paced business world of today.

REFERENCES

Baen, J. (2000). The effects of technology on retail sales. *Journal of Shopping Center Research*, 7, 85–101.

Bosman, J. (2011). Book shopping in stores, then buying online. *The New York Times*.

Burt, S., & Sparks, L. (2003). E-commerce and the retail process: A review. *Journal of Retailing and Consumer Services*, 10, 275–286.

Chalutz Ben-Gal, H. (2019). An ROI-based review of HR analytics: Practical implementation tools. *Personnel Review*, 48(6), 1429–1448.

Dash, G., & Chakraborty, D. (2021). Digital transformation of marketing strategies during a pandemic: Evidence from an emerging economy during COVID-19. *Sustainability*, 13(12), 6735.

Dhanabagiyam, S., Blessy Doe, M., Thamizhselvi, M., Irfan, M., Thalari, S. K., & Libeesh, P. C. (2024). Factors influencing growth of micro entrepreneurship in the hospitality industry: An empirical study in India. *Cogent Business & Management*, 11(1), 2285260.

Fennell, S., Kaur, P., Jhunjhunwala, A., Narayanan, D., Loyola, C., Bedi, J., & Singh, Y. (2018). Examining linkages between Smart Villages and Smart Cities: Learning from rural youth accessing the internet in India. *Telecommunications Policy*, 42(10), 810–823.

Irfan, M., Dhanabagiyam, S., Nayak, S. R., & Dias, R. (2024). Promotion of Rural Tourism Destination for Community and Sustainable Destination Development: An Indigenous Study. In *Achieving Sustainable Transformation in Tourism and Hospitality Sectors* (pp. 268–277). IGI Global.

Jedwab, R., Christiaensen, L., & Gindelsky, M. (2015). *Demography, urbanization and development: Rural push, urban pull and... urban push?* The World Bank.

Ko, G., Routray, J. K., & Ahmad, M. M. (2019). ICT infrastructure for rural community sustainability. *Community Development (Columbus, Ohio)*, 50(1), 51–72.

Manconi, A., Massa, M., & Yasuda, A. (2012). The role of institutional investors in propagating the crisis of 2007–2008. *Journal of Financial Economics*, 104(3), 491–518.

Marler, J. H., & Boudreau, J. W. (2017). An evidence-based review of HR Analytics. *International Journal of Human Resource Management*, 28(1), 3–26.

Parker, D. (2016). Property investment decision making by Australian unlisted property funds: An exploratory study. *Property Management*, 34(5), 381–395.

Rahmawati, D., Rahadi, R. A., Putri, A. D., & Bandung, E. (2021). The Current State of Property Development in Indonesia During the Covid-19 Pandemic. *International Journal of Innovation, Creativity and Change, 15*(7).

Steel, W., Daglish, T., Marriott, L., Gemmell, N., & Howell, B. (2013). *E-Commerce and its effect upon the Retail Industry and Government Revenue.* Academic Press.

Ullah, F., Sepasgozar, S. M., Thaheem, M. J., & Al-Turjman, F. (2021). Barriers to the digitalisation and innovation of Australian Smart Real Estate: A managerial perspective on the technology non-adoption. *Environmental Technology & Innovation*, 22, 101527.

Chapter 9
The Application of AI in New Start-ups:
A Descriptive Inquiry That Emphasizes Sustainable Elements

P. C. Libeesh
https://orcid.org/0009-0006-0369-5460
CMR Institute of Technology, India

Mohammad Irfan
NSB Academy, India

Sylva Alif Rusmita
University of Airlangga, Indonesia

Lissy George
Mount Tabor Training College, Pathanapuram, India

ABSTRACT

This research explores the dynamic interactions between artificial intelligence (AI) and start-ups, with a particular emphasis on sustainable aspects and a thorough investigation of their symbiotic relationship. In order to explore the various ways that AI technologies support the viability of start-ups in a variety of industries, the research uses a descriptive study approach. A detailed examination of the literature is incorporated into the investigation, which analyses accepted theories and models about sustainability, entrepreneurship, and artificial intelligence. The goal of the study is to provide a comprehensive understanding of how AI-driven innovations improve operational efficiency, encourage environmentally friendly practices, and support social inclusion within the entrepreneurial landscape by integrating existing

DOI: 10.4018/979-8-3693-3322-8.ch009

evidence. This descriptive study offers insightful insights for academics and business practitioners alike, adding to the continuing conversation about the complex relationship between artificial intelligence (AI) and the sustainability of start-ups.

INTRODUCTION

Artificial intelligence (AI) is widely used in all most all fields of human's life, like agriculture, business, manufacturing, finance etc. Artificial intelligence is a technology of using machine as intelligence of human being. It means all the work whatever humans are doing can be done by using the machines. Human being are facing lot of problems in solving various complexities in their daily life including financing, investing and utilisation of resources etc. The recent explosion of AI, made possible by ever-rising amounts of data and computing power, has given rise to the field of AI ethics—the study of ethical and societal issues facing developers, producers, consumers, citizens, policy makers, and civil society organizations (van Wynsberghe, 2021). Artificial intelligence can be streamline the entrepreneurs in market research, personalised marketing and customer engagement, increase the operational efficiency, enhancing product development, Financial analysis and Decision making, cyber security and prevention of fraud, Scaling customer support, predictive analytics of business growth, and legal and compliant assistance.

Experience is very big matter to start a business but how experience will make use to adapt to the situation like technological change, consumer taste and preference, and government policy etc. Artificial Intelligence (AI) and internet of things (IOT) are having a major role in sustainability of start-up. Managerial attention on AI and Big Data (BD) – in combination with environmental responsiveness – can affect entrepreneurs expectations regarding available opportunities (Bickley et al., n.d.). Expectations on life is leading the people to live same in the start-up like expectation of the future profit, expansion, diversification modernisation are motivating the people to do more investment and effort on the start-up. There is no doubt on that, there is a higher impact and role of AI in sustainable development of entrepreneurship. Hence it is highly relevant to discuss the role and influence of AI in sustainability of entrepreneurship. Several societal stakeholders must play a central role in advancing the sustainability agenda, and business has an important role to play as sustainability is not a set of requirements but an optimal outcome (Kushwaha, n.d.).

It has been observed that many start-ups have pursued digital transformation strategies, reinforcing their workforce and services to incorporate digital technology (Borges et al. 2021. Digital technology, especially Artificial Intelligence giving wide scope of expansion, growth, modernisation, and diversification according to the requirement of the market and customers. Furthermore, the development of AI-based business models is growing as part of the effort to guarantee the success of digital transformation plans (Verhoef et al. 2021). As every were it enhanced the digital transformation the role of AI having wide coverage in all sectors of business. Artificial Intelligence (AI) encompasses natural language processing, machine learning, and deep learning. It provides broad and varied data analysis capabilities for various industries, making corporate administration, planning, and operations easier (Kasemsap 2017).

Sustainability of Start-Ups and AI

In a variety of industries, artificial intelligence (AI) is a critical component in supporting the viability of companies. The optimization of resource use and operational efficiency is one of the key contributions. Startups may improve their entire environmental footprint by streamlining supply chains, cutting energy costs, and minimizing waste by utilizing predictive analytics and machine learning algorithms. Radical innovators, such as startup entrepreneurs, are needed to assist address today's sustainability concerns. They need to come up with innovative ways to stop illnesses from spreading, pollution from sources, and unsustainable resource use (Tiba et al., 2021). Sustainable business models are further promoted by AI-driven advances in circular economy activities, such as developing items for lifetime and streamlining recycling procedures. Artificial intelligence (AI) improves routes and logistics in the field of supply chain management, which lowers transportation costs and has a less environmental impact. Furthermore, as a means of tackling the issues raised by rapid urbanization, firms that employ AI to improve urban planning and smart building technologies also encourage the growth of eco-friendly infrastructure and smart cities.

AI-powered precision agriculture makes it possible for newcomers in the agricultural industry to implement sustainable farming methods by maximizing resource efficiency and reducing environmental effect. Furthermore, AI makes it easier to create renewable energy solutions by giving entrepreneurs the resources they need to effectively integrate clean energy sources into the electrical grid. AI-driven solutions that improve access to healthcare, education, and other necessities while fostering equality and diversity also address social sustainability. Startups that adopt ethical and responsible AI methods not only help to conserve the environment but also cultivate trust among stakeholders and promote a sustainable culture that extends beyond financial concerns to a more resilient and responsible future. Tools that are in line with well-established management practices—like an environmental management system, supply chain management, risk analysis, sustainability management, and training and education—are the most useful for small enterprises (Halberstadt et al., 2014). Marketing is essential to the viability of startups, and in the context of Marketing 4.0, its importance will only grow. The administration of marketing must penetrate every stage of the startup's development (Petru et al., 2019). The digital communication capabilities have a lot of room for improvement, which will impact the companies' exposure and positioning. Therefore, if these businesses align their corporate identity with ideas connected to the SDGs, CSR, and circular economy for a state of well-being of stakeholders in the present and future, they have a wonderful potential to stand out from the competition (Torres-Mancera et al., 2023).

Review of Literature

AI may help entrepreneurs make better judgments and take better action when exploring chances for profitable gains that benefit them, stakeholders, the environment, and society as a whole. In fact, we went over several ways that AI may support entrepreneurship (Shepherd & Majchrzak, 2022). Industry 4.0 may give an effective and easy customer care experience by employing Chat GPT to construct a chatbot that can comprehend and answer client inquiries and requests organically and conversationally (Javaid et al., 2023).

Artificial intelligence-driven creative solutions provide accurate, insightful data about customer needs and wants, allowing these quickly expanding start-ups to update their current portfolio of goods and services or develop new ones that satisfy customers (Sreenivasan & Suresh, 2023). The digital marketing technology helps businesses get maximum outcomes. One digital marketing service that assists in reaching the target audience at the appropriate moment and ensuring pertinent conversion methods is email marketing. The main benefit of AI in marketing is data analysis (Haleem et al., 2022). There are currently more than two dozen "centres of excellence" promoting evidence-based methods worldwide. Operating under the British Blockchain Association's umbrella, the Centre for Evidence-Based Blockchain (CEBB) is the world's first hub for distributed ledger technologies that promote evidence-based practices (Naqvi, 2020).

The creation and celebration of success stories that highlight our talents will help Italian successful start-ups and companies invest in new technologies through corporate risk capital, which will eventually lead to the realization of an AI ecosystem. (Marinoni, 2019) ("Advances in Global Services and Retail Management: Volume 2," 2021). The comments from the start-up experts' group and the AI experts' group showed clear variances as well as some parallels. At first, the topic was determined by both groups to be the most crucial element. On the other hand, their answers varied greatly about the next most crucial elements (Lee et al., 2023). Behind all the real-world applications (table 1), there is an intelligent agent (IA). It engages in a recurring cycle of sense-think-act with its surroundings. It investigates the incoming data (big data) to find suitable portrayal on several levels, learn correlations, extract features, and find commonalities. Formerly, the development of AI was hampered by the lack of data and effective hardware (Soni et al., 2020). The unique value proposition reflects the goal of the AI systems, emphasizing the customers' problem and the solutions enabled or implemented by the AI systems. The value proposition is realized by several sub-processes inside the key process, which are (1) model requirement, (2) model selection, (3) data preparation and (4) evaluation metrics (Duc et al., n.d.).

The use of artificial intelligence faces fourteen challenges, including a lack of a common understanding of the technology, a lack of expertise and experience in the field, Lack of leadership vision and dedication to investing in AI, Lack of training money, lack of initial cash and investment, lack of funds for managing, storing, and monitoring systems, Absence of education regarding the artificial intelligence framework and standards that Indonesia has adopted, Institutions that provide certifications or guidelines for the application of artificial intelligence do not exist. Absence of comprehensive regulations governing Indonesia's use of artificial intelligence Absence of internal amenities, Lack of systems (hardware/ software), Insufficient cooperation and coordination, Resistance or hostility to the use of artificial intelligence and Unawareness of the advantages (Maulina et al., 2020). Although investors and venture capitalists are very interested in AI start-ups, in order to assure long-term survival and performance, these companies eventually need to discover a strong business model. On the one hand, our findings from recent research indicate that AI start-ups do use unique or distinct business models (Weber et al., 2022). The way that start-ups, small businesses, the supportive ecosystem, and technology interact dynamically is what is going to shape the business environment of the future. Technology has become a driver for transformation, improving productivity through automation, transforming marketing tactics with data-driven customisation, and providing scalable solutions at a reasonable price (Rastogi, 2023). It's feasible that in the further future, AI will have distinct consequences on employment. It's also feasible that big businesses and the startups in this poll have different employment-related effects. However, the data allays worries of widespread unemployment or professional misemployment (Bessen et al., n.d.). The majority of entrepreneurs utilize productivity tools like Trello, Slack, Discord, Click Up, Miro, Zoom, and Teams for internal communication, teamwork, and project management during the value creation process. The application of this program can present challenges for certain individuals, even with its extensive usage (Fuerst et al., 2023).

Research Methodology

This conceptual paper's research design is fundamentally qualitative, with an emphasis on exploring and analysing theoretical frameworks and conceptual findings pertaining to artificial intelligence's (AI) role in sustaining start-ups. The main objective is to combine the various theoretical stances and models that are now in use to offer a thorough comprehension of the topic. More over the paper intent to describe about the various role of AI in sustainability of start-ups. This conceptual paper's main variables include start-ups success factors, AI applications, and sustainability elements (economic, environmental, and social). To investigate the diverse ways in which artificial intelligence (AI) contributes to the sustainability of start-ups, these variables will be conceptually synthesized.

Data Collection and Sources

Hence it is a conceptual study it has focused more on the secondary source of information. This conceptual paper's data comes from theoretical models and current literature. The resources have been collected from websites, research gate, google scholar etc. in order to locate pertinent books, reports, and articles. Instead of emphasizing empirical evidence, theoretical ideas are highlighted. Integrating several theoretical stances from the literature on entrepreneurship, sustainability, and artificial intelligence is part of the conceptual synthesis. The examination will pinpoint overarching themes, interrelationships, and theoretical constructs that aid in comprehending AI's function in promoting sustainability in start-up ecosystems.

AI Applications in Start-Ups

Applications of Artificial intelligence are very wide in start-ups by using Chat bots, Predictive analysis, Image and speech recognition, recommendation system, and fraud detection etc. There are so many recurring activities have to be done by entrepreneurs in dealing with internal and external parties of the business. A start-up has to deal with customers in clarifying their doubts regarding the products and services what they deal with it. Hence chatbots are using natural language processing (NLP) to communicate with customers and leads to provide quick, automated responses to common questions start-ups can deal with their parties very quickly. Prediction of the future is highly complicated as well as necessary to the organisation adapt to the trend. Many start-ups are facing challenges in forecasting and predicting the demand, price fluctuations, market trends, competitor's strategies and policies, consumer behaviour etc. it is important to know all this changes so that predictive analytics application can use for it. This may use machine learning algorithms to analyse data and make predictions about future outcomes.

Image and speech recognition, a subset of computer vision, involves the use of algorithms and machine learning models to identify and interpret objects or patterns within images. As Automation is influencing in all area of human life especially in the field of medicine, education, automobile, logistics, marketing, Human resources and analytics etc. Image and speech recognitions highly possible with AI in all the mentioned area of business. Image recognition may work in the areas of business like Inventory management, Retail and e commerce, Security and surveillance, Quality control in manufacturing, healthcare, marketing and advertising, augmented reality, and customer engagement. And the image recognition is highly significant in voice assistance and customer service, voice biometrics for security, hand free operations in vehicles, voice controlled devices, data analysis and insights and multilingual support.

The strength and capabilities of AI have increased dramatically, and it now has the ability to open up a whole new chapter in the way businesses evaluate and make strategic decisions. While there is growing concern that humans will eventually be replaced by artificial intelligence (AI) in decision-making, this article offers a thorough approach, highlights AI's complimentary role in decision-making, and clarifies that everyone will still contribute their unique strengths to make the decision-making process more effective (Kamyar & Ghiyas Kamyar, n.d.). Recommendation systems of applications are use AI algorithms to suggest products or services to customers based on their past behaviour and preferences. Many start-ups finding difficulties to detecting the fraud. Start-ups are does not having proper information to taking various decisions hence they have to depending on the external paid agencies that may lead to go in wrong decisions as well as wrong operations. AI fraud detections may be more helpful to the start-ups to lead their business in a proper direction to attain their goal.

Benefits of AI in Start-Ups

The benefits AI in start-up is limitless. AI can automate mundane and repetitive tasks related business and freeing up valuable time for start-up teams to focus on more strategic and creative decisions of their business to take in to the next level. AI tools can analyse large datasets quickly and extracting valuable insights. This enables start-ups to make data-driven decisions, understand customer behaviour, and identify market trends. Automation and efficiency improvements brought by AI can lead to cost savings. By optimizing the operations of start-ups can be reducing manual costs including production cost, labor costs, marketing and selling and achieve better resource allocation. All start-ups have to ensure the better experience of the customer. By using the AI- enabled chatbots and virtual assistant's business can provide immediate and personalized customer support. This improves customer satisfaction by addressing queries promptly and enhancing the overall user experience. Customers taste and preference are very unique and it should be fulfilled by good businessman for the sustainability. Major reasons for the failure of start-ups is that less personalisation of the products and services which can reduced by the support of AI. AI enables start-ups to offer personalized experiences to their customers to improve their experience. This can include personalized recommendations, targeted marketing campaigns, and customized product offerings based on individual preferences. Figure 1 gives glimpse on the benefits of AI in start-ups.

Figure 1. Benefits of AI in start-ups

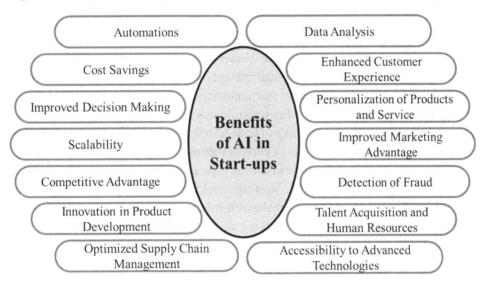

Selecting best alternatives among from the various alternatives is decision making. All the decisions should be based on the information which is collected before. Wrong decision will lead to the failure of the start-ups. Decision making is the one of the complex processes of a businessman. Start-ups can use predictive analytics and machine learning algorithms to forecast trends, identify potential risks, and make informed strategic decisions. Scaling the start-ups is highly required to know the growth and development. This process is very difficult without using the latest technology. AI technologies can scale seamlessly as the start-up grows. Automation and AI-driven processes are often designed to handle increased workloads without a proportional increase in manual effort. AI can optimize supply chain processes, improving inventory management, demand forecasting, and logistics. This ensures that start-ups can meet customer demands efficiently while minimizing costs.

Analysis

It is evident that AI is having a significant role in the sustainability of start-ups in the scenario. Here the researcher uses the qualitative analysis for understanding the role of AI in sustainability of start-ups. All AI Applications like chat bot, Predictive analysis, Image and speech recognition, Recommendation systems, Fraud detections etc. are supporting the entrepreneurs to sustain environmentally, economically and socially. With the help of AI tools, a businessman can analyse all the present situation with available data to the success of business by considering all sustainable elements (economic, environmental, and social). The examination of Artificial Intelligence's (AI) contribution to sustainability in start-up ecosystems reveals a complex setting where cutting-edge technologies meet social, environmental, and economic factors. A thorough grasp of how AI helps businesses remain sustainable is made possible by the synthesis of current theoretical viewpoints. The examination of Artificial Intelligence's (AI) contribution to sustainability in start-up ecosystems reveals a complex setting where cutting-edge technologies meet social, environmental, and economic factors. A thorough grasp of how AI helps businesses remain sustainable is made possible by the synthesis of current theoretical viewpoints.

AI technologies have a key role in cutting expenses, increasing operational effectiveness, and conserving resources. Start-ups can improve supply chain management, expedite production processes, and make well-informed decisions regarding resource optimization by utilizing machine learning algorithms and predictive analytics. This efficiency reduces the negative environmental effects of excessive resource usage while simultaneously enhancing economic sustainability. Sustainable practices are introduced by supply chain management with the use of AI. Algorithms powered by AI optimize routes, cut down on transportation expenses, and lessen environmental impact. Businesses that use artificial intelligence (AI) in their supply chains can advance eco-friendly business practices that support global sustainability objectives.

AI is essential to start-ups' efforts to advance circular economy principles. AI makes it easier to adopt sustainable product life cycles, from product design to end-of-life recycling procedures. Start-ups may support the circular economy by using AI to reduce waste, encourage recycling, and implement environmentally friendly production techniques. AI gives entrepreneurs in the agriculture industry access to precise farming methods. Start-ups may achieve more sustainable farming practices by optimizing pest management, fertilizer, and irrigation with data-driven insights. Artificial Intelligence (AI) in agriculture promotes higher yields while reducing environmental effect, which is consistent with ecological and social sustainability.

AI is having a revolutionary effect on the renewable energy industry as well. In this sector, firms are using advanced analytics to integrate clean energy sources into the power grid. Artificial intelligence (AI)-powered devices boost the effectiveness of renewable energy sources, increasing their viability and aiding in the world's shift to sustainable energy sources.

By tackling issues with accessibility and diversity, AI-driven solutions support social sustainability. AI-powered apps can be created by start-ups to increase access to critical services like healthcare and education. These activities' social impact promotes diversity and advances the narrative surrounding sustainability. It's critical to emphasize the value of moral and responsible AI practices when start-ups incorporate AI into their operations. By upholding the values of justice, accountability, and openness, potential biases and social concerns are reduced, and the revolutionary potential of AI is used responsibly. Start-ups' capacity for innovation and adaptation is intrinsically linked to their financial viability. AI is an innovation catalyst that helps start-ups create new products, break into untapped markets, and gain a competitive edge. Thus, a start-up's ability to use AI to drive sustainable growth is closely related to its financial sustainability. Figure 2 describes the AI applications and role in sustainability of start-ups.

Figure 2. AI and sustainability of start-ups

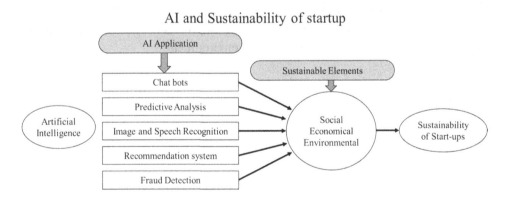

CONCLUSION

To sum up, this descriptive study has offered a thorough investigation of the crucial role that artificial intelligence (AI) plays in the world of start-ups, with an emphasis on the implications that AI has for sustainability. The integration of extant literature and conceptual frameworks has shed light on the complex interactions between AI technology and the core components of social responsibility, environmental effect, and economic feasibility in entrepreneurial endeavours.

The report emphasizes how start-ups can achieve operational efficiency and promote sustainable practices using a revolutionary toolkit provided by AI-driven technologies. Utilizing AI to optimize resource consumption and promote the principles of the circular economy is emerging as a catalyst for eco-friendly entrepreneurship. This study highlights the potential of AI to address societal issues and promote a fairer business environment, further demonstrating the critical role that AI plays in guiding start-ups towards social inclusion.

The results underscore the complex interplay between artificial intelligence (AI) and the viability of start-ups, highlighting the fact that these technologies are revolutionary catalysts for innovation rather than just tools. In order to promote resilience, sustainable growth, and a positive social effect, start-ups must deliberately embrace AI as they traverse the intricacies of the contemporary corporate environment.

Furthermore, the study lays the groundwork for future investigations by encouraging a more thorough examination of particular business applications, moral dilemmas, and the changing terrain of AI-driven entrepreneurship. This study offers insightful information that will help academics, practitioners, and policymakers better understand how to use artificial intelligence (AI) to support sustainable and creative futures for start-ups, as the start-up ecosystem develops. Essentially, artificial intelligence (AI) in start-ups is not just about integrating technology; it's also about creating a route towards sustainable innovation that fits with the larger goals of a robust and socially conscious company environment.

REFERENCES

Bessen, J., Impink, S. M., Paris, H., & Reichensperger, L. (n.d.). *The Business of AI Startups*. Academic Press.

Bickley, S. J., Macintyre, A., & Torgler, B. (n.d.). *Standard-Nutzungsbedingungen.* http://hdl.handle.net/10419/234626

Borges, A., Laurindo, F., Spínola, M., Gonçalves, R. F., & Mattos, C. (2021). The strategic use of artificial intelligence in the digital era: Systematic literature review and future research directions. *International Journal of Information Management*, 57, 102225. 10.1016/j.ijinfomgt.2020.102225

Duc, A. N., Bøe, T., & Sundbø, I. (n.d.). *Understanding the Role of Artificial Intelligence in Digital Startups: A Conceptual Framework.* https://www.angellist.com/

Fuerst, S., Sanchez-Dominguez, O., & Rodriguez-Montes, M. A. (2023). The Role of Digital Technology within the Business Model of Sustainable Entrepreneurship. *Sustainability (Basel)*, 15(14), 10923. Advance online publication. 10.3390/su151410923

Halberstadt, J., & Johnson, M. (2014, September). Sustainability Management for Startups and Micro-Enterprises: Development of a Sustainability-Quick-Check and Reporting Scheme. In *EnviroInfo* (pp. 17-24). Academic Press.

Haleem, A., Javaid, M., Asim Qadri, M., Pratap Singh, R., & Suman, R. (2022). Artificial intelligence (AI) applications for marketing: A literature-based study. In *International Journal of Intelligent Networks* (Vol. 3, pp. 119–132). KeAi Communications Co. 10.1016/j.ijin.2022.08.005

Javaid, M., Haleem, A., & Singh, R. P. (2023). A study on ChatGPT for Industry 4.0: Background, potentials, challenges, and eventualities. *Journal of Economy and Technology*, 1, 127–143. 10.1016/j.ject.2023.08.001

Kamyar, A., & Ghiyas Kamyar, A. (n.d.). Artificial Intelligence Startups in Italy: Their role in Decision-Making. 10.13140/RG.2.2.16272.17929

Kasemsap, K. (2017). Artificial intelligence: Current issues and applications. In *Handbook of Research on Manufacturing Process Modeling and Optimization Strategies* (pp. 454–474). IGI Global. 10.4018/978-1-5225-2440-3.ch022

Kushwaha, R. (n.d.). *Sustainable Entrepreneurship Creating Value with Sustainability.* https://www.researchgate.net/publication/366371306

Lee, B., Kim, B., & Ivan, U. V. (2023). Enhancing the Competitiveness of AI Technology-Based Startups in the Digital Era. *Administrative Sciences*, 14(1), 6. 10.3390/admsci14010006

Maulina, E., Purnomo, M., Wicaksono, A. R., Rizal, M., Program, D., Raya, J., Sumedang, B., Jatinangor, K., Sumedang, K., & Barat, J. (2020). Analysis of the Use of Artificial Intelligence Technology on Digital Startups in Indonesia. *International Journal of Advanced Science and Technology, 29*(3), 750–758. https://www.researchgate.net/publication/343224942

Naqvi, N. (2020). Evidence-Based Blockchain: Findings from a Global Study of Blockchain Projects and Start-up Companies. *The Journal of The British Blockchain Association*, 3(2), 1–13. 10.31585/jbba-3-2-(8)2020

Petru, N., Pavlák, M., & Polák, J. (2019). Factors impacting startup sustainability in the Czech Republic. In *Innovative Marketing* (Vol. 15, Issue 3, pp. 1–15). LLC CPC Business Perspectives. 10.21511/im.15(3).2019.01

Rastogi, P. (2023). *The Role of Technology in Start-ups and Small Businesses*. International Scientific Refereed Research Journal Available Online. 10.32628/SHISRRJ

Shepherd, D. A., & Majchrzak, A. (2022). Machines augmenting entrepreneurs: Opportunities (and threats) at the Nexus of artificial intelligence and entrepreneurship. *Journal of Business Venturing*, 37(4), 106227. 10.1016/j.jbusvent.2022.106227

Soni, N., Sharma, E. K., Singh, N., & Kapoor, A. (2019). Artificial Intelligence in Business: From Research and Innovation to Market Deployment. *Procedia Computer Science*, 167, 2200–2210. 10.1016/j.procs.2020.03.272

Sreenivasan, A., & Suresh, M. (2023). *Adoption of Artificial Intelligence (AI) in Start-ups*. 10.46254/IN02.20220104

Tiba, S., Van Rijnsoever, F. J., & Hekkert, M. P. (2021). Sustainability startups and where to find them: Investigating the share of sustainability startups across entrepreneurial ecosystems and the causal drivers of differences. *Journal of Cleaner Production*, 306, 127054. 10.1016/j.jclepro.2021.127054

Torres-Mancera, R., Martínez-Rodrigo, E., & Santos, C. A. (2023). Female sustainability and startups: Analysis of the leadership in communication by women entrepreneurs in Spain and Portugal. *Revista Latina de Comunicacion Social*, 2023(81), 474–491. 10.4185/rlcs-2023-1978

van Wynsberghe, A. (2021). Sustainable AI: AI for sustainability and the sustainability of AI. *AI and Ethics*, 1(3), 213–218. 10.1007/s43681-021-00043-6

Verhoef, P. C., Broekhuizen, T., Bart, Y., Bhattachary, A., Dong, J. Q., Fabian, N., & Haenlein, M. (2021). Digital transformation: A multidisciplinary reflection and research agenda. *Journal of Business Research*, 122, 889–901. 10.1016/j.jbusres.2019.09.022

Weber, M., Beutter, M., Weking, J., Böhm, M., & Krcmar, H. (2022). AI Startup Business Models: Key Characteristics and Directions for Entrepreneurship Research. *Business & Information Systems Engineering*, 64(1), 91–109. 10.1007/s12599-021-00732-w

Chapter 10
Data Security and Privacy in RegTech

Ruchika Rastogi
(iD) https://orcid.org/0000-0001-7144-4387
Pranveer Singh Institute of Technology, Kanpur, India

Mohammad Ismail Iqbal
University of Technology and Applied Sciences, Oman

ABSTRACT

Regtech, or the use of technology in regulation, compliance, risk management, reporting, and monitoring, is driven by increasing regulatory requirements, rapid and continuous changes, and the digital dynamics of financial markets. The resulting multidimensional framework covers many dimensions. The first is regulation and technology, where technology (such as artificial intelligence, DLT, blockchain, smart contracts, apis) is used to meet one or more laws that do not require financial management. Regtech leverages technology for regulation, compliance, and risk management in finance, driven by regulatory demands and digital market dynamics. It utilizes AI, blockchain, and data automation for efficient data integration. Information sharing fosters an ecosystem benefiting stakeholders, offering increased efficiency, transparency, and reduced costs. Yet, risks like cyber threats and algorithmic bias persist.

INTRODUCTION

Due to innovations in networked digital communication technology, including the emergence of cloud storage systems and the rise of so-called "big data", new social processes called algorithmic rules (Flyverbom et al., 2019). The advantage of

DOI: 10.4018/979-8-3693-3322-8.ch010

regtech is that it meets regulatory requirements more efficiently and effectively than currently available (Fca, 2016). High levels of digital dynamism and their continued evolution are also driving the development of regtech, giving rise to new business ideas and businesses such as regtech startups, which can help support corporate banking in managing new risks, compliance, and new regulations. They are moving towards automation and efficiency. However, advances in digital innovation bring with them new risks, including those related to cybersecurity (Buckley et al., 2020).

Current policy is being reviewed, its suitability is being questioned, and financial stability and risks are also being questioned (Bis, 2021). Regulators, on the other hand, have announced new ways and strategies for the authorities and managements here, aiming to promote innovation and competition, such as regulatory virtual spaces and innovation centres (Fca, 2016; Kurum, 2020), as well as risk management. There is also discussion about the possibility of organizations adopting regtech solutions.

Personal data protection is a significant issue for both businesses and individuals in the current digital landscape (Arner et al 2020). As cyber-attacks and data breaches become more common, it is crucial to safeguard sensitive information (Bansod & Venice 2023). Regulation technology (regtech) is utilized to assist businesses in adhering to regulations. Regulatory agencies worldwide are now utilizing regtech solutions to ensure data privacy and security, making them an essential part of compliance. Regtech solutions can be instrumental in helping businesses protect their data privacy and security. By offering real-time monitoring and access capabilities, regtech platforms can assist in identifying and mitigating data breaches. Companies can receive assistance in implementing data protection measures, such as DPIA (Data Protection Impact Assessment) (Lim 2022).

Privacy in Compliance

In the compliance all over the world, privacy is one of the maximum essential matters to bear in mind. Confidentiality approaches any statistics that must be saved personal and need to not be disclosed to unauthorized parties (Teichmann et al 2023). For compliance functions, confidentiality is important to make certain that each data supplied with the aid of customers is at ease so that nobody can access it without permission. As technology advances, gathering, storing and sharing facts turns into less complicated, however this additionally increases the hazard of records leakage and facts leakage (Grassi et al 2022; Becker et al 2020). Consequently, it's miles critical to apprehend the importance of privacy compliance to preserve accept as true with and shield sensitive facts from unauthorized get right of entry to. Right here are a few factors to consider:

1. Privateness (Cristofari 2023) is crucial to preserving accept as true with between clients and organizations. Failure with the aid of a company to keep statistics private will bring about loss of believe and damage to the popularity of the business enterprise.

2. Confidentiality (Grassi et al 2022) is vital to make certain that sensitive statistics isn't disclosed to unauthorized third parties. This includes any non-public or financial statistics that the customer or customers may additionally offer. It requires organizations to defend the confidentiality of client information. Failure to conform with those rules might also bring about extreme legal consequences.

4. Companies need to implement various measures to protect privateness (Becker et al 2020), along with get right of entry to control, get entry to control, comfy facts storage. This ensures that handiest authorized personnel have get entry to sensitive facts and that it is blanketed from unauthorized get right of entry to.

5. Privateness additionally calls for employees to be trained within the use of sensitive data. This consists of information the importance of confidentiality, a way to pick out exclusive statistics, and the way to accurately control private facts (Cristofari 2023).

6. A breach of confidentiality may have a enormous effect on an organization and its customers. As an example, a facts breach should bring about robbery, monetary loss, and harm to a customer's popularity (Teichmann et al 2023).

Privacy is an important thing of compliance and information its importance is crucial to maintaining accept as true with and protecting touchy facts. By enforcing measures to ensure privateness, groups can reduce the hazard of data breaches and protect customers' personal and economic records.

Encounters in Data Privacy

Making sure the security of personal data is an important component of compliance that has emerge as increasingly harder in recent years. As increasingly more records are created and accumulated, organizations ought to take greater care to defend touchy records from unauthorized get right of entry to and misuse. Solving those issues calls for a multifaceted technique that includes robust policies and procedures in addition to overall performance measurements. From data breaches to birthday celebration risks, there are numerous threats to private facts that agencies need to display to agree with purchasers. Some of the main troubles groups face in ensuring statistics privacy are:

1. Facts breach: one of the maximum important threats to private statistics is the risk of facts breach. Cybercriminals are continuously seeking out methods to exploit system vulnerabilities and gain touchy records. Organizations ought to take steps to prevent facts breaches, such as taking security measures, conducting everyday audits, and training personnel to do their quality (Sumkovski 2023).
2. Celebration risks: companies frequently depend upon partners to manner sensitive statistics. But those events may additionally pose a sizable risk to private facts. Companies ought to evaluate their providers and make sure appropriate information privacy and security measures are in place (Becker et al 2020).
3. Regulatory compliance: complying with statistics privacy legal guidelines is vital for groups handling touchy facts. But preserving up with the changing regulatory environment may be tough. Agencies ought to keep up with new guidelines and make sure they have powerful guidelines and procedures in location to comply with the policies (Grassi et al 2022).
4. Employee schooling: employees can be poor resources of private facts due to the fact they will divulge touchy information via inappropriate behaviour. Offering regular schooling on facts privacy pleasant practices can help reduce this chance and ensure employees recognize their responsibilities (Charoenwong et al 2023)
5. Regional information: in some jurisdictions, nearby statistics legal guidelines require statistics to be stored in a particular geographic region. This could create issues for organizations that perform in one-of-a-kind jurisdictions and need to comply with exceptional regional guidelines.

In conclusion, preserving information non-public is a tough and hard challenge that calls for many methods. By way of taking steps to resolve those issues, corporations can better protect sensitive data and follow records privateness laws.

Data Privacy and Protection for RegTech

Data privacy is significantly vital for businesses of any size to consider. As data breaches and cyberattacks keep on increasing, all businesses are under increasing pressure to ensure data confidentiality, integrity, and availability (Bloushi 2020). Regtech solutions can help businesses comply with data privacy laws by providing solutions that assist in identifying and mitigating data privacy risks. Regtech solutions can assist organizations in improving compliance and reducing associated costs (Johansson et al 2019). In this section, we'll look at the diverse regtech solutions that organizations can use to achieve data compliance.

Data privacy management solution: These solutions are brilliantly designed to assist businesses in managing and protecting sensitive data. These solutions significantly assist businesses in identifying and analysing sensitive data, creating controls, and tracking data usage. Bigid, for instance, is a data privacy management system that utilizes machine learning algorithms to identify and classify sensitive data within an organization's data environment (Grassi and Lanfranchi 2022).

Identity and access management: These extraordinary solutions can assist organizations in managing user identities and access to information and systems. These exceptional solutions can assist organizations in ensuring that only authorized personnel have access to sensitive information. Okta, for example, is a privacy and security management system that provides secure access to your apps and data on any device, at any time (Becker et al 2020).

Data encryption solution: These solutions can remarkably help organizations in protecting sensitive data through encrypting data in transit and at rest. Encryption solutions can significantly help organizations in complying with regulations requiring protection of sensitive data, such as gdpr and ccpa. Cipher cloud, for example, is a data encryption solution that provides industry-class encryption for cloud applications and data (Grassi and Lanfranchi 2022).

Prevent data loss: These phenomenal solutions can assist organizations in preventing the loss of sensitive data by monitoring and auditing data usage and blocking access to data. Symantec data loss prevention is a data loss prevention solution that helps organizations identify, monitor, and protect their data regardless of where it is stored or used. Regtech solutions significantly help organizations comply with privacy laws and protect personal data and sensitive information. By incorporating these solutions, organizations can strengthen compliance, reduce compliance costs, and improve overall security (Grassi and Lanfranchi 2022).

Best Ways to Show the Path

There are some best practices that companies should keep in mind when implementing regtech solutions (Bolton & Mintrom 2023). These practices help ensure compliant implementation of these solutions and protect the confidentiality of sensitive information. It is important to have a good understanding of the regulatory environment and the specific regulations that affect the business. This understanding will help determine the right regtech solution to implement and ensure it is installed correctly.

Conduct a comprehensive evaluation of regtech solutions: before implementing a regtech solution, it is important to evaluate its efficiency, reliability, and effectiveness. This assessment should consider the specific needs of the business and the implement of the solution. It is also important to evaluate the seller's reputation, financial stability, and safety record.

Ensure data privacy: data privacy is critical to compliance, and it is important to ensure that regtech solutions do not compromise the confidentiality of sensitive information. Companies must ensure the regtech solutions they use are secure and that data is encrypted in transitions and at rest. They should also consider implementing controls to prevent anyone from accessing sensitive information.

Provide adequate training: a well-educated workforce is critical to the success of regtech solutions. Companies should provide training to employees on how to use the solution and integrate it into existing compliance processes. This training should include how to identify potential problems and respond to them.

Be flexible and flexible: as your business grows and evolves, your needs will evolve too. Regtech solutions must be scalable and flexible enough to adapt to these changes. Companies need to ensure that the regtech solutions they use are compatible with other systems and can be adapted to meet needs.

Review and update regtech solutions regularly: regulations continue to evolve, and regtech solutions need to be reviewed and updated to ensure they remain current and compliant. Businesses should review solutions regularly and work closely with vendors to ensure solutions are updated and implemented.

Using regtech solutions can help businesses achieve compliance and manage data privacy. However, it is important to follow best practices to ensure these solutions are successfully integrated into the compliance process. The company must evaluate each solution it uses, ensure the confidentiality of information, provide adequate training to employees, ensure capacity and flexibility, and regularly review and update the solutions.

Application of RegTech With Data Privacy and Security

A global financial service implemented a regtech solution to manage data privacy. The innovative tool delivers a total view of data privacy risks and allows for rapid detection. Additionally, it enables the company to set up a personalized data privacy management system based on its unique requirements. This program is then carried out organization-wide, elevating compliance and minimizing risk factors.

The provider utilizes a regtech solution for personal information management. The tool offers the company a centralized view of all data privacy risks and lets the company oversee and control data breaches. The solution also significantly speeds up data processing, hence improving efficiency and cutting down on expenses.

A global retail company utilizes regtech solutions for personal data management (Solms 2021). The tool furnishes the organization with a centralized view of all confidential risk data, making it simpler to identify and resolve potential issues. It also enables the company to establish a customized data privacy management blueprint tailored to its individual needs. The initiative is then executed across the establishment, heightening compliance, and risk mitigation.

The shipping company applied a regtech solution to oversee their personal data. The tool presents the company with a comprehensive outlook of its confidential data and authorizes tracking and management of data breaches. Similar to other companies, this regtech solution allows the company to craft a personal information management strategy that suits its specific requirements (Solms 2021). The plan is then rolled out across the organization, optimizing compliance and risk reduction.

The above-mentioned case studies highlight the perks of regtech in data privacy management. By embracing regtech solutions, companies can adhere to data privacy regulations while reaching their business objectives. These solutions equip companies with a centralized view of confidential risk data, enabling them to quickly identify and tackle potential problems. Moreover, they help companies establish data privacy guidelines tailored to their unique needs, ensuring compliance and risk mitigation.

Data Privacy, Security, and the Future of RegTech

As organizations keep collecting and storing data, data privacy has become a top concern. The increase in data breaches and cyber-attacks have revealed the vulnerability of personal data and the need for tighter controls. Here is some info regarding this topic to ponder:

Focus on privacy laws: as awareness of personal data continues to grow, we can expect regulations to become stricter. For instance, the proposed eu rules on intellectual property, which are expected to come into force in 2022, aim to ensure that intellectual property does not undermine fundamental rights, involving private security. This means organizations need to invest more in privacy compliance to avoid vast fines.

Emergence of pets: pets are technologies that enable organizations to collect, process, and share info while protecting personal privacy. Some examples of pet include homomorphic encryption, distinct secrets, and secure multiparty computing. These technologies are still in their infancy, but they hold great promise for the future of data privacy.

Collaboration between regulators and business staff: regulators and business staff should work together to resolve privacy issues. For example, the eu blockchain observatory and forum is working with partners to develop blockchain and data protection systems. This collaboration is necessary to ensure the effective implementation of data privacy policies.

Better investment in compliance automation: compliance automation involves using technology to streamline compliance processes. This helps organizations save time and resources while maintaining effective control. For instance, some regtech solutions use machine learning to analyse data and identify compliance issues.

Importance of ethical considerations: as artificial intelligence and other technologies are increasingly used; ethical considerations will also become more important. For instance, organizations have to ensure that their ai systems are transparent and explainable. This means that humans must be able to understand how ai systems make decisions.

The future of data privacy and technology management is bright. However, organizations need to keep up with technology and change management processes to ensure compliance.

Data Privacy and Compliance Regulatory Framework

As technology and new ways of collecting and processing information increase, people have become more concerned about the security and privacy of sensitive information. Management processes are in place to ensure data confidentiality and compliance and to protect individuals and organizations from risk and harm. These guidelines are designed to establish procedures and standards for handling and processing information and to hold organizations accountable for protecting sensitive information.

1. GDPR

In 2018, the european union's general data protection regulation (GDPR) is one of the most important data privacy regulations in the world. It applies to all organizations that process personal data of EU citizens, regardless of the location of the organization. GDPR requires organizations to obtain explicit consent from individuals before collecting and processing data and provide clear and transparent information about how the data will be used. It also gives people the right to access, correct and delete their personal information (Goddard 2017).

2. CCPA

The California consumer privacy act (CCPA) is another important law regarding privacy and data compliance (Baik 2020). It gives California residents the right to know what personal information a business has collected about them and to request that their information be deleted. It also requires businesses to disclose the names of the personal data they collect and provide non-disclosure options regarding the sale of personal data.

3. HIPAA

The health insurance portability and accountability act (HIPAA) is a law that regulates the processing of personal health information in the United States (Olukoya 2022). Requires physicians, health plans, and other organizations that handle personal health information to take precautions to protect the confidentiality, integrity, and possession of that information. It also gives people the right to access and control their personal health information.

Table 1. Summary of regulatory framework (Author Compilation)

Parameters	HIPAA	CCPA	HIPAA
Scope	Healthcare organizations in the US	Organizations handling EU/ UK citizen data	Business operating in California
Focus	Protection of protected health information	Protection of personal data	Protection of consumer data rights
Applicability		Applicable to organizations worldwide	Applicable to businesses in California
Consent requirements		Requires explicit consent for data processing	Provides right to opt-out of data sale and right to request deletion
Individual rights			Extensive individual rights including right to opt-out and deletion
Enforcement	Enforced by us department of health and human services' office for civil rights	Enforced by data protection authorities within EU/UK member states	Enforced by California attorney general's office

HIPAA (health insurance portability and accountability act) stands as a cornerstone legislation in the United States, designed to regulate the handling of protected health information (phi) within the healthcare sector. Its primary focus revolves around ensuring the privacy and security of individuals' health data, imposing stringent guidelines and standards on covered entities such as healthcare providers, health plans, and healthcare clearinghouses.

The significance of HIPAA cannot be overstated, as it plays a pivotal role in maintaining trust between patients and healthcare organizations by safeguarding sensitive information like medical histories, billing records, and laboratory results. By establishing rules such as the privacy rule, security rule, and breach notification rule, HIPAA sets forth a comprehensive framework for protecting phi and holding entities accountable for any breaches or violations (Larson 2022).

In comparing HIPAA with other data privacy regulations like GDPR and CCPA, it becomes evident that each framework operates within distinct scopes and jurisdictions. While GDPR, for instance, addresses the broader landscape of personal data protection within the European union and the United Kingdom, encompassing various industries beyond healthcare, HIPAA remains specific to the us healthcare sector (Perumal 2022; Mulgund et al 2021). Furthermore, while both HIPAA and GDPR emphasize the importance of data security and breach notification, they differ significantly in their approaches to consent and individual rights (Perumal 2022).

Similarly, CCPA, as a state-level regulation in California, shares some common objectives with GDPR and HIPAA in terms of empowering consumers with greater control over their personal information (Larson 2022; Mulgund et al 2021). However, CCPA's focus on consumer data rights within the context of commercial activities within California sets it apart from the healthcare-centric focus of hipaa and the broader territorial scope of GDPR.

In essence, HIPAA's role in regulating healthcare data privacy and security serves as a vital component of the broader landscape of data protection laws. While it differs in scope and application from regulations like GDPR and CCPA, its fundamental goal remains consistent: safeguarding individuals' privacy and fostering trust in the handling of sensitive health information within the healthcare ecosystem (Larson 2022).

SUMMARY

The landscape of data privacy has seen increasing scrutiny and regulation globally due to concerns over data breaches, unauthorized access, and misuse of personal information. Companies across various industries have encountered challenges in complying with data privacy laws such as GDPR (general data protection regulation) in Europe, CCPA (California consumer privacy act) in the United States, and similar regulations in other regions (Larson 2022; Mulgund et al 2021). These encounters have necessitated a re-evaluation of data handling practices, implementation of robust security measures, and adoption of compliance frameworks to safeguard sensitive information.

Regtech (regulatory technology) solutions have emerged as a vital tool for companies to navigate the complex landscape of regulatory compliance, including data privacy and protection requirements (Baik 2020). These technologies leverage advanced algorithms, artificial intelligence, and automation to streamline compliance processes, monitor regulatory changes, and ensure adherence to data privacy laws. By integrating data privacy and protection features into regtech platforms, organizations can effectively manage regulatory risks while maintaining data security and privacy standards (Arner et al 2020).

The application of regtech in conjunction with data privacy and security measures offers several benefits for organizations. These include enhanced data governance, real-time monitoring of compliance activities, timely identification of data breaches or privacy violations, and streamlined reporting capabilities (Sumkovski 2023; Buckley et al 2020). By leveraging regtech solutions, companies can mitigate compliance costs, reduce manual errors, and foster trust among customers by demonstrating a commitment to protecting their personal data.

As data privacy regulations continue to evolve and become more stringent, the future of regtech will likely focus on integrating advanced encryption techniques, biometric authentication, and decentralized data storage to enhance security measures. Additionally, there will be an increased emphasis on transparency, accountability, and ethical data practices within regtech solutions to address concerns regarding algorithmic bias and privacy infringement. Collaboration between regulators, industry stakeholders, and technology providers will be crucial in shaping the future direction of regtech to effectively address emerging data privacy and security challenges.

The regulatory framework surrounding data privacy and compliance is dynamic and multifaceted, requiring organizations to stay abreast of evolving requirements and standards. A robust compliance regulatory framework encompasses not only legal mandates but also industry best practices, international guidelines, and voluntary certifications such as ISO 27001 for information security management (Kitsios et al 2023). By adhering to a comprehensive regulatory framework, organizations can mitigate legal risks, protect sensitive data, and uphold the trust and confidence of stakeholders in their data handling practices.

REFERENCES

Al Bloushi, M. (2020). *Cyber-Attacks and Data Integrity Concerns Cripple Large Parts of the Internet on Banking* (Doctoral dissertation, The British University in Dubai).

Anagnostopoulos, I. (2018). Fintech and regtech: Impact on regulators and banks. *Journal of Economics and Business*, 100, 7–25. 10.1016/j.jeconbus.2018.07.003

Arner, D. W., Zetzsche, D. A., Buckley, R. P., & Weber, R. H. (2020). The future of data-driven finance and RegTech: Lessons from EU big bang II. *Stan. JL Bus. & Fin.*, 25, 245.

Baik, J. S. (2020). Data privacy against innovation or against discrimination?: The case of the California Consumer Privacy Act (CCPA). *Telematics and Informatics*, 52, 52. 10.1016/j.tele.2020.101431

Bansod, A., & Venice, A. (2023). Importance of Cybersecurity and RegTech in FinTech. *Telecom Business Review, 16*(1).

Becker, M., Merz, K., & Buchkremer, R. (2020). RegTech—the application of modern information technology in regulatory affairs: Areas of interest in research and practice. *International Journal of Intelligent Systems in Accounting Finance & Management*, 27(4), 161–167. 10.1002/isaf.1479

Bolton, M., & Mintrom, M. (2023). RegTech and creating public value: Opportunities and challenges. *Policy Design and Practice*, 6(3), 266–282. 10.1080/25741292.2023.2213059

Buckley, r. P., Arner, d. W., Zetzsche, d. A., & Weber, R. H. (2020). The road to regtech: the (astonishing) example of the European union. *Journal of Banking Regulation, 21*(1), 26–36.

Charoenwong, B., Kowaleski, Z. T., Kwan, A., & Sutherland, A. (2023). *RegTech*. Academic Press.

Cristofari, G. (2023). *The Politics of Platformization–Amsterdam Dialogues on Platform Theory*. Institute of Network Cultures.

FCA. (2016). *Call for input on supporting the development and adopters of regtech*. Academic Press.

Flyverbom, M., Deibert, R., & Matten, D. (2019). The governance of digital technology, big data, and the internet: new roles and responsibilities for business. *Business & Society, 58*(1), 3-19.

Goddard, M. (2017). The EU General Data Protection Regulation (GDPR): European regulation that has a global impact. *International Journal of Market Research*, 59(6), 703–705. 10.2501/IJMR-2017-050

Grassi, L., & Lanfranchi, D. (2022). RegTech in public and private sectors: The nexus between data, technology and regulation. *Economia e Politica Industriale*, 49(3), 441–479. 10.1007/s40812-022-00226-0

Johansson, E., Sutinen, K., Lassila, J., Lang, V., Martikainen, M., & Lehner, O. M. (2019). Regtech-a necessary tool to keep up with compliance and regulatory changes. *ACRN Journal of Finance and Risk Perspectives. Special Issue Digital Accounting*, 8, 71–85.

Kitsios, F., Chatzidimitriou, E., & Kamariotou, M. (2023). The ISO/IEC 27001 Information security management standard: How to extract value from data in the IT sector. *Sustainability (Basel)*, 15(7), 5828. 10.3390/su15075828

Kurum, E. (2023, April 18). Regtech solutions and AML compliance: What future for financial crime? *Journal of Financial Crime*, 30(3), 776–794. Advance online publication. 10.1108/JFC-04-2020-0051

Larson, J. M. (2022). Data Privacy Laws and Regulatory Drivers. In *Snowflake Access Control: Mastering the Features for Data Privacy and Regulatory Compliance* (pp. 25–42). Apress. 10.1007/978-1-4842-8038-6_3

Lim, H. Y. F. (2022). Regulatory compliance. In *Artificial Intelligence* (pp. 85–108). Edward Elgar Publishing.

Muganyi, T., Yan, L., Yin, Y., Sun, H., Gong, X., & Taghizadeh-Hesary, F. (2022). Fintech, regtech, and financial development: Evidence from China. *Financial Innovation*, 8(1), 1–20. 10.1186/s40854-021-00313-6

Olukoya, O. (2022). Assessing frameworks for eliciting privacy & security requirements from laws and regulations. *Computers & Security*, 117, 102697. 10.1016/j.cose.2022.102697

Perumal, V. (2022). The future of US data privacy: Lessons from the GDPR and State Legislation. *Notre Dame J. Int'l Comp. L.*, 12, 99.

Sumkovski, I. (2023). The use of RegTech in fighting financial crime. *Journal of Financial Compliance*, 6(2), 138–147.

Teichmann, F., Boticiu, S., & Sergi, B. S. (2023). RegTech–Potential benefits and challenges for businesses. *Technology in Society*, 72, 102150. 10.1016/j.techsoc.2022.102150

Von Solms, J. (2021). Integrating Regulatory Technology (RegTech) into the digital transformation of a bank Treasury. *Journal of Banking Regulation*, 22(2), 152–168. 10.1057/s41261-020-00134-0

Chapter 11
The Nexus of Regulation and Technology:
A Strategic Approach to Combating Digital Music Piracy

Kiran Sharma
Galgotias University, India

Shivangi Sharma
Galgotias University, India

Ansari Sarwar Alam
Britts Imperial University College, UAE

ABSTRACT

In the digital age, the proliferation of technology has transformed the landscape of the music industry, enabling unprecedented access to music but also giving rise to rampant piracy. The chapter explores the intricate interplay between regulation and technology in combating digital music piracy. The analysis reveals that while regulatory interventions have played a crucial role in shaping the legal framework, technological advancements have simultaneously presented both opportunities and hurdles in the fight against piracy. Furthermore, the authors examine the strategic approaches adopted by industry players, policymakers, and technology innovators to mitigate piracy, including the development of DRM systems, subscription-based streaming services, and collaborative enforcement efforts.

The digital age has revolutionized music consumption, offering unparalleled access to a vast library of songs at our fingertips. However, this convenience has come at a cost: the rampant spread of digital music piracy. Illegal downloading and

DOI: 10.4018/979-8-3693-3322-8.ch011

streaming deprive artists and rights holders of rightful revenue, hindering investment in new music creation and threatening the entire music ecosystem.

This challenge demands a multi-faceted approach. While regulations form the backbone of efforts against piracy, they need the support of innovative technological solutions. This document explores the strategic intersection of regulation and technology, arguing that a well-coordinated effort is essential to create a sustainable future for the music industry.

DEFINITION AND SCOPE OF REGTECH

RegTech, short for Regulatory Technology involves implementing digital tools and processes that enhance organizations' ability to comply with regulations more efficiently and cost-effectively (Estevez, 2023). It encompasses technologies like artificial intelligence, machine learning, big data analytics, blockchain, cloud computing, and the Internet of Things to streamline compliance management and improve regulatory adherence (Li & Maiti, 2023). RegTech aims to automate manual tasks, enhance risk analysis, prioritize resources effectively, identify fraud patterns, and anticipate regulatory disruptions, ultimately helping organizations navigate the increasingly complex regulatory landscape (Becker; Merz & Buchkremer, 2020).

THE NEXUS OF REGULATION AND TECHNOLOGY

Digital music piracy thrives in a landscape of inconsistent copyright laws and readily available illegal platforms. Artists see their work readily available online without compensation, leading to financial hardship and a stifling effect on creativity (Neu, 2023). Record labels struggle to recoup production and promotion costs, impacting artist development and overall investment in the industry. Piracy also undermines live music experiences, a crucial income source for many artists, as fans who can access music for free may be less inclined to attend concerts (Shah, 2019).

While creativity and human endeavour fuel economic progress, it is intellectual property rights that recognize and reward individuals for such efforts. However, online piracy is a prime hurdle causing severe revenue leakages in the monetisation of music. Piracy in India is estimated at a staggering 67%, down from 94%, causing an annual loss of Rs. 1500 crore for the country's recorded music industry (Sabharwal, 2019)

A STRATEGIC APPROACH TO COMBATING DIGITAL MUSIC PIRACY

Strengthening the regulatory framework is the first step towards combating piracy. International cooperation on copyright enforcement is essential. Harmonized copyright laws across countries can close loopholes exploited by pirates, making enforcement more effective (Pal, 2023). Additionally, requiring transparency from online music platforms regarding music licensing and content removal procedures promotes accountability and deters infringement (Band, 2001). Regulatory bodies can also establish graduated response systems with escalating penalties for piracy offenses. This can range from educational warnings for casual downloaders to hefty fines for large-scale piracy operations (Kilbride, 2022).

Regulations provide the legal framework, but technology offers the tools for enforcement and user education. Secure streaming services with robust Digital Rights Management (DRM) technology offer a convenient legal alternative to piracy by minimizing unauthorized copying (Bytescare, 2024). Advanced AI systems can be leveraged to identify pirated music across various formats with greater accuracy. This disrupts piracy networks and allows for the efficient removal of infringing content. Blockchain technology holds immense promise for the future. Its secure and transparent system for music rights management can ensure artists are fairly compensated regardless of where their music is streamed (Neu, 2023).

A purely regulatory and technological approach, however, has limitations. User adoption and a shift in cultural attitudes are crucial for long-term success. User-centric solutions like flexible licensing models and reward programs incentivize legal music consumption by offering attractive alternatives to piracy (Band, 2001). Additionally, fostering a culture of respect for intellectual property through education and artist advocacy is key. Collaboration between artists, music labels, technology companies, and governments can lead to public awareness campaigns that educate users about the ethical and financial consequences of piracy.

The fight against digital music piracy is an ongoing battle. By strategically combining regulation and technology, a robust defense can be built. This fosters a sustainable music industry where artists are fairly compensated, innovation flourishes, and music lovers can enjoy their favorite tunes legally and ethically. Furthermore, by promoting user education and fostering a culture of respect for intellectual property, we can create a vibrant musical landscape where both artists and music lovers can thrive.

DIGITAL MUSIC PIRACY AND ITS IMPACT ON THE INDUSTRY

The digital age has revolutionized the way we consume music. Gone are the days of bulky record collections and expensive CDs. With a few clicks, we have access to vast libraries of songs, from timeless classics to the latest hits. However, this convenience has come at a cost: the rampant spread of digital music piracy (Janssens; Daele & Beken, 2009). This illegal practice of copying and distributing copyrighted music without permission has inflicted significant damage on the music industry, impacting everything from artists' livelihoods to the future of music itself.

The most immediate consequence of piracy is the financial loss incurred by artists and rights holders. Every unauthorized download or stream translates to lost revenue. Recording labels, the entities that invest in artists, record albums, and handle marketing, are particularly hit hard. Piracy makes it harder for them to recoup the costs associated with artist development, production, and promotion. This can lead to a vicious cycle – declining revenue from piracy can mean smaller budgets for signing new artists, promoting existing ones, and producing high-quality music (Waldfogel, 2012).

The impact goes beyond just record labels. Artists themselves see their income streams dwindle. Royalties from album sales and streaming platforms form a significant portion of an artist's income. When music is readily available for free online, artists receive a fraction of what they deserve for their hard work and creativity. This financial strain can stifle creativity and innovation (Bender & Wang, 2009). Artists may be forced to prioritize commercially viable music overtaking artistic risks and exploring new sounds.

Live performances are another crucial source of revenue for many artists. However, piracy can indirectly affect the live music scene as well. When fans can access music for free online, they may be less likely to purchase albums or attend concerts, which are key sources of income for artists to recoup production costs and sustain their careers(Shah, 2019).

Beyond the direct financial impact, piracy has a broader negative effect on the music industry. With fewer resources available for artist development and promotion, the diversity of music can suffer. Smaller, independent labels and artists may struggle to compete with established names, leading to a homogenization of sound. Additionally, the constant threat of piracy discourages investment in new music production and exploration of innovative formats and distribution models (Akulavičius & Bartkus, 2015).

The argument that piracy benefits artists by exposing them to a wider audience doesn't hold much weight. While some casual listeners may discover new music through unauthorized channels, they rarely convert into paying fans (Bender & Wang, 2009). Moreover, with piracy, artists have no control over how their music is presented or consumed, and they miss out on potential opportunities for collaborations and endorsements that may arise from legitimate streams.

Combating piracy requires a multi-faceted approach. Strengthening copyright laws and fostering international cooperation are crucial steps. However, the industry also needs to adapt and offer consumers compelling alternatives. User-friendly, subscription-based streaming services with extensive music libraries and personalized recommendations have proven to be a successful countermeasure (Koester, 2008). Additionally, fostering a culture that respects intellectual property and the value of creative work is essential. Educating music fans about the negative consequences of piracy and supporting artists through legal channels is key to building a sustainable future for the music industry.

In conclusion, digital music piracy is a complex issue with far-reaching consequences. It weakens the entire music ecosystem, from artists livelihoods to the creation and distribution of new music for fans. While technological advancements offer solutions, a collaborative effort from artists, music labels, technology companies, and policymakers is necessary to create a legal and sustainable environment where creativity can flourish, and music lovers can continue to enjoy their favorite tunes.

IMPORTANCE OF REGTECH IN COMBATING DIGITAL MUSIC PIRACY

RegTechh as emerged as a pivotal industry leveraging cutting-edge technologies to optimize regulatory processes. In the context of the music industry, RegTech plays a crucial role in addressing regulatory challenges related to digital music piracy. By harnessing advancements like artificial intelligence, automation, data analytics, and blockchain, RegTech offers innovative solutions to enhance regulatory compliance, risk assessment, and monitoring (Butler& O'Brien, 2019). These technologies enable the music industry to navigate complex regulatory landscapes efficiently, automate compliance management, and mitigate the risks associated with piracy. RegTech's application in the music sector extends beyond traditional methods, offering a strategic approach to combat digital music piracy effectively while ensuring fair compensation for artists and rights holders.

Regulating technology plays a crucial role in combatting digital music piracy by providing tools and processes to enhance regulatory compliance and enforcement. Using technology, such as RegTech solutions, artificial intelligence, machine learning, and blockchain, enables organizations to streamline compliance management, improve risk analysis, and identify fraudulent activities related to music piracy. By leveraging technology, the music industry can more effectively monitor and combat illegal downloading and sharing of music, ultimately reducing economic losses, protecting intellectual property rights, and ensuring a fair marketplace for artists and content creators. The integration of technology in regulatory efforts is essential to address the challenges posed by digital piracy and to safeguard the music industry from the detrimental effects of copyright infringement (Sinha & Mandel, 2008).

The music industry faces a complex challenge: balancing the need to protect artists' work through copyright law with the realities of a digital age rife with piracy. Here's where RegTech, comes in. RegTech utilizes innovative solutions to streamline compliance and enforcement processes. In the music industry, RegTech could be applied to develop automated rights management systems or AI-powered tools for identifying pirated content (Watson & Leyshon, 2021). By leveraging these technologies, the music industry can potentially streamline copyright enforcement, ensure artists receive fair compensation, and ultimately foster a healthier creative environment.

The importance of regulation and technology in combating digital music piracy is crucial in safeguarding the rights and revenues of artists, record labels, and other stakeholders in the music industry. The impact of music piracy technologies has been significant, leading to a decline in revenue for record labels and artists, as well as the closure of many music stores. Unauthorized copying and distribution of music online have posed a serious threat to the economic health of the music industry, resulting in substantial financial losses and undermining the value of music. Advances in technology, such as DRM, watermarking, and fingerprinting, play a vital role in combating music piracy by tracing and restricting unauthorized distribution of music (Robinson, 2001). By implementing effective regulatory frameworks and leveraging technological solutions like DRM, the industry can mitigate the risks associated with digital music piracy and protect the intellectual property rights of creators. Collaboration with internet service providers, online stores, and the adoption of blockchain technology can further enhance efforts to combat piracy and ensure fair compensation for artists. Overall, the intersection of regulation and technology is essential in creating a sustainable and secure environment for the music industry to thrive while deterring illegal distribution and consumption of copyrighted music (Watson & Leyshon, 2021).

Combating digital music piracy requires a two-pronged attack: strong regulation and innovative technology. Copyright law establishes the foundation, protecting music as intellectual property and outlining penalties for infringement. International cooperation ensures consistent enforcement across borders. However, regulations alone can't win the fight. Technological solutions like DRM and secure streaming services provide user-friendly alternatives to piracy. Regulation empowers technology by providing a clear legal framework for innovation, while technology strengthens enforcement by aiding in identifying and removing pirated content (Robinson, 2001).

CHALLENGES FACED BY REGULATORY BODIES

The key challenges faced by regulatory bodies in working against digital music piracy include:

The rapid evolution of technology and piracy tactics: The search results indicate that as soon as regulatory bodies and the music industry develop solutions to combat one form of piracy, new and more sophisticated methods emerge. The decentralized nature of peer-to-peer file sharing networks and the use of "bulletproof" internet service providers make it difficult for regulators to keep up (Kumar, 2024).

Monitoring and enforcement across the vast digital landscape: The sheer scale of the internet and the widespread availability of pirated music online pose a significant challenge for regulatory bodies to effectively monitor and enforce anti-piracy measures. The dispersed nature of piracy makes it difficult to identify and target all the perpetrators (Singh, Nigam & Sinha, 2020).

Normalization of piracy among consumers: The search results suggest that the widespread availability of pirated music has led to the normalization of piracy among consumers, making it more challenging for regulatory bodies to change public perception and discourage the illegal consumption of copyrighted content (Karamchandani, 2020).

Limitations of legislation and legal actions: The search results indicate that the current legislative framework and legal actions taken by the music industry have had limited success in deterring digital music piracy. The decentralized nature of piracy and the difficulty in prosecuting individual users pose significant obstacles for regulatory bodies (Pham, Dang & Nguyen, 2020).

Collaboration and cooperation challenges: Effective regulation against digital music piracy requires collaboration between various stakeholders, such as internet service providers, online stores, and social media platforms. The search results suggest that regulatory bodies face challenges in securing adequate cooperation and implementation of anti-piracy measures across these diverse entities (Reis, Matos & Ferreira, 2024).

In summary, the rapid technological advancements, the scale and complexity of the digital landscape, the normalization of piracy, the limitations of existing legislation, and the need for effective collaboration pose significant challenges for regulatory bodies in their efforts to combat digital music piracy.

TECHNOLOGICAL SOLUTIONS FOR DIGITAL MUSIC PIRACY

Digital music piracy has been a persistent challenge for the music industry. Here's a breakdown of some technological solutions aimed at curbing it:

Digital Rights Management (DRM) Systems: DRM technologies like Widevine, PlayReady, and FairPlay can be implemented to attach usage restrictions and access controls to digital music files. This prevents unauthorized distribution and copying of copyrighted content. This technology encrypts music files, restricting copying and unauthorized sharing. However, DRM can be inconvenient for users and sometimes cracked by hackers (Mahajan & Tripathi, 2022).

Watermarking and Content Identification: Watermarking solutions embed unique identifiers within digital music files, allowing the source of any pirated content to be traced back. Content recognition systems can also be used to detect and remove infringing content from online platforms and networks. Embedding a digital watermark into audio files allows for tracking the source of leaks and identifying illegal distribution networks (Borland, 2002).

Streaming Services: Subscription-based platforms like Spotify and Apple Music offer extensive music libraries for a monthly fee, providing a convenient and legal alternative to piracy. Some services offer limited free tiers with ads, incentivizing users to upgrade for an ad-free and full-access experience (Harel, 2022).

Anti-Piracy Software and Monitoring: Specialized anti-piracy software can continuously monitor file-sharing networks and websites to detect illegal distribution of copyrighted music. These solutions can then automate the process of sending takedown notices to remove infringing content (Sudler, 2013).

Integrated Workflow Solutions: Anti-piracy technologies can be integrated directly into content creation and distribution workflows, automating the protection process, and making it easier for creators to safeguard their digital assets (Varsani, 2019).

ISP cooperation: Internet Service Providers (ISPs) can collaborate with rights holders to identify and throttle users engaged in large-scale piracy (Bach, 2004).

Public awareness campaigns: Educating users about the legal and ethical implications of music piracy can foster a culture of supporting artists through legitimate channels (Ahlawat, 2019).

Balancing Security and User Experience: While technological solutions are valuable tools, it's important to strike a balance between protecting content and offering a user-friendly experience. Overly restrictive measures can drive users back to piracy (Varsani, 2019).

Respecting Privacy: Some solutions, like ISP monitoring, raise privacy concerns. Finding ways to combat piracy without compromising user privacy is crucial (Mahajan & Tripathi, 2022).

Global Cooperation: Digital music piracy is a global issue. International collaboration among governments, music labels, and technology companies is necessary for effective solutions (Sudler, 2013).

By leveraging a combination of these technological solutions, the music industry can more effectively combat digital music piracy and protect the rights and revenues of artists and content creators. Apart from all this, certain emerging technologies also provide measures against digital music piracy. Here's a look at some emerging technological advancements addressing this issue:

Blockchain-based Rights Management: Blockchain technology such as Mycelia, offers a secure and decentralized ledger system for tracking music ownership and distribution rights. This can improve transparency in royalty payments and make it harder to tamper with ownership records (Bludov, 2024).

Smart Contracts: Smart contracts can automate royalty distribution based on pre-defined rules, ensuring artists receive fair compensation every time their music is streamed or downloaded (Jurkauskas, 2024).

Automated fingerprinting: Services like Audible Magic can identify copyrighted music used in unauthorized uploads on platforms like YouTube, allowing for takedown requests (Rauta, 2022).

Artificial intelligence: AI can be used for more sophisticated content recognition and personalized recommendations within legal music platforms. Machine learning algorithms can analyze vast amounts of music data to identify pirated copies with greater accuracy, even if they've been slightly altered (Bach, 2023).

Audio Steganography: Embedding hidden codes within audio files themselves can be a more robust method for identifying pirated content compared to traditional watermarking techniques (Leight, 2023).

Micro-transactions and Fan Clubs: Platforms allowing fans to directly tip or purchase exclusive content from artists can create new revenue streams and strengthen artist-fan relationships, reducing reliance on traditional distribution models vulnerable to piracy (Rauta, 2022).

Non-Fungible Tokens (NFTs): NFTs can be used to create unique digital collectibles tied to music releases, offering fans a new way to support artists and own exclusive digital assets (Leight, 2023).

By harnessing these emerging technologies and fostering a collaborative environment, the music industry can move towards a future where piracy is less prevalent, and artists are fairly compensated for their work.

REGULATORY FRAMEWORKS FOR COMBATTING DIGITAL MUSIC PIRACY

Digital music piracy has long been a thorn in the side of the music industry. While technological solutions are crucial, a strong regulatory framework forms the foundation for effective enforcement. Here's a breakdown of key areas within copyright law and related regulations:

Copyright Protection: Copyright law grants creators exclusive rights to control the reproduction, distribution, and public performance of their works. This includes musical compositions and recordings. The Indian Copyright Law does not specifically deal with digital work or to be precise digital music. Even though after the commencement of the "Internet Treaties", the Act was amended in 2012 to comply with the treaty and came up with two major provisions i.e. Sec 65 A & 65 B dealing with technological protection measures and rights management information respectively. These two are penal provisions and state that any person who tries to circumvent the technological protection measures taken by the copyright holder to protect their work and any person who tries to remove the information used on the work to protect will be held liable for imprisonment and fine. However, the Act does not define technological protection measures, and the provisions are not elaborated enough to understand the concept unlike in the treaty.

Enforcement Mechanisms: The Copyright Act, 1957 provides both civil and criminal remedies to the copyright holders against infringement. Copyright holders can sue infringers in civil court to recover damages and obtain injunctions to stop further piracy. However, litigation can be expensive and time-consuming. The Act does not provide the criminal penalty specifically for music piracy. It has become the need of an hour to specially mention a provision with piracy taking place in the entertainment industry as this industry is playing a very important role in the GDP of the economy. Every year the country generates crores of revenue from the entertainment industry.

Notice and Takedown Procedures: The Information Technology Act 2000 in India and similar laws in other countries allow copyright holders to request online platforms to remove infringing content upon notification. For this, the person needs to be vigilant all the time as piracy is taking place at such a vast level specifically in this technological era. Moreover, the notice and takedown process itself doesn't determine whether copyright infringement has occurred. It simply removes the content while leaving the legal issues to be resolved elsewhere, potentially in court.

THE NEXUS OF REGULATORY FRAMEWORK AND TECHNOLOGICAL APPROACH TO COMBAT DIGITAL MUSIC PIRACY

The technology and regulations should work hand in hand to fight against music piracy. In today's digital era piracy takes place using all the technological methods, therefore the law is not sufficient to deal with this menace. There is a need to come up with new technologies to curb this menace and to regulate these technologies so that copyright holders can feel safe and protected. The nexus of the regulatory framework and technology in combating digital music piracy are:

Enhance Regulatory Frameworks: Strengthen international laws and conventions, such as the United Nations Convention on the Law of the Sea (UNCLOS), to provide a robust legal foundation for addressing digital music piracy. Collaborate with governments and policymakers to enact stricter copyright laws and enforcement mechanisms to deter illegal downloading and distribution of copyrighted music. Establish clear guidelines and regulations for online platforms, internet service providers, and other intermediaries to ensure their cooperation in identifying and removing pirated content (Robinson, 2001).

Leverage RegTech Solutions: Implement advanced DRM systems to protect digital music files and restrict unauthorized access and distribution. Utilize watermarking and fingerprinting technologies to enable the tracing and monitoring of pirated music, facilitating the identification of the source of illegal distribution. Develop AI-powered content monitoring and takedown systems to automatically detect and remove pirated music from online platforms and websites. Integrate blockchain technology to create secure and transparent music distribution platforms, ensuring fair compensation for artists and rights holders (Neu, 2023).

Enhance Collaboration and Information Sharing: Foster partnerships between the music industry, regulatory bodies, internet service providers, and online platforms to share intelligence, best practices, and coordinate enforcement actions. Participate in regional and international initiatives, such as those led by the International Maritime Organization (IMO), to facilitate the exchange of information and coordinate joint efforts against digital music piracy. Establish centralized databases and reporting systems to track and analyze piracy trends, enabling more informed decision-making and targeted interventions (Robinson, 2001).

Strengthen Enforcement and Legal Actions: Empower regulatory bodies and law enforcement agencies to investigate and prosecute individuals and organizations involved in digital music piracy, serving as a deterrent. Streamline the process of extradition and cross-border prosecution of pirates to ensure effective legal consequences for their actions. Collaborate with online platforms and intermediaries to implement robust notice-and-takedown procedures to remove infringing content expeditiously (Chawla, 2024).

Educate and Engage Consumers: Launch public awareness campaigns to educate consumers about the ethical and legal implications of music piracy, as well as the risks associated with downloading or streaming pirated content. Promote the availability of affordable and convenient legal music streaming and download services to encourage legitimate consumption and reduce the demand for pirated music. Incentivize consumers to report instances of piracy and collaborate with the industry in identifying and addressing the sources of illegal distribution (Alahwat, 2024).

By integrating these regulatory and technological strategies, the music industry can create a comprehensive and multi-pronged approach to effectively combat the threat of digital music piracy, protect the rights and revenues of artists and rights holders, and foster a sustainable and secure digital ecosystem for the creation and consumption of music.

In summary, the nexus of the regulatory framework and technology is essential in combating digital music piracy. This involves updating copyright laws, collaborating with intermediaries, implementing technological solutions, raising public awareness, and fostering industry-wide coordination and cooperation to effectively address the challenges posed by digital piracy.

CASE STUDIES: COMBATING MUSIC PIRACY WITH INNOVATION

The fight against digital music piracy is a constant battle, but some innovative initiatives have shown promise. Here are a couple of successful case studies:

Spotify's Freemium Model and User Experience

Prior to Spotify, music consumption habits were changing rapidly. The decline of physical media like CDs and the rise of the internet created a demand for convenient, on-demand access to music. However, legal alternatives were often clunky, expensive, or lacked the vast libraries that pirates offered. This gap fueled the growth of piracy, particularly among casual listeners who weren't willing to pay a premium for occasional music enjoyment (Arun, 2023).

Spotify addressed this challenge by introducing a freemium model. This model provided users with free, ad-supported access to a massive music library. This was a significant shift – users no longer needed to pay upfront or navigate complex music software to enjoy their favorite tunes legally (Wijayasekara, 2022). The freemium model offered several key advantages:

Convenience: Spotify's user-friendly interface and mobile apps made it easy to browse, search for, and listen to music on the go. This convenience directly challenged the ease of pirated downloads.

Discovery: Spotify's personalized recommendation algorithms exposed users to new music they might not have discovered otherwise. This fostered a sense of exploration and engagement with the platform, keeping users coming back for more.

Limited Free Tier: The free tier wasn't a complete replacement for a paid subscription. Features like unlimited skips, offline listening, and higher-quality audio were reserved for paying users. This created an incentive to upgrade for a more seamless and enjoyable music experience.

Spotify's freemium model proved to be a game-changer. It offered a user-centric and convenient legal alternative to piracy, attracting millions of users and paving the way for a new era of music consumption. The success of Spotify highlights two key takeaways:

The Importance of User Experience: Providing a user-friendly and enjoyable platform is crucial in the fight against piracy. Convenience and ease of use are essential for competing with the simplicity of illegal downloads.

The Power of Freemium: A well-designed freemium model can attract a large user base and convert a significant portion into paying customers. By offering a taste of the benefits, it incentivizes users to invest in the full experience.

The success of Spotify's freemium model has been replicated by other streaming services like Apple Music and YouTube Music. Today, these platforms offer a vast array of legal music options, making piracy a less attractive choice for many users. However, the fight against piracy is ongoing. New technologies and methods continue to emerge. The music industry needs to maintain a focus on user experience, innovation, and collaboration to ensure a sustainable future where artists and music lovers can both thrive.

The Music Modernization Act (US) and International Copyright Collaboration

Digital music piracy thrives in the cracks of inconsistent copyright laws. Previously, these inconsistencies created a global game of whack-a-mole for rights holders. Pirates could exploit loopholes in one country's laws while operating with impunity elsewhere. This challenged the ability to effectively enforce copyright and ensure fair compensation for artists and songwriters (Elton, 2019).

However, two key initiatives have emerged as powerful tools in combating this issue:

The Music Modernization Act (MMA):The MMA, enacted in the US in 2018, addressed the complexities of digital music licensing for streaming services. Before the MMA, licensing music for streaming services was a cumbersome process, often requiring negotiations with multiple entities. The MMA established a standardized licensing system, making it easier and more efficient for streaming platforms to obtain the necessary rights (Gormley, 2020). The MMA recognized the growing importance of streaming and ensured that songwriters, who may not be the performing artists, receive their fair share of royalties in the digital age. This incentivizes songwriters to keep creating high-quality music that fuels the industry.

The Anti-Counterfeiting Trade Agreement (ACTA): Piracy operates on a global scale, so addressing it requires international cooperation. ACTA is a significant agreement that promotes collaboration between member countries in enforcing copyright laws.

ACTA encourages member countries to align their copyright laws with international standards, creating a more consistent legal framework across borders. This makes it more difficult for pirates to exploit loopholes and operate with impunity in certain jurisdictions. The agreement promotes greater cooperation between law enforcement agencies and copyright enforcement bodies across countries. This allows for coordinated efforts to target piracy operations and disrupt their activities on a global scale (Ward & Beard, 2012).

The combined effect of the MMA and ACTA highlights the importance of regulation and collaboration in combating piracy. The MMA ensures fair compensation for the creative forces behind music, while ACTA strengthens enforcement capabilities on a global stage.

However, the fight against piracy is an ongoing battle. New technologies and methods constantly emerge. Moving forward, collaboration between governments, international organizations, and the music industry will be crucial. Continuously adapting regulations and fostering further international cooperation are essential steps to ensure a level playing field for artists and songwriters and a sustainable future for the music industry.

YouTube's Content ID System

In the vast ocean of YouTube videos, the platform faces a constant challenge: ensuring copyrighted music isn't uploaded illegally. Here's where YouTube's Content ID system comes in – a powerful tool that utilizes advanced fingerprinting technology to identify and address potential piracy concerns (Beeson, 2013).

Building the Database: Rights holders, such as record labels, music publishers, and artists themselves, can submit their music files to YouTube's Content ID database. This database acts as a digital reference library containing unique identifiers, or "fingerprints," for copyrighted music.

Scanning Uploads: Whenever someone uploads a video to YouTube, Content ID automatically scans the audio track against the reference database. This scanning process is incredibly fast and efficient, analyzing the audio for its unique characteristics and comparing it to the fingerprints stored in the database.

Matching and Claims: If a match is found between the uploaded video and a copyrighted work in the database, Content ID triggers a claim. This claim can result in various actions depending on the copyright holder's preferences:

Blocking: The video may be blocked from being viewed entirely, essentially removing it from the platform.

Monetization: The copyright holder can claim the ad revenue generated by the video, ensuring they receive some compensation even if the video remains online.

Tracking: The video might be allowed to stay online, but its viewership statistics are tracked and reported to the rights holder.

There are several benefits of Content ID, such as, Content ID automates the process of identifying potential copyright infringement, saving time and resources compared to manual review of every upload. The system can handle the massive volume of video uploads on YouTube, ensuring a consistent response to potential piracy attempts. Content ID empowers artists and copyright holders to protect their work and ensure they are fairly compensated for its use. Content ID provides copyright holders with clear information about claimed videos and gives them control over the actions taken (Beeson, 2013).

There are a few Challenges also, such as, while powerful, Content ID isn't perfect. Occasionally, the system might misidentify a legitimate use of copyrighted material, leading to disputed claims. YouTube offers a system for creators to appeal these claims. Content ID can raise concerns about fair use, where copyrighted material is used for purposes like criticism, commentary, or parody. YouTube provides guidelines to help creators understand fair use principles. Content ID primarily focuses on audio matching. Visual copyright infringement, such as using copyrighted music videos without permission, may require separate reporting mechanisms (Beeson, 2013).

Content ID remains a crucial tool for YouTube in its fight against digital music piracy. As technology evolves, we can expect further advancements in the system. For instance, the ability to identify and match visual content more effectively could broaden its scope. Additionally, ongoing collaboration between YouTube and rights holders can refine the system to minimize false positives and ensure fair treatment for creators who use copyrighted material within the boundaries of fair use.

China's Copyright Crackdown

China's aggressive campaign against digital music piracy is a complex issue with both positive and negative implications. The Positive Impact shows a substantial decrease in illegal music downloads. This benefits artists and rights holders who receive fairer compensation for their work. With fewer illegal downloads, legal music streaming services have seen a surge in popularity. This injects much-needed revenue into the music industry, fostering investment in new music creation and artist development. The aggressive approach sends a strong message that copyright infringement is taken seriously. This can deter potential pirates and encourage users to turn to legal alternatives (Wodecki, 2020).

On the other hand, the Concerns show that China's approach often relies on heavy-handed tactics like internet surveillance and content blocking. This raises concerns about user privacy and freedom of expression. Some argue that China's regulations stifle innovation and limit user access to diverse music. This can have a chilling effect on artistic expression and creativity. The enforcement process in China can be opaque, making it difficult to assess the fairness and effectiveness of the measures taken. This lack of transparency fuels concerns about potential abuse of power (Xinhua, 2021).

Finding the right balance is crucial. For which China can collaborate with other countries to develop more effective and consistent anti-piracy measures that respect user privacy and intellectual property rights. Instead of solely relying on enforcement, China could invest in creating a more user-friendly and affordable legal music ecosystem. Greater transparency in enforcement procedures and increased accountability for government agencies can address concerns about arbitrary power and censorship (Xinhua, 2023).

China's copyright crackdown has shown that aggressive tactics can be effective in reducing piracy. However, the concerns about user privacy and the overall regulatory environment cannot be ignored. Moving forward, a more balanced approach that prioritizes both copyright protection and user rights is essential for creating a sustainable music industry in China and fostering a global environment that respects creativity and innovation.

These cases showcase how innovation in regulation and technology, coupled with user-centric solutions, can create a more balanced landscape for the music industry. As technology continues to evolve, ongoing collaboration and adaptation will be crucial in the ongoing fight against digital music piracy.

Potential challenges, ethical considerations, and future trends in the intersection of regulation, technology, and piracy prevention

While regulation and technology offer powerful tools for combating digital music piracy, their intersection presents its own set of challenges and ethical considerations. Here's a breakdown of some key areas to consider:

Challenges

Finding the right balance between protecting artists' rights and fostering innovation, user access, and fair use is crucial. Overly restrictive regulations can stifle creativity and impede technological advancement.

1. Enforcing copyright laws effectively in a globalized digital space remains a challenge. Jurisdictional differences and the anonymity of online activity can make it difficult to track down and prosecute piracy operations.
2. Piracy methods and technology constantly evolve, requiring continuous adaptation of regulations and technological solutions. Staying ahead of the curve is a never-ending battle.
3. Technologies like AI-powered fingerprinting and content scanning can raise concerns about user privacy and data collection practices. Ensuring appropriate safeguards is crucial.
4. Regulations requiring internet platforms to actively monitor user activity and remove infringing content can be resource-intensive and raise issues related to freedom of expression.

Ethical Considerations

1. Both regulatory frameworks and technological solutions need to be transparent in their operations and accountable to the public.
2. Regulations and technological solutions should not create barriers to access music, particularly for users in developing countries with limited internet resources.
3. When addressing piracy, it's crucial to ensure a fair and balanced approach that protects the rights of both copyright holders and users.
4. Regulations and technological solutions shouldn't stifle innovation in music creation and distribution models.

Future Trends

1. Blockchain technology offers a promising avenue for secure and transparent music rights management, ensuring artists receive fair compensation regardless of where their music is streamed.
2. Advanced AI systems can be used not only for content identification but also for proactive measures like detecting and disrupting piracy operations.
3. The focus will likely shift towards building user trust and loyalty by providing legal alternatives that are convenient, affordable, and offer high-quality music experiences.
4. Public awareness campaigns that educate users about the ethical and financial consequences of piracy will become increasingly important.
5. Stronger international cooperation on copyright enforcement and the development of harmonized regulations will be crucial in addressing the global nature of piracy.

By addressing these challenges and ethical considerations, and by embracing future trends, we can create a more sustainable future for the music industry. One where artists are fairly compensated, technology fosters innovation, and music lovers can enjoy their favorite tunes legally and ethically.

CONCLUSION

In summary, the key findings from the information provided highlight the critical role of integrating regulation and technology to effectively combat the threat of digital music piracy. The rapid evolution of technology has significantly exacerbated the issue of music piracy, enabling the widespread and instantaneous distribution of copyrighted content without the consent of rights holders. This has led to substantial financial losses for the music industry, undermining the value of music and discouraging innovation and creative expression.

Regulatory bodies face numerous challenges in working against digital music piracy, including the rapid pace of technological change, the vast and decentralized nature of the digital landscape, the normalization of piracy among consumers, and the limitations of existing legislation. To address these challenges, the music industry has had to leverage innovative RegTech solutions, such as advanced DRM systems, watermarking, and AI-powered content monitoring and takedown tools.

Successful initiatives have involved a combination of legal actions, industry collaborations, public awareness campaigns, and the strengthening of copyright laws and enforcement mechanisms. However, potential challenges remain, including ethical considerations around the unauthorized use of copyrighted material and the need to balance the interests of artists, creators, and consumers.

Looking to the future, the intersection of regulation, technology, and piracy prevention is expected to see continued advancements in RegTech solutions, increased collaboration among stakeholders, the expansion of RegTech applications to other regulated industries, and the potential integration of emerging technologies like blockchain to create more secure and transparent music distribution platforms. By addressing these evolving trends and challenges, the music industry can work towards a more sustainable and secure digital ecosystem that protects the rights and revenues of artists and rights holders while fostering innovation and creativity.

Combatting digital music piracy requires a strategic marriage of regulation and technology. Stronger international copyright laws and transparency requirements for online platforms establish a firm legal foundation. This is bolstered by technological advancements like secure streaming with DRM and AI-powered content identification that can pinpoint pirated music across formats. Blockchain offers a promising path for the future, ensuring artists are fairly compensated through its secure and transparent rights management system. However, regulations alone are not enough. User-centric solutions like flexible licensing models and reward programs incentivize legal music consumption. Ultimately, fostering a culture of respect for intellectual property through education and artist advocacy is key to creating a sustainable music ecosystem where piracy risks are minimized. This combined approach ensures both artists and music lovers thrive in a fair and vibrant musical landscape.

REFERENCES

Ahlawat, S. (n.d.). Music Piracy: The Looming Peril for Music Industries in the Digital Age. https://subhashahlawat.com/blog/music-piracy

Akulavičius, M., & Vaclovas, E. (2015). Possibilities of Digital Piracy Management in Music Records Industry. *Procedia: Social and Behavioral Sciences*, 213, 716–721. 10.1016/j.sbspro.2015.11.492

Arun, R. (2023). A Case Study on Spotify Marketing Strategy. *Simplilearn.* https://www.simplilearn.com/tutorials/marketing-case-studies-tutorial/spotify-marketing -strategy

Bach, D. (2004). The Double Punch of Law and Technology: Fighting Music Piracy or Remaking Copyright in a Digital Age? *Business and Politics*, 6(2), 3–3. 10.2202/1469-3569.1089

Band, J. (2001). The Copyright Paradox: Fighting Content Piracy in the Digital Era. *Brookings.* https://www.brookings.edu/articles/the-copyright-paradox-fighting -content-piracy-in-the-digital-era/

Becker, M., Merz, K., & Buchkremer, R. (2024). RegTech—the application of modern information technology in regulatory affairs: Areas of interest in research and practice. *ResearchGate.* https://www.researchgate.net/publication/341821781 _RegTech_the_Application_of_Modern_Information_Technology_Solutions_in _Regulatory_Affairs_Areas_of_Interest_in_Research_and_Practice

Beeson, S. (2023). YouTube Content ID explained. *Uppbeat.* https://uppbeat.io/ blog/youtube-content-id/

Bender, M. T., & Wang, Y. (2009). The Impact of Digital Piracy on Music Sales: A Cross-Country Analysis. *International Social Science Review*, 84(3/4), 157–170. https://www.jstor.org/stable/41887409

Bludov, S. (2024). Music Streaming Trends: 7 Innovations and Strategies in the Digital Music Industry to Watch for in 2024. *Dataart.* https://www.dataart.com/ blog/music-streaming-trends

Borland, J. (2002). New technology could help squelch digital music piracy. *CNET.* https://www.cnet.com/tech/services-and-software/new-technology-could-help -squelch-digital-music-piracy/

Butler, T., & Brien, L. (2019). *Understanding RegTech for Digital Regulatory Compliance: FinTech and Strategy in the 21st Century.* 10.1007/978-3-030-02330-0_6

Chawla, S. (2014). Digital Piracy & Copyright Enforcement: Approaches to Tackling Online. *TaxGuru*. https://taxguru.in/corporate-law/digital-piracy-copyright-enforcement-approaches-tackling-online-infringement.html

Elton, S. (2019). Mechanical Licensing Before and After the Music Modernization Act. *Journal of the Music & Entertainment Industry Educators Association*, 19(1), 13–35. 10.25101/19.1

Estevez, E. (2020). RegTech: Definition, Who Uses It and Why, and Example Companies. *Investopedia*. https://www.investopedia.com/terms/r/regtech.asp

Gormley, H. (2020). *The Breakdown: What Songwriters Need to Know about the Music Modernization Act and Royalty Payments*. https://blogs.loc.gov/copyright/2020/04/the-breakdown-what-songwriters-need-to-know-about-the-music-modernization-act-and-royalty-payments/

Granados, N. (2016). How Online Piracy Hurts Emerging Artists. *Forbes*. https://www.forbes.com/sites/nelsongranados/2016/02/01/how-online-piracy-hurts-emerging-artists/?sh=1a68e7d17774

Harel, M. (2022). 6 Ways to Stop Digital Piracy. *Viaccess*. https://www.viaccess-orca.com/blog/six-ways-to-stop-digital-piracy

Janssens, E., Daele, S., & Vander, T. (2009). The Music Industry on (the) Line? *Journal of Crime, Criminal Law and Criminal Justice*, *17*, 77–96. https://www.researchgate.net/publication/228223919_The_Music_Industry_on_the_Line_Surviving_Music_Piracy_in_a_Digital_Era

Jurkauskas, L. (2015). Digital Piracy as an innovation in Recording Industry Linas. *Projekter*. https://projekter.aau.dk/projekter/files/213765961/Digital_Piracy_as_an_Innovation_in_Recording_Industry_by_L._Jurkauskas.pdf

Karamchandani, S. Protecting Music from Digital Exploitation: Challenges to Copyright Laws in Digital India. *Legalserviceindia*. https://www.legalserviceindia.com/legal/article-11107-protecting-music-from-digital-exploitation-challenges-to-copyright-laws-in-digital-india.html#google_vignette

Kumar, S. (2024). Tackling digital piracy: The Indian context. The complexities of hate speech laws in India. *Linkedin*. https://www.linkedin.com/pulse/tackling-digital-piracy-indian-context-complexities-nyiac/

Leight, E. (2023). Music Piracy Is Rising — And the U.S. Is a Trouble Spot. *BillBoard*. https://www.billboard.com/pro/music-piracy-2022-stream-ripping/

Li, J., Maiti, A., & Fei, J. (2023). Features and Scope of Regulatory Technologies: Challenges and Opportunities with Industrial Internet of Things. *Future Internet*, 15(8), 256. 10.3390/fi15080256

Mahajan, S., & Tripathi, V. (n.d.). Three Solutions to Curb Piracy in the Music Industry. *WNS*. https://www.wns.com/perspectives/articles/articledetail/706/three -solutions-to-curb-piracy-in-the-music-industry

Neu, M. (2023). Understanding Music Piracy and its Impact on the Industry. *Reprtoir*.https://www.reprtoir.com/blog/music-piracy

Pal, L. (2023). Digital Piracy and Intellectual Property Protection, *Bytescare*. https:// bytescare.com/blog/digital-piracy-intellectual-property-protection

Patrick, K. (2022). Digital piracy jeopardises India's flourishing creative economy. *TOI.* https://timesofindia.indiatimes.com/blogs/voices/digital-piracy-jeopardises -indias-flourishing-creative-economy/

Pham, Q. T., Dang, N. M., & Nguyen, D. T. (2020). Factors Affecting on the Digital Piracy Behavior: An Empirical Study in Vietnam. *Journal of Theoretical and Applied Electronic Commerce Research*, 15(2), 0. Advance online publication. 10.4067/S0718-18762020000200108

Rauta, A. (2022). Digital Music Piracy: Trends, Challenges and the Way Forward. *IPRMentLaw*. https://iprmentlaw.com/guest-column/guest-interview-in-conversation -with-ms-melissa-morgia-of-ifpi-on-digital-music-piracy-trends-challenges-and-the -way-forward/

Reis, F., Matos, M. G., & Ferreira, P. (2024). Controlling digital piracy via domain name system blocks: A natural experiment. *Journal of Economic Behavior & Organization*, 218, 89–103. 10.1016/j.jebo.2023.12.005

Shah, U. (2019). Digital Music Piracy in India: Issues and Challenges. *International Journal of Research in Social Sciences*, 9(6). https://www.ijmra.us/project%20doc/ 2019/IJRSS_JUNE2019/IJMRA-15747.pdf

Singh, M., Nigam, A., & Sinha, S. (2020). Combating Copyright Online Piracy in India: Government's Initiatives and Judicial Enforcement. *Lexorbis*. https:// lexorbis.com/combating-copyright-online-piracy-in-india-governments-initiatives -and-judicial-enforcement/

Sinha, R. K., & Mandel, N. (2008). Preventing Digital Music Piracy: The Carrot or the Stick? *Journal of Marketing*, 72(1), 1–15. 10.1509/jmkg.72.1.001

Sudler, H. (2013). Effectiveness of anti-piracy technology: Finding appropriate solutions for evolving online piracy. *Business Horizons*, 56(2), 149–157. 10.1016/j. bushor.2012.11.001

Varsani, J. (2019). Fighting against Digital Piracy in the Streaming Age. *Cartesian.* https://www.cartesian.com/fighting-against-digital-piracy-in-the-streaming-age/

Waldfogel, J. Music Piracy and Its Effects on Demand, Supply, and Welfare. *Carlson School and Department of Economics, University of Minnesota.* https://www.journals .uchicago.edu/doi/epdf/10.1086/663157

Ward, P., & Beard, J. (2012). The Anti-Counterfeiting Trade Agreement (ACTA). *CommonsLibrary.* https://commonslibrary.parliament.uk/research-briefings/sn06248/

Watson, A., & Leyshon, A. (2021). *Negotiating platformisation: MusicTech, intellectual property rights and third wave platform reintermediation in the music industry.* 10.1080/17530350.2022.2028653

Wijayasekara, K. (2022). How Spotify's freemium business model made $11.42B in revenue in 2021? *Linkedin.* https://www.linkedin.com/pulse/how-spotifys-freemium -business-model-made-1142b-2021-wijayasekara/

Wodecki, B. (2020). *China begins 'nationwide' copyright crackdown.* https://www .i-law.com/ilaw/doc/view.htm?id=410125

Xinhua. (2021). *Crackdown on pirated-video platform signals China's resolve on copyright protection.* http://www.xinhuanet.com/english/2021-02/05/c_139722134 .htm

Chapter 12
Automated Vehicles Landscape and India Through a Regulatory Lens

Smita Gupta
Galgotias University, India

Lavanya Bhagra
Maharashtra National Law University, Nagpur, India

ABSTRACT

This chapter examines various perspectives and challenges related to the integration of artificial intelligence (AI) in the transportation industry, particularly focusing on automated. The chapter also addresses the governance of AI, emphasizing the importance of responsible, ethical, and transparent control mechanisms. The chapter then explores AV 4.0, the latest guidance from the US Department of Transportation, which outlines efforts to support and advance autonomous vehicles while ensuring accountability. The legal status of automated vehicles is analysed under different regimes, including international conventions, national regulations, and state vehicle codes. The chapter recommends measures to increase legal certainty for automated vehicles, such as the development of common definitions and monitoring of relevant conventions.

DOI: 10.4018/979-8-3693-3322-8.ch012

I. INTRODUCTION

The technologically advanced sensory facilities have become a future of artificially driven transportation. Since long, the AI regulated world has been discerned to be captivating by many futurists and aficionados. Yet, according to the present circumstances in the transportation industry all over the globe, the revolution of the world towards automated future of AI regulated or self-driven vehicle is already being accepted by many. The environmental hazards such as blooming population, overcrowding on city roads, reduction in resources and shooting operational costs are on hike. Briefly, taking conscious steps towards preceding and many other rising intricacies that the globe is facing or might face in the near future, the advanced emerging technologies are jointly working on bring into existence vehicles having divergent sizes, shapes and automation for commuting. This is where the autonomous vehicles come into existence.

In comparison to human-driven automobiles, automation may indeed be capable of offering significant perks. One possible benefit is reduction in collisions which becomes a reason for countless lives annually, thus driverless vehicles might substantially decrease the number of casualties make fewer errors than people, (de Sio, 2017). Self-driving cars to a large limit assure to propose solutions to these traffic problems of longer vehicular queueing, slower speeds and even decreasing the mortalities. Driverless vehicles can indeed be the best solutions to humanistic behaviours which produce roadblocks.

Additional potential advantage of driverless vehicles will be to old age or disabled individuals who can more conveniently operate automated automobiles for transportation. Indeed, it also include the Added benefits of automated vehicles include the eradication of driving exhaustion due to which many cases of sleep over long travels occurs.

Artificial Intelligence is being created as a supplement towards the digital online economy, which it could eventually control. There seems to be no doubt that there is a distinction to be made between both the technical edifice of Internet to integrate people and information in corollary to what is happening on the Internet, just as there is a distinction to be made between the conceptual development of AI for better and the relevance and objectives with which it is successfully invented by many who govern its advancement, (Nemitz, n.d.).

Broadly, AI is an effective tool in the enforcement of the law. Other areas wherein legislators need to observe utmost caution is data security. The benefits of AI encompass better justice delivery system in the world if law-making authorities can take into consideration these problems and build regulatory framework accordingly.

For instance, in Indian perspective policy development in regard to Artificial Intelligence (AI) is rapidly growing. The geographical significance of the country, expanding AI domain, and significant legislative AI programmes, make it quite an essential country, to be examined, (Hubbard, 2014). Even though established regulatory mechanisms aims to motivate the accelerated advancement for economic growth and social gain, an integrated and holistic phenomenon continues in India as well as several other territories: the restrictions and threats of information decision - making remain observational concerns for AI application building and implementation (Calo, 2015).

II. LITERATURE REVIEW

There has been a wave of AI technology influence in the transportation industry across all countries. Automated vehicles future AI technology is already initiated in few countries. The uncertainty of introduction of emotional AI in automobiles and how well to control such innovations has been emphasised by McStay A. & Urquhart L. (2022). They have further studied the approaches on automobile driver-monitoring technology that assess bodies to predict and response to emotions, weariness, and attention are also examined by them.

Critics of Artificial Intelligence have pointed out AI is on its way to create intelligent computers that are considerably more competent than humans and may result in drastic and unanticipated consequences for humans. The nexus, according to some experts, might happen in around 2030, Amitai E., Oren E (2017).

Etzioni, O. (2018) pin-points the absence of any kind of regulatory authority to oversee AI applications, which are likely to come up in future. Assignment of appropriate regulatory authority is an urgent need and even a shift, as to how we perceive rules, from cumbersome administration to well-being guardians, is required. According to him that the primary goal must be to safeguard persons and civilization from damage. E. Scherer, M.U. (2015) stressed in his study that AI pervades our lives in a variety of subtle and not-so-subtle manner. There have been countries where automated vehicles have already been certified for road use, it is not too far when emergence of these vehicles in the mainstream market may revolutionise transportation system.

Cath, C. (2018) has focussed his work on Governing AI, such as integrated AI in robots and artificial intelligence techniques, can help to enhance financial, social, and human rights outcomes. The paper emphasised on the demand to control AI in a way that is responsible, ethical, and transparent. Levine, J. and Yergin, R. (2020) in their work have tried to explain AV 4.0 which is the newest guidance from the US Department of Transportation regarding the advancement and implementation of autonomous vehicles. Its purpose is to outline the government's efforts to support and advance the use of such vehicles, while also ensuring accountability for those who use and are impacted by them. The guidance compiles information from various sources rather than providing strict regulations. Smith, B. (2014) have focused their work to analyse the legal status of automated vehicles under three key regimes are "the 1949 Geneva Convention on Road Traffic, regulations by the National Highway Traffic Safety Administration (NHTSA), and the vehicle codes of all 50 US states". As per the Convention held in Geneva, automated driving is not prohibited but requires a driver who can always control the vehicle. NHTSA regulations do not generally prohibit automated vehicles. State vehicle codes may complicate automated driving by assuming the presence of human drivers and requiring specific actions. The article recommends five near-term measures to increase legal certainty for automated vehicles, including the development of common definitions and close monitoring of the 1969 Vienna Convention. Brady, M. (2019) in his article suggests that the current privacy framework will not be effective in preserving personal information in data generated by automated land vehicles. The existing privacy laws in Australia are not equipped to handle the protection of personal information generated by automated vehicles. As automation technology advances, these vehicles will collect, transmit, and disperse more data about vehicle and its passengers. This data, when analysed through data mining techniques, can reveal personal information about individuals. A recent court case, "Privacy Commissioner v. Telstra Corporation Ltd," has shown that current Australian law does not acknowledge personal information that is not contained in a single data stream, and lacks guidelines for identifying personal information in data with multiple subjects. Contissa, G., Lagioia, F., & Sartor, G. (2017) article proposes a new approach to addressing the ethical challenges posed by autonomous vehicle accidents. Instead of programming the self-driving cars to make ethical decisions, the authors suggest that the responsibility be given to the user or passenger through an "Ethical Knob." This device would allow the passenger to customize the ethical approach taken by the AV in unavoidable accidents. The manufacturers would then be responsible for enabling the passenger's choice and ensuring that it is implemented by the vehicle. This approach shifts the decision-making from the manufacturer to the passenger and presents a unique solution to the ethical and legal concerns surrounding autonomous vehicles. Abraham K. & Rabin R (2019) the authors understand that with the advancement of technology in the automotive industry will eventually replace present driver focussed liability system. However, before this happens, there will be a period where accidents will occur involving conventional vehicles (CVs), highly automated vehicles (HAVs), and third parties. During this transitional period, the authors suggest using traditional tort law to address these accidents. But as HAVs become more widespread and dominant, a new legal framework that better fits the new reality of accidents will be required. The authors propose that the Modified Enterprise Responsibility (MER) system can fill this role and believe that although this shift away from the traditional tort system may be unsettling, it will ultimately prove to be beneficial, similar to the introduction of workers' compensation in the past.

METHODOLOGY

This a conceptual paper beginning with introduction and reviews literature that addresses contemporary issues on artificial intelligence and automated transportation. The scheme of this paper is divided into eight parts. Section 3 deals with examining peculiarities of smart future. Section 4 discusses regulations existing around the world on this dimension. Section 5 sheds light on Indian current scenario along with challenges. Section 6 specifically delves into legal-ethical challenges. Section 7 traverse's regulatory options & the potential pace of change and lastly section 8 covers concluding remarks.

III. PECULIARITIES OF SMART FUTURE

An advanced technology sensory facility vehicle which can perceive its surroundings, with a potential to run itself and dispense vital functions without any human intervention is known as autonomous vehicle (AV) (Geistfeld, 2017). Through this- 'technologically-advanced sensory facility to perceive its surroundings' such a vehicle is made competent to react to the external surroundings like what a human driven vehicle would do.

To understand the differences between the technologically advanced and autonomous vehicles (AV)s. Any vehicle's independency and operating competencies are usually governed by six stages of automation. These are numbered from zero to five and are described as follows: (Foot, 1967).

Level Zero: At this level a vehicle's automation and various other operations are completely reliant on a human driver.

Level One: With an effective ADAS (Advanced Driver Assistance System) the upgraded experience by assisting the driver with one or more of the following processes: accelerating, steering, or braking is improved.

Level Two: Coming to this stage, the ADAS examines all three functions of accelerating, steering, and braking under specific conditions. But still the controlling edge remains with the human driver, who examines the additional tasks involved in driving a vehicle.

Level Three: As ADS (advanced driving system) becomes operational, this is the first step of true advancement in automobile technology. Until it asks the human driver to take charge of the operation, ADS can handle practically all of the responsibilities associated with driving. In such a case it is expected that a human driver is the one who follows instructions.

Level Four: ADS at this level, can self-automate all driving functions with least of human intervention in most cases.

Level Five: ADS in this level, without any human assistance can fully operate and control vehicular motion. This level of automation can be achieved through usage of 5G technology, which opens a new corridor for vehicle to interact with other vehicles and even with traffic signals, signs, and roadways, (Paul Keller, 2018).

Maintaining the vehicle's speed is another vital element to mention while talking about driving achieved by the technique of adaptive cruise control, which helps in maintaining safe distance and automatically modifies the speed, if two vehicles are very close by.[1]

The greatest revolutionizing technology of this century is indeed both labour-saving and accident-reductive. Although, the legal implications of these advanced robotic motors are undoubtedly huge and cannot be neglected. There are rules controlling the handling of technology-driven cars in these nations because the revolution began mostly in the industrialised world.[2]

V. REGULATIONS AROUND THE WORLD

For a long time, tests in regard to automated driving test were not considered by any government across globe due to the majority of global states adopting at "Vienna Convention on Road Traffic in 1968", which demanded a human operator to be present at all times when they drove this car on the road. "This lasted until an amendment to Article 8 of the Convention was enacted in 2014, in which nations recognized the changing and expanding technology and deemed it as permitted, to drive a car as long as it could be 'overridden' or 'turned off' by a human driver" (Smith, 2017).

National governments have committed to considerably expanding public funding for AI through increasing R&D spending, establishing industrial and investment funds for AI companies, and expanding in networks and services, as well as AI-related public contracts.[3] China, the United States, France, and Japan have all pledged considerable public funds to AI research and development.

Dentons, the largest legal firm of the world, highlighted the fact that, with an ideological change in global automotive sector, nations around the world are voicing for framing of policy and guidelines to address issues such as security, accountability, and user privacy, mentioned in report - "Global Guide to Autonomous Vehicles," (Huber & Litan, 1991). Despite the fact that policies are not present in many of the countries, "the governments of the United States of America, the United Kingdom, Australia, Canada, New Zealand, China, and Germany have initiated deliberating a developed jurisprudence related to the new technological discovery that is seen as the future of global transit". Some of which are mentioned below: (Gogoll & Muller, 2016).

A. CANADA

The government of Canada is divided into three levels: federal, provincial or territorial, and municipal. According to the research, autonomous vehicle regulations are accessible throughout all three levels, with the federal level focusing on regions such as 'Ontario, Quebec, British Columbia', and some few other cities. The study also reported that when it comes to the law and policies regulating autonomous vehicles, safety seems to be a major concern for Canadian politicians, who would like to encourage this innovation without jeopardizing humanity or safety, (TWI, n.d.).

B. USA

Interestingly, the United States of America is well advanced of the rest of the globe in terms of driverless car testing, but much behind in terms of having a relevant statutory structure in place for AVs. In a federal system such as the United States, inter-state acceptance is critical, and government law is critical for proper national implementation of AV regulations. A majority of states have already approved their own legislative laws or presidential directives, and enacting a national legislation is viewed as a top priority. Nevada was the first state in the world to allow autonomous vehicles on the roads in 2011[4]

C. CHINA

China has become one of the countries spearheading the charge toward driverless mobility and is well ahead of the curve in terms of enacting legislation to govern it. At both the national and municipal levels of governance, there are existing road safety standards that include AVs. The Ministry of Industry and Information Technology, in collaboration with the Ministries of Public Security and Transport, has issued Regulations on the Administration of Road Testing of Autonomous Vehicles, which is aiding the country's innovative advancement, (Goodall, 2016). The fundamental goal of the Chinese government in enacting these rules, according to the research, is to create its existence with an innovative, high-tech industrial model.

D. AUSTRALIA

Different rules apply to road safety and vehicle usage on a state and territorial level in Australia, resulting in a legislative structure that is inconsistent throughout the states. To address this issue, the Australian government issued Australian Road Rules (or ARRs) in 2018 mostly on proposal of the National Transport Commission for pan-Australian implementation. According to the article, the Commission is also vehemently considering incorporating the existing challenges and alternatives linked with automated vehicles into their rules and amending them to accommodate innovation.[5]

E. NEW ZEALAND

While the New Zealand government is eager and encouraging the operation of wholly or semi-autonomous cars, the nation seems to have no legislation or rules surrounding self-driving vehicles and transporting. The notion that there really is no stringent law or restrictions prohibiting the implementation or test for this modern technology is a significant reality.

F. UNITED KINGDOMS

The United Kingdom has an administration that is pro-autonomous vehicles and had earlier targeted to have self-driving cars on the streets by the year 2021. The administration believes that such cars will make life easier, safer, and more accessible for all. The Department of Transport of the United Kingdom oversees overseeing autonomous cars, their testing, and installation.

Aside from these, nations including as Japan, Sweden, Switzerland, Singapore, and the United Arab Emirates have made substantial progress in developing AVs and associated regulatory frameworks. In 2014, France unveiled its roadmap for AVs that included designation of specific zones for experimentation, as well as R&D initiatives related to AVs and driverless vehicles, (Lin, 2014).

G. GERMANY

Germany is not just a pioneer in automotive production, but is also a lead in self-driving vehicles. According to the paper, the government has a legislative plan in place for driverless cars, but it needs to be extended countrywide for efficient execution.

H. ARGENTINA

Artificial intelligence (AI) and big data analytics are already common for intellectual discourse with its branches deepening into the legal system across the globe. "Prometea[6] is an artificially intelligent tool developed in Argentina by the Innovation and Artificial Intelligence Laboratory of the University of Buenos Aires, School of Law, and the Buenos Aires Public Prosecutor's Office. Its goal is to speed up bureaucratic processes so that more time may be spent on difficult case analysis. It can also find critical instances in enormous amounts of data in well under few minutes," (Sreejani, 2021).

I. INDIA

The Indian car industry, which accounts for 7.1% of the nation's GDP, is indeed one of the world's biggest, contributing significantly to domestic service, manufacturing and distribution, exports, international trade, and income. Without a question, innovation, development, and, most crucially, automation are the keys to this essential industry's prospects. As a result, many of the foreign as well domestic firms are thinking to get involve in financing of autonomous cars and bringing them to India.

Several automotive manufacturers and technological behemoths, including Tesla, General Motors, Audi, Mercedes-Benz, Nissan, Uber, Toyota, and others, are pouring resources and effort into the development of self - driving vehicles on a worldwide scale. However, in comparison to its worldwide counterparts, the Indian car sector is still lagging and developing at a snail's pace. Furthermore, due to worries of enormous job losses, the existing administration has demonstrated a clear lack of desire to bring driverless vehicles on Indian roads, (Millar, 2015).

In India, the government has been actively promoting the development, expansion, and adoption of autonomous vehicles. The Ministry of Road Transport & Highways has set up a committee to examine the legal and regulatory structure planned for autonomous vehicles in India. The committee has proposed several measures such as the creation of a national level test track for autonomous vehicles, the development of a national policy on autonomous vehicles, and the creation of a dedicated fund for the development of autonomous vehicle technology. In addition, several Indian companies and startups are working on developing autonomous vehicle technology, including Tata Motors, Mahindra & Mahindra, and Ola. However, the deployment of autonomous vehicles in India is still in its infancy with many challenges to be faced, such as infrastructure development, cyber-security, and the regulation of autonomous vehicles.

Mr Nitin Gadkari, the Hon'ble Minister of Road Transport and Highways, discusses the reason of the government that it is not opposed to technology but it would jeopardise lakh drivers jobs where there is already shortage of 25 lakh. As one of the key revenues for many is driving skill. Government claims that the deployment of AVs would result in losing almost more than 1 crore people's job. Due to this attitude of government, many financiers do not consider India to be a promising market for self-driving vehicles, and so do not consider it worthwhile to invest in.[7]

Another hindrance to this innovative endeavour is the poor condition of country's roads and highways, which show infrastructure flaws and lead to high accident fatalities. Nonetheless, numerous indigenous start-ups and major giants like Tata and Mahindra are investing in the AV sector's expansion despite the difficulties and inadequacies. Indeed, it must not be ignored that that the introduction of AV technology in India will to some extent address issues like as pollution, carbon emissions, fuel use, road congestion, improved urban planning, road and transportation system development, and improved network connection.

V. CHALLENGES IN CONTEXT TO INDIA

India's automotive industry has witnessed remarkable growth in recent years, solidifying its position as the third-largest auto market globally, surpassing Japan. There are several contributory factors, including a burgeoning middle class with increased purchasing power, a growing urban population, and a robust demand for affordable and fuel-efficient vehicles. Indian automakers have adeptly responded to these market dynamics by producing innovative and competitive models tailored to the needs of the Indian consumer, thus it is pertinent to mention India when it comes to discussing the future of AI regulated vehicles. Additionally, the Indian Government's initiatives aimed at boosting the automotive sector, such as the 'Make in India' campaign, have further propelled India's ascent in the global auto market rankings. With the continued expansion of the Indian automotive industry and a focus on sustainable mobility solutions, India's position as a major player in the global automotive landscape is likely to strengthen even further in the years to come.[8] The present legal structure in India that controls autos is a significant impediment to the implementation of autonomous vehicles, and a significant legal-policy shift is required to obtain the necessary results.

Currently, in India, automobiles and their operation are controlled and overseen by the 'Motor Vehicles Act, 1988', which prohibits the use of autonomous vehicles. Apart from this, the legal framework is so rigid and convoluted that even AV testing is prohibited in India. Testing is included in the proposed Motor Vehicles

(Amendment) Bill of 2017. However, after the bill's introduction, no movement has been accomplished.

The distribution of culpability in the event that a self-driving car collides with a pedestrian or another vehicle on the road is another key problem that emerges when granting legal sanction to AVs. 'Section 140 of the Motor Vehicle Act, 1988' imposes no-fault liability on the owners or insurance company in the event of death or permanent disability, according to current Indian regulations. Additionally concern also expand to privacy issues that may come with the advent of AVs, since these cars require a massive quantity of private information and user preferences. These challenges faced by self-driving cars in India is a deafening call for inclusivity under the Indian legal system which shall be discussed in the following pages.

- India: A Promising Global Hub for Autonomous Vehicles

In June this year, Quantron AG, a German company in the field of electric mobility, has teamed up with Goldstone Technologies (GTL) as part of its strategy in India. Michael Perschke, the CEO of Quantron AG, shared why they picked India as the base for their mobility as a service platform instead of Germany. With his extensive experience at major European automakers like Mercedes Benz and Audi, Perschke recognized India's potential as it moves towards a carbon-neutral future. India holds a pivotal role in their plans, benefiting from its talent pool and innovative capacity. Quantron's future includes the possibility of going public around 2025, with India playing a significant part, particularly in the platform sector.[9]

The automotive industry in India is experiencing significant growth and transformation as compared to other countries around the globe. This transformation is driven by various factors and government initiatives, some of these factors are discussed by the authors as below:

- Rising Government Support

The Indian government is increasingly backing sustainable and safe solutions in the automotive sector, creating promising opportunities for industry players. In India, we are still in the early stages of adopting autonomous vehicles. However, there is a concerted effort between the AI and automotive industries to drive significant progress in this domain.[10] The government is playing a pivotal role in fostering innovation in autonomous vehicles (AVs) and drone technologies. For instance, organizations like the Aeronautical Development Establishment (ADE) of the DRDO, Hindustan Aeronautics Limited, and BEL are collaborating to develop advanced UAVs (Unmanned Aerial Vehicles) with capabilities such as synthetic aperture radar, electronic intelligence systems, and situational awareness payloads.

Moreover, the Indian government is actively involved in various projects and initiatives, including the development of advanced underwater vehicles for the Navy, the National Electric Mobility Mission Plan 2020, and collaborations with organizations like the Automotive Research Association of India.

- High Vehicle Costs

While autonomous vehicles hold the promise of significantly reducing road accidents caused by human errors, the high production costs associated with these vehicles pose a significant challenge. Many components used in autonomous vehicles, such as communication devices, radar systems, high-quality cameras, and sensors, are considerably more expensive compared to traditional vehicle parts. For example, LIDAR sensors,[11] which are essential for autonomous vehicles, can cost more than twice the price of the vehicle itself. This cost barrier makes it challenging for manufacturers to bring self-driving vehicles to market at an affordable price point.

However, there is potential to address this cost constraint by promoting ride-sharing, rentals, and vehicle-for-hire services. By adopting shared mobility models, similar to modern taxi services, the operational expenses of autonomous vehicles can be distributed among a larger number of users, making them more economically accessible to the public. This practice has been adopted in India and has even been propagated by the State Governments.

- Rise in Demand for Autonomous Vehicles

The demand for autonomous vehicles in India is on the rise, driven by the potential benefits they offer. These vehicles can navigate and operate without human intervention, thanks to the integration of artificial intelligence. Thus, India's automotive industry is poised for growth, driven by government support, the demand for autonomous vehicles, and efforts to address cost constraints. These developments are not only transforming the way we travel but also contributing to road safety and sustainability in the country. While India is indeed making strides in the field of artificial intelligence (AI) and is emerging as a significant player in the global technology landscape, it's important to note that India is not necessarily the primary hub for AI vehicles. Instead, countries like China, the United States, and some European nations have traditionally been at the forefront of AI development in the automotive industry. However, India is actively involved in AI research and development and has the potential to become a significant player in the future.[12]

- Tech Talent Pool

India is known for its large pool of skilled software engineers and data scientists. The country produces a significant number of IT professionals who are well-equipped to work on AI-related projects. India has several leading research institutions and technology companies that are actively engaged in AI research and development. These organizations collaborate with global partners and contribute to the advancement of AI technologies. [13]Another factor which contributes to India becoming a global hub when we talk about AI vehicles, we reckon is its cost-effective development capabilities. Many multinational companies outsource AI-related projects and research to Indian firms due to cost-efficiency.[14]

• Market Potential

India is a large and growing market for automobiles. As the Indian middle class continues to expand, there is a growing demand for advanced features and technologies in vehicles, including AI-driven systems.

• Start-up Ecosystem

India has a vibrant start-up ecosystem, and many start-ups are focusing on AI applications in various industries, including automotive. These start-ups contribute to innovation and technology adoption in the sector.

• Diverse Geographic Conditions

India has diverse geographical conditions, from dense urban areas to rural settings and a wide range of terrains. This diversity allows for testing and developing AI vehicles in varied environments, which is crucial for their robustness and adaptability. When we come to talk about the challenges India might face when it comes to AI vehicles, we cannot miss a few, for example, India's road network is extensive, and it often faces challenges related to road quality, signage, and traffic management. Inconsistent infrastructure can pose difficulties for AI vehicles, which rely heavily on clear and well-maintained roads. Traffic congestion is another challenge faced by many Indian cities, which can be a complex environment for AI vehicles to navigate. Further India experiences a wide range of weather conditions, from extreme heat to heavy monsoon rains. Adapting AI vehicles to function reliably in these diverse weather conditions can be challenging. Thus, India has both advantages and challenges when it comes to becoming a hub for AI vehicles. Its diverse conditions, large market, and skilled workforce are positive factors, but it needs to address infrastructure issues, traffic congestion, and regulatory concerns to fully leverage its potential in the AI vehicle sector.

- Position in India

When we talk about the leading jurisprudence on AI vehicles it is pertinent to discuss Britain and Germany. Britain has been at the forefront of regulating self-driving cars. In 2018, they passed the Automated and Electric Vehicles Act. Notably, Section 2(2) of this act[15] explicitly places liability on the owner of an automated car in the event of an accident caused by the car's automation. This principle extends to cases where an automated car causes a fatality. Furthermore, Section 4 of the act[16] addresses insurance in the context of autonomous cars. If such a vehicle is insured, but an accident occurs due to unauthorized software updates or failure to update the software, the liability of the insurer decreases. However, the act does not adequately address the liability of the autonomous car manufacturer, leaving all liability squarely on the owner's shoulders. This allocation of liability creates numerous issues, not only for the owner but also in the realm of justice administration.

Germany, was one of the pioneers in enacting legislation to regulate autonomous vehicles. The German Road Traffic (Amendment) Act of 2017 is a notable piece of legislation worldwide for its regulation of autonomous cars. Section 1 of the act allows drivers to transfer control of the car to an automated driving system if it complies with international requirements, particularly those outlined in the Vienna Convention on Road Traffic of 1968. The Convention, updated in March 2016, now applies to self-driving cars, making it applicable to autonomous vehicles.

Section 63A of the act mandates the installation of a black box in cars. This device, connected to a GPS system, records vital information such as vehicle speed, direction, distance travelled, driving speed, and time of day. This black box helps establish responsibility in case of accidents. If the accident is caused by the driver, the driver is held accountable. If the self-driving system fails and leads to an accident, the manufacturer of the car bears the blame. Moreover, according to Section 12 of the act, in cases of death or injury due to the self-driving system, victims can recover a maximum of 10 million dollars.

India on the other hand has developed no such jurisprudence when it comes to AI vehicles, the legal landscape governing motor vehicles in India primarily relies on two major laws: a. The Motor Vehicles Act of 1988 and b. The Consumer Protection Act of 1986. The former regulates various aspects of motor vehicles, including driver eligibility, vehicle registration, and liability. Meanwhile, the latter deals with issues related to damages resulting from negligence, industrial errors, construction defects, and unfair trade practices. At present, India lacks dedicated legislation to address self-driving cars adequately. Even the 2019 amendment to the Motor Vehicles Act has made no discernible impact on the regulation of self-driving or autonomous vehicles. This regulatory gap raises pertinent questions about accountability, personhood, and agency when it comes to AI. There has been minimal debate regarding the accountability of AI systems. Notably, in 2018, NITI Aayog released a policy paper titled "National Strategy for Artificial Intelligence," which explores the integration of AI across various sectors, including healthcare, agriculture, and automobiles.

On the lines of the German model, the recently enacted Consumer Protection Act of 2019, Section 2(34) defines product liability as the responsibility of a product manufacturer or seller to compensate consumers for harm caused by defective products or deficient services. If we consider AI as a product, the manufacturer would bear full liability for any resulting damage. But before we even address this concern, a more nuanced issue surfaces regarding whether AI should be classified as a service or a product. AI primarily consists of complex programming code, typically considered a service rather than a tangible product. In such cases, legal disputes are often treated as breaches of warranty rather than traditional product liability claims.

Coming back to the Motor Vehicle Act,[17] yet, an even more profound question arises, should the principle of 'no-fault liability' apply to accidents involving self-driving cars? This principle implies that a defendant can be held liable without demonstrating any fault on their part. Section 140 of the Motor Vehicle Act, 1988, stipulates compensation of Rs. 50,000 in cases of death and Rs. 25,000 in cases of permanent damage. However, the case of *Haji Zakaria v. Naoshir Cama*[18] has challenged this notion, asserting that liability cannot be imposed on the owner or driver in the absence of negligence. Applying this judgment to accidents involving self-driving cars, it becomes evident that the manufacturer, not the owner or driver, should be held liable due to the absence of negligence on their part. Similarly, the case of *United States v. Athlone Indus Inc.*[19] sets a precedent by establishing that robots cannot be prosecuted for their faults. Instead, the legal liability is imputed on the manufacturer due to a faulty robotic system. Yet we still have not addressed a major concern when it comes to AI vehicles, given India's alarming road accident statistics, where approximately 4.5 lakh road crashes occur annually, resulting in at least 1.5 lakh fatalities, there is an urgent need for comprehensive legislation with a clear demarcation of liability.

- The Way Forward

To address the challenges posed by autonomous vehicles in the Indian context, it is imperative to consider other relevant laws that will play a crucial role. One such aspect pertains to privacy and confidentiality, especially concerning the handling of sensitive personal data. In this regard, it is essential to examine the implications of the Information Technology Act, 2000, particularly Section 66, which deals with hacking, as autonomous vehicle technology is susceptible to cyber threats. However, the current provisions of the IT Act do not encompass autonomous vehicles, necessitating an expansion of the definition of hacking and the introduction of stringent regulations. Automakers should be mandated to implement anti-hacking systems and safety features to protect against potential cyber-attacks.

Another significant piece of legislation to consider is the Geospatial Information Regulation Bill of 2016. This bill aims to regulate the acquisition, transmission, publishing, and delivery of geospatial information. It outlines restrictions on entities seeking to acquire geospatial data/maps, emphasizing that such data should be sourced exclusively from Indian entities for serving Indian customers. The use of APIs is mandated to view this data, preventing it from flowing through restricted entities or their servers. Reselling or reusing such information is prohibited. Restricted entities are also prohibited from conducting ground verification within Indian territories to safeguard national security and privacy. While this bill is currently under negotiation, it has the potential to address certain aspects related to autonomous vehicles, particularly in terms of data privacy and usage.

When it comes to challenges, the foremost question that arises is whether India should adopt the British model, where the owner remains liable even if the AI system commits an error, or follow the German model, which places liability on the manufacturer when AI-driven mistakes occur. Answering the question, the government should consider amending the Motor Vehicles Act, 1988, to accommodate self-driving cars or drafting a dedicated legislation specifically for self-driving cars, similar to the approaches taken by Britain or Germany. Such legislation should clearly define rules pertaining to liability in accidents and charging mechanisms, this is pertinent if India is looking to overtake other developed countries when it comes to being the global hub for AI vehicles. The Indian Legislature also needs to align existing provisions of the Motor Vehicle Act and the Consumer Protection Act with the regulatory framework for autonomous vehicles. Amendments to these regulations will be necessary to facilitate the proper implementation of autonomous vehicles within the regulatory framework. Furthermore, provisions should be introduced to hold companies accountable for the performance of their self-driving cars on Indian roads. Companies failing to meet the required standards for safety and suitability on Indian roads should face higher penalties, and in severe cases, their licenses could be revoked.

VI. LEGAL-ETHICAL CHALLENGES

The shift to autonomous vehicles raises a variety of policy concerns, with safety being the primary issue currently. As the technology advances, other concerns such as privacy, data security, infrastructure, and environmental impact will become more significant. Privacy is a concern as the communication between vehicles can track the location, time and activity of its users. There are also worries about the impact of autonomous vehicles on roads and the infrastructure required. The environmental impact of increased car usage is also a concern. However, the effects of autonomous vehicles on these issues will depend on how they are introduced and regulated. Research is still less to sufficient around the policy implications of autonomous vehicles, (Lin, 2016).

The supporters and manufacturers of Connected and Automated Vehicles (CAVs) claim that CAVs have the capability to decrease human errors which are considered to be the cause of almost 94% of accidents. Even though there is some debate about this statistic, many people opine that it may significantly enhance road safety. However, queries have been piling up in regard to requirement of extra safety regulations during the testing phase and for the widespread adoption of CAVs, (Naughton, 2016). In case any CAV is involved into accidents which had resulted in fatalities, consumer safety organizations have called for stricter safety policies. Developing safety policies for CAVs will be over a foundation built on existing standards of International systems, which are developed by the "U.S Federal Motor Vehicle Safety Standards and the United Nations Economic Commission for Europe and the EU," (Contissa, Lagioia, & Sartor, 2017).

However, two perspectives debate in issues relating to automotive safety: "functional safety with respect to internal faults" and "driving behaviour competency to deal with external hazards in the driving environment".[20] Other important aspects of safety include 'mechanisms for communication with other road users, passenger mediation for other road user communication with AVs, and the provision for detailed reporting of data for test vehicles to gather information on potential safety risks and make improvements'.[21]

A. THE ETHICAL CONUNDRUM

Complex ethical and legal issues crop up when autonomous vehicles (AVs) involve in accidents. Arguments propose for setting up programmed self-driving cars, to make decisions on sacrificing lives in unavoidable accidents.[22] It can be suggested here that, where the user/passenger can decide the ethical approach for the AV to take in such scenarios, should be given. This would involve equipping AVs with an "Ethical Knob" which would enable passengers to choose between different moral approaches or principles. The AV would then implement the user's ethical choice, while manufacturers and programmers would be responsible for ensuring that the user's choice is enabled and implemented by the AV.[23]

Recent studies have examined the ethical dilemmas that arise from potential accident scenarios involving autonomous vehicles (AVs) and the decisions they make involving the lives of passengers and third parties. These studies have used the "trolley problem", a classic ethical thought experiment, to frame the ethical and legal issues surrounding AVs in these situations.[24] In particular, researchers have considered scenarios where harm is unavoidable and a choice must be made about who will be harmed, such as passengers, pedestrians or passers. This raises in turn another question of who should be responsible for setting the ethical criteria for AVs in these situations, whether it should be a mandatory ethics setting for all cars or if each driver should have the choice to select their own personal ethics setting, (Nyholm & Smids, 2016).

A study by Bonnefon et al. (2016) found that people generally support the idea of autonomous vehicles being programmed to make decisions that result in the least number of deaths, also known as a utilitarian approach. However, participants in the study showed a preference for cars that prioritize the safety of their passengers. This creates a paradox where individuals want others to use vehicles with a utilitarian approach but would personally choose a car that prioritizes their own safety (Thompson, 1976). Regulations may help solve this issue, but people tend to be against regulations that require a utilitarian approach for autonomous vehicles. This could lead to problems if such regulations were implemented, as many people may choose not to use autonomous vehicles despite their potential benefits over human-driven cars. If the ethical decision-making process is left up to manufacturers, market pressures may lead to the creation of cars that prioritize passenger safety, putting the lives of pedestrians at risk, (Rawls, 1999).

B. PRIVACY AND DATA USE

"Disclosed in [locational] data . . . will be trips of indisputably private nature . . .. trips to the psychiatrist, the plastic surgeon, the abortion clinic, . . . the union meeting, the mosque, synagogue or church, the gay bar and on and on[.] . . . [I]t will be possible to tell ... with ever increasing precision who we are and are not with, [and] when we are and are not with them."

Autonomous vehicles will generate and transmit a large amount of personal data, which raises privacy concerns. Even if the data is cleansed of unique individual identifying markers, data mining techniques can still reconstruct personal identifying information. The use and storage of this data will be a subject of legal regulations and controversies, particularly with regard to government access to and use of locational and other personal data, and the private, mainly commercial, use of personal data. These concerns are similar to those already present with the use of personal data generated by mobile phones, GPS devices and internet usage, and may be resolved before autonomous vehicles are ready for the market. The resolution of these issues is uncertain and will have an impact on the rate of autonomous vehicle adoption.[25]

The use of vehicle routing and locational data raises concerns about privacy and autonomy in relation to the government. If the government has access to users' routing information, it can easily obtain personal information that could have a negative impact on the expression of free speech and political dissent. If a vehicle's navigation route is determined by a centralized government network, there may be concerns about whether this infringes on individual rights to privacy and physical autonomy. Rerouting may be used for questionable purposes, such as diverting traffic away from public protests. Additionally, individuals may object to being consistently routed on slower routes for the sake of overall traffic efficiency at the expense of their time. The government may also reserve faster routes for those who are willing and able to pay for the privilege. Additionally, if the government controls the decision-making process for vehicle routing, there may be concerns about infringement of individuals' right to privacy and physical autonomy. This could lead to potential misuse of the technology, such as rerouting traffic away from public protests or offering faster routes to those who can afford it. These issues have not yet been fully addressed and will likely be a point of contention as autonomous vehicles become more prevalent. It is important for policymakers and industry leaders to consider these ethical concerns and develop regulations and guidelines that protect the privacy and autonomy of individuals.

C. SECURITY, TERRORISM, AND CYBER-ATTACKS

There are concerns about the vulnerability of connected vehicles to cyber-attacks, such as the ability for hackers to take control of the braking, acceleration, and steering of a car. Additionally, researchers have found that newer cars are also susceptible to wireless attacks through their tire pressure monitoring systems and emergency data recording systems. This presents a significant risk in a world with fully automated vehicles, as coordinated traffic flow could be disrupted by a sudden change in a vehicle's path, potentially causing major damage and disruption, and even leading to terror on a large scale.

Cyber-attacks on autonomous vehicles are a growing concern as the technology becomes more prevalent. These attacks can take many forms as discussed, including hacking into the vehicle's control systems to take control of the car, stealing personal information or data from the vehicle, or using the car's network to launch attacks on other connected devices. One major concern is that autonomous cars rely heavily on communication between vehicles, infrastructure, and the cloud, which can make them vulnerable to cyber-attacks. For example, if an attacker is able to gain access to the communication network used by autonomous cars, they could potentially disrupt traffic flow, cause accidents, or steal sensitive information.

Another concern is that as cars become increasingly connected, they are also becoming more vulnerable to remote attacks. For example, researchers have shown that it is possible to hack into a car's electronic control units (ECUs) through its wireless tire pressure monitoring system or event data recorder (EDR). This could allow an attacker to take control of the car's braking, acceleration, and steering systems.

Overall, the increasing use of autonomous vehicles and the integration of connected technologies makes it more important than ever to ensure that these cars are secure from cyber-attacks. Many governments and organizations around the world are working to develop regulations, standards, and best practices to protect autonomous vehicles from cyber threats.

There is ongoing research and development globally to address the issue of cyber security in autonomous vehicles. Governments and industry players are investing resources to understand and develop strategies to protect vehicles from cyber-attacks. The National Highway Traffic Safety Administration (NHTSA) in the United States, for example, has stated its goal of developing a "initial baseline set of requirements" to ensure that the electronic control units (ECUs) in contemporary and future vehicles, including autonomous vehicles, are secure from cyber-attack. Other countries and international organizations, such as the European Union, are also working on developing regulations and guidelines for cyber security in autonomous vehicles. Additionally, many companies in the automotive industry are working on developing their own security measures to protect against cyber-attacks on their vehicles.[26]

VII. REGULATORY OPTIONS AND THE POTENTIAL PACE OF CHANGE

The implementation of autonomous vehicles technology is influenced by various factors such as improved safety, driver's willingness to give up control, high cost of technology, and lack of cyber-security. These factors are considered as obstacles to achieving advanced levels of automation. Furthermore, there are concerns about determining liability for accidents caused by these vehicles, and privacy concerns are also seen as potential barriers. It is suggested that enough resources should be allocated to tackle these issues and establish liability within the existing legal system, (Bigelow & Foxx, 2016).

There are several factors that can affect the deployment of autonomous vehicles globally, which industry analysts have attempted to anticipate. These factors include the limitations of technology, costs, cyber-security, and legal issues:[27]

- The willingness of drivers to give up control of their vehicles to the technology is a crucial factor in the deployment of autonomous vehicles. Consumers need to be assured that the technology is completely safe and reliable before they give up control. The high cost of the technology and the infrastructure required for autonomous vehicles is also a significant obstacle to widespread adoption. A survey shows that only 20% of consumers are willing to spend as much as $3,000 on automated vehicle features.
- Cyber-security is also a significant concern, especially with respect to V2V and V21 technologies that involve multiple vehicles. The National Highway Traffic Safety Administration (NHTSA) and the Department of Transportation (DOT) in United States of America are working with the industry to establish a secure V2V credentialing system that may alleviate these concerns, (Bonnefon, Shariff, & Rahwan, 2016).
- The availability of aftermarket technologies for autonomous vehicles is also an important factor in their widespread adoption. Efforts should be made to develop a plan for insuring these types of vehicles.
- There is uncertainty about who will be held liable for accidents caused by autonomous vehicles, which is a concern for the implementation of fully autonomous Level 4 vehicles. However, as automation reduces crash rates and insurance claims, the risk for insurance companies will decrease. Additionally, concerns about privacy of data collected by autonomous vehicles are not unique to this technology and should be addressed in a broader context
- Ethical concerns surrounding autonomous vehicles include how the vehicles should be programmed to make decisions in unavoidable accident scenarios, and who should be responsible for making those decisions. One approach is to give the user or passenger control over the ethical approach taken by the vehicle through an 'Ethical Knob,' a device that allows them to choose between different settings corresponding to different moral principles, (Kohler & Coblert-Taylor, 2014). This approach raises questions about the manufacturers' and programmers' responsibility to ensure the ethical choices made by the user are implemented correctly by the vehicle. Another ethical concern is the potential for autonomous vehicles to prioritize the safety of their occupants over that of pedestrians or other road users. This raises the question of whether there should be mandatory ethical standards for all autonomous vehicles, or if individuals should have the freedom to choose their own ethical settings.[28]

There are several ways to improve human-automated vehicle interactions in order to address ethical concerns. One approach is to give the user/passenger the task (and burden) of deciding what ethical approach should be taken by AVs in unavoidable accident scenarios. Additionally, AVs can be programmed to prioritize the safety of vulnerable road users, such as pedestrians and cyclists, rather than just the passengers. Another approach is to involve ethical experts in the development and design of AVs to ensure that the technology is aligned with widely accepted moral principles. Furthermore, there should be regular evaluations and audits of AVs to ensure that they are following ethical guidelines and regulations. Some of the following suggestions can be incorporated:[29]

- IMPROVE THE USER INTERFACE

The user interface of automated vehicles should be designed in a way that is intuitive and easy to understand for the average person. This will help users feel more comfortable and in control when interacting with the vehicle.

- PROVIDE CLEAR AND CONCISE FEEDBACK

Automated vehicles should provide clear and concise feedback to the user on the status of the vehicle and its actions, (Nayyer, Rodriguez, & Sutherland, 2020). This will help users understand what the vehicle is doing and why, which will in turn increase their trust in the vehicle.

- DEVELOP A COMPREHENSIVE TRAINING PROGRAM

Automated vehicles should come with a comprehensive training program that educates users on how to interact with the vehicle, its capabilities, and its limitations. This will help users understand the vehicle better and feel more comfortable using it.

- IMPLEMENT A ROBUST TESTING AND CERTIFICATION PROCESS

To ensure that automated vehicles are safe and reliable, a robust testing and certification process should be implemented. This process should include both laboratory and on-road testing, as well as a thorough review of the vehicle's software and hardware.

- ADDRESS ETHICAL CONCERNS

Automated vehicles raise a number of ethical concerns, such as how the vehicle should make decisions in emergency situations. These concerns should be addressed through research and development, as well as through public engagement and education.[30]

- DEVELOP ETHICAL GUIDELINES

A set of ethical guidelines should be developed to address the ethical concerns raised by automated vehicles.[31] These guidelines should be developed in consultation with experts in ethics, philosophy, and law, and should be reviewed and updated as necessary.

Thus, the deployment of automated vehicle technology is affected by a variety of factors including consumer acceptance, technology costs, cyber-security concerns and liability issues. While safety improvements are a key driver for the development of these technologies, it is crucial for stakeholders to address these other concerns in order to ensure successful deployment, (Nayyer, Rodriguez, & Sutherland, 2020). To improve human-automated vehicle interactions, it is important for manufacturers to prioritize user-centered design, and for regulators to establish clear guidelines and regulations for the use of these technologies. Additionally, addressing privacy concerns and finding solutions for insuring autonomous vehicle systems can help alleviate some of the ethical concerns surrounding their implementation.[32]

CONCLUSION

It is expected that Artificial intelligence will become more sophisticated in the coming years than it is today. Presently also we observe that AI can now perform more and for less money than ever before owing to considerably faster specialised computers, better technology, and greater data sets. As a result, AI is becoming more widespread and omnipresent, prompting increased governmental concern. Equality, prejudice, inequality, multiculturalism, and security are all issues that certain policymakers are concerned with AI as well. For instance, learning that has been scrutinised by policymakers and many others for possible social prejudice is a crucial element of today's AI.

India's innovation in AI has so far been a disjointed legislative exercise. There is no one regulatory authority, ministry, or department entrusted with comprehending all consequences and challenges afforded by artificial intelligence. Nevertheless, initiatives have been largely haphazard, with hardly any awareness of how alternative activities should be coordinated or related. At the global level, AI rules are a combative. If one nation or area can establish the worldwide norm for AI legislation, it may provide local firms a competitive assistance while putting foreigners at a loss.

REFERENCES

Abraham, K. S., & Rabin, R. L. (2019, March). Automated Vehicles and Manufacturer Responsibility for Accidents: A New Legal Regime for a New Era. *Virginia Law Review*, 105(1), 127–172.

Amitai, E., & Oren, E. (2017). *Should Artificial Intelligence be Regulated? Issues in Science and Technology.* National Academies of Sciences, Engineering, and Medicine, The University of Texas at Dallas, Arizona State University.

Andrew & Urquhart. (2022). In cars (are we really safest of all?): Interior sensing and emotional opacity. *International Review of Law Computers & Technology*.

Bigelow, P., & Foxx, A. (2016). Coolness Aside, Self-Driving Focus Should Be on Safety. *Car & Driver.* http:// blog.caranddriver.com/anthony-foxx-coolness-aside -self-driving-focus-should-beon-safety

Bonnefon, J. F., Shariff, A., & Rahwan, I. (2015) Autonomous vehicles need experimental ethics: are we ready for utilitarian cars? arXiv preprint arXiv:151003346.

Bonnefon, J. F., Shariff, A., & Rahwan, I. (2016). The social dilemma of autonomous vehicles. *Science*, 352(6293), 1573–1576. 10.1126/science.aaf265427339987

Brady, M. (2019). Data Privacy and Automated Vehicles: Navigating the Privacy Continuum. *Monash University Law Review. Monash University. Faculty of Law*, 45(3), 589–625.

Calo, R. (2015). Robotics and the Lessons of Cyberlaw, 103 Calif. L. *Rev.*, 513, 535–537.

Cath, C. (2018). Governing artificial intelligence: Ethical, legal and technical opportunities and challenges. *Philosophical Transactions. Series A, Mathematical, Physical, and Engineering Sciences*, 376(2133), 20180080. 10.1098/rsta.2018.008030322996

Contissa, G., Lagioia, F., & Sartor, G. (2017). The ethical knob: Ethically-customisable automated vehicles and the law. *Artificial Intelligence and Law*, 25(3), 365–378. 10.1007/s10506-017-9211-z

Electronic Vehicles Act, sec. 2(2) (2018).

Etzioni, O. (2018). Point: Should AI technology be regulated? yes, and here's how. *Communications of the ACM*, 61(12), 30–32. 10.1145/3197382

Foot, P. (1967). The problem of abortion and the doctrine of double effect. *Oxford Review*, 5(1), 5–15.

Gogoll, J., & Muller, J. F. (2016). Autonomous cars: In favor of a mandatory ethics setting. *Science and Engineering Ethics*. Advance online publication. 10.1007/si1948-016-9806-x27417644

Goodall, N. J. (2016). Away from trolley problems and toward risk management. *Applied Artificial Intelligence*, 30(8), 810–821. 10.1080/08839514.2016.1229922

India surpasses Japan to become 3rd largest market globally. (n.d.). ETauto. Available at https://auto.economictimes.indiatimes.com/news/industry/india-surpasses-japan-to-become-3rd-largest-auto-market-

Keller, P. (2018, March-April). Autonomous Vehicles, Artificial Intelligence, and the Law. *RAIL: The Journal of Robotics Artificial Intelligence and Law*, 1(2), 101–110.

Kohler, W. J., & Colbert-Taylor, A. (2014). Current law and potential legal issues pertaining to automated, autonomous and connected vehicles. *Santa Clara High-Technology Law Journal*, 31(1), 99–138.

Levine, J. (2020, May-June). Rebecca Yergin, "DOT Introduces Fourth Round of Automated Vehicles Guidance," RAIL: The Journal of Robotics. *Artificial Intelligence and Law*, 3(3), 171–174.

Lin, P. (2014). *Here's a terrible idea: robot cars with adjustable ethics settings*. Available via https://www.wired.com/2014/08/heres-a-terrible-idea-robot-cars-with-adjustable-ethics-settings

Lin, P. (2016). Why ethics matters for autonomous cars. In Maurer, M., Gerdes, J. C., Lenz, B., & Winner, H. (Eds.), *Autonomous driving* (pp. 69–85). Springer.

Mark, A. (2017). Geistfeld, A Roadmap for Autonomous Vehicles: State Tort Liability, Automobile Insurance, and Federal Safety Regulation. *Calif. L.Rev.*, 1611, 1612.

Millar, J. (2015). Technology as moral proxy: Autonomy and paternalism by design. *IEEE Technology and Society Magazine*, 34(2), 47–55. 10.1109/MTS.2015.2425612

Naughton, K. (2016). Regulator Says Self-Driving Cars Must Be Twice as Safe. *Bloomberg*. https://www.bloomberg.com/news/ articles/20 16-06-08/u-s-auto-regulator-says-self-driving-cars-must-be-twice-as-safe

Nayyer, K. P., Rodriguez, M., & Sutherland, S. (2020, May/June). Artificial Intelligence & Implicit Bias: With Great Power Comes Great Responsibility: Addressing the Biases Inherent in the Datasets That Drive AI Applications and Their Algorithms. *AALL Spectrum*, 24(5), 14–16.

Nemitz, P. (2018). Constitutional democracy and technology in the age of artificial intelligence. *Phil. Trans. R. Soc. A, 376.* .10.1098/rsta.2018.0089

Nyholm, S., & Smids, J. (2016). *The ethics of accident-algorithms for self-driving cars: an applied trolley problem? Ethical theory and moral practice.* .10.1007/s10677-016-9745-2

Patrick Hubbard, F. (2014). "Sophisticated Robots": Balancing Liability, Regulation, and Innovation. *Fla. L.Rev.*, 1803, 1866–1867.

Rawls, J. (1999). *A Theory of Justice* (revised edn.). Oxford University Press. 10.4159/9780674042582

Santoni de Sio, F. (2017). Killing by autonomous vehicles and the legal doctrine of necessity. *Ethical Theory and Moral Practice*, 20(2), 411–429. 10.1007/s10677-017-9780-7

Scherer, E. (2015). M. U., Regulating artificial intelligence systems: Risks, challenges, competencies, and strategies. *SSRN*, 29, 353. 10.2139/ssrn.2609777

Smith, B. (2014). Automated vehicles are probably legal in the United States. Texas A&M. *Law Review*, 1(3), 411–522.

Smith, B. W. (2017). Automated Driving and Product Liability. *Detroit College of Law at Michigan State University Law Review*, 2017(1), 1–74.

Sreejani, B. (2021). Can AI Revolutionise India's Judicial System? *Analytics India Magazine.*

The Motor Vehicles Act, Gazette of India (1988)

Thomson, J. J. (1976). Killing, letting die, and the trolley problem. *The Monist*, 59(2), 204–217. 10.5840/monist19765922411662247

United States v. Athlone Industries, Inc., 746 F.2d 977 (3d Cir. 1984).

What is Autonomous Vehicle? (n.d.). TWI. https://www.twi-global.com/technical-knowledge/faqs/what-is-an-autonomous-vehicle

Zakaria & Ors. v. Naoshir Cama & Ors., AIR 1976 AP 171.

ENDNOTES

[1] Ibid.

[2] Ibid.

[3] Ibid.

[4] Ibid.

[5]   Ibid.

[6]   Ibid.

[7]   Ibid.

[8]   India surpasses Japan to become 3rd largest market globally, ETauto, available at https://auto.economictimes.indiatimes.com/news/industry/india-surpasses-japan-to-become-3rd-largest-auto-market-globally/96786895

[9]   https://www.autocarpro.in/interview/metaverse-experience-should-be-akin-to-online-marketing-campaign-sukrit-singh-115591

[10]   https://www.precedenceresearch.com/automotive-artificial-intelligence-market

[11]   Ibid.

[12]   https://lawreview.nmims.edu/self-driving-cars-and-india-a-call-for-inclusivity-under-the-indian-legal-position/#:~:text=In%202018%2C%20the%20Automated%20and,is%20liable%20for%20the%20accident.

[13]   Ibid

[14]   Ibid.

[15]   Electronic Vehicles Act, sec. 2(2) (2018).

[16]   Ibid

[17]   The Motor Vehicles Act, Gazette of India (1988)

[18]   Zakaria & Ors. v. Naoshir Cama & Ors., AIR 1976 AP 171.

[19]   United States v. Athlone Industries, Inc., 746 F.2d 977 (3d Cir. 1984).

[20]   Ibid.

[21]   Ibid.

[22]   The Trolley Problem which is a hypothetical choice that a trolley driver must make between striking multiple people on the trolley's track and affirmatively shunting onto another track and striking only one person. Seminal work on the problem can be found in Philippa Foot, Virtues and Vices and Other Essays in Moral Philosophy 23 (1978), and Judith Jarvis Thomson, The Trolley Problem, 94 Yale L.J. 1395 (1985). The problem extensively deals with the ethical conundrum a driver faces in such challenging situations.

[23]   Ibid.

[24]   Ibid.

[25]   Ibid.

[26]   Ibid.

[27]   Ibid.

[28]   Ibid

[29]   Ibid.

[30]   Ibid.

[31]   Ibid.

[32]   Ibid.

Compilation of References

Abdel-Basset, M., Chang, V., & Nabeeh, N. A. (2021). An intelligent framework using disruptive technologies for COVID-19 analysis. *Technological Forecasting and Social Change*, 163, 120431. 10.1016/j.techfore.2020.120431

Abdullah, Z., Anumudu, C. E., & Raza, S. H. (2022). Examining the digital organizational identity through content analysis of missions and vision statements of Malaysian and Singaporean SME company websites. *The Bottom Line (New York, N.Y.)*, 35(2–3), 137–158. 10.1108/BL-12-2021-0108

Abraham, K. S., & Rabin, R. L. (2019, March). Automated Vehicles and Manufacturer Responsibility for Accidents: A New Legal Regime for a New Era. *Virginia Law Review*, 105(1), 127–172.

Accenture. (2018). Mind the gap: the challenges to fintech adaptation. In *FinTech Innovation Lab*. Accenture.

Accenture-Going beyond extended reality. (n.d.). https://www.accenture.com/de-de/about/going-beyond-extended-reality

Aggarwal, M., Nayak, K. M., & Bhatt, V. (2023). Examining the factors influencing fintech adoption behaviour of gen Y in India. *Cogent Economics & Finance*, 11(1), 2197699. 10.1080/23322039.2023.2197699

Agrawal, S., & Singh, R. K. (2019). Analyzing disposition decisions for sustainable reverse logistics: Triple Bottom Line approach. *Resources, Conservation and Recycling*, 150, 104448. 10.1016/j.resconrec.2019.104448

Ahlawat, S. (n.d.). Music Piracy: The Looming Peril for Music Industries in the Digital Age. https://subhashahlawat.com/blog/music-piracy

Ahluwalia, S., Mahto, R. V. & Guerrero, M. (2020). Blockchain technology and startup financing: A transaction cost economics perspective. *Technological Forecasting and Social Change*. .10.1016/j.techfore.2019.119854

AI Now Institute. (n.d.). https://ainowinstitute.org/

Akçay, S. (2019). Remittances and financial development in Bangladesh: Substitutes or complements? *Applied Economics Letters*, 27(16), 1206–1214.

Akulavičius, M., & Vaclovas, E. (2015). Possibilities of Digital Piracy Management in Music Records Industry. *Procedia: Social and Behavioral Sciences*, 213, 716–721. 10.1016/j.sbspro.2015.11.492

Al Bloushi, M. (2020). *Cyber-Attacks and Data Integrity Concerns Cripple Large Parts of the Internet on Banking* (Doctoral dissertation, The British University in Dubai).

Alabi, K. (2017). Digital blockchain networks appear to be following Metcalfe's Law. *Electronic Commerce Research and Applications*, 24(June), 23–29. 10.1016/j.elerap.2017.06.003

Al-Amri, R., Zakaria, N. H., Habbal, A., & Hassan, S. (2019). Cryptocurrency adoption: Current stage, opportunities, and open challenges. *International Journal of Advanced Computer Research*, 9(44), 293–307. 10.19101/IJACR.PID43

Alexander, C., & Dakos, M. (2020). A critical investigation of cryptocurrency data and analysis. *Quantitative Finance*, 20(2), 173–188. 10.1080/14697688.2019.1641347

Ali, O., Ally, M., Clutterbuck, , & Dwivedi, Y. (2019). Clutterbuck and Dwivedi, Y. (2020), "The state of play of blockchain technology in the financial services sector: A systematic literature review. *International Journal of Information Management*, 54(August), 102199. 10.1016/j.ijinfomgt.2020.102199

Al-Khawaja, H. A., Yamin, I., & Alshehadeh, A. (2023). The COVID-19 Pandemic's Effects on Fintech in Banking Sector. *Revue d'Economie Financiere*, 21, 1.

Alkhawaldeh, B., Alhawamdeh, H., Al-Afeef, M., Al-Smadi, A., Almarshad, M., Fraihat, B., & Alaa, A. (2023). The effect of financial technology on financial performance in Jordanian SMEs: The role of financial satisfaction. *Uncertain Supply Chain Management*, 11(3), 1019–1030. 10.5267/j.uscm.2023.4.020

Alt, R. (2020). Electronic Markets on sustainability. *Electronic Markets*, 30(4), 667–674. 10.1007/s12525-020-00451-2

Alt, R., & Wende, E. (2020). Blockchain technology in energy markets – An interview with the European Energy Exchange. *Electronic Markets*, 30(2), 325–330. 10.1007/s12525-020-00423-6

Amitai, E., & Oren, E. (2017). *Should Artificial Intelligence be Regulated? Issues in Science and Technology*. National Academies of Sciences, Engineering, and Medicine, The University of Texas at Dallas, Arizona State University.

Ammous, S. (2018). Can cryptocurrencies fulfil the functions of money? *The Quarterly Review of Economics and Finance*, 70, 38–51. 10.1016/j.qref.2018.05.010

Anagnostopoulos, I. (2018). Fintech and regtech: Impact on regulators and banks. *Journal of Economics and Business*, 100, 7–25. 10.1016/j.jeconbus.2018.07.003

Compilation of References

Andreassen, T. W., Lervik-Olsen, L., Snyder, H., Van Riel, A. C. R., Sweeney, J. C., & Van Vaerenbergh, Y. (2018). Business model innovation and value-creation: The triadic way. *Journal of Service Management*, 29(5), 883–906. 10.1108/JOSM-05-2018-0125

Andrew & Urquhart. (2022). In cars (are we really safest of all?): Interior sensing and emotional opacity. *International Review of Law Computers & Technology*.

Angelis, J., & Ribeiro da Silva, E. (2019). Blockchain adoption: A value driver perspective. *Business Horizons*, 62(3), 307–314. 10.1016/j.bushor.2018.12.001

Angerer, M., Hoffmann, C. H., Neitzert, F., & Kraus, S. (2020). Objective and subjective risks of investing into cryptocurrencies. *Finance Research Letters*, 40, 101737. 10.1016/j.frl.2020.101737

Ansari, S., & Krop, P. (2012). Incumbent performance in the face of a radical innovation: towards a framework for incumbent challenger dynamics. SSRN *Electronic Journal, 41*, 1357–1374. 10.2139/ssrn.2034266

Antonakakis, N., Chatziantoniou, I., & Gabauer, D. (2019). Cryptocurrency market contagion: Market uncertainty, market complexity, and dynamic portfolios. *Journal of International Financial Markets, Institutions and Money*, 61, 37–51. 10.1016/j.intfin.2019.02.003

Antweiler, W., & Frank, M. Z. (2011). Do US Stock Markets Typically Overreact to Corporate News Stories? SSRN *Electronic Journal*. 10.2139/ssrn.878091

Appiah-Otoo, I. (2023). The Impact of the Russia-Ukraine War on the Cryptocurrency Market. *Asian Economics Letters*, 4(1). Advance online publication. 10.46557/001c.53110

Arner, D. W., Barberis, J., & Buckey, R. P. (2016). FinTech, RegTech, and the Reconceptualization of Financial Regulation. *Northwestern Journal of International Law & Business*, 37, 371.

Arner, D. W., Barberis, J., & Buckley, R. P. (2018). RegTech: Building a Better Financial System. In Lee Kuo Chuen, D., & Deng, R. (Eds.), *Handbook of Blockchain, Digital Finance, and Inclusion* (Vol. 1, pp. 359–373). Academic Press. 10.1016/B978-0-12-810441-5.00016-6

Arner, D. W., Zetzsche, D. A., Buckley, R. P., & Weber, R. H. (2020). The future of data-driven finance and RegTech: Lessons from EU big bang II. *Stan. JL Bus. & Fin.*, 25, 245.

Arun, R. (2023). A Case Study on Spotify Marketing Strategy. *Simplilearn*. https://www.simplilearn.com/tutorials/marketing-case-studies-tutorial/spotify-marketing-strategy

Asif, M., Khan, M. N., Tiwari, S., Wani, S. K., & Alam, F. (2023). The impact of fintech and digital financial services on financial inclusion in India. *Journal of Risk and Financial Management*, 16(2), 122. 10.3390/jrfm16020122

Aslanidis, N., Bariviera, A. F., & Martínez-Ibañez, O. (2019). An analysis of cryptocurrencies conditional cross correlations. *Finance Research Letters*, 31, 130–137. 10.1016/j.frl.2019.04.019

Attaran, M., & Gunasekaran, A. (2019). Blockchain-enabled technology: The emerging technology set to reshape and decentralise many industries. *International Journal of Applied Decision Sciences*, 12(4), 424–444. 10.1504/IJADS.2019.102642

Babich, V., & Hilary, G. (2020). Distributed ledgers and operations: What operations management researchers should know about blockchain technology. *Manufacturing & Service Operations Management*, 22(2), 223–240. 10.1287/msom.2018.0752

Bach, D. (2004). The Double Punch of Law and Technology: Fighting Music Piracy or Remaking Copyright in a Digital Age? *Business and Politics*, 6(2), 3–3. 10.2202/1469-3569.1089

Baen, J. (2000). The effects of technology on retail sales. *Journal of Shopping Center Research*, 7, 85–101.

Baik, J. S. (2020). Data privacy against innovation or against discrimination?: The case of the California Consumer Privacy Act (CCPA). *Telematics and Informatics*, 52, 52. 10.1016/j.tele.2020.101431

Bajwa, I. A., Ur Rehman, S., Iqbal, A., Anwar, Z., Ashiq, M., & Khan, M. A. (2022). Past, Present and Future of FinTech Research: A Bibliometric Analysis. *SAGE Open*, 12(4), 1–22. 10.1177/21582440221131242

Band, J. (2001). The Copyright Paradox: Fighting Content Piracy in the Digital Era. *Brookings*. https://www.brookings.edu/articles/the-copyright-paradox-fighting-content-piracy-in-the-digital -era/

Bansod, A., & Venice, A. (2023). Importance of Cybersecurity and RegTech in FinTech. *Telecom Business Review, 16*(1).

Bariviera, A. F., & Merediz-Solà, I. (2021). Where Do We Stand in Cryptocurrencies Economic Research? a Survey Based on Hybrid Analysis. *Journal of Economic Surveys*, 35(2), 377–407. 10.1111/joes.12412

Basdekis, C., Christopoulos, A., Katsampoxakis, I., & Vlachou, A. (2022). FinTech's rapid growth and its effect on the banking sector. *Journal of Banking and Financial Technology*, 6(2), 159–176. 10.1007/s42786-022-00045-w

Baur, D. G., Hong, K., & Lee, A. D. (2018). Bitcoin : Medium of Exchange or Speculative Assets? *Journal of International Financial Markets, Institutions and Money*, 54, 177–189. 10.1016/j.intfin.2017.12.004

Becker, M., Merz, K., & Buchkremer, R. (2024). RegTech—the application of modern information technology in regulatory affairs: Areas of interest in research and practice. *ResearchGate*. https://www.researchgate.net/publication/341821781_RegTech_the_Application_of_Modern _Information_Technology_Solutions_in_Regulatory_Affairs_Areas_of_Interest_in_Research _and_Practice

Compilation of References

Becker, M., Merz, K., & Buchkremer, R. (2020). RegTech—the application of modern information technology in regulatory affairs: Areas of interest in research and practice. *International Journal of Intelligent Systems in Accounting Finance & Management*, 27(4), 161–167. 10.1002/isaf.1479

Beeson, S. (2023). YouTube Content ID explained. *Uppbeat*. https://uppbeat.io/blog/youtube-content-id/

Belotti, M., Božić, N., Pujolle, G., & Secci, S. (2019). A Vademecum on Blockchain Technologies: When, Which, and How. *IEEE Communications Surveys and Tutorials*, 21(4), 3796–3838. 10.1109/COMST.2019.2928178

Bender, M. T., & Wang, Y. (2009). The Impact of Digital Piracy on Music Sales: A Cross-Country Analysis. *International Social Science Review*, 84(3/4), 157–170. https://www.jstor.org/stable/41887409

Berger, A. N., Bouwman, C. H. S., & Kim, D. (2017). Small bank comparative advantages in alleviating financial constraints and providing liquidity insurance over time. *Review of Financial Studies*, 30(9), 3416–3454. 10.1093/rfs/hhx038

Bessen, J., Impink, S. M., Paris, H., & Reichensperger, L. (n.d.). *The Business of AI Startups*. Academic Press.

Bhutto, S. A., Jamal, Y., & Ullah, S. (2023). FinTech adoption, HR competency potential, service innovation and firm growth in banking sector. *Heliyon*, 9(3), e13967. 10.1016/j.heliyon.2023.e1396736915496

Biancone, P., Saiti, B., Petricean, D., & Chmet, F. (2020). The bibliometric analysis of Islamic banking and finance. *Journal of Islamic Accounting and Business Research*, 11(9), 2069–2086. 10.1108/JIABR-08-2020-0235

Bickley, S. J., Macintyre, A., & Torgler, B. (n.d.). *Standard-Nutzungsbedingungen*. http://hdl.handle.net/10419/234626

Bigelow, P., & Foxx, A. (2016). Coolness Aside, Self-Driving Focus Should Be on Safety. *Car & Driver*. http:// blog.caranddriver.com/anthony-foxx-coolness-aside-self-driving-focus-should-beon-safety

Bitterli, M. (2017). Is Regtech "The next big thing"? First part. Available at: https://blogs.deloitte.ch/banking/2017/11/is-regtech-the-next-big-thing-first-part.html

Blau, B. M. (2017). Research in International Business and Finance Price dynamics and speculative trading in bitcoin. *Research in International Business and Finance*, 41(May), 493–499. 10.1016/j.ribaf.2017.05.010

Bludov, S. (2024). Music Streaming Trends: 7 Innovations and Strategies in the Digital Music Industry to Watch for in 2024. *Dataart*. https://www.dataart.com/blog/music-streaming-trends

Bollani, L., & Chmet, F. (2020). Bibliometric Analysis of Islamic Finance. *European Journal of Islamic Finance*, 19(1), 1–11.

Bolton, M., & Mintrom, M. (2023). RegTech and creating public value: Opportunities and challenges. *Policy Design and Practice*, 6(3), 266–282. 10.1080/25741292.2023.2213059

Bonnefon, J. F., Shariff, A., & Rahwan, I. (2015) Autonomous vehicles need experimental ethics: are we ready for utilitarian cars? arXiv preprint arXiv:151003346.

Bonnefon, J. F., Shariff, A., & Rahwan, I. (2016). The social dilemma of autonomous vehicles. *Science*, 352(6293), 1573–1576. 10.1126/science.aaf265427339987

Boonsiritomachai, W., & Pitchayadejanant, K. (2019). Determinants affecting mobile banking adoption by generation Y based on the Unified Theory of Acceptance and Use of Technology Model modified by the Technology Acceptance Model concept. *Kasetsart Journal of Social Sciences*, 40(2), 349–358.

Borges, A., Laurindo, F., Spínola, M., Gonçalves, R. F., & Mattos, C. (2021). The strategic use of artificial intelligence in the digital era: Systematic literature review and future research directions. *International Journal of Information Management*, 57, 102225. 10.1016/j.ijinfomgt.2020.102225

Borland, J. (2002). New technology could help squelch digital music piracy. *CNET*. https://www.cnet.com/tech/services-and-software/new-technology-could-help-squelch-digital-music-piracy/

Borri, N. (2019). Conditional Tail-Risk in Cryptocurrency Markets. *Journal of Empirical Finance*, 50, 1–19. 10.1016/j.jempfin.2018.11.002

Bosman, J. (2011). Book shopping in stores, then buying online. *The New York Times*.

Bouri, E., Gupta, R., & Roubaud, D. (2018). Spillovers between Bitcoin and other assets during bear and bull markets. *Applied Economics*, 50(55), 5935–5949. 10.1080/00036846.2018.1488075

Bouri, E., Jalkh, N., Molnár, P., & Roubaud, D. (2017). Bitcoin for energy commodities before and after the December 2013 crash : Diversifier, hedge or safe haven? *Applied Economics*, 49(50), 5063–5073. 10.1080/00036846.2017.1299102

Bouri, E., Jawad, S., Shahzad, H., & Roubaud, D. (2018). *"Co-explosivity in the cryptocurrency market", Finance Research Letters.* Elsevier Inc., 10.1016/j.frl.2018.07.005

Bouri, E., Molnár, P., Azzi, G., Roubaud, D., & Hagfors, L. I. (2017). On the hedge and safe haven properties of Bitcoin: Is it really more than a diversifier? Forthcoming in Finance Research Letters On the hedge and safe haven properties of Bitcoin: Is it really more than a diversifier? *Finance Research Letters*, 20, 1–12. 10.1016/j.frl.2016.09.025

Brady, M. (2019). Data Privacy and Automated Vehicles: Navigating the Privacy Continuum. *Monash University Law Review. Monash University. Faculty of Law*, 45(3), 589–625.

Breitung, J. (2000). The local power of some unit root tests for panel data. *Advances in Econometrics*, 15, 161–177. Advance online publication. 10.1016/S0731-9053(00)15006-6

Breusch, T., & Pagan, A. (1980). The Lagrange multiplier test and its application to model specification in econometrics. *The Review of Economic Studies*, 47(1), 239–253. 10.2307/2297111

Compilation of References

Broadus, R. N. (1987). Toward a definition of 'bibliometrics'. *Scientometrics*, 12(5–6), 373–379. 10.1007/BF02016680

Buckley, r. P., Arner, d. W., Zetzsche, d. A., & Weber, R. H. (2020). The road to regtech: the (astonishing) example of the European union. *Journal of Banking Regulation, 21*(1), 26–36.

Burt, S., & Sparks, L. (2003). E-commerce and the retail process: A review. *Journal of Retailing and Consumer Services*, 10, 275–286.

Butler, T., & O'Brien, L. (2019). Understanding RegTech for Digital Regulatory Compliance. In Lynn, T., Mooney, J. G., Rosati, P., & Cummins, M. (Eds.), *Disrupting Finance: FinTech and Strategy in the 21st Century* (pp. 85–102). Springer International Publishing. 10.1007/978-3-030-02330-0_6

Caliskan, K. (2020). Data money: The socio-technical infrastructure of cryptocurrency blockchains. *Economy and Society*, 49(4), 540–561. 10.1080/03085147.2020.1774258

Calo, R. (2015). Robotics and the Lessons of Cyberlaw, 103 Calif. L. *Rev.*, 513, 535–537.

Caporale, G. M., & Plastun, A. (2019). On stock price overreactions: Frequency, seasonality and information content. *Journal of Applied Econometrics*, 22(1), 602–621. Advance online publication. 10.1080/15140326.2019.1692509

Cath, C. (2018). Governing artificial intelligence: Ethical, legal and technical opportunities and challenges. *Philosophical Transactions. Series A, Mathematical, Physical, and Engineering Sciences*, 376(2133), 20180080. 10.1098/rsta.2018.008030322996

Chalutz Ben-Gal, H. (2019). An ROI-based review of HR analytics: Practical implementation tools. *Personnel Review*, 48(6), 1429–1448.

Chang, V., Baudier, P., Zhang, H., Xu, Q., Zhang, J., & Arami, M. (2020). How Blockchain can impact financial services – The overview, challenges and recommendations from expert interviewees. *Technological Forecasting and Social Change*, 158(June), 120166. 10.1016/j.techfore.2020.120166

Charoenwong, B., Kowaleski, Z. T., Kwan, A., & Sutherland, A. (2023). *RegTech*. Academic Press.

Chawla, S. (2014). Digital Piracy & Copyright Enforcement: Approaches to Tackling Online. *TaxGuru*. https://taxguru.in/corporate-law/digital-piracy-copyright-enforcement-approaches -tackling-online-infringement.html

Cheng, T. E., Lam, D. Y., & Yeung, A. C. (2006). Adoption of internet banking: An empirical study in Hong Kong. *Decision Support Systems*, 42(3), 1558–1572. 10.1016/j.dss.2006.01.002

Chen, J. (2023). Transaction. Available at: https://www.investopedia.com/terms/t/transaction.asp

Chen, M. W., & Zhu, J. (2005). Do Investors in Chinese Stock Market Overreact? *Journal of Accounting and Finance Research*, 13(3).

Chen, Y., Wang, Q., Chen, H., Song, X., Tang, H., & Tian, M. (2019, June). An overview of augmented reality technology. *Journal of Physics: Conference Series*, 1237(2), 022082. 10.1088/1742-6596/1237/2/022082

Chettri, Y. (2022). RegTech-A Beginner's Guide to Regulation Technology. Available at: https://signalx.ai/blog/a-beginners-guide-to-regtech/

Chiratae. (2024). *FinTech Report 2024*. Retrieved from https://www.chiratae.com/fintech-report-2024/

Choi, I. (2001). Unit root tests for panel data. *Journal of International Money and Finance*, 20(2), 249–272. 10.1016/S0261-5606(00)00048-6

Chouhan, V., Ali, S., Sharma, R. B., & Sharma, A. (2023). The effect of financial technology (Fin-tech) on the conventional banking industry in India. *International Journal of Innovative Research and Scientific Studies*, 6(3), 538–544. 10.53894/ijirss.v6i3.1578

Christensen, C. M. (2016). *The innovator's dilemma: When new technologies cause great firms to fail*. Harvard Business Review Press.

Cole, R. A., Cumming, D. J., & Taylor, J. R. (2019). Does FinTech compete with or complement bank finance? *SSRN*. 10.2139/ssrn.3302975

Cole, R. A., Gao, L., & Strobel, J. (2019). Fintech credit markets around the world: Size, drivers and policy issues. *Journal of Financial Stability*, 42, 100–113.

Contissa, G., Lagioia, F., & Sartor, G. (2017). The ethical knob: Ethically-customisable automated vehicles and the law. *Artificial Intelligence and Law*, 25(3), 365–378. 10.1007/s10506-017-9211-z

Corallo, A., Lazoi, M., Lezzi, M., & Luperto, A. (2022). Cybersecurity awareness in the context of the Industrial Internet of Things: A systematic literature review. *Computers in Industry*, 137, 103614. 10.1016/j.compind.2022.103614

Corbet, S., Lucey, B., Urquhart, A., & Yarovaya, L. (2019). Cryptocurrencies as a financial asset: A systematic analysis. *International Review of Financial Analysis*, 62, 182–199. 10.1016/j.irfa.2018.09.003

Cristofari, G. (2023). *The Politics of Platformization–Amsterdam Dialogues on Platform Theory*. Institute of Network Cultures.

Cui, J., & Maghyereh, A. (2022). Time–frequency co-movement and risk connectedness among cryptocurrencies: New evidence from the higher-order moments before and during the COVID-19 pandemic. *Financial Innovation*, 8(1), 90. Advance online publication. 10.1186/s40854-022-00395-w

da Gama, P. V. J., Silva, M. C., & Klotzle, A. C. F. P. (2019). Herding Behavior and Contagion in the Cryptocurrency Market Pontifical Catholic University of Rio de Janeiro. *Journal of Behavioral and Experimental Finance*, 22, 41–50. 10.1016/j.jbef.2019.01.006

Compilation of References

Dabla-Norris, E., & Srivisal, N. (2013). *Revisiting the link between finance and macroeconomic volatility*. IMF Working Paper, 13/29.

Dash, G., & Chakraborty, D. (2021). Digital transformation of marketing strategies during a pandemic: Evidence from an emerging economy during COVID-19. *Sustainability*, 13(12), 6735.

Dashkevich, N., Counsell, S., & Destefanis, G. (2020). Blockchain Application for Central Banks: A Systematic Mapping Study. *IEEE Access : Practical Innovations, Open Solutions*, 8, 139918–139952. 10.1109/ACCESS.2020.3012295

De Bondt, W. F. M., & Thaler, R. H. (2012). Do Analysts Overreact? *Heuristics and Biases*. 10.1017/CBO9780511808098.040

De Bondt, W. F. M., & Thaler, R. (1985). Does the Stock Market Overreact? *The Journal of Finance*, 40(3), 793–805. Advance online publication. 10.1111/j.1540-6261.1985.tb05004.x

De Bondt, W. F. M., & Thaler, R. H. (1987). Further Evidence on Investor Overreaction and Stock Market Seasonality. *The Journal of Finance*, 42(3), 557–581. Advance online publication. 10.1111/j.1540-6261.1987.tb04569.x

de Moraes, G. H. S. M., Pelegrini, G. C., de Marchi, L. P., Pinheiro, G. T., & Cappellozza, A. (2022). Antecedents of big data analytics adoption: An analysis with future managers in a developing country. *The Bottom Line (New York, N.Y.)*, 35(2/3), 73–89. 10.1108/BL-06-2021-0068

De Vries, A., Gallersdörfer, U., Klaaßen, L., & Stoll, C. (2021). The true costs of digital currencies: Exploring impact beyond energy use. *One Earth*, 4(6), 786–789. 10.1016/j.oneear.2021.05.009

Dhanabagiyam, S., Blessy Doe, M., Thamizhselvi, M., Irfan, M., Thalari, S. K., & Libeesh, P. C. (2024). Factors influencing growth of micro entrepreneurship in the hospitality industry: An empirical study in India. *Cogent Business & Management*, 11(1), 2285260.

Di Francesco Maesa, D., & Mori, P. (2020). Blockchain 3.0 applications survey. *Journal of Parallel and Distributed Computing*, 138, 99–114. 10.1016/j.jpdc.2019.12.019

Dias, R., Horta, N., Chambino, M., Alexandre, P., & Heliodoro, P. (2022). A Multiple Fluctuations and Detrending Analysis of Financial Market Efficiency: Comparison of Central and Eastern European Stock Indexes. *International Scientific-Business Conference – LIMEN 2022: Vol 8.Conference Proceedings*, 11–21. 10.31410/LIMEN.2022.11

Dias, R., Pereira, J. M., & Carvalho, L. C. (2022). Are African Stock Markets Efficient? A Comparative Analysis Between Six African Markets, the UK, Japan and the USA in the Period of the Pandemic. *Naše Gospodarstvo/Our Economy, 68*(1), 35–51. 10.2478/ngoe-2022-0004

Dias, R. M. T. S., Chambino, M., Alexandre, P., Morais da Palma, C., & Almeida, L. (2023). Unveiling Bitcoin's Safe Haven and Hedging Properties Beyond Diversification. *Advances in Web Technologies and Engineering*, (November), 380–410. Advance online publication. 10.4018/978-1-6684-9039-6.ch018

Dias, R. T., Chambino, M., Palma, C., Almeida, L., & Alexandre, P. (2023). Overreaction, Underreaction, and Short-Term Efficient Reaction Evidence for Cryptocurrencies. *Advances in Web Technologies and Engineering*, (November), 288–312. 10.4018/978-1-6684-9039-6.ch014

Dias, R., Chambino, M., & Rebolo Horta, N. (2023). Long-Term Dependencies in Central European Stock Markets: A Crisp-Set Analysis. *Economic Analysis Letters*, 2(February), 10–17. 10.58567/eal02010002

Dias, R., Horta, N. R., & Chambino, M. (2023). Portfolio rebalancing in times of stress: Capital markets vs. Commodities. *Journal of Economic Analysis*, 9(1), 129–151. 10.58567/jea02010005

Dias, R., Horta, N., & Chambino, M. (2023). Clean Energy Action Index Efficiency: An Analysis in Global Uncertainty Contexts. *Energies*, 16(9), 3937. Advance online publication. 10.3390/en16093937

Dias, R., Teixeira, N., Machova, V., Pardal, P., Horak, J., & Vochozka, M. (2020). Random walks and market efficiency tests: Evidence on US, Chinese and European capital markets within the context of the global Covid-19 pandemic. *Oeconomia Copernicana*, 11(4), 585–608. Advance online publication. 10.24136/oc.2020.024

Dickey, D., & Fuller, W. (1981). Likelihood ratio statistics for autoregressive time series with a unit root. *Econometrica*, 49(4), 1057–1072. 10.2307/1912517

Diemers, D., Lamaa, A., Salamat, J., & Stefens, T. (2015). *Developing a FinTech ecosystem in the GCC*. Strategy.

Dierksmeier, C., & Seele, P. (2018). Cryptocurrencies and Business Ethics. *Journal of Business Ethics*, 152(1), 1–14. 10.1007/s10551-016-3298-0

Ding, D., Chong, G., & Chuen, L. K. D., & Cheng, T. L. (2018). From Ant Financial to Alibaba's rural Taobao strategy—how Fintech is transforming social inclusion. In D. Lee & R. H. Deng (Eds.), *Handbook of blockchain, digital finance, and inclusion* (Vol. 1, pp. 19–35). Academic Press.

Dobson, W., & Westland, T. (2018). Financial liberalisation and trade: An examination of moving up value chains in the Asia-Pacific region. In Armstrong, S., & Westland, T. (Eds.), *Asian economic integration in an era of global uncertainty*. ANU Press. 10.22459/AEIEGU.01.2018.05

Donthu, N., Kumar, S., Mukherjee, D., Pandey, N., & Lim, W. M. (2021). How to conduct a bibliometric analysis: An overview and guidelines. *Journal of Business Research*, 133(May), 285–296. 10.1016/j.jbusres.2021.04.070

Dorfleitner, G., Hornuf, L., Schmitt, M., & Weber, M. (2017). Definition of FinTech and Description of the FinTech Industry. In Dorfleitner, G., Hornuf, L., Schmitt, M., & Weber, M. (Eds.), *FinTech in Germany* (pp. 5–10). Springer International Publishing., 10.1007/978-3-319-54666-7_2

Drasch, B. J., Schweizer, A., & Urbach, N. (2018). Integrating the 'Troublemakers': A taxonomy for cooperation between banks and fintechs. *Journal of Economics and Business*, 100, 26–42. 10.1016/j.jeconbus.2018.04.002

Compilation of References

Drljevic, N., Aranda, D. A., & Stantchev, V. (2020). Perspectives on risks and standards that affect the requirements engineering of blockchain technology. *Computer Standards & Interfaces*, 69, 103409. 10.1016/j.csi.2019.103409

Drummer, D., Jerenz, A., Siebelt, P., & Thaten, M. (2016). *Fintech—challenges and opportunities. How digitization is transforming the financial sector*. McKinsey & Company.

Duan, R., & Guo, L. (2021). Application of Blockchain for Internet of Things: A Bibliometric Analysis. *Mathematical Problems in Engineering*, 2021, 1–16. 10.1155/2021/5547530

Duc, A. N., Bøe, T., & Sundbø, I. (n.d.). *Understanding the Role of Artificial Intelligence in Digital Startups: A Conceptual Framework*. https://www.angellist.com/

Dwyer, G. P. (2015). The economics of Bitcoin and similar private digital currencies. *Journal of Financial Stability*, 17, 81–91. 10.1016/j.jfs.2014.11.006

Ediagbonya, V., & Tioluwani, C. (2023). The role of fintech in driving financial inclusion in developing and emerging markets: Issues, challenges and prospects. *Technological Sustainability*, 2(1), 100–119. 10.1108/TECHS-10-2021-0017

Electronic Vehicles Act, sec. 2(2) (2018).

Ellegaard, O., & Wallin, J. A. (2015). *The bibliometric analysis of scholarly production: How great is the impact?Scientometrics*, *105*(3), 1809–1831. 10.1007/s11192-015-1645-z

Elton, S. (2019). Mechanical Licensing Before and After the Music Modernization Act. *Journal of the Music & Entertainment Industry Educators Association*, 19(1), 13–35. 10.25101/19.1

Ergashev, A. (2023). Financial technologies in the remote banking system. *Science and Innovation,2*(A6), 197-201.

Ernst & Young. (2019). *EY 2019 global fintech adoption index*. Author.

Esmaeilian, B., Sarkis, J., Lewis, K., & Behdad, S. (2020). Blockchain for the future of sustainable supply chain management in Industry 4.0. *Resources, Conservation and Recycling*, 163, 105064. 10.1016/j.resconrec.2020.105064

Estevez, E. (2020). RegTech: Definition, Who Uses It and Why, and Example Companies. *Investopedia*. https://www.investopedia.com/terms/r/regtech.asp

Etzioni, O. (2018). Point: Should AI technology be regulated? yes, and here's how. *Communications of the ACM*, 61(12), 30–32. 10.1145/3197382

European Data Protection Supervisor. (n.d.). https://www.edps.europa.eu/_en

European Union Agency for Cybersecurity (ENISA). (n.d.). https://www.enisa.europa.eu/ publications/industry-4-0-cybersecurity-challenges-and-recommendations

Ewens, M., Xiao, K., & Xu, T. (2024). Regulatory costs of being public: Evidence from bunching estimation. *Journal of Financial Economics*, 153, 103775. 10.1016/j.jfineco.2023.103775

EY. (2022). *$1 Tn India FinTech Opportunity: Chiratae Ventures-EY FinTech Report*. Retrieved from https://assets.ey.com/content/dam/ey-sites/ey-com/en_in/topics/financial-services/2022/ey-one-trillion-dollars-india-fintech-opportunity-chiratae-ventures-ey-fintech-report_v1.pdf

Eze, S. C., Olatunji, S., Chinedu-Eze, V. C., Bello, A. O., Ayeni, A., & Peter, F. (2019). Determinants of perceived information need for emerging ICT adoption: A study of UK small service businesses. *The Bottom Line (New York, N.Y.)*, 32(2), 158–183. 10.1108/BL-01-2019-0059

Fama, E. F. (1965). Random Walks in Stock Market Prices. *Financial Analysts Journal*, 21(5), 55–59. Advance online publication. 10.2469/faj.v21.n5.55

Fama, E. F. (1970). Efficient Capital Markets: A Review of Theory and Empirical Work. *The Journal of Finance*, 25(2), 383. Advance online publication. 10.2307/2325486

Fama, E. F., & French, K. R. (1993). Common risk factors in the returns on stocks and bonds. *Journal of Financial Economics*, 33(1), 3–56. 10.1016/0304-405X(93)90023-5

FCA. (2016). *Call for input on supporting the development and adopters of regtech*. Academic Press.

Fennell, S., Kaur, P., Jhunjhunwala, A., Narayanan, D., Loyola, C., Bedi, J., & Singh, Y. (2018). Examining linkages between Smart Villages and Smart Cities: Learning from rural youth accessing the internet in India. *Telecommunications Policy*, 42(10), 810–823.

Ferenhof, H. A., Durst, S., Zaniboni Bialecki, M., & Selig, P. M. (2015). Intellectual capital dimensions: State of the art in 2014. *Journal of Intellectual Capital*, 16(1), 58–100. 10.1108/JIC-02-2014-0021

Fintech. (2018). Regtech and the importance of cybersecurity. *Issues in Information Systems*. Advance online publication. 10.48009/3_iis_2018_220-225

Fintechs in India. (n.d.). Deloitte India. Retrieved January 7, 2024, from https://www2.deloitte.com/in/en/pages/financial-services/articles/in-banking-fintechs-in-india-key-trends-noexp.html

Firdaus, A., Razak, M. F. A., Feizollah, A., Hashem, I. A. T., Hazim, M., & Anuar, N. B. (2019). *The Rise of "Blockchain": Bibliometric Analysis of Blockchain Study, Scientometrics* (Vol. 120). Springer International Publishing. 10.1007/s11192-019-03170-4

Flyverbom, M., Deibert, R., & Matten, D. (2019). The governance of digital technology, big data, and the internet: new roles and responsibilities for business. *Business & Society, 58*(1), 3-19.

Foot, P. (1967). The problem of abortion and the doctrine of double effect. *Oxford Review*, 5(1), 5–15.

Freij, Å. (2020). Using technology to support financial services regulatory compliance: Current applications and future prospects of regtech. *Journal of Investment Compliance*, 21(2/3), 181–190. 10.1108/JOIC-10-2020-0033

Compilation of References

Fry, J. (2018). Booms, busts and heavy-tails: The story of Bitcoin and cryptocurrency markets? *Economics Letters*, 171, 225–229. 10.1016/j.econlet.2018.08.008

Fuerst, S., Sanchez-Dominguez, O., & Rodriguez-Montes, M. A. (2023). The Role of Digital Technology within the Business Model of Sustainable Entrepreneurship. *Sustainability (Basel)*, 15(14), 10923. Advance online publication. 10.3390/su151410923

Functional safety standards-An overview. (n.d.). https://www.tuvsud.com/en-us/services/functional-safety/about

Gabor, D., & Brooks, S. (2016). The digital revolution in financial inclusion: International development in the fintech era. *New Political Economy*, 22(4), 423–436. 10.1080/13563467.2017.1259298

Ganguly, A. K., & Arcot, P. P. (2023). Models of technology adoption and growth of fintech in India: A review. *European Chemical Bulletin*, 12, 2153–2168.

García-Corral, F. J., Cordero-García, J. A., de Pablo-Valenciano, J., & Uribe-Toril, J. (2022). A bibliometric review of cryptocurrencies: How have they grown? *Financial Innovation*, 8(1), 2. Advance online publication. 10.1186/s40854-021-00306-5

GDPR-fines and penalties. (n.d.). https://gdpr.eu/fines/

Gil-Alana, L. A., Abakah, E. J. A., & Rojo, M. F. R. (2020). Cryptocurrencies and stock market indices. Are they related? *Research in International Business and Finance*, 51, 101063. Advance online publication. 10.1016/j.ribaf.2019.101063

Goddard, M. (2017). The EU General Data Protection Regulation (GDPR): European regulation that has a global impact. *International Journal of Market Research*, 59(6), 703–705. 10.2501/IJMR-2017-050

Gogoll, J., & Muller, J. F. (2016). Autonomous cars: In favor of a mandatory ethics setting. *Science and Engineering Ethics*. Advance online publication. 10.1007/si1948-016-9806-x27417644

Goodall, N. J. (2016). Away from trolley problems and toward risk management. *Applied Artificial Intelligence*, 30(8), 810–821. 10.1080/08839514.2016.1229922

Goode, A. (2018). Biometrics for banking: Best practices and barriers to adoption. *Biometric Technology Today*, 2018(10), 5–7. 10.1016/S0969-4765(18)30156-5

Gopalan, S., & Sasidharan, S. (2020). Financial liberalization and access to credit in emerging and developing economies: A firm-level empirical investigation. *Journal of Economics and Business*, 107, 105861. 10.1016/j.jeconbus.2019.105861

Gopal, S., Gupta, P., & Minocha, A. (2023). Advancements in Fin-Tech and Security Challenges of Banking Industry. *4th International Conference on Intelligent Engineering and Management (ICIEM)*, 1-6 10.1109/ICIEM59379.2023.10165876

Gorkhali, A., Li, L., & Shrestha, A. (2020). Blockchain: A literature review. *Journal of Management Analytics, Taylor & Francis*, 7(3), 321–343. 10.1080/23270012.2020.1801529

Gormley, H. (2020). *The Breakdown: What Songwriters Need to Know about the Music Modernization Act and Royalty Payments.* https://blogs.loc.gov/copyright/2020/04/the-breakdown -what-songwriters-need-to-know-about-the-music-modernization-act-and-royalty-payments/

Granados, N. (2016). How Online Piracy Hurts Emerging Artists. *Forbes.* https://www.forbes.com/ sites/nelsongranados/2016/02/01/how-online-piracy-hurts-emerging-artists/?sh=1a68e7d17774

Grassi, L., & Lanfranchi, D. (2022). RegTech in public and private sectors: The nexus between data, technology and regulation. *Economia e Politica Industriale,* 49(3), 441–479. 10.1007/ s40812-022-00226-0

Guedes, E. F., Santos, R. P. C., Figueredo, L. H. R., Da Silva, P. A., Dias, R. M. T. S., & Zebende, G. F. (2022). Efficiency and Long-Range Correlation in G-20 Stock Indexes: A Sliding Windows Approach. *Fluctuation and Noise Letters,* 21(4), 2250033. Advance online publication. 10.1142/ S021947752250033X

Guo, Y. M., Huang, Z. L., Guo, J., Guo, X. R., Li, H., Liu, M. Y., Ezzeddine, S., & Nkeli, M. J. (2021). "A bibliometric analysis and visualization of blockchain", *Future Generation Computer Systems. Future Generation Computer Systems,* 116, 316–332. 10.1016/j.future.2020.10.023

Haddad, C., & Hornuf, L. (2018). The emergence of the global fintech market: Economic and technological determinants. *Small Business Economics,* 53(1), 81–105. 10.1007/s11187-018-9991-x

Hair, J. F., Jr., & Black, W. C. (2010). *Multivariate data analysis* (7th ed.). Pearson Prentice Hall.

Hairudin, A., Sifat, I. M., Mohamad, A., & Yusof, Y. (2020). Cryptocurrencies: A survey on acceptance, governance and market dynamics. *International Journal of Finance & Economics,* (December). Advance online publication. 10.1002/ijfe.2392

Ha, L. T. (2022). Effects of digitalization on financialization: Empirical evidence from European countries. *Technology in Society,* 68(C), 101851. 10.1016/j.techsoc.2021.101851

Halberstadt, J., & Johnson, M. (2014, September). Sustainability Management for Startups and Micro-Enterprises: Development of a Sustainability-Quick-Check and Reporting Scheme. In *EnviroInfo* (pp. 17-24). Academic Press.

Haleem, A., Javaid, M., Asim Qadri, M., Pratap Singh, R., & Suman, R. (2022). Artificial intelligence (AI) applications for marketing: A literature-based study. In *International Journal of Intelligent Networks* (Vol. 3, pp. 119–132). KeAi Communications Co. 10.1016/j.ijin.2022.08.005

Hanley-Giersch, B. J. (2019). *RegTech and Financial Crime Prevention.* The RegTech Book. 10.1002/9781119362197.ch4

Harel, M. (2022). 6 Ways to Stop Digital Piracy. *Viaccess.* https://www.viaccess-orca.com/blog/ six-ways-to-stop-digital-piracy

Compilation of References

Haris, M., & Dhobale, S. (2023). Revolutionising Compliance: The Role Of RegTech In Reshaping India's Regulatory Landscape. Available at: https://www.news18.com/business/revolutionising-compliance-the-role-of-regtech-in-reshaping-indias-regulatory-landscape-8645348.html#:~:text=The%20Future%20of%20RegTech%20in%20India&text=In%20the%20coming%20years,%20we,stay%20ahead%20of%20the%20curve

Haykir, O., & Yagli, I. (2022). Speculative bubbles and herding in cryptocurrencies. *Financial Innovation*, 8(1), 78. 10.1186/s40854-022-00383-0

Hota, P. K., Subramanian, B., & Narayanamurthy, G. (2020). Mapping the intellectual structure of social entrepreneurship research. *Journal of Business Ethics*, 166(1), 89–114. 10.1007/s10551-019-04129-4

Huang, Y., & Ji, Y. (2017). How will financial liberalization change the Chinese economy? Lessons from middle-income countries. *Journal of Asian Economics*, 50, 27–45. 10.1016/j.asieco.2017.04.001

Huo, X., & Qiu, Z. (2020). How does China's stock market react to the announcement of the COVID-19 pandemic lockdown? *Economic and Political Studies*, 8(4), 436–461. Advance online publication. 10.1080/20954816.2020.1780695

Huynh, T. L. D., Shahbaz, M., Nasir, M. A., & Ullah, S. (2022). Financial modelling, risk management of energy instruments and the role of cryptocurrencies. *Annals of Operations Research*, 313(1), 47–75. 10.1007/s10479-020-03680-y

Hu, Z., Ding, S., Li, S., Chen, L., & Yang, S. (2019). Adoption intention of fintech services for bank users: An empirical examination with an extended technology acceptance model. *Symmetry*, 11(3), 340. 10.3390/sym11030340

Iansiti, M., & Lakhani, K. R. (2017). The truth about blockchain. *Harvard Business Review*.

IBM. (n.d.). Cost of a Data Breach Report 2023. https://www.ibm.com/reports/data-breach/

IDC spending guide forecasts. (n.d.). https://www.idc.com/getdoc.jsp?containerId=prUS50386323

Im, K. S., Pesaran, M. H., & Shin, Y. (2003). Testing for unit roots in heterogeneous panels. *Journal of Econometrics*, 115(1), 53–74. Advance online publication. 10.1016/S0304-4076(03)00092-7

Inci, A. C., & Lagasse, R. (2019). Cryptocurrencies: Applications and investment opportunities. *Journal of Capital Markets Studies*, 3(2), 98–112. 10.1108/JCMS-05-2019-0032

India surpasses Japan to become 3rd largest market globally. (n.d.). ETauto. Available at https://auto.economictimes.indiatimes.com/news/industry/india-surpasses-japan-to-become-3rd-largest-auto-market-

Inegbedion, H. E. (2021). Digital divide in the major regions of the world and the possibility of convergence. *The Bottom Line (New York, N.Y.)*, 34(1), 68–85. 10.1108/BL-09-2020-0064

Insights, C. (2019). *Global Fintech Report Q2 2019*. CB Insights.

IoT Security Best Practices. (n.d.). https://codalien.com/blog/ internet-of-things-iot-security-best-practices/

Irfan, M., Dhanabagiyam, S., Nayak, S. R., & Dias, R. (2024). Promotion of Rural Tourism Destination for Community and Sustainable Destination Development: An Indigenous Study. In *Achieving Sustainable Transformation in Tourism and Hospitality Sectors* (pp. 268–277). IGI Global.

Jagtiani, J., & Lemieux, C. (2018). *Fintech Lending: Financial Inclusion, Risk Pricing, and Alternative Information.* Federal Reserve Bank of Philadelphia Working Paper, (18-20).

Jagtiani, J., & Lemieux, C. (2018). Do fintech lenders penetrate areas that are underserved by traditional banks? *Journal of Economics and Business*, 100, 43–54. 10.1016/j.jeconbus.2018.03.001

Jalal, R. N. U. D., Alon, I., & Paltrinieri, A. (2021). A bibliometric review of cryptocurrencies as a financial asset. *Technology Analysis and Strategic Management*, 0(0), 1–16. 10.1080/09537325.2021.1939001

Janssens, E., Daele, S., & Vander, T. (2009). The Music Industry on (the) Line? *Journal of Crime, Criminal Law and Criminal Justice*, 17, 77–96. https://www.researchgate.net/publication/228223919_The_Music_Industry_on_the_Line_Surviving_Music_Piracy_in_a_Digital_Era

Jarque, C. M., & Bera, A. K. (1980). Efficient tests for normality, homoscedasticity and serial independence of regression residuals. *Economics Letters*, 6(3), 255–259. 10.1016/0165-1765(80)90024-5

Javaid, M., Haleem, A., & Singh, R. P. (2023). A study on ChatGPT for Industry 4.0: Background, potentials, challenges, and eventualities. *Journal of Economy and Technology*, 1, 127–143. 10.1016/j.ject.2023.08.001

Jedwab, R., Christiaensen, L., & Gindelsky, M. (2015). *Demography, urbanization and development: Rural push, urban pull and… urban push?* The World Bank.

Johannesson, J., & Clowes, D. (2022). Energy Resources and Markets - Perspectives on the Russia-Ukraine War. *European Review (Chichester, England)*, 30(1), 4–23. 10.1017/S1062798720001040

Johansson, E., Sutinen, K., Lassila, J., Lang, V., Martikainen, M., & Lehner, O. M. (2019). Regtech-a necessary tool to keep up with compliance and regulatory changes. *ACRN Journal of Finance and Risk Perspectives. Special Issue Digital Accounting*, 8, 71–85.

Jordão, R. V. D., & Novas, J. C. (2017). Knowledge management and intellectual capital in networks of small- and medium-sized enterprises. *Journal of Intellectual Capital*, 18(3), 667–692. 10.1108/JIC-11-2016-0120

Jugurnath, B., Hemshika, P., & Štraupaitė, S. (2023). Fintech challenges and opportunities in banking. *Management/Vadyba, 39*(1), 16487974.

Compilation of References

Jurkauskas, L. (2015). Digital Piracy as an innovation in Recording Industry Linas. *Projekter.* https://projekter.aau.dk/projekter/files/213765961/Digital_Piracy_as_an_Innovation_in _Recording_Industry_by_L._Jurkauskas.pdf

Kamyar, A., & Ghiyas Kamyar, A. (n.d.). Artificial Intelligence Startups in Italy: Their role in Decision-Making. 10.13140/RG.2.2.16272.17929

Kapasi, S. (2023). The Effects of Data Privacy Bills on Healthcare: Safeguarding Patient Information. Available at: https://health.economictimes.indiatimes.com/news/health-it/the-effects-of -data-privacy-bills-on-healthcare-safeguarding-patient-information-in-the-digital-age/100748897

Karamchandani, S. Protecting Music from Digital Exploitation: Challenges to Copyright Laws in Digital India. *Legalserviceindia.* https://www.legalserviceindia.com/legal/article-11107 -protecting-music-from-digital-exploitation-challenges-to-copyright-laws-in-digital-india.html #google_vignette

Kasemsap, K. (2017). Artificial intelligence: Current issues and applications. In *Handbook of Research on Manufacturing Process Modeling and Optimization Strategies* (pp. 454–474). IGI Global. 10.4018/978-1-5225-2440-3.ch022

Katsiampa, P. (2017). Volatility estimation for Bitcoin : A comparison of GARCH models. *Economics Letters*, 158, 3–6. 10.1016/j.econlet.2017.06.023

Keller, P. (2018, March-April). Autonomous Vehicles, Artificial Intelligence, and the Law. *RAIL: The Journal of Robotics Artificial Intelligence and Law*, 1(2), 101–110.

Kent Baker, H., Pandey, N., Kumar, S., & Haldar, A. (2020). A bibliometric analysis of board diversity: Current status, development, and future research directions. *Journal of Business Research*, 108, 232–246. 10.1016/j.jbusres.2019.11.025

Key Data From Regulatory Sandboxes Across The Globe. (n.d.). https://www.worldbank.org/ en/topic/fintech/brief/key-data-from-regulatory-sandboxes-across-the-globe

Khalfaoui, R., Gozgor, G., & Goodell, J. W. (2023). Impact of Russia-Ukraine war attention on cryptocurrency: Evidence from quantile dependence analysis. *Finance Research Letters*, 52, 103365. Advance online publication. 10.1016/j.frl.2022.103365

Khan, R., & Hakami, T. A. (2022). Cryptocurrency: Usability perspective versus volatility threat. *Journal of Money and Business*, 2(1), 16–28. 10.1108/JMB-11-2021-0051

Kim, H. & So, K.K.F. (2022). Two decades of customer experience research in hospitality and tourism: A bibliometric analysis and thematic content analysis. *International Journal of Hospitality Management*, 100. .10.1016/j.ijhm.2021.103082

Kim, S. J. (2023). An Overview of Fintech, Pandemic and the Financial System: Challenges and Opportunities. *Fintech, Pandemic, and the Financial System. Challenges and Opportunities*, 22, 3–9.

Kitsios, F., Chatzidimitriou, E., & Kamariotou, M. (2023). The ISO/IEC 27001 Information security management standard: How to extract value from data in the IT sector. *Sustainability (Basel)*, 15(7), 5828. 10.3390/su15075828

Kline, R. (2010). *Principles and practice of structural equation modelling*. The Guilford Press.

Klose, J. (2022). Comparing cryptocurrencies and gold - a system-GARCH-approach. *Springer International Publishing*, 12(4), 653–679. 10.1007/s40822-022-00218-4

Ko, G., Routray, J. K., & Ahmad, M. M. (2019). ICT infrastructure for rural community sustainability. *Community Development (Columbus, Ohio)*, 50(1), 51–72.

Kohler, W. J., & Colbert-Taylor, A. (2014). Current law and potential legal issues pertaining to automated, autonomous and connected vehicles. *Santa Clara High-Technology Law Journal*, 31(1), 99–138.

Krueckeberg, S., & Scholz, P. (2019). *Cryptocurrencies as an Asset Class?* Springer International Publishing., 10.2139/ssrn.3162800

Kulkarni, V., Sunkle, S., Kholkar, D., Roychoudhury, S., Kumar, R., & Raghunandan, M. (2021). Toward automated regulatory compliance. *CSI Transactions on ICT*, 9(2), 95–104. 10.1007/s40012-021-00329-4

Kumar, S. (2024). Tackling digital piracy: The Indian context. The complexities of hate speech laws in India. *Linkedin*. https://www.linkedin.com/pulse/tackling-digital-piracy-indian-context-complexities-nyiac/

Kurum, E. (2023, April 18). Regtech solutions and AML compliance: What future for financial crime? *Journal of Financial Crime*, 30(3), 776–794. Advance online publication. 10.1108/JFC-04-2020-0051

Kushwaha, R. (n.d.). *Sustainable Entrepreneurship Creating Value with Sustainability*. https://www.researchgate.net/publication/366371306

Laksamana, P., Suharyanto, S., & Cahaya, Y. F. (2023). Determining factors of continuance intention in mobile payment: Fintech industry perspective. *Asia Pacific Journal of Marketing and Logistics*, 35(7), 1699–1718. 10.1108/APJML-11-2021-0851

Lardo, A., Corsi, K., Varma, A., & Mancini, D. (2022). Exploring blockchain in the accounting domain: A bibliometric analysis. *Accounting, Auditing & Accountability Journal*, 35(9), 204–233. 10.1108/AAAJ-10-2020-4995

Larson, J. M. (2022). Data Privacy Laws and Regulatory Drivers. In *Snowflake Access Control: Mastering the Features for Data Privacy and Regulatory Compliance* (pp. 25–42). Apress. 10.1007/978-1-4842-8038-6_3

Lee, B., Kim, B., & Ivan, U. V. (2023). Enhancing the Competitiveness of AI Technology-Based Startups in the Digital Era. *Administrative Sciences*, 14(1), 6. 10.3390/admsci14010006

Compilation of References

Lee, C.-C., Lin, C.-W., & Zeng, J.-H. (2016). Financial liberalization, insurance market, and the likelihood of financial crises. *Journal of International Money and Finance*, 62, 25–51. 10.1016/j.jimonfin.2015.12.002

Lee, C., Kim, S., & Park, J. (2021). The Impact of Fintech on Customer Satisfaction in the Banking Sector. *Journal of Financial Services*, 25(3), 129–147.

Lee, I., & Shin, Y. J. (2018). Fintech: Ecosystem, business models, investment decisions, and challenges. *Business Horizons*, 61(1), 35–46. 10.1016/j.bushor.2017.09.003

Leight, E. (2023). Music Piracy Is Rising — And the U.S. Is a Trouble Spot. *BillBoard*. https://www.billboard.com/pro/music-piracy-2022-stream-ripping/

Leong, C. W., Tan, G. W., Chong, S. C., Ooi, K. B., & Lin, B. (2017). Predicting the determinants of users' intention for using mobile-based financial services: A structural equation modeling (SEM) approach. *International Journal of Information Management*, 37(3), 252–261.

Leong, C., Tan, B., Xiao, X., Tan, F. T. C., & Sun, Y. (2017). Nurturing a FinTech ecosystem: The case of a youth microloan startup in China. *International Journal of Information Management*, 37(2), 92–97. 10.1016/j.ijinfomgt.2016.11.006

Leonidou, C. N., & Leonidou, L. C. (2011). Research into environmental marketing/management: A bibliographic analysis. *European Journal of Marketing*, 45(1), 68–103. 10.1108/03090561111095603

Levin, A., Lin, C. F., & Chu, C. S. J. (2002). Unit root tests in panel data: Asymptotic and finite-sample properties. *Journal of Econometrics*, 108(1), 1–24. Advance online publication. 10.1016/S0304-4076(01)00098-7

Levine, J. (2020, May-June). Rebecca Yergin, "DOT Introduces Fourth Round of Automated Vehicles Guidance," RAIL: The Journal of Robotics. *Artificial Intelligence and Law*, 3(3), 171–174.

Levine, R. (2005). Finance and growth: Theory and evidence. In Aghion, P., & Durlauf, S. (Eds.), *Handbook of Economic Growth* (pp. 865–934). Elsevier.

Li, G. Z., Xiong, D. H., & Liu, L. (2016). How does SMBs' development affect SMEs' financing? *Journal of Financial Research*, 12, 78–94.

Li, H., Tao, Q., Xiao, H., & Li, G. (2019). Money market funds, bank loans and interest rate liberalization: Evidence from an emerging market. *Finance Research Letters*, 30, 426–435. 10.1016/j.frl.2019.04.020

Li, J., Maiti, A., & Fei, J. (2023). Features and Scope of Regulatory Technologies: Challenges and Opportunities with Industrial Internet of Things. *Future Internet*, 15(8), 8. Advance online publication. 10.3390/fi15080256

Lim, H. Y. F. (2022). Regulatory compliance. In *Artificial Intelligence* (pp. 85–108). Edward Elgar Publishing.

Lim, M. K., Li, Y., Wang, C., & Tseng, M. L. (2021). A literature review of blockchain technology applications in supply chains: A comprehensive analysis of themes, methodologies and industries. *Computers & Industrial Engineering*, 154, 107133. 10.1016/j.cie.2021.107133

Lin, P. (2014). *Here's a terrible idea: robot cars with adjustable ethics settings.* Available via https://www.wired.com/2014/08/heres-a-terrible-idea-robot-cars-with-adjustable-ethics-settings

Linnenluecke, M. K., Marrone, M., & Singh, A. K. (2020). Conducting systematic literature reviews and bibliometric analyses. *Australian Journal of Management*, 45(2), 175–194. 10.1177/0312896219877678

Lin, P. (2016). Why ethics matters for autonomous cars. In Maurer, M., Gerdes, J. C., Lenz, B., & Winner, H. (Eds.), *Autonomous driving* (pp. 69–85). Springer.

Li, Z. (2023). Digitalization of RegTech - Critical Review in China. *Journal of Applied Economics and Policy Studies.*, 1(1), 57–65. 10.54254/2977-5701/1/2023006

Lo, A. W., & MacKinlay, A. C. (1988). Stock Market Prices Do Not Follow Random Walks: Evidence from a Simple Specification Test. *Review of Financial Studies*, 1(1), 41–66. Advance online publication. 10.1093/rfs/1.1.41

Lombardi, R., de Villiers, C., Moscariello, N., & Pizzo, M. (2022). The disruption of blockchain in auditing – a systematic literature review and an agenda for future research. *Accounting, Auditing & Accountability Journal*, 35(7), 1534–1565. 10.1108/AAAJ-10-2020-4992

Mahajan, S., & Tripathi, V. (n.d.). Three Solutions to Curb Piracy in the Music Industry. *WNS.* https://www.wns.com/perspectives/articles/articledetail/706/three-solutions-to-curb-piracy-in-the-music-industry

Mahoney, J. (2019). *The rise of Chinese fintech: Lessons for the United States.* Colombia Business School.

Makina, D. (Ed.). (2019). *Extending financial inclusion in Africa.* Academic Press.

Manconi, A., Massa, M., & Yasuda, A. (2012). The role of institutional investors in propagating the crisis of 2007–2008. *Journal of Financial Economics*, 104(3), 491–518.

Mark, A. (2017). Geistfeld, A Roadmap for Autonomous Vehicles: State Tort Liability, Automobile Insurance, and Federal Safety Regulation. *Calif. L.Rev.*, 1611, 1612.

Marler, J. H., & Boudreau, J. W. (2017). An evidence-based review of HR Analytics. *International Journal of Human Resource Management*, 28(1), 3–26.

Maulina, E., Purnomo, M., Wicaksono, A. R., Rizal, M., Program, D., Raya, J., Sumedang, B., Jatinangor, K., Sumedang, K., & Barat, J. (2020). Analysis of the Use of Artificial Intelligence Technology on Digital Startups in Indonesia. *International Journal of Advanced Science and Technology, 29*(3), 750–758. https://www.researchgate.net/publication/343224942

Mbonihankuye, S., Nkunzimana, A., & Ndagijimana, A. (2019). Healthcare data security technology: HIPAA compliance. *Wireless Communications and Mobile Computing*, 2019, 1–7. 10.1155/2019/1927495

McGraw, D., & Mandl, K. D. (2021). Privacy protections to encourage use of health-relevant digital data in a learning health system. *NPJ Digital Medicine*, 4(1), 2. 10.1038/s41746-020-00362-833398052

McWaters, R. J., Bruno, G., Lee, A., & Blake, M. (2015). The future of financial services: How disruptive innovations are reshaping the way financial services are structured, provisioned and consumed. *World Economic Forum,125*, 1-178.

Meijering, E. (2002). A chronology of interpolation: From ancient astronomy to modern signal and image processing. *Proceedings of the IEEE*, 90(3), 319–342. 10.1109/5.993400

Mengfei, L. I. U., Jie, F. E. N. G., & Xiaowei, L. U. O. (2022). RegTech: Theory and Practice in Technology Driven Financial Regulation. *Frontiers of Economics in China*, 17(1).

Mention, A.-L. (2019). The Future of Fintech. *Research Technology Management*, 62(4), 59–63. 10.1080/08956308.2019.1613123

Merediz-Solá, I., & Bariviera, A. F. (2019). A bibliometric analysis of bitcoin scientific production. *Research in International Business and Finance*, 50, 294–305. 10.1016/j.ribaf.2019.06.008

Millar, J. (2015). Technology as moral proxy: Autonomy and paternalism by design. *IEEE Technology and Society Magazine*, 34(2), 47–55. 10.1109/MTS.2015.2425612

Mnif, E., Jarboui, A., & Mouakhar, K. (2020). How the cryptocurrency market has performed during COVID 19? A multifractal analysis. *Finance Research Letters*, 36, 101647. 10.1016/j.frl.2020.101647

Mohamed, H., & Yildirim, R. (2021). RegTech and Regulatory Change Management for Financial Institutions. In Hamdan, A., Hassanien, A. E., Razzaque, A., & Alareeni, B. (Eds.), *The Fourth Industrial Revolution: Implementation of Artificial Intelligence for Growing Business Success* (pp. 153–168). Springer International Publishing. 10.1007/978-3-030-62796-6_8

Mohammad Saif, A. N., & Islam, M. A. (2022). Blockchain in human resource management: A systematic review and bibliometric analysis. *Technology Analysis and Strategic Management*, 2021(March), 1–16. 10.1080/09537325.2022.2049226

Muganyi, T., Yan, L., Yin, Y., Sun, H., Gong, X., & Taghizadeh-Hesary, F. (2022). Fintech, regtech, and financial development: Evidence from China. *Financial Innovation*, 8(1), 1–20. 10.1186/s40854-021-00313-6

Müller, R., & Antoni, C. H. (2020). Individual Perceptions of Shared Mental Models of Information and Communication Technology (ICT) and Virtual Team Coordination and Performance — The Moderating Role of Flexibility in ICT Use. *Group Dynamica:Theory, Research, and Practices*, 24(3), 186–200. 10.1037/gdn0000130

Musigmann, B., Von Der Gracht, H., & Hartmann, E. (2020). Blockchain Technology in Logistics and Supply Chain Management - A Bibliometric Literature Review from 2016 to January 2020. *IEEE Transactions on Engineering Management*, 67(4), 988–1007. 10.1109/TEM.2020.2980733

Nagariya, R., Kumar, D., & Kumar, I. (2021). Service supply chain: From bibliometric analysis to content analysis, current research trends and future research directions. *Benchmarking*, 28(1), 333–369. 10.1108/BIJ-04-2020-0137

Naqvi, N. (2020). Evidence-Based Blockchain: Findings from a Global Study of Blockchain Projects and Start-up Companies. *The Journal of The British Blockchain Association*, 3(2), 1–13. 10.31585/jbba-3-2-(8)2020

Nasir, A., Shaukat, K., Khan, K. I., Hameed, I. A., Alam, T. M., & Luo, S. (2021). What is Core and What Future Holds for Blockchain Technologies and Cryptocurrencies: A Bibliometric Analysis. *IEEE Access : Practical Innovations, Open Solutions*, 9, 989–1004. 10.1109/ACCESS.2020.3046931

Naughton, K. (2016). Regulator Says Self-Driving Cars Must Be Twice as Safe. *Bloomberg*. https://www.bloomberg.com/news/ articles/20 16-06-08/u-s-auto-regulator-says-self-driving-cars-must-be-twice-as-safe

Nayyer, K. P., Rodriguez, M., & Sutherland, S. (2020, May/June). Artificial Intelligence & Implicit Bias: With Great Power Comes Great Responsibility: Addressing the Biases Inherent in the Datasets That Drive AI Applications and Their Algorithms. *AALL Spectrum*, 24(5), 14–16.

Nemitz, P. (2018). Constitutional democracy and technology in the age of artificial intelligence. *Phil. Trans. R. Soc. A, 376.* .10.1098/rsta.2018.0089

Neu, M. (2023). Understanding Music Piracy and its Impact on the Industry. *Reprtoir*.https://www.reprtoir.com/blog/music-piracy

Nicoletti, B. (2017). Financial services and fintech. In B. Nicoletti, W. Nicoletti, & Weis (Eds.), *The Future of FinTech* (pp. 3–29). Springer. 10.1007/978-3-319-51415-4_2

Nicoletti, B., & Nicoletti, B. (2021). Future of Insurance 4.0 and Insurtech. *Insurance 4.0: Benefits and Challenges of Digital Transformation*, 389-431.

Nobanee, H., & Ellili, N. O. D. (2023). Non-fungible tokens (NFTs): A bibliometric and systematic review, current streams, developments, and directions for future research. *International Review of Economics & Finance*, 84(January), 460–473. 10.1016/j.iref.2022.11.014

Noor, A. (2022). Adoption of Blockchain Technology Facilitates a Competitive Edge for Logistic Service Providers. *Sustainability (Basel)*, 14(23), 15543. Advance online publication. 10.3390/su142315543

Nyholm, S., & Smids, J. (2016). *The ethics of accident-algorithms for self-driving cars: an applied trolley problem? Ethical theory and moral practice.* .10.1007/s10677-016-9745-2

Compilation of References

Olukoya, O. (2022). Assessing frameworks for eliciting privacy & security requirements from laws and regulations. *Computers & Security*, 117, 102697. 10.1016/j.cose.2022.102697

Pahlevan Sharif, S., Mura, P. & Wijesinghe, S.N.R. (2019). *Systematic Reviews in Asia: Introducing the 'PRISMA' Protocol to Tourism and Hospitality Scholars.* .10.1007/978-981-13-2463-5_2

Pahlevan-Sharif, S., Mura, P., & Wijesinghe, S. N. R. (2019). A systematic review of systematic reviews in tourism. *Journal of Hospitality and Tourism Management*, 39(March), 158–165. 10.1016/j.jhtm.2019.04.001

Pal, L. (2023). Digital Piracy and Intellectual Property Protection, *Bytescare*. https://bytescare .com/blog/digital-piracy-intellectual-property-protection

Papantoniou, A. A. (2022). Regtech: Steering the regulatory spaceship in the right direction? *Journal of Banking and Financial Technology*, 6(1), 1–16. 10.1007/s42786-022-00038-9

Parino, F., Beiró, M. G., & Gauvin, L. (2018). Analysis of the Bitcoin blockchain: Socio-economic factors behind the adoption. *EPJ Data Science*, 7(1), 38. Advance online publication. 10.1140/epjds/s13688-018-0170-8

Parker, D. (2016). Property investment decision making by Australian unlisted property funds: An exploratory study. *Property Management*, 34(5), 381–395.

Park, S. Y. (2009). An analysis of the technology acceptance model in understanding university students' behavioral intention to use e-learning. *Journal of Educational Technology & Society*, 12(3), 150–162.

Parmentola, A., Petrillo, A., Tutore, I., & De Felice, F. (2022). Is blockchain able to enhance environmental sustainability? A systematic review and research agenda from the perspective of Sustainable Development Goals (SDGs). *Business Strategy and the Environment*, 31(1), 194–217. 10.1002/bse.2882

Patrick Hubbard, F. (2014). "Sophisticated Robots": Balancing Liability, Regulation, and Innovation. *Fla. L.Rev.*, 1803, 1866–1867.

Patrick, K. (2022). Digital piracy jeopardises India's flourishing creative economy. *TOI*. https://timesofindia.indiatimes.com/blogs/voices/digital-piracy-jeopardises-indias-flourishing-creative -economy/

Paul, M., Maglaras, L., Ferrag, M. A., & AlMomani, I. (2023). *Digitization of healthcare sector: A study on privacy and security concerns.* ICT Express.

Perumal, V. (2022). The future of US data privacy: Lessons from the GDPR and State Legislation. *Notre Dame J. Int'l Comp. L.*, 12, 99.

Pesaran, M. H. (2004). *General diagnostic tests for cross section dependence in panels.* Cambridge Working Papers in Economics. University of Cambridge, Faculty of Economics.

Pesaran, M. H. (2014). Testing weak cross-sectional dependence in large panels. *Econometric Reviews*, 34(6-10), 1089–1117. 10.1080/07474938.2014.956623

Pesaran, M., & Yamagata, T. (2008). Testing slope homogeneity in large panels. *Journal of Econometrics*, 142(1), 50–93. 10.1016/j.jeconom.2007.05.010

Petru, N., Pavlák, M., & Polák, J. (2019). Factors impacting startup sustainability in the Czech Republic. In *Innovative Marketing* (Vol. 15, Issue 3, pp. 1–15). LLC CPC Business Perspectives. 10.21511/im.15(3).2019.01

Pham, Q. T., Dang, N. M., & Nguyen, D. T. (2020). Factors Affecting on the Digital Piracy Behavior: An Empirical Study in Vietnam. *Journal of Theoretical and Applied Electronic Commerce Research*, 15(2), 0. Advance online publication. 10.4067/S0718-18762020000200108

Phillips, P. C. B., & Perron, P. (1988). Testing for a unit root in time series regression. *Biometrika*, 75(2), 335–346. 10.1093/biomet/75.2.335

Piñeiro-Chousa, J., López-Cabarcos, M. Á., & Šević, A. (2022). Green bond market and Sentiment: Is there a switching Behaviour? *Journal of Business Research*, 141, 520–527. Advance online publication. 10.1016/j.jbusres.2021.11.048

Pivoto, D. G., de Almeida, L. F., da Rosa Righi, R., Rodrigues, J. J., Lugli, A. B., & Alberti, A. M. (2021). Cyber-physical systems architectures for industrial internet of things applications in Industry 4.0: A literature review. *Journal of Manufacturing Systems*, 58, 176–192. 10.1016/j.jmsy.2020.11.017

Pizzi, S., Caputo, A., Venturelli, A., & Caputo, F. (2022). Embedding and managing blockchain in sustainability reporting: A practical framework. *Sustainability Accounting, Management and Policy Journal*, 13(3), 545–567. 10.1108/SAMPJ-07-2021-0288

Platanakis, E., & Urquhart, A. (2019). Portfolio management with cryptocurrencies: The role of estimation risk. *Economics Letters*, 177, 76–80. 10.1016/j.econlet.2019.01.019

Ponemon Institute. (2019). Global State of Cybersecurity in Small to Medium-sized Businesses Report. Author.

Pritchard, A. (1969). Statistical bibliography or bibliometrics. *The Journal of Documentation*, 25, 348.

Quantum Computing for the Quantum Era. (n.d.). McKinsey & Company. https://www.mckinsey.com/featured-insights/the-rise-of-quantum-computing

Rahmawati, D., Rahadi, R. A., Putri, A. D., & Bandung, E. (2021). The Current State of Property Development in Indonesia During the Covid-19 Pandemic. *International Journal of Innovation, Creativity and Change, 15*(7).

Rajan, R. G., & Zingales, L. (2003). The great reversals: The politics of financial development in the twentieth century. *Journal of Financial Economics*, 69(1), 5–50. 10.1016/S0304-405X(03)00125-9

Compilation of References

Rangaswamy, E., Yong, W. S., & Joy, G. V. (2023). The evaluation of challenges and impact of digitalisation on consumers in Singapore. *International Journal of System Assurance Engineering and Management,* 1-13.

Rastogi, P. (2023). *The Role of Technology in Start-ups and Small Businesses.* International Scientific Refereed Research Journal Available Online. 10.32628/SHISRRJ

Rauta, A. (2022). Digital Music Piracy: Trends, Challenges and the Way Forward. *IPRMentLaw.* https://iprmentlaw.com/guest-column/guest-interview-in-conversation-with-ms-melissa-morgia -of-ifpi-on-digital-music-piracy-trends-challenges-and-the-way-forward/

Rawls, J. (1999). *A Theory of Justice* (revised edn.). Oxford University Press. 10.4159/9780674042582

RegTech Survey: PricewaterhouseCoopers. (n.d.). https://www.pwc.com/us/en/industries/ financial-services/regulatory-services/regtech.html

RegTech. (n.d.). A New Way to Manage Risks. https://www.hbs.edu/faculty/Shared%20Documents/ conferences/2022-imo/Andrew%20Sutherland%20paper.pdf

Regulatory Divergence. (n.d.). Costs, Risks and Impacts. https://www. ifac.org/knowledge -gateway/contributing-global-economy/publications/

Regulatory sandbox lessons learnt-report. (n.d.). https://www.fca.org.uk/publication/ research-and-data/regulatory-sandbox-lessons-learned-report.pdf

Reis, F., Matos, M. G., & Ferreira, P. (2024). Controlling digital piracy via domain name system blocks: A natural experiment. *Journal of Economic Behavior & Organization,* 218, 89–103. 10.1016/j.jebo.2023.12.005

Rejeb, A., Rejeb, K., & Keogh, , J. (2021). Cryptocurrencies in Modern Finance: A Literature Review. *Etikonomi,* 20(1), 93–118. 10.15408/etk.v20i1.16911

Reserve Bank of India—RBI Bulletin. (n.d.). Retrieved January 24, 2024, from https://www.rbi .org.in/Scripts/BS_ViewBulletin.aspx?Id=19899

Riaz, M., Mehmood, A., Shabbir, U., & Kazmi, S. M. A. (2023). Social Interactions Leading Role in Adopting the Fintech: A Case of Banking Sector. *Pakistan Journal of Humanities and Social Sciences,* 11(2), 1467–1476. 10.52131/pjhss.2023.1102.0449

Rodríguez-López, M. E., Alcántara-Pilar, J. M., Del Barrio-García, S., & Muñoz-Leiva, F. (2020). A review of restaurant research in the last two decades: A bibliometric analysis. *International Journal of Hospitality Management,* 87(April), 102387. 10.1016/j.ijhm.2019.102387

Rogers, E. M. (1983). *Diffusion of Innovation* (3rd ed.). Academic Press.

Rohan, R., Pal, D., Hautamäki, J., Funilkul, S., Chutimaskul, W., & Thapliyal, H. (2023). A systematic literature review of cybersecurity scales assessing information security awareness. *Heliyon,* 9(3), e14234. 10.1016/j.heliyon.2023.e1423436938452

Roh, T., Park, B. I., & Xiao, S. S. (2023). Adoption of AI-enabled Robo-advisors in Fintech: Simultaneous Employment of UTAUT and the Theory of Reasoned Action. *Journal of Electronic Commerce Research*, 24(1), 29–47.

Rosenthal, L. (1983). An empirical test of the efficiency of the ADR market. *Journal of Banking & Finance*, 7(1), 17–29. 10.1016/0378-4266(83)90053-5

Ryan, P., Crane, M., & Brennan, R. (2021). GDPR compliance tools: best practice from RegTech. In *International Conference on Enterprise Information Systems* (pp. 905-929). Cham: Springer International Publishing. 10.1007/978-3-030-75418-1_41

Ryan, R. M., O'Toole, C. M., & McCann, F. (2014). Does bank market power affect SME financing constraints? *Journal of Banking & Finance*, 49, 495–505. 10.1016/j.jbankfin.2013.12.024

Sabharwal, A. (2023). India's Digital Personal Data Protection Act (DPDPA) Demystified. Available at: https://www.forbes.com/sites/forbestechcouncil/2023/11/15/indias-digital-personal-data-protection-act-dpdpa-demystified/?sh=6651b27c5c1c

Sahay, M. R., Cihak, M. M., N'Diaye, M. P., Barajas, M. A., Kyobe, M. A., Mitra, M. S., Mooi, M. N., & Yousef, M. R. (2015). *Rethinking financial deepening: Stability and growth in emerging markets*. IMF Working Paper, SDN.

Sahay, R., Čihák, M., N'Diaye, P., Barajas, A., Bi, R., Ayala, D., & Yousefi, S. R. (2015). *Rethinking financial deepening: Stability and growth in emerging markets*. International Monetary Fund.

Sahoo, S., Kumar, S., Sivarajah, U., Lim, W.M., Westland, J.C. & Kumar, A. (2022), *Blockchain for Sustainable Supply Chain Management: Trends and Ways Forward, Electronic Commerce Research*. Springer US. .10.1007/s10660-022-09569-1

Saji, T. G. (2023). Mean reversals and stock market overreactions: Further evidence from India. *Afro-Asian Journal of Finance and Accounting*, 13(4), 467–477. Advance online publication. 10.1504/AAJFA.2023.132959

Sakhare, C. A., Somani, N. N., Patel, B. L., Khorgade, S. N., & Parchake, S. (2023). What drives FinTech Adoption? A study on Perception, Adoption, and Constraints of FinTech Services. *European Economic Letters*, 13(3), 1216–1230.

Santana, T. P., Horta, N., Revez, C., Dias, R. M. T. S., & Zebende, G. F. (2023). Effects of Interdependence and Contagion on Crude Oil and Precious Metals According to ρDCCA: A COVID-19 Case Study. *Sustainability (Basel)*, 15(5), 3945. Advance online publication. 10.3390/su15053945

Santoni de Sio, F. (2017). Killing by autonomous vehicles and the legal doctrine of necessity. *Ethical Theory and Moral Practice*, 20(2), 411–429. 10.1007/s10677-017-9780-7

Sarafidis, V., & Wansbeek, T. (2011). Cross-sectional dependence in panel data analysis. *Econometric Reviews*, 31(5), 483–531. 10.1080/07474938.2011.611458

Schellinger, B. (2020). Optimization of special cryptocurrency portfolios. *The Journal of Risk Finance*, 21(2), 127–157. 10.1108/JRF-11-2019-0221

Compilation of References

Scherer, E. (2015). M. U., Regulating artificial intelligence systems: Risks, challenges, competencies, and strategies. *SSRN*, 29, 353. 10.2139/ssrn.2609777

Secinaro, S., Dal Mas, F., Brescia, V., & Calandra, D. (2021). Blockchain in the accounting, auditing and accountability fields: A bibliometric and coding analysis. *Accounting, Auditing & Accountability Journal*, 35(9), 168–203. 10.1108/AAAJ-10-2020-4987

Shahbazi, Z., & Byun, Y. C. (2022). Machine Learning-Based Analysis of Cryptocurrency Market Financial Risk Management. *IEEE Access : Practical Innovations, Open Solutions*, 10, 37848–37856. 10.1109/ACCESS.2022.3162858

Shahbaz, M., Bhattacharya, M., & Mahalik, M. K. (2017). Financial development, industrialization, the role of institutions and government: A comparative analysis between India and China. *Applied Economics*, 50(17), 1952–1977. 10.1080/00036846.2017.1383595

Shah, U. (2019). Digital Music Piracy in India: Issues and Challenges. *International Journal of Research in Social Sciences*, 9(6). https://www.ijmra.us/project%20doc/2019/IJRSS_JUNE2019/IJMRA-15747.pdf

Shanaev, S., Sharma, S., Ghimire, B., & Shuraeva, A. (2020). Taming the blockchain beast? Regulatory implications for the cryptocurrency Market. *Research in International Business and Finance*, 51, 101080. 10.1016/j.ribaf.2019.101080

Sharma, G. D., Jain, M., Mahendru, M., Bansal, S., & Kumar, G. (2019). Emergence of Bitcoin as an Investment Alternative: A Systematic Review and Research Agenda. *International Journal of Business and Information*, 14(1), 47–84. 10.6702/ijbi.201903

Shen, D., Urquhart, A. & Wang, P. (2020). A three-factor pricing model for cryptocurrencies. *Finance Research Letters*, 34. .10.1016/j.frl.2019.07.021

Sheng, T. (2020). The effect of fintech on banks' credit provision to SMEs: Evidence from China. *Finance Research Letters*, 39, 101558. 10.1016/j.frl.2020.101558

Shepherd, D. A., & Majchrzak, A. (2022). Machines augmenting entrepreneurs: Opportunities (and threats) at the Nexus of artificial intelligence and entrepreneurship. *Journal of Business Venturing*, 37(4), 106227. 10.1016/j.jbusvent.2022.106227

Shibano, K., & Mogi, G. (2022). An analysis of the acquisition of a monetary function by cryptocurrency using a multi-agent simulation model. *Financial Innovation*, 8(1), 87. Advance online publication. 10.1186/s40854-022-00389-8

Shiller, R. J. (2003). From Efficient Markets Theory to Behavioral Finance The 1980s and Excess Volatility. *Journal of Economic Perspectives, 17*(1).

Shtovba, S., Shtovba, O., & Filatova, L. (2020). The current state of brand management research: An overview of leaders and trends in branding research over the past 20 years. *The Bottom Line (New York, N.Y.)*, 33(1), 1–11. 10.1108/BL-08-2019-0106

Sian, D. (2023). RegTech adoption is accelerating fast, but who's in the driving seat? Available at: https://iqeq.com/insights/regtech-adoption-accelerating-fast-whos-driving-seat/

Singh, M., Nigam, A., & Sinha, S. (2020). Combating Copyright Online Piracy in India: Government's Initiatives and Judicial Enforcement. *Lexorbis*. https://lexorbis.com/combating-copyright -online-piracy-in-india-governments-initiatives-and-judicial-enforcement/

Sinha, R. K., & Mandel, N. (2008). Preventing Digital Music Piracy: The Carrot or the Stick? *Journal of Marketing*, 72(1), 1–15. 10.1509/jmkg.72.1.001

Smith, A., & Johnson, B. (2022). Customer Perceptions of Fintech Services. *Journal of Financial Innovation*, 10(2), 75–92.

Smith, B. (2014). Automated vehicles are probably legal in the United States. Texas A&M. *Law Review*, 1(3), 411–522.

Smith, B. W. (2017). Automated Driving and Product Liability. *Detroit College of Law at Michigan State University Law Review*, 2017(1), 1–74.

Soni, N., Sharma, E. K., Singh, N., & Kapoor, A. (2019). Artificial Intelligence in Business: From Research and Innovation to Market Deployment. *Procedia Computer Science*, 167, 2200–2210. 10.1016/j.procs.2020.03.272

Soon, L. K. (2023). A review of literature on the impact of fintech firms on the banking industry. *Informative Journal of Management Sciences,2*(2).

Sreejani, B. (2021). Can AI Revolutionise India's Judicial System? *Analytics India Magazine*.

Sreenivasan, A., & Suresh, M. (2023). *Adoption of Artificial Intelligence (AI) in Start-ups*. 10.46254/IN02.20220104

Steel, W., Daglish, T., Marriott, L., Gemmell, N., & Howell, B. (2013). *E-Commerce and its effect upon the Retail Industry and Government Revenue*. Academic Press.

Sudler, H. (2013). Effectiveness of anti-piracy technology: Finding appropriate solutions for evolving online piracy. *Business Horizons*, 56(2), 149–157. 10.1016/j.bushor.2012.11.001

Sumkovski, I. (2023). The use of RegTech in fighting financial crime. *Journal of Financial Compliance*, 6(2), 138–147.

Sun, H., Edziah, B. K., Kporsu, A. K., Sarkodie, S. A., & Taghizadeh-Hesary, F. (2021). Energy efficiency: The role of technological innovation and knowledge spillover. *Technological Forecasting and Social Change*, 167, 120659. 10.1016/j.techfore.2021.120659

Sun, H., Kporsu, A. K., Taghizadeh-Hesary, F., & Edziah, B. K. (2020). Estimating environmental efficiency and convergence: 1980 to 2016. *Energy*, 208, 118224. 10.1016/j.energy.2020.118224

Sun, Y., Chen, L., Sun, H., & Taghizadeh-Hesary, F. (2020). Low-carbon financial risk factor correlation in the belt and road PPP project. *Finance Research Letters*, 35, 101491. 10.1016/j. frl.2020.101491

Svirydzenka, K. (2016). *Introducing a new broad-based index of financial development.* IMF Working Paper.

Tandon, A., Kaur, P., Mäntymäki, M., & Dhir, A. (2021). Blockchain applications in management: A bibliometric analysis and literature review. *Technological Forecasting and Social Change*, 166(January), 120649. Advance online publication. 10.1016/j.techfore.2021.120649

Tan, E., & Leby Lau, J. (2016). Behavioural intention to adopt mobile banking among the millennial generation. *Young Consumers*, 17(1), 18–31. 10.1108/YC-07-2015-00537

Teichmann, F., Boticiu, S., & Sergi, B. S. (2023). RegTech–Potential benefits and challenges for businesses. *Technology in Society*, 72, 102150. 10.1016/j.techsoc.2022.102150

TerJi-Xi, J., Salamzadeh, Y., & Teoh, A. P. (2021). Behavioral intention to use cryptocurrency in Malaysia: An empirical study. *The Bottom Line (New York, N.Y.)*, 34(2), 170–197. 10.1108/BL-08-2020-0053

The Motor Vehicles Act, Gazette of India (1988)

The regulatory technology "RegTech" and money laundering prevention in Islamic and conventional banking industry—PMC. (n.d.). Retrieved January 8, 2024, from https://www.ncbi.nlm.nih.gov/pmc/articles/PMC7550909/

The Role of RegTech in Organizations. (n.d.). https://www.doxee.com/blog/regtech/ the-role-of-regtech-in-organizations/

Thomson, J. J. (1976). Killing, letting die, and the trolley problem. *The Monist*, 59(2), 204–217. 10.5840/monist197659224 11662247

Thriving in a digital world. (n.d.). https://kpmg.com/xx/en/home/about/corporate-reporting/thriving-in-a-digital-world.html

Tianhong. (2019). http://www.thfund.com.cn/en/about.html

Tiba, S., Van Rijnsoever, F. J., & Hekkert, M. P. (2021). Sustainability startups and where to find them: Investigating the share of sustainability startups across entrepreneurial ecosystems and the causal drivers of differences. *Journal of Cleaner Production*, 306, 127054. 10.1016/j.jclepro.2021.127054

Tips for Selecting RegTec Solutions. (n.d.). https://infobelt.com/ tips-for-selecting-regulatory-technology-regtech-solutions/

Tönnissen, S., Beinke, J. H., & Teuteberg, F. (2020). Understanding token-based ecosystems – a taxonomy of blockchain-based business models of start-ups. *Electronic Markets*, 30(2), 307–323. 10.1007/s12525-020-00396-6

Torres-Mancera, R., Martínez-Rodrigo, E., & Santos, C. A. (2023). Female sustainability and startups: Analysis of the leadership in communication by women entrepreneurs in Spain and Portugal. *Revista Latina de Comunicacion Social*, 2023(81), 474–491. 10.4185/rlcs-2023-1978

Turki, M., Hamdan, A., Cummings, R. T., Sarea, A., Karolak, M., & Anasweh, M. (2020, October 8). The regulatory technology "RegTech" and money laundering prevention in Islamic and conventional banking industry. *Heliyon*, 6(10), e04949. 10.1016/j.heliyon.2020.e0494933083582

Ullah, F., Sepasgozar, S. M., Thaheem, M. J., & Al-Turjman, F. (2021). Barriers to the digitalisation and innovation of Australian Smart Real Estate: A managerial perspective on the technology non-adoption. *Environmental Technology & Innovation*, 22, 101527.

United States v. Athlone Industries, Inc., 746 F.2d 977 (3d Cir. 1984).

Urquhart, A. (2016). The inefficiency of Bitcoin. *Economics Letters*, 148, 80–82. 10.1016/j.econlet.2016.09.019

Van Veldhoven, Z., & Vanthienen, J. (2023). Best practices for digital transformation based on a systematic literature review. *Digital Transformation and Society*, 2(2), 104–128. 10.1108/DTS-11-2022-0057

van Wynsberghe, A. (2021). Sustainable AI: AI for sustainability and the sustainability of AI. *AI and Ethics*, 1(3), 213–218. 10.1007/s43681-021-00043-6

Varsani, J. (2019). Fighting against Digital Piracy in the Streaming Age. *Cartesian.* https://www.cartesian.com/fighting-against-digital-piracy-in-the-streaming-age/

Verhoef, P. C., Broekhuizen, T., Bart, Y., Bhattachary, A., Dong, J. Q., Fabian, N., & Haenlein, M. (2021). Digital transformation: A multidisciplinary reflection and research agenda. *Journal of Business Research*, 122, 889–901. 10.1016/j.jbusres.2019.09.022

Verma, A., Tiwari, D., Lohchab, P., Khan, M., & Pandey, A. (2023). *Fintech and digital finance: opportunities and challenges in Indian banking sector.* Academic Press.

Vijai, C., Bhuvaneswari, L., Sathyakala, S., Dhinakaran, D. P., Arun, R., & Lakshmi, M. R. (2023). The Effect of Fintech on Customer Satisfaction Level. *Journal of Survey in Fisheries Sciences*, 10(3S), 6628–6634.

Vivek, D., Rakesh, S., Walimbe, R. S., & Mohanty, A. (2020). The Role of CLOUD in FinTech and RegTech. *Annals of the University Dunarea de Jos of Galati: Fascicle: I, Economics & Applied Informatics, 26*(3).

Von Solms, J. (2021). Integrating Regulatory Technology (RegTech) into the digital transformation of a bank Treasury. *Journal of Banking Regulation*, 22(2), 152–168. 10.1057/s41261-020-00134-0

Waldfogel, J. Music Piracy and Its Effects on Demand, Supply, and Welfare. *Carlson School and Department of Economics, University of Minnesota.* https://www.journals.uchicago.edu/doi/epdf/10.1086/663157

Wang, Y., Han, J. H., Beynon-davies, P., Wang, Y., Han, J. H., & Beynon-davies, P. (2019). Understanding blockchain technology for future supply chains : A systematic literature review and research agenda. *Supply Chain Management*, 24(1), 62–84. 10.1108/SCM-03-2018-0148

Compilation of References

Ward, P., & Beard, J. (2012). The Anti-Counterfeiting Trade Agreement (ACTA). *CommonsLibrary.* https://commonslibrary.parliament.uk/research-briefings/sn06248/

Warner, K. S. R., & Wäger, M. (2019). Building dynamic capabilities for digital transformation: An ongoing process of strategic renewal. *Long Range Planning*, 52(3), 326–349. 10.1016/j.lrp.2018.12.001

Watson, A., & Leyshon, A. (2021). *Negotiating platformisation: MusicTech, intellectual property rights and third wave platform reintermediation in the music industry.* 10.1080/17530350.2022.2028653

Weber, M., Beutter, M., Weking, J., Böhm, M., & Krcmar, H. (2022). AI Startup Business Models: Key Characteristics and Directions for Entrepreneurship Research. *Business & Information Systems Engineering*, 64(1), 91–109. 10.1007/s12599-021-00732-w

WEF. (n.d.-a). Global cybersecurity outlook, 2024. https://www.weforum.org/publications/global-cybersecurity-outlook-2024/

WEF. (n.d.-b). Regulatory technology for the 21st century. https://www.weforum.org/publications/regulatory-technology-for-the-21st-century/

What is Autonomous Vehicle? (n.d.). TWI. https://www.twi-global.com/technical-knowledge/faqs/what-is-an-autonomous-vehicle

Wijayasekara, K. (2022). How Spotify's freemium business model made $11.42B in revenue in 2021? *Linkedin.* https://www.linkedin.com/pulse/how-spotifys-freemium-business-model-made-1142b-2021-wijayasekara/

Wodecki, B. (2020). *China begins 'nationwide' copyright crackdown.* https://www.i-law.com/ilaw/doc/view.htm?id=410125

Wooldridge, J. M. (2010). *Econometric Analysis of Cross Section and Panel Data.* The MIT Press.

World Bank. (2018). *Global Financial Inclusion (Global Findex) Database.* https://www.worldbank.org/en/publication/gfdr/data/global-financial-development-database

Xinhua. (2021). *Crackdown on pirated-video platform signals China's resolve on copyright protection.* http://www.xinhuanet.com/english/2021-02/05/c_139722134.htm

Yang, F., & Gu, S. (2021). Industry 4.0, a revolution that requires technology and national strategies. *Complex & Intelligent Systems*, 7(3), 1311–1325. 10.1007/s40747-020-00267-9

Yin, H. H. S., Langenheldt, K., Harlev, M., Mukkamala, R. R., & Vatrapu, R. (2019). Regulating Cryptocurrencies: A Supervised Machine Learning Approach to De-Anonymizing the Bitcoin Blockchain. *Journal of Management Information Systems*, 36(1), 37–73. 10.1080/07421222.2018.1550550

Yousaf, I., & Yarovaya, L. (2022). Herding behavior in conventional cryptocurrency market, non-fungible tokens, and DeFi assets. *Finance Research Letters*, 50, 103299. 10.1016/j.frl.2022.103299

Yue, Y., Li, X., Zhang, D., & Wang, S. (2021). How cryptocurrency affects economy? A network analysis using bibliometric methods. *International Review of Financial Analysis*, 77(71988101), 101869. 10.1016/j.irfa.2021.101869

Zaefarian, G., Kadile, V., Henneberg, S. C., & Leischnig, A. (2017). Endogeneity bias in marketing research: Problem, causes and remedies. *Industrial Marketing Management*, 65, 39–46. 10.1016/j.indmarman.2017.05.006

Zakaria & Ors. v. Naoshir Cama & Ors., AIR 1976 AP 171.

Zhang, W., Siyal, S., Riaz, S., Ahmad, R., Hilmi, M. F., & Li, Z. (2023). Data security, customer trust and intention for adoption of fintech services: An empirical analysis from commercial bank users in Pakistan. *SAGE Open*, 13(3). 10.1177/21582440231181388

Related References

To continue our tradition of advancing information science and technology research, we have compiled a list of recommended IGI Global readings. These references will provide additional information and guidance to further enrich your knowledge and assist you with your own research and future publications.

Abdul Razak, R., & Mansor, N. A. (2021). Instagram Influencers in Social Media-Induced Tourism: Rethinking Tourist Trust Towards Tourism Destination. In M. Dinis, L. Bonixe, S. Lamy, & Z. Breda (Eds.), *Impact of New Media in Tourism* (pp. 135-144). IGI Global. https://doi.org/10.4018/978-1-7998-7095-1.ch009

Abir, T., & Khan, M. Y. (2022). Importance of ICT Advancement and Culture of Adaptation in the Tourism and Hospitality Industry for Developing Countries. In Ramos, C., Quinteiro, S., & Gonçalves, A. (Eds.), *ICT as Innovator Between Tourism and Culture* (pp. 30–41). IGI Global. https://doi.org/10.4018/978-1-7998-8165-0.ch003

Abtahi, M. S., Behboudi, L., & Hasanabad, H. M. (2017). Factors Affecting Internet Advertising Adoption in Ad Agencies. *International Journal of Innovation in the Digital Economy*, 8(4), 18–29. 10.4018/IJIDE.2017100102

Afenyo-Agbe, E., & Mensah, I. (2022). Principles, Benefits, and Barriers to Community-Based Tourism: Implications for Management. In Mensah, I., & Afenyo-Agbe, E. (Eds.), *Prospects and Challenges of Community-Based Tourism and Changing Demographics* (pp. 1–29). IGI Global. 10.4018/978-1-7998-7335-8.ch001

Agbo, V. M. (2022). Distributive Justice Issues in Community-Based Tourism. In Mensah, I., & Afenyo-Agbe, E. (Eds.), *Prospects and Challenges of Community-Based Tourism and Changing Demographics* (pp. 107–129). IGI Global. https://doi.org/10.4018/978-1-7998-7335-8.ch005

Agrawal, S. (2017). The Impact of Emerging Technologies and Social Media on Different Business(es): Marketing and Management. In Rishi, O., & Sharma, A. (Eds.), *Maximizing Business Performance and Efficiency Through Intelligent Systems* (pp. 37–49). Hershey, PA: IGI Global. 10.4018/978-1-5225-2234-8.ch002

Ahmad, A., & Johari, S. (2022). Georgetown as a Gastronomy Tourism Destination: Visitor Awareness Towards Revisit Intention of Nasi Kandar Restaurant. In Valeri, M. (Ed.), *New Governance and Management in Touristic Destinations* (pp. 71–83). IGI Global. https://doi.org/10.4018/978-1-6684-3889-3.ch005

Alkhatib, G., & Bayouq, S. T. (2021). A TAM-Based Model of Technological Factors Affecting Use of E-Tourism. *International Journal of Tourism and Hospitality Management in the Digital Age*, 5(2), 50–67. https://doi.org/10.4018/IJTHMDA.20210701.oa1

Altinay Ozdemir, M. (2021). Virtual Reality (VR) and Augmented Reality (AR) Technologies for Accessibility and Marketing in the Tourism Industry. In C. Eusébio, L. Teixeira, & M. Carneiro (Eds.), *ICT Tools and Applications for Accessible Tourism* (pp. 277-301). IGI Global. https://doi.org/10.4018/978-1-7998-6428-8.ch013

Anantharaman, R. N., Rajeswari, K. S., Angusamy, A., & Kuppusamy, J. (2017). Role of Self-Efficacy and Collective Efficacy as Moderators of Occupational Stress Among Software Development Professionals. *International Journal of Human Capital and Information Technology Professionals*, 8(2), 45–58. 10.4018/IJHCITP.2017040103

Aninze, F., El-Gohary, H., & Hussain, J. (2018). The Role of Microfinance to Empower Women: The Case of Developing Countries. *International Journal of Customer Relationship Marketing and Management*, 9(1), 54–78. 10.4018/IJCRMM.2018010104

Antosova, G., Sabogal-Salamanca, M., & Krizova, E. (2021). Human Capital in Tourism: A Practical Model of Endogenous and Exogenous Territorial Tourism Planning in Bahía Solano, Colombia. In Costa, V., Moura, A., & Mira, M. (Eds.), *Handbook of Research on Human Capital and People Management in the Tourism Industry* (pp. 282–302). IGI Global. https://doi.org/10.4018/978-1-7998-4318-4.ch014

Arsenijević, O. M., Orčić, D., & Kastratović, E. (2017). Development of an Optimization Tool for Intangibles in SMEs: A Case Study from Serbia with a Pilot Research in the Prestige by Milka Company. In Vemić, M. (Ed.), *Optimal Management Strategies in Small and Medium Enterprises* (pp. 320–347). Hershey, PA: IGI Global. 10.4018/978-1-5225-1949-2.ch015

Aryanto, V. D., Wismantoro, Y., & Widyatmoko, K. (2018). Implementing Eco-Innovation by Utilizing the Internet to Enhance Firm's Marketing Performance: Study of Green Batik Small and Medium Enterprises in Indonesia. *International Journal of E-Business Research*, 14(1), 21–36. 10.4018/IJEBR.2018010102

Asero, V., & Billi, S. (2022). New Perspective of Networking in the DMO Model. In Valeri, M. (Ed.), *New Governance and Management in Touristic Destinations* (pp. 105–118). IGI Global. https://doi.org/10.4018/978-1-6684-3889-3.ch007

Atiku, S. O., & Fields, Z. (2017). Multicultural Orientations for 21st Century Global Leadership. In Baporikar, N. (Ed.), *Management Education for Global Leadership* (pp. 28–51). Hershey, PA: IGI Global. 10.4018/978-1-5225-1013-0.ch002

Atiku, S. O., & Fields, Z. (2018). Organisational Learning Dimensions and Talent Retention Strategies for the Service Industries. In Baporikar, N. (Ed.), *Global Practices in Knowledge Management for Societal and Organizational Development* (pp. 358–381). Hershey, PA: IGI Global. 10.4018/978-1-5225-3009-1.ch017

Atsa'am, D. D., & Kuset Bodur, E. (2021). Pattern Mining on How Organizational Tenure Affects the Psychological Capital of Employees Within the Hospitality and Tourism Industry: Linking Employees' Organizational Tenure With PsyCap. *International Journal of Tourism and Hospitality Management in the Digital Age*, 5(2), 17–28. https://doi.org/10.4018/IJTHMDA.2021070102

Ávila, L., & Teixeira, L. (2018). The Main Concepts Behind the Dematerialization of Business Processes. In M. Khosrow-Pour, D.B.A. (Ed.), *Encyclopedia of Information Science and Technology, Fourth Edition* (pp. 888-898). Hershey, PA: IGI Global. https://doi.org/10.4018/978-1-5225-2255-3.ch076

Ayorekire, J., Mugizi, F., Obua, J., & Ampaire, G. (2022). Community-Based Tourism and Local People's Perceptions Towards Conservation: The Case of Queen Elizabeth Conservation Area, Uganda. In Mensah, I., & Afenyo-Agbe, E. (Eds.), *Prospects and Challenges of Community-Based Tourism and Changing Demographics* (pp. 56–82). IGI Global. https://doi.org/10.4018/978-1-7998-7335-8.ch003

Baleiro, R. (2022). Tourist Literature and the Architecture of Travel in Olga Tokarczuk and Patti Smith. In R. Baleiro & R. Pereira (Eds.), *Global Perspectives on Literary Tourism and Film-Induced Tourism* (pp. 202-216). IGI Global. https://doi.org/10.4018/978-1-7998-8262-6.ch011

Barat, S. (2021). Looking at the Future of Medical Tourism in Asia. *International Journal of Tourism and Hospitality Management in the Digital Age*, 5(1), 19–33. https://doi.org/10.4018/IJTHMDA.2021010102

Barbosa, C. A., Magalhães, M., & Nunes, M. R. (2021). Travel Instagramability: A Way of Choosing a Destination? In M. Dinis, L. Bonixe, S. Lamy, & Z. Breda (Eds.), *Impact of New Media in Tourism* (pp. 173-190). IGI Global. https://doi.org/10.4018/978-1-7998-7095-1.ch011

Bari, M. W., & Khan, Q. (2021). Pakistan as a Destination of Religious Tourism. In E. Alaverdov & M. Bari (Eds.), *Global Development of Religious Tourism* (pp. 1-10). IGI Global. https://doi.org/10.4018/978-1-7998-5792-1.ch001

Bartens, Y., Chunpir, H. I., Schulte, F., & Voß, S. (2017). Business/IT Alignment in Two-Sided Markets: A COBIT 5 Analysis for Media Streaming Business Models. In De Haes, S., & Van Grembergen, W. (Eds.), *Strategic IT Governance and Alignment in Business Settings* (pp. 82–111). Hershey, PA: IGI Global. 10.4018/978-1-5225-0861-8.ch004

Bashayreh, A. M. (2018). Organizational Culture and Organizational Performance. In Lee, W., & Sabetzadeh, F. (Eds.), *Contemporary Knowledge and Systems Science* (pp. 50–69). Hershey, PA: IGI Global. 10.4018/978-1-5225-5655-8.ch003

Bechthold, L., Lude, M., & Prügl, R. (2021). Crisis Favors the Prepared Firm: How Organizational Ambidexterity Relates to Perceptions of Organizational Resilience. In Zehrer, A., Glowka, G., Schwaiger, K., & Ranacher-Lackner, V. (Eds.), *Resiliency Models and Addressing Future Risks for Family Firms in the Tourism Industry* (pp. 178–205). IGI Global. https://doi.org/10.4018/978-1-7998-7352-5.ch008

Bedford, D. A. (2018). Sustainable Knowledge Management Strategies: Aligning Business Capabilities and Knowledge Management Goals. In Baporikar, N. (Ed.), *Global Practices in Knowledge Management for Societal and Organizational Development* (pp. 46–73). Hershey, PA: IGI Global. 10.4018/978-1-5225-3009-1.ch003

Bekjanov, D., & Matyusupov, B. (2021). Influence of Innovative Processes in the Competitiveness of Tourist Destination. In Soares, J. (Ed.), *Innovation and Entrepreneurial Opportunities in Community Tourism* (pp. 243–263). IGI Global. https://doi.org/10.4018/978-1-7998-4855-4.ch014

Bharwani, S., & Musunuri, D. (2018). Reflection as a Process From Theory to Practice. In M. Khosrow-Pour, D.B.A. (Ed.), *Encyclopedia of Information Science and Technology, Fourth Edition* (pp. 1529-1539). Hershey, PA: IGI Global. 10.4018/978-1-5225-2255-3.ch132

Bhatt, G. D., Wang, Z., & Rodger, J. A. (2017). Information Systems Capabilities and Their Effects on Competitive Advantages: A Study of Chinese Companies. *Information Resources Management Journal*, 30(3), 41–57. 10.4018/IRMJ.2017070103

Bhushan, M., & Yadav, A. (2017). Concept of Cloud Computing in ESB. In Bhadoria, R., Chaudhari, N., Tomar, G., & Singh, S. (Eds.), *Exploring Enterprise Service Bus in the Service-Oriented Architecture Paradigm* (pp. 116–127). Hershey, PA: IGI Global. 10.4018/978-1-5225-2157-0.ch008

Bhushan, S. (2017). System Dynamics Base-Model of Humanitarian Supply Chain (HSCM) in Disaster Prone Eco-Communities of India: A Discussion on Simulation and Scenario Results. *International Journal of System Dynamics Applications*, 6(3), 20–37. 10.4018/IJSDA.2017070102

Binder, D., & Miller, J. W. (2021). A Generations' Perspective on Employer Branding in Tourism. In Costa, V., Moura, A., & Mira, M. (Eds.), *Handbook of Research on Human Capital and People Management in the Tourism Industry* (pp. 152–174). IGI Global. https://doi.org/10.4018/978-1-7998-4318-4.ch008

Birch Freeman, A. A., Mensah, I., & Antwi, K. B. (2022). Smiling vs. Frowning Faces: Community Participation for Sustainable Tourism in Ghanaian Communities. In Mensah, I., & Afenyo-Agbe, E. (Eds.), *Prospects and Challenges of Community-Based Tourism and Changing Demographics* (pp. 83–106). IGI Global. https://doi.org/10.4018/978-1-7998-7335-8.ch004

Biswas, A., & De, A. K. (2017). On Development of a Fuzzy Stochastic Programming Model with Its Application to Business Management. In Trivedi, S., Dey, S., Kumar, A., & Panda, T. (Eds.), *Handbook of Research on Advanced Data Mining Techniques and Applications for Business Intelligence* (pp. 353–378). Hershey, PA: IGI Global. 10.4018/978-1-5225-2031-3.ch021

Boragnio, A., & Faracce Macia, C. (2021). "Taking Care of Yourself at Home": Use of E-Commerce About Food and Care During the COVID-19 Pandemic in the City of Buenos Aires. In Korstanje, M. (Ed.), *Socio-Economic Effects and Recovery Efforts for the Rental Industry: Post-COVID-19 Strategies* (pp. 45–71). IGI Global. https://doi.org/10.4018/978-1-7998-7287-0.ch003

Borges, V. D. (2021). Happiness: The Basis for Public Policy in Tourism. In Perinotto, A., Mayer, V., & Soares, J. (Eds.), *Rebuilding and Restructuring the Tourism Industry: Infusion of Happiness and Quality of Life* (pp. 1–25). IGI Global. https://doi.org/10.4018/978-1-7998-7239-9.ch001

Bücker, J., & Ernste, K. (2018). Use of Brand Heroes in Strategic Reputation Management: The Case of Bacardi, Adidas, and Daimler. In Erdemir, A. (Ed.), *Reputation Management Techniques in Public Relations* (pp. 126–150). Hershey, PA: IGI Global. 10.4018/978-1-5225-3619-2.ch007

Buluk Eşitti, B. (2021). COVID-19 and Alternative Tourism: New Destinations and New Tourism Products. In Demir, M., Dalgıç, A., & Ergen, F. (Eds.), *Handbook of Research on the Impacts and Implications of COVID-19 on the Tourism Industry* (pp. 786–805). IGI Global. https://doi.org/10.4018/978-1-7998-8231-2.ch038

Bureš, V. (2018). Industry 4.0 From the Systems Engineering Perspective: Alternative Holistic Framework Development. In Brunet-Thornton, R., & Martinez, F. (Eds.), *Analyzing the Impacts of Industry 4.0 in Modern Business Environments* (pp. 199–223). Hershey, PA: IGI Global. 10.4018/978-1-5225-3468-6.ch011

Buzady, Z. (2017). Resolving the Magic Cube of Effective Case Teaching: Benchmarking Case Teaching Practices in Emerging Markets – Insights from the Central European University Business School, Hungary. In Latusek, D. (Ed.), *Case Studies as a Teaching Tool in Management Education* (pp. 79–103). Hershey, PA: IGI Global. 10.4018/978-1-5225-0770-3.ch005

Camillo, A. (2021). *Legal Matters, Risk Management, and Risk Prevention: From Forming a Business to Legal Representation*. IGI Global. 10.4018/978-1-7998-4342-9.ch004

Căpusneanu, S., & Topor, D. I. (2018). Business Ethics and Cost Management in SMEs: Theories of Business Ethics and Cost Management Ethos. In Oncioiu, I. (Ed.), *Ethics and Decision-Making for Sustainable Business Practices* (pp. 109–127). Hershey, PA: IGI Global. 10.4018/978-1-5225-3773-1.ch007

Chan, R. L., Mo, P. L., & Moon, K. K. (2018). Strategic and Tactical Measures in Managing Enterprise Risks: A Study of the Textile and Apparel Industry. In Strang, K., Korstanje, M., & Vajjhala, N. (Eds.), *Research, Practices, and Innovations in Global Risk and Contingency Management* (pp. 1–19). Hershey, PA: IGI Global. 10.4018/978-1-5225-4754-9.ch001

Charlier, S. D., Burke-Smalley, L. A., & Fisher, S. L. (2018). Undergraduate Programs in the U.S: A Contextual and Content-Based Analysis. In Mendy, J. (Ed.), *Teaching Human Resources and Organizational Behavior at the College Level* (pp. 26–57). Hershey, PA: IGI Global. 10.4018/978-1-5225-2820-3.ch002

Chumillas, J., Güell, M., & Quer, P. (2022). The Use of ICT in Tourist and Educational Literary Routes: The Role of the Guide. In Ramos, C., Quinteiro, S., & Gonçalves, A. (Eds.), *ICT as Innovator Between Tourism and Culture* (pp. 15–29). IGI Global. https://doi.org/10.4018/978-1-7998-8165-0.ch002

Dahlberg, T., Kivijärvi, H., & Saarinen, T. (2017). IT Investment Consistency and Other Factors Influencing the Success of IT Performance. In De Haes, S., & Van Grembergen, W. (Eds.), *Strategic IT Governance and Alignment in Business Settings* (pp. 176–208). Hershey, PA: IGI Global. 10.4018/978-1-5225-0861-8.ch007

Damnjanović, A. M. (2017). Knowledge Management Optimization through IT and E-Business Utilization: A Qualitative Study on Serbian SMEs. In Vemić, M. (Ed.), *Optimal Management Strategies in Small and Medium Enterprises* (pp. 249–267). Hershey, PA: IGI Global. 10.4018/978-1-5225-1949-2.ch012

Daneshpour, H. (2017). Integrating Sustainable Development into Project Portfolio Management through Application of Open Innovation. In Vemić, M. (Ed.), *Optimal Management Strategies in Small and Medium Enterprises* (pp. 370–387). Hershey, PA: IGI Global. 10.4018/978-1-5225-1949-2.ch017

Daniel, A. D., & Reis de Castro, V. (2018). Entrepreneurship Education: How to Measure the Impact on Nascent Entrepreneurs. In Carrizo Moreira, A., Guilherme Leitão Dantas, J., & Manuel Valente, F. (Eds.), *Nascent Entrepreneurship and Successful New Venture Creation* (pp. 85–110). Hershey, PA: IGI Global. 10.4018/978-1-5225-2936-1.ch004

David, R., Swami, B. N., & Tangirala, S. (2018). Ethics Impact on Knowledge Management in Organizational Development: A Case Study. In Baporikar, N. (Ed.), *Global Practices in Knowledge Management for Societal and Organizational Development* (pp. 19–45). Hershey, PA: IGI Global. 10.4018/978-1-5225-3009-1.ch002

De Uña-Álvarez, E., & Villarino-Pérez, M. (2022). Fostering Ecocultural Resources, Identity, and Tourism in Inland Territories (Galicia, NW Spain). In G. Fernandes (Ed.), *Challenges and New Opportunities for Tourism in Inland Territories: Ecocultural Resources and Sustainable Initiatives* (pp. 1-16). IGI Global. https://doi.org/10.4018/978-1-7998-7339-6.ch001

Delias, P., & Lakiotaki, K. (2018). Discovering Process Horizontal Boundaries to Facilitate Process Comprehension. *International Journal of Operations Research and Information Systems*, 9(2), 1–31. 10.4018/IJORIS.2018040101

Denholm, J., & Lee-Davies, L. (2018). Success Factors for Games in Business and Project Management. In *Enhancing Education and Training Initiatives Through Serious Games* (pp. 34–68). Hershey, PA: IGI Global. 10.4018/978-1-5225-3689-5.ch002

Deshpande, M. (2017). Best Practices in Management Institutions for Global Leadership: Policy Aspects. In Baporikar, N. (Ed.), *Management Education for Global Leadership* (pp. 1–27). Hershey, PA: IGI Global. 10.4018/978-1-5225-1013-0.ch001

Deshpande, M. (2018). Policy Perspectives for SMEs Knowledge Management. In Baporikar, N. (Ed.), *Knowledge Integration Strategies for Entrepreneurship and Sustainability* (pp. 23–46). Hershey, PA: IGI Global. 10.4018/978-1-5225-5115-7.ch002

Dezdar, S. (2017). ERP Implementation Projects in Asian Countries: A Comparative Study on Iran and China. *International Journal of Information Technology Project Management*, 8(3), 52–68. 10.4018/IJITPM.2017070104

Domingos, D., Respício, A., & Martinho, R. (2017). Reliability of IoT-Aware BPMN Healthcare Processes. In Reis, C., & Maximiano, M. (Eds.), *Internet of Things and Advanced Application in Healthcare* (pp. 214–248). Hershey, PA: IGI Global. 10.4018/978-1-5225-1820-4.ch008

Dosumu, O., Hussain, J., & El-Gohary, H. (2017). An Exploratory Study of the Impact of Government Policies on the Development of Small and Medium Enterprises in Developing Countries: The Case of Nigeria. *International Journal of Customer Relationship Marketing and Management*, 8(4), 51–62. 10.4018/IJCRMM.2017100104

Durst, S., Bruns, G., & Edvardsson, I. R. (2017). Retaining Knowledge in Smaller Building and Construction Firms. *International Journal of Knowledge and Systems Science*, 8(3), 1–12. 10.4018/IJKSS.2017070101

Edvardsson, I. R., & Durst, S. (2017). Outsourcing, Knowledge, and Learning: A Critical Review. *International Journal of Knowledge-Based Organizations*, 7(2), 13–26. 10.4018/IJKBO.2017040102

Edwards, J. S. (2018). Integrating Knowledge Management and Business Processes. In M. Khosrow-Pour, D.B.A. (Ed.), *Encyclopedia of Information Science and Technology, Fourth Edition* (pp. 5046-5055). Hershey, PA: IGI Global. 10.4018/978-1-5225-2255-3.ch437

Eichelberger, S., & Peters, M. (2021). Family Firm Management in Turbulent Times: Opportunities for Responsible Tourism. In Zehrer, A., Glowka, G., Schwaiger, K., & Ranacher-Lackner, V. (Eds.), *Resiliency Models and Addressing Future Risks for Family Firms in the Tourism Industry* (pp. 103–124). IGI Global. https://doi.org/10.4018/978-1-7998-7352-5.ch005

Eide, D., Hjalager, A., & Hansen, M. (2022). Innovative Certifications in Adventure Tourism: Attributes and Diffusion. In R. Augusto Costa, F. Brandão, Z. Breda, & C. Costa (Eds.), *Planning and Managing the Experience Economy in Tourism* (pp. 161-175). IGI Global. https://doi.org/10.4018/978-1-7998-8775-1.ch009

Ejiogu, A. O. (2018). Economics of Farm Management. In *Agricultural Finance and Opportunities for Investment and Expansion* (pp. 56–72). Hershey, PA: IGI Global. 10.4018/978-1-5225-3059-6.ch003

Ekanem, I., & Abiade, G. E. (2018). Factors Influencing the Use of E-Commerce by Small Enterprises in Nigeria. *International Journal of ICT Research in Africa and the Middle East*, 7(1), 37–53. 10.4018/IJICTRAME.2018010103

Ekanem, I., & Alrossais, L. A. (2017). Succession Challenges Facing Family Businesses in Saudi Arabia. In Zgheib, P. (Ed.), *Entrepreneurship and Business Innovation in the Middle East* (pp. 122–146). Hershey, PA: IGI Global. 10.4018/978-1-5225-2066-5. ch007

El Faquih, L., & Fredj, M. (2017). Ontology-Based Framework for Quality in Configurable Process Models. *Journal of Electronic Commerce in Organizations*, 15(2), 48–60. 10.4018/JECO.2017040104

Faisal, M. N., & Talib, F. (2017). Building Ambidextrous Supply Chains in SMEs: How to Tackle the Barriers? *International Journal of Information Systems and Supply Chain Management*, 10(4), 80–100. 10.4018/IJISSCM.2017100105

Fernandes, T. M., Gomes, J., & Romão, M. (2017). Investments in E-Government: A Benefit Management Case Study. *International Journal of Electronic Government Research*, 13(3), 1–17. 10.4018/IJEGR.2017070101

Figueira, L. M., Honrado, G. R., & Dionísio, M. S. (2021). Human Capital Management in the Tourism Industry in Portugal. In Costa, V., Moura, A., & Mira, M. (Eds.), *Handbook of Research on Human Capital and People Management in the Tourism Industry* (pp. 1–19). IGI Global. 10.4018/978-1-7998-4318-4.ch001

Gao, S. S., Oreal, S., & Zhang, J. (2018). Contemporary Financial Risk Management Perceptions and Practices of Small-Sized Chinese Businesses. In I. Management Association (Ed.), *Global Business Expansion: Concepts, Methodologies, Tools, and Applications* (pp. 917-931). Hershey, PA: IGI Global. 10.4018/978-1-5225-5481-3.ch041

Garg, R., & Berning, S. C. (2017). Indigenous Chinese Management Philosophies: Key Concepts and Relevance for Modern Chinese Firms. In Christiansen, B., & Koc, G. (Eds.), *Transcontinental Strategies for Industrial Development and Economic Growth* (pp. 43–57). Hershey, PA: IGI Global. 10.4018/978-1-5225-2160-0.ch003

Gencer, Y. G. (2017). Supply Chain Management in Retailing Business. In Akkucuk, U. (Ed.), *Ethics and Sustainability in Global Supply Chain Management* (pp. 197–210). Hershey, PA: IGI Global. 10.4018/978-1-5225-2036-8.ch011

Gera, R., Arora, S., & Malik, S. (2021). Emotional Labor in the Tourism Industry: Strategies, Antecedents, and Outcomes. In Costa, V., Moura, A., & Mira, M. (Eds.), *Handbook of Research on Human Capital and People Management in the Tourism Industry* (pp. 73–91). IGI Global. https://doi.org/10.4018/978-1-7998-4318-4.ch004

Giacosa, E. (2018). The Increasing of the Regional Development Thanks to the Luxury Business Innovation. In Carvalho, L. (Ed.), *Handbook of Research on Entrepreneurial Ecosystems and Social Dynamics in a Globalized World* (pp. 260–273). Hershey, PA: IGI Global. 10.4018/978-1-5225-3525-6.ch011

Glowka, G., Tusch, M., & Zehrer, A. (2021). The Risk Perception of Family Business Owner-Manager in the Tourism Industry: A Qualitative Comparison of the Intra-Firm Senior and Junior Generation. In Zehrer, A., Glowka, G., Schwaiger, K., & Ranacher-Lackner, V. (Eds.), *Resiliency Models and Addressing Future Risks for Family Firms in the Tourism Industry* (pp. 126–153). IGI Global. https://doi.org/10.4018/978-1-7998-7352-5.ch006

Glykas, M., & George, J. (2017). Quality and Process Management Systems in the UAE Maritime Industry. *International Journal of Productivity Management and Assessment Technologies*, 5(1), 20–39. 10.4018/IJPMAT.2017010102

Glykas, M., Valiris, G., Kokkinaki, A., & Koutsoukou, Z. (2018). Banking Business Process Management Implementation. *International Journal of Productivity Management and Assessment Technologies*, 6(1), 50–69. 10.4018/IJPMAT.2018010104

Gomes, J., & Romão, M. (2017). The Balanced Scorecard: Keeping Updated and Aligned with Today's Business Trends. *International Journal of Productivity Management and Assessment Technologies*, 5(2), 1–15. 10.4018/IJPMAT.2017070101

Gomes, J., & Romão, M. (2017). Aligning Information Systems and Technology with Benefit Management and Balanced Scorecard. In De Haes, S., & Van Grembergen, W. (Eds.), *Strategic IT Governance and Alignment in Business Settings* (pp. 112–131). Hershey, PA: IGI Global. 10.4018/978-1-5225-0861-8.ch005

Goyal, A. (2021). Communicating and Building Destination Brands With New Media. In M. Dinis, L. Bonixe, S. Lamy, & Z. Breda (Eds.), *Impact of New Media in Tourism* (pp. 1-20). IGI Global. https://doi.org/10.4018/978-1-7998-7095-1.ch001

Grefen, P., & Turetken, O. (2017). Advanced Business Process Management in Networked E-Business Scenarios. *International Journal of E-Business Research*, 13(4), 70–104. 10.4018/IJEBR.2017100105

Guasca, M., Van Broeck, A. M., & Vanneste, D. (2021). Tourism and the Social Reintegration of Colombian Ex-Combatants. In J. da Silva, Z. Breda, & F. Carbone (Eds.), *Role and Impact of Tourism in Peacebuilding and Conflict Transformation* (pp. 66-86). IGI Global. https://doi.org/10.4018/978-1-7998-5053-3.ch005

Haider, A., & Saetang, S. (2017). Strategic IT Alignment in Service Sector. In Rozenes, S., & Cohen, Y. (Eds.), *Handbook of Research on Strategic Alliances and Value Co-Creation in the Service Industry* (pp. 231–258). Hershey, PA: IGI Global. 10.4018/978-1-5225-2084-9.ch012

Hajilari, A. B., Ghadaksaz, M., & Fasghandis, G. S. (2017). Assessing Organizational Readiness for Implementing ERP System Using Fuzzy Expert System Approach. *International Journal of Enterprise Information Systems*, 13(1), 67–85. 10.4018/IJEIS.2017010105

Haldorai, A., Ramu, A., & Murugan, S. (2018). Social Aware Cognitive Radio Networks: Effectiveness of Social Networks as a Strategic Tool for Organizational Business Management. In Bansal, H., Shrivastava, G., Nguyen, G., & Stanciu, L. (Eds.), *Social Network Analytics for Contemporary Business Organizations* (pp. 188–202). Hershey, PA: IGI Global. 10.4018/978-1-5225-5097-6.ch010

Hall, O. P.Jr. (2017). Social Media Driven Management Education. *International Journal of Knowledge-Based Organizations*, 7(2), 43–59. 10.4018/IJKBO.2017040104

Hanifah, H., Halim, H. A., Ahmad, N. H., & Vafaei-Zadeh, A. (2017). Innovation Culture as a Mediator Between Specific Human Capital and Innovation Performance Among Bumiputera SMEs in Malaysia. In Ahmad, N., Ramayah, T., Halim, H., & Rahman, S. (Eds.), *Handbook of Research on Small and Medium Enterprises in Developing Countries* (pp. 261–279). Hershey, PA: IGI Global. 10.4018/978-1-5225-2165-5.ch012

Hartlieb, S., & Silvius, G. (2017). Handling Uncertainty in Project Management and Business Development: Similarities and Differences. In Raydugin, Y. (Ed.), *Handbook of Research on Leveraging Risk and Uncertainties for Effective Project Management* (pp. 337–362). Hershey, PA: IGI Global. 10.4018/978-1-5225-1790-0.ch016

Hass, K. B. (2017). Living on the Edge: Managing Project Complexity. In Raydugin, Y. (Ed.), *Handbook of Research on Leveraging Risk and Uncertainties for Effective Project Management* (pp. 177–201). Hershey, PA: IGI Global. 10.4018/978-1-5225-1790-0.ch009

Hawking, P., & Carmine Sellitto, C. (2017). Developing an Effective Strategy for Organizational Business Intelligence. In Tavana, M. (Ed.), *Enterprise Information Systems and the Digitalization of Business Functions* (pp. 222–237). Hershey, PA: IGI Global. 10.4018/978-1-5225-2382-6.ch010

Hawking, P., & Sellitto, C. (2017). A Fast-Moving Consumer Goods Company and Business Intelligence Strategy Development. *International Journal of Enterprise Information Systems*, 13(2), 22–33. 10.4018/IJEIS.2017040102

Hawking, P., & Sellitto, C. (2017). Business Intelligence Strategy: Two Case Studies. *International Journal of Business Intelligence Research*, 8(2), 17–30. 10.4018/IJBIR.2017070102

Hee, W. J., Jalleh, G., Lai, H., & Lin, C. (2017). E-Commerce and IT Projects: Evaluation and Management Issues in Australian and Taiwanese Hospitals. *International Journal of Public Health Management and Ethics*, 2(1), 69–90. 10.4018/IJPHME.2017010104

Hernandez, A. A. (2018). Exploring the Factors to Green IT Adoption of SMEs in the Philippines. *Journal of Cases on Information Technology*, 20(2), 49–66. 10.4018/JCIT.2018040104

Hollman, A., Bickford, S., & Hollman, T. (2017). Cyber InSecurity: A Post-Mortem Attempt to Assess Cyber Problems from IT and Business Management Perspectives. *Journal of Cases on Information Technology*, 19(3), 42–70. 10.4018/JCIT.2017070104

Ibrahim, F., & Zainin, N. M. (2021). Exploring the Technological Impacts: The Case of Museums in Brunei Darussalam. *International Journal of Tourism and Hospitality Management in the Digital Age*, 5(1), 1–18. https://doi.org/10.4018/IJTHMDA.2021010101

Igbinakhase, I. (2017). Responsible and Sustainable Management Practices in Developing and Developed Business Environments. In Fields, Z. (Ed.), *Collective Creativity for Responsible and Sustainable Business Practice* (pp. 180–207). Hershey, PA: IGI Global. 10.4018/978-1-5225-1823-5.ch010

Iwata, J. J., & Hoskins, R. G. (2017). Managing Indigenous Knowledge in Tanzania: A Business Perspective. In Jain, P., & Mnjama, N. (Eds.), *Managing Knowledge Resources and Records in Modern Organizations* (pp. 198–214). Hershey, PA: IGI Global. 10.4018/978-1-5225-1965-2.ch012

Jain, P. (2017). Ethical and Legal Issues in Knowledge Management Life-Cycle in Business. In Jain, P., & Mnjama, N. (Eds.), *Managing Knowledge Resources and Records in Modern Organizations* (pp. 82–101). Hershey, PA: IGI Global. 10.4018/978-1-5225-1965-2.ch006

James, S., & Hauli, E. (2017). Holistic Management Education at Tanzanian Rural Development Planning Institute. In Baporikar, N. (Ed.), *Management Education for Global Leadership* (pp. 112–136). Hershey, PA: IGI Global. 10.4018/978-1-5225-1013-0.ch006

Janošková, M., Csikósová, A., & Čulková, K. (2018). Measurement of Company Performance as Part of Its Strategic Management. In Leon, R. (Ed.), *Managerial Strategies for Business Sustainability During Turbulent Times* (pp. 309–335). Hershey, PA: IGI Global. 10.4018/978-1-5225-2716-9.ch017

Jean-Vasile, A., & Alecu, A. (2017). Theoretical and Practical Approaches in Understanding the Influences of Cost-Productivity-Profit Trinomial in Contemporary Enterprises. In Jean Vasile, A., & Nicolò, D. (Eds.), *Sustainable Entrepreneurship and Investments in the Green Economy* (pp. 28–62). Hershey, PA: IGI Global. 10.4018/978-1-5225-2075-7.ch002

Joia, L. A., & Correia, J. C. (2018). CIO Competencies From the IT Professional Perspective: Insights From Brazil. *Journal of Global Information Management*, 26(2), 74–103. 10.4018/JGIM.2018040104

Juma, A., & Mzera, N. (2017). Knowledge Management and Records Management and Competitive Advantage in Business. In Jain, P., & Mnjama, N. (Eds.), *Managing Knowledge Resources and Records in Modern Organizations* (pp. 15–28). Hershey, PA: IGI Global. 10.4018/978-1-5225-1965-2.ch002

K., I., & A, V. (2018). Monitoring and Auditing in the Cloud. In K. Munir (Ed.), *Cloud Computing Technologies for Green Enterprises* (pp. 318-350). Hershey, PA: IGI Global. https://doi.org/10.4018/978-1-5225-3038-1.ch013

Kabra, G., Ghosh, V., & Ramesh, A. (2018). Enterprise Integrated Business Process Management and Business Intelligence Framework for Business Process Sustainability. In Paul, A., Bhattacharyya, D., & Anand, S. (Eds.), *Green Initiatives for Business Sustainability and Value Creation* (pp. 228–238). Hershey, PA: IGI Global. 10.4018/978-1-5225-2662-9.ch010

Kaoud, M. (2017). Investigation of Customer Knowledge Management: A Case Study Research. *International Journal of Service Science, Management, Engineering, and Technology*, 8(2), 12–22. 10.4018/IJSSMET.2017040102

Katuu, S. (2018). A Comparative Assessment of Enterprise Content Management Maturity Models. In Gwangwava, N., & Mutingi, M. (Eds.), *E-Manufacturing and E-Service Strategies in Contemporary Organizations* (pp. 93–118). Hershey, PA: IGI Global. 10.4018/978-1-5225-3628-4.ch005

Khan, M. Y., & Abir, T. (2022). The Role of Social Media Marketing in the Tourism and Hospitality Industry: A Conceptual Study on Bangladesh. In Ramos, C., Quinteiro, S., & Gonçalves, A. (Eds.), *ICT as Innovator Between Tourism and Culture* (pp. 213–229). IGI Global. https://doi.org/10.4018/978-1-7998-8165-0.ch013

Kinnunen, S., Ylä-Kujala, A., Marttonen-Arola, S., Kärri, T., & Baglee, D. (2018). Internet of Things in Asset Management: Insights from Industrial Professionals and Academia. *International Journal of Service Science, Management, Engineering, and Technology*, 9(2), 104–119. 10.4018/IJSSMET.2018040105

Klein, A. Z., Sabino de Freitas, A., Machado, L., Freitas, J. C.Jr, Graziola, P. G.Jr, & Schlemmer, E. (2017). Virtual Worlds Applications for Management Education. In Tomei, L. (Ed.), *Exploring the New Era of Technology-Infused Education* (pp. 279–299). Hershey, PA: IGI Global. 10.4018/978-1-5225-1709-2.ch017

Kővári, E., Saleh, M., & Steinbachné Hajmásy, G. (2022). The Impact of Corporate Digital Responsibility (CDR) on Internal Stakeholders' Satisfaction in Hungarian Upscale Hotels. In Valeri, M. (Ed.), *New Governance and Management in Touristic Destinations* (pp. 35–51). IGI Global. https://doi.org/10.4018/978-1-6684-3889-3 .ch003

Kożuch, B., & Jabłoński, A. (2017). Adopting the Concept of Business Models in Public Management. In Lewandowski, M., & Kożuch, B. (Eds.), *Public Sector Entrepreneurship and the Integration of Innovative Business Models* (pp. 10–46). Hershey, PA: IGI Global. 10.4018/978-1-5225-2215-7.ch002

Kumar, J., Adhikary, A., & Jha, A. (2017). Small Active Investors' Perceptions and Preferences Towards Tax Saving Mutual Fund Schemes in Eastern India: An Empirical Note. *International Journal of Asian Business and Information Management*, 8(2), 35–45. 10.4018/IJABIM.2017040103

Latusi, S., & Fissore, M. (2021). Pilgrimage Routes to Happiness: Comparing the Camino de Santiago and Via Francigena. In Perinotto, A., Mayer, V., & Soares, J. (Eds.), *Rebuilding and Restructuring the Tourism Industry: Infusion of Happiness and Quality of Life* (pp. 157–182). IGI Global. https://doi.org/10.4018/978-1-7998 -7239-9.ch008

Lavassani, K. M., & Movahedi, B. (2017). Applications Driven Information Systems: Beyond Networks toward Business Ecosystems. *International Journal of Innovation in the Digital Economy*, 8(1), 61–75. 10.4018/IJIDE.2017010104

Lazzareschi, V. H., & Brito, M. S. (2017). Strategic Information Management: Proposal of Business Project Model. In Jamil, G., Soares, A., & Pessoa, C. (Eds.), *Handbook of Research on Information Management for Effective Logistics and Supply Chains* (pp. 59–88). Hershey, PA: IGI Global. 10.4018/978-1-5225-0973-8.ch004

Lechuga Sancho, M. P., & Martín Navarro, A. (2022). Evolution of the Literature on Social Responsibility in the Tourism Sector: A Systematic Literature Review. In Fernandes, G. (Ed.), *Challenges and New Opportunities for Tourism in Inland Territories: Ecocultural Resources and Sustainable Initiatives* (pp. 169–186). IGI Global. https://doi.org/10.4018/978-1-7998-7339-6.ch010

Lederer, M., Kurz, M., & Lazarov, P. (2017). Usage and Suitability of Methods for Strategic Business Process Initiatives: A Multi Case Study Research. *International Journal of Productivity Management and Assessment Technologies*, 5(1), 40–51. 10.4018/IJPMAT.2017010103

Lee, I. (2017). A Social Enterprise Business Model and a Case Study of Pacific Community Ventures (PCV). In Potocan, V., Üngan, M., & Nedelko, Z. (Eds.), *Handbook of Research on Managerial Solutions in Non-Profit Organizations* (pp. 182–204). Hershey, PA: IGI Global. 10.4018/978-1-5225-0731-4.ch009

Leon, L. A., Seal, K. C., Przasnyski, Z. H., & Wiedenman, I. (2017). Skills and Competencies Required for Jobs in Business Analytics: A Content Analysis of Job Advertisements Using Text Mining. *International Journal of Business Intelligence Research*, 8(1), 1–25. 10.4018/IJBIR.2017010101

Levy, C. L., & Elias, N. I. (2017). SOHO Users' Perceptions of Reliability and Continuity of Cloud-Based Services. In Moore, M. (Ed.), *Cybersecurity Breaches and Issues Surrounding Online Threat Protection* (pp. 248–287). Hershey, PA: IGI Global. 10.4018/978-1-5225-1941-6.ch011

Levy, M. (2018). Change Management Serving Knowledge Management and Organizational Development: Reflections and Review. In Baporikar, N. (Ed.), *Global Practices in Knowledge Management for Societal and Organizational Development* (pp. 256–270). Hershey, PA: IGI Global. 10.4018/978-1-5225-3009-1.ch012

Lewandowski, M. (2017). Public Organizations and Business Model Innovation: The Role of Public Service Design. In Lewandowski, M., & Kożuch, B. (Eds.), *Public Sector Entrepreneurship and the Integration of Innovative Business Models* (pp. 47–72). Hershey, PA: IGI Global. 10.4018/978-1-5225-2215-7.ch003

Lhannaoui, H., Kabbaj, M. I., & Bakkoury, Z. (2017). A Survey of Risk-Aware Business Process Modelling. *International Journal of Risk and Contingency Management*, 6(3), 14–26. 10.4018/IJRCM.2017070102

Li, J., Sun, W., Jiang, W., Yang, H., & Zhang, L. (2017). How the Nature of Exogenous Shocks and Crises Impact Company Performance?: The Effects of Industry Characteristics. *International Journal of Risk and Contingency Management*, 6(4), 40–55. 10.4018/IJRCM.2017100103

Lopez-Fernandez, M., Perez-Perez, M., Serrano-Bedia, A., & Cobo-Gonzalez, A. (2021). Small and Medium Tourism Enterprise Survival in Times of Crisis: "El Capricho de Gaudí. In Toubes, D., & Araújo-Vila, N. (Eds.), *Risk, Crisis, and Disaster Management in Small and Medium-Sized Tourism Enterprises* (pp. 103–129). IGI Global. 10.4018/978-1-7998-6996-2.ch005

Mahajan, A., Maidullah, S., & Hossain, M. R. (2022). Experience Toward Smart Tour Guide Apps in Travelling: An Analysis of Users' Reviews on Audio Odigos and Trip My Way. In R. Augusto Costa, F. Brandão, Z. Breda, & C. Costa (Eds.), *Planning and Managing the Experience Economy in Tourism* (pp. 255-273). IGI Global. https://doi.org/10.4018/978-1-7998-8775-1.ch014

Malega, P. (2017). Small and Medium Enterprises in the Slovak Republic: Status and Competitiveness of SMEs in the Global Markets and Possibilities of Optimization. In Vemić, M. (Ed.), *Optimal Management Strategies in Small and Medium Enterprises* (pp. 102–124). Hershey, PA: IGI Global. 10.4018/978-1-5225-1949-2.ch006

Malewska, K. M. (2017). Intuition in Decision-Making on the Example of a Non-Profit Organization. In Potocan, V., Üngan, M., & Nedelko, Z. (Eds.), *Handbook of Research on Managerial Solutions in Non-Profit Organizations* (pp. 378–399). Hershey, PA: IGI Global. 10.4018/978-1-5225-0731-4.ch018

Maroofi, F. (2017). Entrepreneurial Orientation and Organizational Learning Ability Analysis for Innovation and Firm Performance. In Baporikar, N. (Ed.), *Innovation and Shifting Perspectives in Management Education* (pp. 144–165). Hershey, PA: IGI Global. 10.4018/978-1-5225-1019-2.ch007

Marques, M., Moleiro, D., Brito, T. M., & Marques, T. (2021). Customer Relationship Management as an Important Relationship Marketing Tool: The Case of the Hospitality Industry in Estoril Coast. In M. Dinis, L. Bonixe, S. Lamy, & Z. Breda (Eds.), *Impact of New Media in Tourism* (pp. 39-56). IGI Global. https://doi.org/10.4018/978-1-7998-7095-1.ch003

Martins, P. V., & Zacarias, M. (2017). A Web-based Tool for Business Process Improvement. *International Journal of Web Portals*, 9(2), 68–84. 10.4018/IJWP.2017070104

Matthies, B., & Coners, A. (2017). Exploring the Conceptual Nature of e-Business Projects. *Journal of Electronic Commerce in Organizations*, 15(3), 33–63. 10.4018/JECO.2017070103

Mayer, V. F., Fraga, C. C., & Silva, L. C. (2021). Contributions of Neurosciences to Studies of Well-Being in Tourism. In Perinotto, A., Mayer, V., & Soares, J. (Eds.), *Rebuilding and Restructuring the Tourism Industry: Infusion of Happiness and Quality of Life* (pp. 108–128). IGI Global. https://doi.org/10.4018/978-1-7998-7239-9.ch006

McKee, J. (2018). Architecture as a Tool to Solve Business Planning Problems. In M. Khosrow-Pour, D.B.A. (Ed.), *Encyclopedia of Information Science and Technology, Fourth Edition* (pp. 573-586). Hershey, PA: IGI Global. 10.4018/978-1-5225-2255-3.ch050

McMurray, A. J., Cross, J., & Caponecchia, C. (2018). The Risk Management Profession in Australia: Business Continuity Plan Practices. In Bajgoric, N. (Ed.), *Always-On Enterprise Information Systems for Modern Organizations* (pp. 112–129). Hershey, PA: IGI Global. 10.4018/978-1-5225-3704-5.ch006

Meddah, I. H., & Belkadi, K. (2018). Mining Patterns Using Business Process Management. In Hamou, R. (Ed.), *Handbook of Research on Biomimicry in Information Retrieval and Knowledge Management* (pp. 78–89). Hershey, PA: IGI Global. 10.4018/978-1-5225-3004-6.ch005

Melian, A. G., & Camprubí, R. (2021). The Accessibility of Museum Websites: The Case of Barcelona. In Eusébio, C., Teixeira, L., & Carneiro, M. (Eds.), *ICT Tools and Applications for Accessible Tourism* (pp. 234–255). IGI Global. https://doi.org/10.4018/978-1-7998-6428-8.ch011

Mendes, L. (2017). TQM and Knowledge Management: An Integrated Approach Towards Tacit Knowledge Management. In Jaziri-Bouagina, D., & Jamil, G. (Eds.), *Handbook of Research on Tacit Knowledge Management for Organizational Success* (pp. 236–263). Hershey, PA: IGI Global. 10.4018/978-1-5225-2394-9.ch009

Menezes, V. D., & Cavagnaro, E. (2021). Communicating Sustainable Initiatives in the Hotel Industry: The Case of the Hotel Jakarta Amsterdam. In F. Brandão, Z. Breda, R. Costa, & C. Costa (Eds.), *Handbook of Research on the Role of Tourism in Achieving Sustainable Development Goals* (pp. 224-234). IGI Global. https://doi.org/10.4018/978-1-7998-5691-7.ch013

Menezes, V. D., & Cavagnaro, E. (2021). Communicating Sustainable Initiatives in the Hotel Industry: The Case of the Hotel Jakarta Amsterdam. In F. Brandão, Z. Breda, R. Costa, & C. Costa (Eds.), *Handbook of Research on the Role of Tourism in Achieving Sustainable Development Goals* (pp. 224-234). IGI Global. https://doi.org/10.4018/978-1-7998-5691-7.ch013

Mitas, O., Bastiaansen, M., & Boode, W. (2022). If You're Happy, I'm Happy: Emotion Contagion at a Tourist Information Center. In R. Augusto Costa, F. Brandão, Z. Breda, & C. Costa (Eds.), *Planning and Managing the Experience Economy in Tourism* (pp. 122-140). IGI Global. https://doi.org/10.4018/978-1-7998-8775-1.ch007

Mnjama, N. M. (2017). Preservation of Recorded Information in Public and Private Sector Organizations. In Jain, P., & Mnjama, N. (Eds.), *Managing Knowledge Resources and Records in Modern Organizations* (pp. 149–167). Hershey, PA: IGI Global. 10.4018/978-1-5225-1965-2.ch009

Mokoqama, M., & Fields, Z. (2017). Principles of Responsible Management Education (PRME): Call for Responsible Management Education. In Fields, Z. (Ed.), *Collective Creativity for Responsible and Sustainable Business Practice* (pp. 229–241). Hershey, PA: IGI Global. 10.4018/978-1-5225-1823-5.ch012

Monteiro, A., Lopes, S., & Carbone, F. (2021). Academic Mobility: Bridging Tourism and Peace Education. In J. da Silva, Z. Breda, & F. Carbone (Eds.), *Role and Impact of Tourism in Peacebuilding and Conflict Transformation* (pp. 275-301). IGI Global. https://doi.org/10.4018/978-1-7998-5053-3.ch016

Muniapan, B. (2017). Philosophy and Management: The Relevance of Vedanta in Management. In Ordóñez de Pablos, P. (Ed.), *Managerial Strategies and Solutions for Business Success in Asia* (pp. 124–139). Hershey, PA: IGI Global. 10.4018/978-1-5225-1886-0.ch007

Murad, S. E., & Dowaji, S. (2017). Using Value-Based Approach for Managing Cloud-Based Services. In Turuk, A., Sahoo, B., & Addya, S. (Eds.), *Resource Management and Efficiency in Cloud Computing Environments* (pp. 33–60). Hershey, PA: IGI Global. 10.4018/978-1-5225-1721-4.ch002

Mutahar, A. M., Daud, N. M., Thurasamy, R., Isaac, O., & Abdulsalam, R. (2018). The Mediating of Perceived Usefulness and Perceived Ease of Use: The Case of Mobile Banking in Yemen. *International Journal of Technology Diffusion*, 9(2), 21–40. 10.4018/IJTD.2018040102

Naidoo, V. (2017). E-Learning and Management Education at African Universities. In Baporikar, N. (Ed.), *Management Education for Global Leadership* (pp. 181–201). Hershey, PA: IGI Global. 10.4018/978-1-5225-1013-0.ch009

Naidoo, V., & Igbinakhase, I. (2018). Opportunities and Challenges of Knowledge Retention in SMEs. In Baporikar, N. (Ed.), *Knowledge Integration Strategies for Entrepreneurship and Sustainability* (pp. 70–94). Hershey, PA: IGI Global. 10.4018/978-1-5225-5115-7.ch004

Naumov, N., & Costandachi, G. (2021). Creativity and Entrepreneurship: Gastronomic Tourism in Mexico. In Soares, J. (Ed.), *Innovation and Entrepreneurial Opportunities in Community Tourism* (pp. 90–108). IGI Global. https://doi.org/10.4018/978-1-7998-4855-4.ch006

Nayak, S., & Prabhu, N. (2017). Paradigm Shift in Management Education: Need for a Cross Functional Perspective. In Baporikar, N. (Ed.), *Management Education for Global Leadership* (pp. 241–255). Hershey, PA: IGI Global. 10.4018/978-1-5225-1013-0.ch012

Nedelko, Z., & Potocan, V. (2017). Management Solutions in Non-Profit Organizations: Case of Slovenia. In Potocan, V., Ünğan, M., & Nedelko, Z. (Eds.), *Handbook of Research on Managerial Solutions in Non-Profit Organizations* (pp. 1–22). Hershey, PA: IGI Global. 10.4018/978-1-5225-0731-4.ch001

Nedelko, Z., & Potocan, V. (2017). Priority of Management Tools Utilization among Managers: International Comparison. In Wang, V. (Ed.), *Encyclopedia of Strategic Leadership and Management* (pp. 1083–1094). Hershey, PA: IGI Global. 10.4018/978-1-5225-1049-9.ch075

Nedelko, Z., Raudeliūnienė, J., & Črešnar, R. (2018). Knowledge Dynamics in Supply Chain Management. In Baporikar, N. (Ed.), *Knowledge Integration Strategies for Entrepreneurship and Sustainability* (pp. 150–166). Hershey, PA: IGI Global. 10.4018/978-1-5225-5115-7.ch008

Nguyen, H. T., & Hipsher, S. A. (2018). Innovation and Creativity Used by Private Sector Firms in a Resources-Constrained Environment. In Hipsher, S. (Ed.), *Examining the Private Sector's Role in Wealth Creation and Poverty Reduction* (pp. 219–238). Hershey, PA: IGI Global. 10.4018/978-1-5225-3117-3.ch010

Obicci, P. A. (2017). Risk Sharing in a Partnership. In *Risk Management Strategies in Public-Private Partnerships* (pp. 115–152). Hershey, PA: IGI Global. 10.4018/978-1-5225-2503-5.ch004

Obidallah, W. J., & Raahemi, B. (2017). Managing Changes in Service Oriented Virtual Organizations: A Structural and Procedural Framework to Facilitate the Process of Change. *Journal of Electronic Commerce in Organizations*, 15(1), 59–83. 10.4018/JECO.2017010104

Ojo, O. (2017). Impact of Innovation on the Entrepreneurial Success in Selected Business Enterprises in South-West Nigeria. *International Journal of Innovation in the Digital Economy*, 8(2), 29–38. 10.4018/IJIDE.2017040103

Okdinawati, L., Simatupang, T. M., & Sunitiyoso, Y. (2017). Multi-Agent Reinforcement Learning for Value Co-Creation of Collaborative Transportation Management (CTM). *International Journal of Information Systems and Supply Chain Management*, 10(3), 84–95. 10.4018/IJISSCM.2017070105

Olivera, V. A., & Carrillo, I. M. (2021). Organizational Culture: A Key Element for the Development of Mexican Micro and Small Tourist Companies. In Soares, J. (Ed.), *Innovation and Entrepreneurial Opportunities in Community Tourism* (pp. 227–242). IGI Global. 10.4018/978-1-7998-4855-4.ch013

Ossorio, M. (2022). Corporate Museum Experiences in Enogastronomic Tourism. In R. Augusto Costa, F. Brandão, Z. Breda, & C. Costa (Eds.), *Planning and Managing the Experience Economy in Tourism* (pp. 107-121). IGI Global. https://doi .org/10.4018/978-1-7998-8775-1.ch006

Ossorio, M. (2022). Enogastronomic Tourism in Times of Pandemic. In Fernandes, G. (Ed.), *Challenges and New Opportunities for Tourism in Inland Territories: Eco-cultural Resources and Sustainable Initiatives* (pp. 241–255). IGI Global. https:// doi.org/10.4018/978-1-7998-7339-6.ch014

Özekici, Y. K. (2022). ICT as an Acculturative Agent and Its Role in the Tourism Context: Introduction, Acculturation Theory, Progress of the Acculturation Theory in Extant Literature. In Ramos, C., Quinteiro, S., & Gonçalves, A. (Eds.), *ICT as Innovator Between Tourism and Culture* (pp. 42–66). IGI Global. https://doi.org/ 10.4018/978-1-7998-8165-0.ch004

Pal, K. (2018). Building High Quality Big Data-Based Applications in Supply Chains. In Kumar, A., & Saurav, S. (Eds.), *Supply Chain Management Strategies and Risk Assessment in Retail Environments* (pp. 1–24). Hershey, PA: IGI Global. 10.4018/978-1-5225-3056-5.ch001

Palos-Sanchez, P. R., & Correia, M. B. (2018). Perspectives of the Adoption of Cloud Computing in the Tourism Sector. In Rodrigues, J., Ramos, C., Cardoso, P., & Henriques, C. (Eds.), *Handbook of Research on Technological Developments for Cultural Heritage and eTourism Applications* (pp. 377–400). Hershey, PA: IGI Global. 10.4018/978-1-5225-2927-9.ch018

Papadopoulou, G. (2021). Promoting Gender Equality and Women Empowerment in the Tourism Sector. In F. Brandão, Z. Breda, R. Costa, & C. Costa (Eds.), *Handbook of Research on the Role of Tourism in Achieving Sustainable Development Goals* (pp. 152-174). IGI Global. https://doi.org/10.4018/978-1-7998-5691-7.ch009

Papp-Váry, Á. F., & Tóth, T. Z. (2022). Analysis of Budapest as a Film Tourism Destination. In R. Baleiro & R. Pereira (Eds.), *Global Perspectives on Literary Tourism and Film-Induced Tourism* (pp. 257-279). IGI Global. https://doi.org/10 .4018/978-1-7998-8262-6.ch014

Patiño, B. E. (2017). New Generation Management by Convergence and Individual Identity: A Systemic and Human-Oriented Approach. In Baporikar, N. (Ed.), *Innovation and Shifting Perspectives in Management Education* (pp. 119–143). Hershey, PA: IGI Global. 10.4018/978-1-5225-1019-2.ch006

Patro, C. S. (2021). Digital Tourism: Influence of E-Marketing Technology. In M. Dinis, L. Bonixe, S. Lamy, & Z. Breda (Eds.), *Impact of New Media in Tourism* (pp. 234-254). IGI Global. https://doi.org/10.4018/978-1-7998-7095-1.ch014

Pawliczek, A., & Rössler, M. (2017). Knowledge of Management Tools and Systems in SMEs: Knowledge Transfer in Management. In Bencsik, A. (Ed.), *Knowledge Management Initiatives and Strategies in Small and Medium Enterprises* (pp. 180–203). Hershey, PA: IGI Global. 10.4018/978-1-5225-1642-2.ch009

Pejic-Bach, M., Omazic, M. A., Aleksic, A., & Zoroja, J. (2018). Knowledge-Based Decision Making: A Multi-Case Analysis. In Leon, R. (Ed.), *Managerial Strategies for Business Sustainability During Turbulent Times* (pp. 160–184). Hershey, PA: IGI Global. 10.4018/978-1-5225-2716-9.ch009

Perano, M., Hysa, X., & Calabrese, M. (2018). Strategic Planning, Cultural Context, and Business Continuity Management: Business Cases in the City of Shkoder. In Presenza, A., & Sheehan, L. (Eds.), *Geopolitics and Strategic Management in the Global Economy* (pp. 57–77). Hershey, PA: IGI Global. 10.4018/978-1-5225-2673-5.ch004

Pereira, R., Mira da Silva, M., & Lapão, L. V. (2017). IT Governance Maturity Patterns in Portuguese Healthcare. In De Haes, S., & Van Grembergen, W. (Eds.), *Strategic IT Governance and Alignment in Business Settings* (pp. 24–52). Hershey, PA: IGI Global. 10.4018/978-1-5225-0861-8.ch002

Pérez-Uribe, R. I., Torres, D. A., Jurado, S. P., & Prada, D. M. (2018). Cloud Tools for the Development of Project Management in SMEs. In Perez-Uribe, R., Salcedo-Perez, C., & Ocampo-Guzman, D. (Eds.), *Handbook of Research on Intrapreneurship and Organizational Sustainability in SMEs* (pp. 95–120). Hershey, PA: IGI Global. 10.4018/978-1-5225-3543-0.ch005

Petrisor, I., & Cozmiuc, D. (2017). Global Supply Chain Management Organization at Siemens in the Advent of Industry 4.0. In Saglietto, L., & Cezanne, C. (Eds.), *Global Intermediation and Logistics Service Providers* (pp. 123–142). Hershey, PA: IGI Global. 10.4018/978-1-5225-2133-4.ch007

Pierce, J. M., Velliaris, D. M., & Edwards, J. (2017). A Living Case Study: A Journey Not a Destination. In Silton, N. (Ed.), *Exploring the Benefits of Creativity in Education, Media, and the Arts* (pp. 158–178). Hershey, PA: IGI Global. 10.4018/978-1-5225-0504-4.ch008

Pipia, S., & Pipia, S. (2021). Challenges of Religious Tourism in the Conflict Region: An Example of Jerusalem. In E. Alaverdov & M. Bari (Eds.), *Global Development of Religious Tourism* (pp. 135-148). IGI Global. https://doi.org/10.4018/978-1-7998-5792-1.ch009

Poulaki, P., Kritikos, A., Vasilakis, N., & Valeri, M. (2022). The Contribution of Female Creativity to the Development of Gastronomic Tourism in Greece: The Case of the Island of Naxos in the South Aegean Region. In Valeri, M. (Ed.), *New Governance and Management in Touristic Destinations* (pp. 246–258). IGI Global. https://doi.org/10.4018/978-1-6684-3889-3.ch015

Radosavljevic, M., & Andjelkovic, A. (2017). Multi-Criteria Decision Making Approach for Choosing Business Process for the Improvement: Upgrading of the Six Sigma Methodology. In Stanković, J., Delias, P., Marinković, S., & Rochhia, S. (Eds.), *Tools and Techniques for Economic Decision Analysis* (pp. 225–247). Hershey, PA: IGI Global. 10.4018/978-1-5225-0959-2.ch011

Radovic, V. M. (2017). Corporate Sustainability and Responsibility and Disaster Risk Reduction: A Serbian Overview. In Camilleri, M. (Ed.), *CSR 2.0 and the New Era of Corporate Citizenship* (pp. 147–164). Hershey, PA: IGI Global. 10.4018/978-1-5225-1842-6.ch008

Raghunath, K. M., Devi, S. L., & Patro, C. S. (2018). Impact of Risk Assessment Models on Risk Factors: A Holistic Outlook. In Strang, K., Korstanje, M., & Vajjhala, N. (Eds.), *Research, Practices, and Innovations in Global Risk and Contingency Management* (pp. 134–153). Hershey, PA: IGI Global. 10.4018/978-1-5225-4754-9.ch008

Raman, A., & Goyal, D. P. (2017). Extending IMPLEMENT Framework for Enterprise Information Systems Implementation to Information System Innovation. In Tavana, M. (Ed.), *Enterprise Information Systems and the Digitalization of Business Functions* (pp. 137–177). Hershey, PA: IGI Global. 10.4018/978-1-5225-2382-6.ch007

Rao, Y., & Zhang, Y. (2017). The Construction and Development of Academic Library Digital Special Subject Databases. In Ruan, L., Zhu, Q., & Ye, Y. (Eds.), *Academic Library Development and Administration in China* (pp. 163–183). Hershey, PA: IGI Global. 10.4018/978-1-5225-0550-1.ch010

Ravasan, A. Z., Mohammadi, M. M., & Hamidi, H. (2018). An Investigation Into the Critical Success Factors of Implementing Information Technology Service Management Frameworks. In Jakobs, K. (Ed.), *Corporate and Global Standardization Initiatives in Contemporary Society* (pp. 200–218). Hershey, PA: IGI Global. 10.4018/978-1-5225-5320-5.ch009

Rezaie, S., Mirabedini, S. J., & Abtahi, A. (2018). Designing a Model for Implementation of Business Intelligence in the Banking Industry. *International Journal of Enterprise Information Systems*, 14(1), 77–103. 10.4018/IJEIS.2018010105

Richards, V., Matthews, N., Williams, O. J., & Khan, Z. (2021). The Challenges of Accessible Tourism Information Systems for Tourists With Vision Impairment: Sensory Communications Beyond the Screen. In Eusébio, C., Teixeira, L., & Carneiro, M. (Eds.), *ICT Tools and Applications for Accessible Tourism* (pp. 26–54). IGI Global. https://doi.org/10.4018/978-1-7998-6428-8.ch002

Rodrigues de Souza Neto, V., & Marques, O. (2021). Rural Tourism Fostering Welfare Through Sustainable Development: A Conceptual Approach. In Perinotto, A., Mayer, V., & Soares, J. (Eds.), *Rebuilding and Restructuring the Tourism Industry: Infusion of Happiness and Quality of Life* (pp. 38–57). IGI Global. https://doi.org/10.4018/978-1-7998-7239-9.ch003

Romano, L., Grimaldi, R., & Colasuonno, F. S. (2017). Demand Management as a Success Factor in Project Portfolio Management. In Romano, L. (Ed.), *Project Portfolio Management Strategies for Effective Organizational Operations* (pp. 202–219). Hershey, PA: IGI Global. 10.4018/978-1-5225-2151-8.ch008

Rubio-Escuderos, L., & García-Andreu, H. (2021). Competitiveness Factors of Accessible Tourism E-Travel Agencies. In Eusébio, C., Teixeira, L., & Carneiro, M. (Eds.), *ICT Tools and Applications for Accessible Tourism* (pp. 196–217). IGI Global. https://doi.org/10.4018/978-1-7998-6428-8.ch009

Rucci, A. C., Porto, N., Darcy, S., & Becka, L. (2021). Smart and Accessible Cities?: Not Always – The Case for Accessible Tourism Initiatives in Buenos Aries and Sydney. In Eusébio, C., Teixeira, L., & Carneiro, M. (Eds.), *ICT Tools and Applications for Accessible Tourism* (pp. 115–145). IGI Global. https://doi.org/10.4018/978-1-7998-6428-8.ch006

Ruhi, U. (2018). Towards an Interdisciplinary Socio-Technical Definition of Virtual Communities. In M. Khosrow-Pour, D.B.A. (Ed.), *Encyclopedia of Information Science and Technology, Fourth Edition* (pp. 4278-4295). Hershey, PA: IGI Global. 10.4018/978-1-5225-2255-3.ch371

Ryan, L., Catena, M., Ros, P., & Stephens, S. (2021). Designing Entrepreneurial Ecosystems to Support Resource Management in the Tourism Industry. In Costa, V., Moura, A., & Mira, M. (Eds.), *Handbook of Research on Human Capital and People Management in the Tourism Industry* (pp. 265–281). IGI Global. https://doi.org/10.4018/978-1-7998-4318-4.ch013

Sabuncu, I. (2021). Understanding Tourist Perceptions and Expectations During Pandemic Through Social Media Big Data. In Demir, M., Dalgıç, A., & Ergen, F. (Eds.), *Handbook of Research on the Impacts and Implications of COVID-19 on the Tourism Industry* (pp. 330–350). IGI Global. https://doi.org/10.4018/978-1 -7998-8231-2.ch016

Safari, M. R., & Jiang, Q. (2018). The Theory and Practice of IT Governance Maturity and Strategies Alignment: Evidence From Banking Industry. *Journal of Global Information Management*, 26(2), 127–146. 10.4018/JGIM.2018040106

Sahoo, J., Pati, B., & Mohanty, B. (2017). Knowledge Management as an Academic Discipline: An Assessment. In Gunjal, B. (Ed.), *Managing Knowledge and Scholarly Assets in Academic Libraries* (pp. 99–126). Hershey, PA: IGI Global. 10.4018/978-1-5225-1741-2.ch005

Saini, D. (2017). Relevance of Teaching Values and Ethics in Management Education. In Baporikar, N. (Ed.), *Management Education for Global Leadership* (pp. 90–111). Hershey, PA: IGI Global. 10.4018/978-1-5225-1013-0.ch005

Sambhanthan, A. (2017). Assessing and Benchmarking Sustainability in Organisations: An Integrated Conceptual Model. *International Journal of Systems and Service-Oriented Engineering*, 7(4), 22–43. 10.4018/IJSSOE.2017100102

Sambhanthan, A., & Potdar, V. (2017). A Study of the Parameters Impacting Sustainability in Information Technology Organizations. *International Journal of Knowledge-Based Organizations*, 7(3), 27–39. 10.4018/IJKBO.2017070103

Sánchez-Fernández, M. D., & Manríquez, M. R. (2018). The Entrepreneurial Spirit Based on Social Values: The Digital Generation. In Isaias, P., & Carvalho, L. (Eds.), *User Innovation and the Entrepreneurship Phenomenon in the Digital Economy* (pp. 173–193). Hershey, PA: IGI Global. 10.4018/978-1-5225-2826-5.ch009

Sanchez-Ruiz, L., & Blanco, B. (2017). Process Management for SMEs: Barriers, Enablers, and Benefits. In Vemić, M. (Ed.), *Optimal Management Strategies in Small and Medium Enterprises* (pp. 293–319). Hershey, PA: IGI Global. 10.4018/978-1-5225-1949-2.ch014

Sanz, L. F., Gómez-Pérez, J., & Castillo-Martinez, A. (2018). Analysis of the European ICT Competence Frameworks. In Ahuja, V., & Rathore, S. (Eds.), *Multidisciplinary Perspectives on Human Capital and Information Technology Professionals* (pp. 225–245). Hershey, PA: IGI Global. 10.4018/978-1-5225-5297-0.ch012

Sarvepalli, A., & Godin, J. (2017). Business Process Management in the Classroom. *Journal of Cases on Information Technology*, 19(2), 17–28. 10.4018/JCIT.2017040102

Saxena, G. G., & Saxena, A. (2021). Host Community Role in Medical Tourism Development. In Singh, M., & Kumaran, S. (Eds.), *Growth of the Medical Tourism Industry and Its Impact on Society: Emerging Research and Opportunities* (pp. 105–127). IGI Global. https://doi.org/10.4018/978-1-7998-3427-4.ch006

Saygili, E. E., Ozturkoglu, Y., & Kocakulah, M. C. (2017). End Users' Perceptions of Critical Success Factors in ERP Applications. *International Journal of Enterprise Information Systems*, 13(4), 58–75. 10.4018/IJEIS.2017100104

Saygili, E. E., & Saygili, A. T. (2017). Contemporary Issues in Enterprise Information Systems: A Critical Review of CSFs in ERP Implementations. In Tavana, M. (Ed.), *Enterprise Information Systems and the Digitalization of Business Functions* (pp. 120–136). Hershey, PA: IGI Global. 10.4018/978-1-5225-2382-6.ch006

Schwaiger, K. M., & Zehrer, A. (2021). The COVID-19 Pandemic and Organizational Resilience in Hospitality Family Firms: A Qualitative Approach. In Zehrer, A., Glowka, G., Schwaiger, K., & Ranacher-Lackner, V. (Eds.), *Resiliency Models and Addressing Future Risks for Family Firms in the Tourism Industry* (pp. 32–49). IGI Global. https://doi.org/10.4018/978-1-7998-7352-5.ch002

Scott, N., & Campos, A. C. (2022). Cognitive Science of Tourism Experiences. In R. Augusto Costa, F. Brandão, Z. Breda, & C. Costa (Eds.), *Planning and Managing the Experience Economy in Tourism* (pp. 1-21). IGI Global. https://doi.org/10.4018/978-1-7998-8775-1.ch001

Seidenstricker, S., & Antonino, A. (2018). Business Model Innovation-Oriented Technology Management for Emergent Technologies. In M. Khosrow-Pour, D.B.A. (Ed.), *Encyclopedia of Information Science and Technology, Fourth Edition* (pp. 4560-4569). Hershey, PA: IGI Global. 10.4018/978-1-5225-2255-3.ch396

Selvi, M. S. (2021). Changes in Tourism Sales and Marketing Post COVID-19. In Demir, M., Dalgıç, A., & Ergen, F. (Eds.), *Handbook of Research on the Impacts and Implications of COVID-19 on the Tourism Industry* (pp. 437–460). IGI Global. 10.4018/978-1-7998-8231-2.ch021

Senaratne, S., & Gunarathne, A. D. (2017). Excellence Perspective for Management Education from a Global Accountants' Hub in Asia. In Baporikar, N. (Ed.), *Management Education for Global Leadership* (pp. 158–180). Hershey, PA: IGI Global. 10.4018/978-1-5225-1013-0.ch008

Sensuse, D. I., & Cahyaningsih, E. (2018). Knowledge Management Models: A Summative Review. *International Journal of Information Systems in the Service Sector*, 10(1), 71–100. 10.4018/IJISSS.2018010105

Seth, M., Goyal, D., & Kiran, R. (2017). Diminution of Impediments in Implementation of Supply Chain Management Information System for Enhancing its Effectiveness in Indian Automobile Industry. *Journal of Global Information Management*, 25(3), 1–20. 10.4018/JGIM.2017070101

Seyal, A. H., & Rahman, M. N. (2017). Investigating Impact of Inter-Organizational Factors in Measuring ERP Systems Success: Bruneian Perspectives. In Tavana, M. (Ed.), *Enterprise Information Systems and the Digitalization of Business Functions* (pp. 178–204). Hershey, PA: IGI Global. 10.4018/978-1-5225-2382-6.ch008

Shaqrah, A. A. (2018). Analyzing Business Intelligence Systems Based on 7s Model of McKinsey. *International Journal of Business Intelligence Research*, 9(1), 53–63. 10.4018/IJBIR.2018010104

Sharma, A. J. (2017). Enhancing Sustainability through Experiential Learning in Management Education. In Baporikar, N. (Ed.), *Management Education for Global Leadership* (pp. 256–274). Hershey, PA: IGI Global. 10.4018/978-1-5225-1013-0.ch013

Shetty, K. P. (2017). Responsible Global Leadership: Ethical Challenges in Management Education. In Baporikar, N. (Ed.), *Innovation and Shifting Perspectives in Management Education* (pp. 194–223). Hershey, PA: IGI Global. 10.4018/978-1-5225-1019-2.ch009

Sinthupundaja, J., & Kohda, Y. (2017). Effects of Corporate Social Responsibility and Creating Shared Value on Sustainability. *International Journal of Sustainable Entrepreneurship and Corporate Social Responsibility*, 2(1), 27–38. 10.4018/IJSECSR.2017010103

Škarica, I., & Hrgović, A. V. (2018). Implementation of Total Quality Management Principles in Public Health Institutes in the Republic of Croatia. *International Journal of Productivity Management and Assessment Technologies*, 6(1), 1–16. 10.4018/IJPMAT.2018010101

Skokic, V. (2021). How Small Hotel Owners Practice Resilience: Longitudinal Study Among Small Family Hotels in Croatia. In Zehrer, A., Glowka, G., Schwaiger, K., & Ranacher-Lackner, V. (Eds.), *Resiliency Models and Addressing Future Risks for Family Firms in the Tourism Industry* (pp. 50–73). IGI Global. 10.4018/978-1-7998-7352-5.ch003

Smuts, H., Kotzé, P., Van der Merwe, A., & Loock, M. (2017). Framework for Managing Shared Knowledge in an Information Systems Outsourcing Context. *International Journal of Knowledge Management*, 13(4), 1–30. 10.4018/IJKM.2017100101

Sousa, M. J., Cruz, R., Dias, I., & Caracol, C. (2017). Information Management Systems in the Supply Chain. In Jamil, G., Soares, A., & Pessoa, C. (Eds.), *Handbook of Research on Information Management for Effective Logistics and Supply Chains* (pp. 469–485). Hershey, PA: IGI Global. 10.4018/978-1-5225-0973-8.ch025

Spremic, M., Turulja, L., & Bajgoric, N. (2018). Two Approaches in Assessing Business Continuity Management Attitudes in the Organizational Context. In Bajgoric, N. (Ed.), *Always-On Enterprise Information Systems for Modern Organizations* (pp. 159–183). Hershey, PA: IGI Global. 10.4018/978-1-5225-3704-5.ch008

Steenkamp, A. L. (2018). Some Insights in Computer Science and Information Technology. In *Examining the Changing Role of Supervision in Doctoral Research Projects: Emerging Research and Opportunities* (pp. 113–133). Hershey, PA: IGI Global. 10.4018/978-1-5225-2610-0.ch005

Stipanović, C., Rudan, E., & Zubović, V. (2022). Reaching the New Tourist Through Creativity: Sustainable Development Challenges in Croatian Coastal Towns. In Valeri, M. (Ed.), *New Governance and Management in Touristic Destinations* (pp. 231–245). IGI Global. https://doi.org/10.4018/978-1-6684-3889-3.ch014

Tabach, A., & Croteau, A. (2017). Configurations of Information Technology Governance Practices and Business Unit Performance. *International Journal of IT/Business Alignment and Governance*, 8(2), 1–27. 10.4018/IJITBAG.2017070101

Talaue, G. M., & Iqbal, T. (2017). Assessment of e-Business Mode of Selected Private Universities in the Philippines and Pakistan. *International Journal of Online Marketing*, 7(4), 63–77. 10.4018/IJOM.2017100105

Tam, G. C. (2017). Project Manager Sustainability Competence. In *Managerial Strategies and Green Solutions for Project Sustainability* (pp. 178–207). Hershey, PA: IGI Global. 10.4018/978-1-5225-2371-0.ch008

Tambo, T. (2018). Fashion Retail Innovation: About Context, Antecedents, and Outcome in Technological Change Projects. In I. Management Association (Ed.), *Fashion and Textiles: Breakthroughs in Research and Practice* (pp. 233-260). Hershey, PA: IGI Global. https://doi.org/10.4018/978-1-5225-3432-7.ch010

Tantau, A. D., & Frățilă, L. C. (2018). Information and Management System for Renewable Energy Business. In *Entrepreneurship and Business Development in the Renewable Energy Sector* (pp. 200–244). Hershey, PA: IGI Global. 10.4018/978-1-5225-3625-3.ch006

Teixeira, N., Pardal, P. N., & Rafael, B. G. (2018). Internationalization, Financial Performance, and Organizational Challenges: A Success Case in Portugal. In Carvalho, L. (Ed.), *Handbook of Research on Entrepreneurial Ecosystems and Social Dynamics in a Globalized World* (pp. 379–423). Hershey, PA: IGI Global. 10.4018/978-1-5225-3525-6.ch017

Teixeira, P., Teixeira, L., Eusébio, C., Silva, S., & Teixeira, A. (2021). The Impact of ICTs on Accessible Tourism: Evidence Based on a Systematic Literature Review. In Eusébio, C., Teixeira, L., & Carneiro, M. (Eds.), *ICT Tools and Applications for Accessible Tourism* (pp. 1–25). IGI Global. 10.4018/978-1-7998-6428-8.ch001

Trad, A., & Kalpić, D. (2018). The Business Transformation Framework, Agile Project and Change Management. In M. Khosrow-Pour, D.B.A. (Ed.), *Encyclopedia of Information Science and Technology, Fourth Edition* (pp. 620-635). Hershey, PA: IGI Global. https://doi.org/10.4018/978-1-5225-2255-3.ch054

Trad, A., & Kalpić, D. (2018). The Business Transformation and Enterprise Architecture Framework: The Financial Engineering E-Risk Management and E-Law Integration. In Sergi, B., Fidanoski, F., Ziolo, M., & Naumovski, V. (Eds.), *Regaining Global Stability After the Financial Crisis* (pp. 46–65). Hershey, PA: IGI Global. 10.4018/978-1-5225-4026-7.ch003

Trengereid, V. (2022). Conditions of Network Engagement: The Quest for a Common Good. In R. Augusto Costa, F. Brandão, Z. Breda, & C. Costa (Eds.), *Planning and Managing the Experience Economy in Tourism* (pp. 69-84). IGI Global. https://doi.org/10.4018/978-1-7998-8775-1.ch004

Turulja, L., & Bajgoric, N. (2018). Business Continuity and Information Systems: A Systematic Literature Review. In Bajgoric, N. (Ed.), *Always-On Enterprise Information Systems for Modern Organizations* (pp. 60–87). Hershey, PA: IGI Global. 10.4018/978-1-5225-3704-5.ch004

Vargas-Hernández, J. G. (2017). Professional Integrity in Business Management Education. In Baporikar, N. (Ed.), *Management Education for Global Leadership* (pp. 70–89). Hershey, PA: IGI Global. 10.4018/978-1-5225-1013-0.ch004

Varnacı Uzun, F. (2021). The Destination Preferences of Foreign Tourists During the COVID-19 Pandemic and Attitudes Towards: Marmaris, Turkey. In Demir, M., Dalgıç, A., & Ergen, F. (Eds.), *Handbook of Research on the Impacts and Implications of COVID-19 on the Tourism Industry* (pp. 285–306). IGI Global. https://doi.org/10.4018/978-1-7998-8231-2.ch014

Vasista, T. G., & AlAbdullatif, A. M. (2017). Role of Electronic Customer Relationship Management in Demand Chain Management: A Predictive Analytic Approach. *International Journal of Information Systems and Supply Chain Management*, 10(1), 53–67. 10.4018/IJISSCM.2017010104

Vieru, D., & Bourdeau, S. (2017). Survival in the Digital Era: A Digital Competence-Based Multi-Case Study in the Canadian SME Clothing Industry. *International Journal of Social and Organizational Dynamics in IT*, 6(1), 17–34. 10.4018/IJSODIT.2017010102

Vijayan, G., & Kamarulzaman, N. H. (2017). An Introduction to Sustainable Supply Chain Management and Business Implications. In Khan, M., Hussain, M., & Ajmal, M. (Eds.), *Green Supply Chain Management for Sustainable Business Practice* (pp. 27–50). Hershey, PA: IGI Global. 10.4018/978-1-5225-0635-5.ch002

Vlachvei, A., & Notta, O. (2017). Firm Competitiveness: Theories, Evidence, and Measurement. In Vlachvei, A., Notta, O., Karantininis, K., & Tsounis, N. (Eds.), *Factors Affecting Firm Competitiveness and Performance in the Modern Business World* (pp. 1–42). Hershey, PA: IGI Global. 10.4018/978-1-5225-0843-4.ch001

Wang, C., Schofield, M., Li, X., & Ou, X. (2017). Do Chinese Students in Public and Private Higher Education Institutes Perform at Different Level in One of the Leadership Skills: Critical Thinking?: An Exploratory Comparison. In Wang, V. (Ed.), *Encyclopedia of Strategic Leadership and Management* (pp. 160–181). Hershey, PA: IGI Global. 10.4018/978-1-5225-1049-9.ch013

Wang, J. (2017). Multi-Agent based Production Management Decision System Modelling for the Textile Enterprise. *Journal of Global Information Management*, 25(4), 1–15. 10.4018/JGIM.2017100101

Wiedemann, A., & Gewald, H. (2017). Examining Cross-Domain Alignment: The Correlation of Business Strategy, IT Management, and IT Business Value. *International Journal of IT/Business Alignment and Governance*, 8(1), 17–31. 10.4018/IJITBAG.2017010102

Wolf, R., & Thiel, M. (2018). Advancing Global Business Ethics in China: Reducing Poverty Through Human and Social Welfare. In Hipsher, S. (Ed.), *Examining the Private Sector's Role in Wealth Creation and Poverty Reduction* (pp. 67–84). Hershey, PA: IGI Global. 10.4018/978-1-5225-3117-3.ch004

Yablonsky, S. (2018). Innovation Platforms: Data and Analytics Platforms. In *Multi-Sided Platforms (MSPs) and Sharing Strategies in the Digital Economy: Emerging Research and Opportunities* (pp. 72–95). Hershey, PA: IGI Global. 10.4018/978-1-5225-5457-8.ch003

Yaşar, B. (2021). The Impact of COVID-19 on Volatility of Tourism Stocks: Evidence From BIST Tourism Index. In Demir, M., Dalgıç, A., & Ergen, F. (Eds.), *Handbook of Research on the Impacts and Implications of COVID-19 on the Tourism Industry* (pp. 23–44). IGI Global. https://doi.org/10.4018/978-1-7998-8231-2.ch002

Yusoff, A., Ahmad, N. H., & Halim, H. A. (2017). Agropreneurship among Gen Y in Malaysia: The Role of Academic Institutions. In Ahmad, N., Ramayah, T., Halim, H., & Rahman, S. (Eds.), *Handbook of Research on Small and Medium Enterprises in Developing Countries* (pp. 23–47). Hershey, PA: IGI Global. 10.4018/978-1-5225-2165-5.ch002

Zacher, D., & Pechlaner, H. (2021). Resilience as an Opportunity Approach: Challenges and Perspectives for Private Sector Participation on a Community Level. In Zehrer, A., Glowka, G., Schwaiger, K., & Ranacher-Lackner, V. (Eds.), *Resiliency Models and Addressing Future Risks for Family Firms in the Tourism Industry* (pp. 75–102). IGI Global. https://doi.org/10.4018/978-1-7998-7352-5.ch004

Zanin, F., Comuzzi, E., & Costantini, A. (2018). The Effect of Business Strategy and Stock Market Listing on the Use of Risk Assessment Tools. In *Management Control Systems in Complex Settings: Emerging Research and Opportunities* (pp. 145–168). Hershey, PA: IGI Global. 10.4018/978-1-5225-3987-2.ch007

Zgheib, P. W. (2017). Corporate Innovation and Intrapreneurship in the Middle East. In Zgheib, P. (Ed.), *Entrepreneurship and Business Innovation in the Middle East* (pp. 37–56). Hershey, PA: IGI Global. 10.4018/978-1-5225-2066-5.ch003

About the Contributors

Swati Gupta is an accomplished academician, Mentor for Change, and a beacon of inspiration in the world of education. With over a decade of experience, she has made significant contributions to the academic landscape. As an Associate Professor at Universal AI University, her passion for teaching and commitment to academic excellence have been instrumental in shaping the minds of aspiring leaders. She has taught courses in entrepreneurial finance, entrepreneurial leadership, Excel, and corporate finance, instilling not only subject knowledge but also ethical values in her students. Beyond the hallowed halls of Universal AI University, Dr. Gupta's influence extends internationally, as she has been associated with prestigious institutions, where she imparts her expertise in analytics. Additionally, she has organized workshops on entrepreneurship, design thinking, and finance for renowned institutes, including DST, Niti Ayog, to name a few. Dr. Gupta's mentoring prowess shines as she nurtures budding entrepreneurs, providing unwavering support to bring their innovative ideas to life. Her dedication to fostering positive change has earned her immense respect among her peers and students alike. In summary, Dr. Swati Gupta's journey in academia and mentorship exemplifies a tireless pursuit of knowledge, an unwavering commitment to education, and a passion for empowering the next generation of leaders. Her impact in both teaching and mentoring is a testament to her valuable contributions to the academic and entrepreneurial ecosystems.

* * *

Anubha is a Professor of Marketing at Jaipuria Institute of Management, Ghaziabad, India. Her research interests include social media marketing, Islamic marketing, electronic word of mouth, advertising, and consumer behaviour. She has published many scholarly "ABS 3 level", "ABDC" and "Scopus-indexed research papers in various journals of Wiley, Emerald, Taylor & Francis, and Sage publications including Psychology and Marketing, Journal of Islamic Marketing, Journal of Internet Commerce, Global Knowledge, Memory & Communication. She has been an active reviewer of journals of Elsevier and Emerald. She has presented papers at various National and International conferences at MDI Murshidabad, IIM Indore, IIT Delhi, XLRI Jamshedpur, and Curtin University. Recently her edited book, indexed in Scopus was published by IGI Global.

Lavanya Bhagra is a Ph.D. Scholar at MNLU, Nagpur, in her last year of Ph.D. In AI and IPR. She has been a double gold medalist in LLB and LLM from GGSIPU and ILI, New Delhi, specializing in Intellectual Property Rights.

Shilpa Bhide is Associate Professor, Department of Management Sciences, Savitribai Phule Pune University.

About the Contributors

Jyoti Kumar Chandel is Assistant Professor with Birla Institute of Technology Mesra, Jaipur Campus. He has rich experience in the domains of teaching, training, research and administration. He holds Ph. D. in Commerce and Management Studies from Himachal Pradesh University, Shimla, India. His current research interests are in Services Marketing, Tourism Management and Digital Businesses. He has published in many peer reviewed refereed international journals and conference proceedings. He reviews research papers for many reputed journals.

Rui Manuel Teixeira Santos Dias has a Postdoctoral degree in Economics/Finance at the State University of Feira de Santana (BR), Department of Exact Sciences. Doctor of Finance at the University of Évora—Institute of Research and Advanced Training (PT). Diploma of Advanced Studies in Doctoral Studies (DEA), at the University of Extremadura (ES), in the scientific area of Financial Economics. He served as Chief Financial Officer in various companies for 26 years. He is currently a guest associate professor at the ISG Business & Economics School and ESCE at the Polytechnic Institute of Setúbal. In terms of research, it is an Integrated Member of CIGEST—Centre for Research in Management—Business & Economics School.

Rosa Galvão is a Guest Adjunct Professor of the Department of Accounting and Finance at School of Business and Administration of the Polytechnic Institute of Setubal (IPS), Portugal. Researcher, and Consultant in Finance and Accounting. Master's degree in Accounting and Finance, Polytechnic Institute of Setúbal. Doctoral student in Management at the University of Évora. Finance Specialist (DL 206/2009).

Lissy George is presently working as an Assistant Professor Grade II in Commerce Education at Mount Tabor Training College, Pathanapuram, affiliated with the University of Kerala, India. She has more than 18 years of teaching experience as a Commerce Educator and has created many excellent commerce teachers in Kerala. She had completed M.Com., M.Ed., and has submitted a thesis on Commerce Education for Ph.D. She is a dedicated educationist who finds happiness in teaching and research. To develop and update her professional knowledge, she has participated in and presented many papers at international and national levels, attended refresher courses, seminars, and workshops, and also published research papers and books. As an educator, she is very passionate about creating an inclusive classroom environment that facilitates learning, positive social interaction, and self-motivation among all levels of learners.

Mithilesh Gidage is an accomplished professional with three years of experience in data analytics and fixed income. Currently serving as a Senior Data Analyst, Fixed Income in Morningstar's Fixed Income Engineering team, he plays a pivotal role in driving strategic insights. Concurrently, Mithilesh is pursuing a PhD in Financial Management at the Department of Management Sciences (PUMBA), Savitribai Phule Pune University. Moreover, he contributes as a visiting faculty at ITM Institute, Kharghar, where he imparts knowledge and shares industry insights with students. Mithilesh's research interests span across diverse areas including ESG, Sustainable Finance, Behavioral Finance, and Diversity, Equity, and Inclusion (DEI), reflecting his passion for exploring innovative solutions in the financial domain.

Mohammad Irfan is presently working as an Associate Professor at NSB Academy Business School, Bangalore. He was associated with the School of Business, AURO University, Surat, Gujarat for five years. He is MBA (Finance) and M.Com (Account and Law). Dr. Irfan has done this Ph.D. from the Central University of Haryana. He has qualified UGC-JRF/SRF/NET in Management and Commerce. Dr. Irfan certified NSEs (NCFM) and BSEs certification. He has experience of sixteen years in the area of SAPM, Artificial Intelligence, Machine Learning, Blockchain, Cryptocurrency, Financial Engineering, Fintech, Green Finance, and Alternative Finance. He has to his credit more than 30 Scopus Indexed articles, includes The Journal of Economic Cooperation and Development (Q2), International Journal of Business Excellence (IJBEX), International Journal of Economics and Management (IJEM), Montenegrin Journal of Economics (Q2), Cogent Business & Management (Taylor & Francis) (Q2), Indian Journal of Finance (IJF) and Journal of Islamic Monetary Economics and Finance (JIMF). His citations reached 200+ along with 7 H-index. Dr. Irfan has published 6 books in Springer, IGI Global Publication (Scopus indexed).

Padma Iyenghar is an "Entwicklungsprofessorin" (Engl. equiv. Development professor) at the University of Applied Sciences, Osnabrueck, Germany where she is active in teaching and research. In tandem, she is also a functional safety engineering consultant at Innotec GmbH, with her work time equally divided between university and industry. She was a post-doctoral researcher at the university of Osnabrueck, in the software engineering research group between 2014 and 2020, where she also received her doctoral degree in Computer Science (Dr. rer. nat.) in 2012. Her research interests include, among others, software engineering and quality assurance (with focus on AI), functional safety software engineering; model-based software development and embedded software engineering.

Ramji Nagariya is an Assistant Professor in the School of Business and Management, CHRIST(Deemed to be University), Delhi-NCR, Ghaziabad, India. He holds a Ph.D. in area of sustainable service supply chain from the Department of Management Studies, Malaviya National Institute of Technology, Jaipur, India. He holds a M. Tech in Industrial Management from Indian Institute of Technology (BHU), Varanasi and bachelor's degree in Aeronautical Engineering. His research papers are published in Business Process Management Journal, Benchmarking: An International Journal, Journal of Humanitarian Logistics and Supply Chain Management, Decision, International Journal of Services & Operations Management, and International Journal of Productivity & Performance Management. He has published several Scopus indexed book chapters also. His research interest includes service supply chain, buyer-supplier relationship and sustainability in supply chain.

Libeesh P. C. is a passionate professor of management and commerce subjects. He has cleared UGC-NET and Kerala SET. He holds a bachelor's degree in commerce and education. He has around Thirteen years of teaching experience, which includes 4.5 years of experience as a HOD of the Department of Commerce in TTGI Coimbatore. He is doing his Ph.D. in finance from Dr. NGP Arts and Science College Coimbatore. His teaching interests include Accounting, Taxation, Financial Management, and Business Economics. He has more than Eight years of experience in training and motivation, and he worked as a trainer and training coordinator of WWTA (World Wide Teacher Academy) for more than Three years and trained so many teachers.

Ruchika Rastogi, Ph.D., is an Associate Professor in Department of Business Administration, Pranveer Singh Institute of Technology, Kanpur. She has been teaching Production & Operation and Economics and Marketing at Post Graduate Level since 2005.She did her Ph.D. from AKTU, Lucknow in microfinance.

Abhineet Saxena is a seasoned academician, research. and banking industry professional with over 12 Years of extensive experience. He has Post-Doctoral. Ph.D., UGC NET qualified, MBA (Finance),M. com (EAFM).He has published many research papers Scopus, National, International journals and Conference proceedings.

Kiran Sharma is currently associated with ICFAI Law School, IFHE, Hyderabad in the capacity of Assistant Professor of Law. She has worked as a copyright examiner in the Intellectual Property Office in India for more than two years. She has also been associated with Prof. D S Sengar, Professor, IIM Noida as an Academic Associate and also has experience of working as a Law Researcher in Delhi State Legal Services Authority. She has also worked briefly with Standing Government Counsel, Ms. Geetanjali Sharma at Delhi District Court, Central Administrative Tribunal, and the Hon'ble High Court. She graduated from VIPS, GGSIPU, Delhi and she has completed her post-graduation from Hidayatullah National Law University, Raipur in Intellectual Property Rights. She is currently pursuing her PhD. She has published a few papers in various journals and edited books. She herself is the editor of a book and a conference proceeding. She has also presented papers in various national and international conferences. She has presented papers in IPIRA, an international conference on IPR, twice held in Singapore and Vietnam respectively. She has also coordinated an IPR awareness program with the Indian Government under the NIPAM Scheme.

About the Contributors

Priyanshu Sharma is Associate Lecturer in the Department of Management, Birla Institute of Technology Mesra, Jaipur Campus and has been teaching Finance Management and Taxation since 2009. He is a post graduate in Commerce and also in Business Administration. He holds Ph. D. in Commerce and Management Studies. His current research interests are in Blockchain Technology, Goods and services tax (GST) and Digital Finance. He has published many research papers Scopus, National, International journals and Conference proceedings.

Diksha Sinha is a Research Scholar in the Department of Management at Birla Institute of Technology, Mesra, Jaipur Campus. She is currently pursuing her Ph.D. in Management. She has qualified NET-JRF exam in Commerce. She has completed her graduation and post-graduation degree in Commerce from Banaras Hindu University, Varanasi. Her area of interest lies in the domain of international business and marketing. She has also presented papers and coordinated various international conferences and seminars. She has also published papers in national journals and conference proceedings.

Index

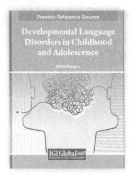

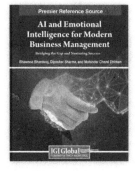

Ensure Quality Research is Introduced to the Academic Community

Become a Reviewer for IGI Global Authored Book Projects

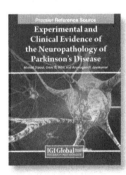

The overall success of an authored book project is dependent on quality and timely manuscript evaluations.

Applications and Inquiries may be sent to:
development@igi-global.com

Applicants must have a doctorate (or equivalent degree) as well as publishing, research, and reviewing experience. Authored Book Evaluators are appointed for one-year terms and are expected to complete at least three evaluations per term. Upon successful completion of this term, evaluators can be considered for an additional term.

If you have a colleague that may be interested in this opportunity, we encourage you to share this information with them.

Printed in the United States
by Baker & Taylor Publisher Services